Programming for the World

A Guide to Internationalization

Sandra Martin O'Donnell

PTR Prentice Hall
Upper Saddle River, New Jersey 07458

Library of Congress Cataloging-in-Publication Data

```
O'Donnell, Sandra Martin
     Programming for the world : a guide to internationalization /
Sandra Martin O'Donnell
     p.    cm.
     Includes bibliographical references and index.
     ISBN 0-13-722190-8
     1. Electronic digital computers--Programming.  2. Linguistics.
I. Title.
QA76.6.O37    1994                                  93-39034
005.1--dc20                                         CIP
```

Editorial/production supervision: *Harriet Tellem*
Cover design: *Bruce Kenselaar*
Manufacturing manager: *Alexis Heydt*
Acquisitions editor: *Mike Meehan*
Editorial assistant: *Nancy Boylan*
Cover photo: *Masterfile* © IMPEK Imagineering-1

© 1994 by P T R Prentice Hall
Prentice-Hall, Inc.
A Pearson Education Company
Upper Saddle River, NJ 07458

The publisher offers discounts on this book in bulk quantities. For more information contact:
Corporate Sales Department, P T R Prentice Hall, 113 Sylvan Avenue, Englewood Cliffs, New Jersey 07632.
Phone: 201-5922863, FAX: 201-592-2249.

Apple, the Apple Logo, and Macintosh are trademarks of Apple Computer, Inc., registered in the United States and other countries. DEC and DIGITAL are registered trademarks of Digital Equipment Corporation. VMS is a trademark of Digital Equipment Corporation. HP and Hewlett-Packard are trademarks of Hewlett-Packard Company. Interleaf is a trademark of Interleaf, Inc. IBM is a registered trademark of International Business Machines Corporation. MS-DOS is a registered trademark of Microsoft Corporation. Open Software Foundation, OSF, the OSF logo, OSF/1, OSF/Motif, and Motif are trademarks of the Open Software Foundation Inc. UNIX is a registered trademark, licensed exclusively by X/Open Company Ltd. X/Open is a trademark of the X/Open Company Ltd. in the United Kingdom and other countries. X Window System is a trademark of the Massachusetts Institute of Technology. Postscript is a trademark of Adobe Systems Incorporated. Uniforum is a trademark of Uniforum.

Printed in the United States of America
10 9 8 7 6 5 4 3 2 1

ISBN 0-13-722190-8

Prentice-Hall International (UK) Limited,London
Prentice-Hall of Australia Pty. Limited, Sydney
Prentice-Hall Canada Inc., Toronto
Prentice-Hall Hispanoamericana, S.A., Mexico
Prentice-Hall of India Private Limited, New Delhi
Prentice-Hall of Japan, Inc., Tokyo
Pearson Education Asia Pte. Ltd., Singapore
Editora Prentice-Hall do Brasil, Ltda., Rio de Janeiro

Contents

Contents

Contents   xi

Preface

Programming for the World: A Guide to Internationalization provides information about cultural and linguistic requirements around the world, and the changes necessary in computer systems to handle those requirements.

Audience

For an author to suggest that everyone needs to read his or her book usually indicates either an overblown ego or that the author has lost all sense of perspective. People writing about black holes, or Mediterranean fruit flies, or cinematographers of the 1930s may think the world revolves around their topic, but most of us can make it through life without becoming experts on those topics.

Books in the computer field also usually are intended for niche audiences—whatever the author's delusions to the contrary. While there definitely are people who need and want to read about operating system locking techniques or communication protocols, most of us don't need to know these topics to any great depth.

It is therefore with some trepidation that I say this book is intended for most computer programmers, technical writers, and project managers. Nearly all software intended for use in multiple countries needs some work to make it usable across regions. Similarly, the documentation that accompanies software needs attention to accommodate international readers' needs—regardless of whether the documentation is translated. Also, project managers need at least a rudimentary understanding of the functional requirements for software that will run throughout the world in order to manage projects that include such functionality.

If your software currently only sells in one country, you may think you can skip this book. However, the reality of global economics means that if you are only sell-ing in one place today, you may need to branch out in the future in order to survive. It is helpful then, to understand other users' needs and the programming techniques you can use to meet those needs.

Assumptions and Caveats

This book examines varying user requirements around the world and describes programming techniques and routines in international standards and common industry specifications for meeting those requirements. Familiarity with the C programming language and a UNIX-like operating system are helpful, but readers with other backgrounds probably also will be able to follow most of the text. In addition, I assume typical readers are familiar with American conventions and characteristics of the English language, but that they may not know the characteristics of other languages and cultures. Despite this assumption, non-American readers probably also will learn quite a bit.

Note that unlike many linguistics texts, this book does not cover all languages and cultures equally. For example, more people speak Bengali natively than speak French, but this book contains more information about French and other European languages than it has about Bengali and other South Asian languages. That is because the amount of software that handles South Asian languages and the potential market for it still is quite small compared to that of languages (like French) that have fewer speakers, but are spoken in countries with more developed computer industries. In addition, the international standards and specifications this book covers have addressed the needs of European and some Asian languages, but still are in the formative stage for other languages and cultures.

The chapters that follow describe many functions or utilities available for use in systems intended for international audiences. However, I do not include the manual pages for these functions or utilities. For detailed descriptions, consult the referenced standards or specifications.

Typographic Conventions

This book uses these typographic conventions:

italic   *Italic* type is used for new terms where they are defined, for variable values that you must supply, and, occasionally, for emphasis.

bold	**Bold** type represents utility and function names, and other keywords that you must use literally. Trailing parentheses distinguish a function name [for example, **isalpha( )**].
`constant width`	C source code, information that the system displays, file names and locale names appear in `constant width` type.
UPPERCASE	Environment variable names appear in UPPERCASE letters.
0x	A leading "0x" precedes hexadecimal numbers (for example, 0x4a).

Acknowledgements

A lucky author is one who finds people who generously share their time and expertise to turn the author's dream of a book into reality. I have been lucky.

Tom McFarland worked with me throughout this project, reviewing draft chapters (multiple times!), offering suggestions, and catching potentially embarrassing errors. He also has been a good friend. Thank you, Tom.

Jeanette Horan, my manager at the Open Software Foundation, consistently supported me and helped make it possible for me to find the time to work on the manuscript. Everyone should have such a good manager.

Many people generously answered questions about their native languages and provided text samples. Thanks to Mariko Romagna, Takashi Ogura, Daniel Dardailler, Mike Feldman, Chih-Chung Ko, Kyuho Kim, Young Hae Rhim, and Martin Gosejacob. Others reviewed some or all of the chapters, providing very helpful suggestions. Thanks to Jim Kumorek, Howard Melman, Sue Kline, Mike Collins, Gary Miller, Josh Goldman, and Glenn Adams.

Thanks to the Open Software Foundation for permission to use the character map and locale definition in Appendix A.

Greg Doench and Mike Meehan, my editors at Prentice Hall, were supportive throughout the project. I appreciate Greg's patience and Mike's effort during the home-stretch stage. Thanks also to Harriet Tellem, the production editor for the book.

Thanks also to Marjorie Martin, who listened when the book was going well and when it wasn't, and who never once told me to shut up.

A different kind of thanks go to Brian O'Donnell, who I met and ended up marrying while working on this book, and who gave me lots of good reasons not to work on it. Never has a slipped schedule been so much fun.

Despite the generous support of so many people, any mistakes in this book are, of course, my responsibility.

Introducing the World

1

Imagine sitting down in front of a computer system to work. For most people, an ordinary sequence of start-up tasks involves typing some English-based commands, and reading or responding to messages like these:

```
Please log in:
Logged in 3:45 p.m., Tue, Aug 24, 1993
```

Such routine tasks and responses occur countless times on systems all over the world. If you are an American, you probably don't really notice the information on your screen. If you are not an American, though, or if your native language happens to be something other than English, you probably are aware of how culturally biased these responses are.

Now imagine you sit down at the computer and see one of these messages:

```
Identification:
Connecté à 15:45, mardi, le 24 août 1993
```

ログ・インして下さい：
１９９３年８月２４日（火）午後３時４５分にログ・インしました。

These provide the same information as the English example above, but since they are in French and Japanese, respectively, there is a fairly good chance that one or more of the three variations would leave you mystified and unable to work with the machine.

1.1   Cultural Biases

It usually is easy to determine a computer system's country of origin; the evidence is as plain as the prompt on your screen. As the first example above shows, for many "Made in the USA" systems, program messages appear in English, while dates appear in the American month/day/year order and use the English names for weekdays and months. In addition, the software may only know how to handle the English letters A–Z and a–z, and stumble when asked to process other characters. Numeric and monetary formats typically use American conventions.

American software often exhibits this culturally biased behavior because that is what is hard-coded into the program logic. This usually is fine for American users, but it is not acceptable for many computer users around the world.

Americans are not alone in their tendency to produce culturally biased systems. A German software package may produce program messages in German only. A Japanese package may handle Japanese text easily, but be unable to process other languages. A French system may only accept dates in the French *jour-mois-année* (day-month-year) order. Throughout the world, programmers write software that addresses local requirements. The problem comes when the users aren't local.

While culturally biased software has never been an ideal solution for international users, several trends are making it less and less acceptable. These trends range from economic considerations to changes in system functionality to the ever-increasing use of computers in everyday life.

1.2   Worldwide Markets, Local Needs

While most computer programmers produce software that is tuned to their local needs, many computer companies sell into much more than local markets. Indeed, they may do business all over the world. An American company might sell products in Western Europe, Canada, Mexico, and Japan. A Japanese firm may sell to the United States, South Korea, Singapore, and Indonesia. A German company probably sells into the multilingual European marketplace, and also may do business in North and South America. Such distributed markets are more than just a theoretical possibility. It is common for major American computer manufacturers to have market shares like one of those in Figure 1.1.

In many cases, economic necessity drives companies to try to sell products beyond their national borders. When this book was written, the American computer market had lower growth rates than those in Europe and the Pacific Rim, which helped convince many companies to seek business elsewhere. However, when

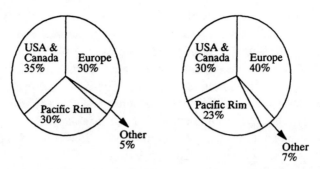

Figure 1.1   Sample Market Shares

markets span national or language boundaries, that means there are multiple user requirements.

Users in Germany and Japan probably both request software that processes their language. The requests appear identical, but the software necessary to meet each request is not. In addition, if you already have culturally biased software, it most likely cannot meet the varying requirements without significant revisions.

A product that produces only American English messages may be unusable in Japan, while a Japanese-only product is even more unusable in the United States. (Many Japanese people understand some English, which is why English-only software *may* be accepted, but very few Americans understand any Japanese.) You may need to change software to meet the local needs of current markets, or the markets you want to get into.

1.2.1   Just Part of Doing Business

The requirement that products meet local needs is not unique to the computer industry. Companies that do business around the world have always had to tailor products for the local marketplace. When building cars for the American market or other places where people drive on the right side of the road, manufacturers put the steering wheel on the left side of the car. Markets like England or Japan, however, require cars with steering wheels on the right because people drive on the left side of the road. Manufacturers who want to sell into these markets make sure they have a product that fits local requirements.

The consumer electronics industry also customizes products for individual markets. The language of text on labels and in instruction manuals changes as the target country changes. Similarly, the type of electrical plug the product uses and the voltage it draws varies depending on the market.

There are countless other examples of industries that must respond in some way to local consumers' requirements. Writing software or producing hardware that meets local needs is just a part of doing business.

It may also be the law. Some countries have laws regarding functionality that must be present in computer systems. For example, Spain requires that all computer keyboards include a keycap for the letter ñ. Other countries require that documentation accompanying a computer be in the local language. (Documentation sent separately may not face the same requirement.) In order to do business in some markets, you may be required to make revisions to your system.

In addition to country-specific requirements, regions may have their own set of rules. Software that handles monetary amounts needs to accommodate the unified European Currency Unit (ECU) if it is to be accepted in Western Europe. As more details of the European Community's (EC) unified market get worked out, software may have to change or face being shut out of that market.

1.3   Results from Culturally Biased Systems

Since so many computer systems are biased toward their country of origin, they may be difficult or impossible for international customers to use. In the past, such customers usually have:

- rejected the product; or
- accepted (perhaps grudgingly) the products' limitations; or
- obtained a rewritten version of the software that handles specific local needs.

All these choices have serious drawbacks.

1.3.1   Rejection

From a company's point of view, the worst thing customers can do is reject their product. However, if the product doesn't meet those customers' needs, that is exactly what can happen. This is likely in the case of culturally biased software, and even more likely when the software in question is intended for nontechnical end-users. Such users often are fluent only in their native language, and thus unable to use software that doesn't handle that language. Of course, the degree of familiarity with nonnative languages depends greatly on the country or region in question. European users often understand one or more languages in addition to the one they speak natively. Many Pacific Rim users study English extensively in school, but they have varying degrees of fluency with that language. Americans, unfortunately, often have *no* level of fluency in other languages; they usually understand only English. When users don't understand the language that software produces or processes, they can't use it, and they therefore will reject it.

Customers may also reject software even if they do understand the language it produces. A Japanese user may understand an English-biased word processing package without difficulty, but that doesn't help if the user needs to produce Japanese text. In that case, the English product is unacceptable.

1.3.2   Limited Software Has Limited Appeal

When faced with biased software, one option is simply to accept the software's limitations and find some way to work around them. Accepting limitations can work if local users are relatively fluent in the language the software supports. A sophisticated graphics modeling package that only handles English text may be acceptable because technical users around the world often understand English. However, accepting limitations means making a compromise. This makes it likely that customers will choose a more functionally complete product if it becomes available.

1.3.3   Customized Software and Worldwide Needs

While users sometimes accept software's cultural limitations, their need for support of local requirements often leads to a different solution: customized software. Either the company that sells the product, or the customers buying it, may create a customized version that meets local needs. Thus, an American company may open a branch in Japan and hire programmers there to produce a Japanized version of a given software package. A French company may create multiple versions of its software including Spanish, English, German, Italian, and others.

These local versions can make otherwise-unusable software usable, but they are costly to create and maintain. (See Chapter 3 for more details.) In addition, they simply replace one set of cultural biases with another. This is particularly troublesome when it comes time to connect sites. Consider computer networks. They are breaking free of physical locations and stretching to include multiple buildings, cities, and even countries. Processing is being distributed across the widely distributed nodes of these networks. However, this new functionality can't work correctly if the different sites have made conflicting changes in software to meet local users' needs. For example, if Japanese, Korean, and Taiwanese sites on a network all have separately customized versions of a software package that originally handled American English, the versions may not interoperate.

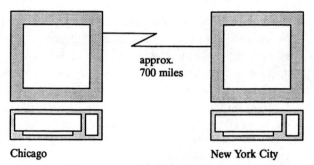

Figure 1.2 Connection Across State Boundaries

While a network that stretches across countries may seem unusual, it actually is becoming increasingly common. Figure 1.2 shows a USA-only connection, while Figure 1.3 shows an international counterpart.

In the first example, a company has operations in Chicago and New York City and connects the computer systems between those two cities. The two sites are about 700 miles apart. In the second, the company networks together its European sites in London, Paris, and Berlin. This multinational connection only spans about 600 miles.

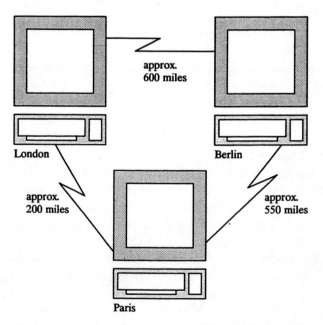

Figure 1.3 Connections Across Country Boundaries

A network doesn't even need to stretch across the street in order to encounter international needs. The population at some international research facilities—or even many computer manufacturers—resembles a mini-United Nations. Since scientists and developers at such sites speak multiple languages, they often have varying computing requirements. Of course, just as the United Nations has a small set of "official" languages, most individual sites do a majority of work in a single language. However, a varied work force using a single network means that software customized for individual languages may cause confusion on the network.

1.4   A New Programming Model

While the old way of writing software may lead to customer rejection, compromises, maintenance problems, and systems that can't interoperate, there is a new programming paradigm that helps eliminate these problems. This new model is called *internationalization*.

Internationalization involves breaking some old programming habits to remove cultural biases and replacing them with the flexibility needed to handle users' differing requirements. This book describes how to write internationalized programs and covers related topics including:

- Linguistic and cultural conventions used in many parts of the world—from Japanese to German to Arabic—and why current programming practices are often inadequate to handle the variety.
- Two common programming models for handling cultural and linguistic differences, and their advantages and disadvantages.
- New routines, concepts, and character encoding methods that have been added to international standards, the C programming language, and UNIX-like operating systems to meet worldwide user demands.
- Advice for changing existing programs to use the new programming model.
- Advice for documenting internationalized functionality and for removing cultural biases from existing documentation.
- An overview of the special requirements that multilingual and distributed computing add to the internationalization picture.

With this information, you can write internationalized software that is capable of taking on much of the world.

A World
of Differences

2

This chapter is about assumptions. Assumptions that may find their way into your everyday programming practices. Assumptions like: *A–Z includes every letter*. Or: *spaces separate words*. Or how about: *"characters" and "bytes" are the same thing*.

There are dozens of others. The only problem is, they are wrong.

The fact that they are wrong and that you probably don't even question these assumptions has serious consequences. It means most software can only handle data in one language, and that if you want the software to handle other languages, you must rewrite it.

Rewriting a program that works just fine for their language is not most programmers' idea of fun. But you can write software in such a way that a major rewrite is not necessary if your company suddenly moves into new international markets. First, though, you need to know what assumptions you probably are making, and why most don't fit today's global markets. This chapter covers linguistic and cultural conventions that affect the software most engineers are likely to write, including:

- The characters used to write languages, and numbering systems
- Language-specific characteristics, including character classification, collation, directionality, punctuation, and grammar
- Culture-specific characteristics, including date and time formatting, calendars, numeric and monetary formatting, measurement systems, and conventions for personal information such as names and addresses

Note that this chapter just points out differences around the world that can impact software; it doesn't tell how to handle them. After all, you can't design software properly until you know what it needs to do. Once you understand those

9

needs, it is up to you to decide whether to handle all or just some of them. Later chapters cover methods for giving software an international flair.

2.1   A Hundred Ways to Write

Over the centuries, different cultures have developed thousands of languages, and hundreds of *scripts* to express those languages on paper. A script is a collection of related graphic symbols used for writing. Most European languages use the Latin script, while Middle Eastern languages often use the Arabic script, and some Asian languages use Han ideographs. While the variety is apparent to anyone who has ever seen printed multilingual text, it has been difficult to get the written languages available on computer systems. Many systems seem stuck in a linguistic dark age, only able to handle American English or maybe the local language (whatever that is) and American English.

The following sections describe characteristics of some of the major scripts and writing systems used throughout the world.

2.2   Latin Scripts

Many European languages are descendants of Latin, which was the official language of the Roman Empire. Those languages tend to be written using some variant of the Latin (or Roman) script. Examples include French, Italian, and Romanian. There also are many languages that are not related to Latin but still use its script. Northern European languages such as German, Danish, and English all are twigs on the Germanic, rather than Latin, branch of the language tree, but they all use the Latin script. Similarly, Eastern European regions or countries that are predominantly Roman Catholic tend to use the Latin script. Examples of these languages include Polish and Hungarian.

The Latin script is used for other languages as well. European missionaries devised a script using Latin letters for Vietnamese, while Malay picked up its Latin-based script when under British rule. And the common African language Swahili, which is not related to Latin, also can be written with the Latin characters.

2.2.1   The Latin Alphabets

When beginning to read Latin scripts, the first thing a child learns is the alphabet. The letters are the foundation on which everything else builds. Once mastered, there are no surprises when opening a book—all words consist of the same set of symbols. The child may not be able to sound out a word (especially in English, with its famously irregular spelling), or may not know the meaning of a given word, but at least the letters all look safely familiar.

So it is a fairly safe assumption that people feel they know the alphabet. There's only one problem. They only know *their* alphabet.

If you ask people who speak, say, English or French, to describe the alphabet, they would say it begins with *A* and ends with *Z*. However, while the English speakers would only be envisioning plain letters, the French speakers would know that certain letters might include an accent or other mark. But at least the French and English speakers would be thinking of the same base set of letters.

Not so with, say, the Danes. They would agree that the alphabet begins with *A*, but for them it ends with Å. Though the two letters look similar, they are considered separate and distinct entries in the Danish alphabet. (It is a little startling for an English-speaking visitor to see the two volumes of the Copenhagen telephone book: A–K and L–Å.)

Poles would agree that the last letter is Z, but it would be a Z with a dot over it rather than a plain Z. The plain Z comes two letters before the Z-with-dot. The Icelandic alphabet has only one form of Z, but it does have two characters that are unfamiliar to modern English speakers, although they existed in Old English: þ (*thorn*) and ð (*eth*).

While some languages that use Latin scripts include more characters than does the English alphabet that most computers process, these same languages omit some letters that are familiar to English readers. Hungarian doesn't include *Q* or *W*. Polish omits *Q*, *V*, and *X*. Spaniards reciting the alphabet wouldn't include *W*, although the letter can appear in words of foreign origin. Vietnamese doesn't include *F*, *J*, *W*, or *Z*.

2.2.2 Diacritics

English is one of the few languages using the Latin script that includes only plain letters. Most other languages include groups of letters that can take a variety of accent marks, dots, and other symbols. Collectively, these symbols are called *diacritics*. Table 2.1 shows common diacritics in Latin scripts.

Diacritics often are used to indicate a special phonetic value. In a way, they are pronunciation aids, because they can indicate which syllable to stress, or how a particular letter should be pronounced. In French, a plain *c* often has a hard *k* sound (for example, *crudité*), while a ç is always pronounced as a soft *s* (*façade*). However, it is not always the case that a letter with a diacritic is pronounced differently

Table 2.1   Common Diacritics

Diacritic	Name(s)
´	acute accent
˘	breve
ˇ	caron
˙	dot above
˝	double acute accent
¸	cedilla
ˆ	circumflex
¨	diaeresis, umlaut
`	grave accent
°	ring
˛	ogonek
~	tilde

from its plain counterpart. Sometimes a diacritic simply differentiates two words that sound the same but have different meanings. Again, using French as an example, there are the words *ou* (or) and *où* (where).

In any case, diacritics are common in nearly all languages that use the Latin script. Among the few exceptions are English, Hawaiian, and Swahili.

The differences described so far prove that there is no such thing as *the* Latin alphabet. Rather, there are dozens of different Latin alphabets. Table 2.2 shows the alphabet (lowercase only) as it exists in four languages. Note that each letter listed is considered a separate entry in the alphabet. For example, while the French consider both plain *a*'s and those with diacritics to be different versions of the same letter, the Poles, Vietnamese, and Danes classify their versions as completely different characters. They are as different from each other as *a* is from *b*.

2.3   Other Alphabetic Scripts

While the Latin script is used today for many languages, it is by no means the only alphabetic script in wide use. This section describes some other major alphabetic writing systems.

Table 2.2   Sample Latin-Based Alphabets

English	Danish	Polish	Vietnamese
a	a	a	a
b	b	ą	ă
c	c	b	â
d	d	c	b
e	e	ć	c
f	f	d	d
g	g	e	đ
h	h	ę	e
i	i	f	ê
j	j	g	g
k	k	h	h
l	l	i	i
m	m	j	k
n	n	k	l
o	o	l	m
p	p	ł	n
q	q	m	o
r	r	n	ô
s	s	ń	ơ
t	t	o	p
u	u	ó	q
v	v	p	r
w	w	r	s
x	x	s	t
y	y	ś	u
z	z	t	ư
	æ	u	v
	ø	w	x
	å	y	y
		z	
		ź	
		ż	

2.3.1 Greek

Before there was a Latin script, there was one in Greece, and the Latin version is a direct descendant of its Greek ancestor. The Greek script was in common use more than 2500 years ago, and continues (with minor modifications) to be used today in its native country.

Greek characters also are familiar to mathematicians and computer scientists, who frequently use letters like α, θ, and σ (alpha, theta, and sigma), and to members of American fraternities and sororities. (Such organizations almost always have names like ΑΓΔ.)

Table 2.3 shows the Greek script.

Table 2.3   The Greek Script

Uppercase	Lowercase	Name
A	α	alpha
B	β	beta
Γ	γ	gamma
Δ	δ	delta
E	ε	epsilon
Z	ζ	zeta
H	η	eta
Θ	θ	theta
I	ι	iota
K	κ	kappa
Λ	λ	lambda
M	μ	mu
N	ν	nu
Ξ	ξ	xi
O	o	omicron
Π	π	pi
P	ρ	rho
Σ	σς*	sigma
T	τ	tau
Υ	υ	upsilon
Φ	φ	phi
X	χ	chi
Ψ	ψ	psi
Ω	ω	omega

* lowercase sigma has two forms

Ancient Greek used a wide variety of diacritics, mostly to indicate pronunciation, but modern Greek generally only uses two: an accent (usually written as a dot over a vowel) and a diaeresis. However, it is not uncommon to include quotes from ancient Greek in a modern text, so a fully functional Greek text editor needs to handle the more complex ancient Greek forms.

2.3.2 Cyrillic

As the Greek script played parent to the Latin script, it also gave birth to another child: the Cyrillic script. Cyrillic is based on Greek characters, but also includes some descendants of Hebrew letters, as well as a few letters that were invented to handle sounds that didn't exist in Greek or Hebrew.

As noted earlier, regions that accepted Roman Catholicism tend to use Latin letters. In contrast, areas that followed the Byzantine, or Eastern Orthodox, branch of Christianity usually use Cyrillic characters. This leads to some interesting anomalies, where languages that are members of the same linguistic family use different scripts. Polish, Hungarian, Croatian, Serbian, and Russian all are Slavic languages, but the first three are written with Latin characters, while the last two use Cyrillic. In fact, Serbian and Croatian are nearly identical when spoken, but look completely different when written.

Figure 2.1 shows the Russian alphabet. The first and third lines are uppercase letters, while the second and fourth show the equivalent lowercase letters.

А Б В Г Д Е Ё Ж З И Й К Л М Н О П Р С Т У Ф

а б в г д е ё ж з и й к л м н о п р с т у ф

Х Ц Ч Ш Щ Ъ Ы Ь Э Ю Я

х ц ч ш щ ъ ы ь э ю я

Figure 2.1   Russian Alphabet

2.3.3 Hebrew

The Hebrew script dates back over 2,000 years and is the primary writing system for Hebrew and Yiddish. It includes 22 consonants, which are written right-to-left. In addition to the consonants, Hebrew vowels look like dots or other marks and they can appear above and below the consonants. However, it is very common to omit the vowels and leave it as an "exercise to the reader" to fill in the marks mentally. Texts that usually do include vowels include religious books, maps, and some children's reading textbooks. Here are examples of the same phrase in Hebrew—the first with vowels and the second without:

מְטַפֵּס הֶהָרִים הָאַמִיץ תִּרְגֵּם: אָבִיב יוֹרְק

לְפִינוֹקִיוֹ הִתְחַשֵׁק לָצֵאת לְטִיּוּל. וְלֹא סְתָם טִיּוּל, כִּי אִם מַסָּע אָרֹךְ שֶׁיִּגָּמֵר רַק עִם רֶדֶת הַחֲשֵׁכָה. וְכַךְ הוּא יָצָא לַדֶּרֶךְ.

מטפס ההרים האמיץ תרגם: אביב יורק

לפינוקיו התחשק לצאת לטיול. ולא סתם טיול, כי אם מסע ארך שיגמר רק עם רדת החשכה. וכך הוא יצא לדרך

2.3.4 Arabic

Arabic is the script for many languages including Arabic, Farsi (Persian), Pashto, and Urdu. The script consists of 28 letters, and, as with Hebrew, these characters represent consonant sounds only. Marks that can appear above, below, or beside the consonants are the vowels. However, vowels usually are used only if the text would be ambiguous without them.

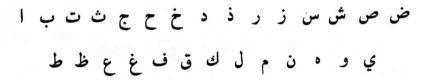

Figure 2.2   The Arabic Alphabet

The Arabic script is written right-to-left, with letters often being joined together to form a cursive writing style. Figure 2.2 shows the consonants of the Arabic alphabet.

2.3.5 Indian and Other South Asian Scripts

As with the Latin and Cyrillic scripts, which are used to write a variety of languages, there is a common writing system for a number of Indian languages.

The Indian subcontinent is home to a large family of related scripts. The oldest of these, Devanagari, was developed for Sanskrit, an Indo-European language. Sanskrit has relatively few speakers today, but the Devanagari script is also used for many living Indian languages, including Hindi, Nepali, and Marathi. The other Indian scripts—Bengali, Gujarati, Gurmukhi, Kannada, Malayalam, Oriya, Tamil, and Telugu—are related to Devanagari, but all have distinct characteristics and appearances.

The top of each Devanagari letter includes a horizontal line, so the letters in words appear to be attached. In the related Oriya script, instead of a horizontal line, nearly every character has a semicircle on top. Figure 2.3 shows the Devanagari script.

क ख ग घ ङ
च छ ज झ ञ
ट ठ ड ढ ण
त थ द ध न
प फ ब भ म
य र ल व
श ष स
ह

ก ข ฃ ค ฅ ฆ ง
จ ฉ ช ซ ฌ ญ
ฎ ฏ ฐ ฑ ฒ ณ
ด ต ถ ท ธ น
บ ป ผ ฝ พ ฟ ภ ม
ย ร ล ว ศ ษ ส ห ฬ อ ฮ

Figure 2.3   The Devanagari Script   **Figure 2.4**   The Thai Alphabet

Indian scripts contain vowels and consonants, and are written left-to-right.

Other scripts in use in South Asia include Thai, Lao, and Burmese. In the Thai script, the base letters are consonants, and vowels can be added above, below, or beside the consonants. There also are four tone marks that appear above and slightly to the right of the consonant. When both a vowel and tone mark appear with a consonant, the vowel is written first and the tone mark written above it. Figure 2.4 shows the Thai alphabet.

2.3.6 African Scripts

Although hundreds of languages are spoken in Africa, most are written in three major scripts: Arabic, Latin, and Ethiopian. The Arabic script is most common in northern Africa, covering countries such as Algeria, Egypt, and Morocco. South of the Sahara, most languages are written with variations of the Latin script. Examples include Hausa and Swahili, among the most common languages in West and East Africa, respectively, and Fulani, Malinke, and Afrikaans.

The Ethiopian script is used to write several languages including Amharic and Oromo.

2.4   Context Dependency in Alphabetic Scripts

Just as many scripts are in use around the world, alphabetic scripts include features that may seem unusual to nonnative speakers. A good example is *context-dependency*. In a context-dependent writing system, some or most of the letters in the alphabet take multiple forms. The form to use depends on where the letter appears in a word, and any adjacent letters.

Arabic and Hebrew both include letters that take multiple forms, although Arabic has much more variety than does Hebrew. In Arabic, most letters have four forms: initial (when it appears at the beginning of a word), medial (in the middle of a word), final (at the end), and isolated (stand-alone). In contrast, only five Hebrew consonants have multiple forms, and they have only two each: regular and final. Figure 2.5 shows the forms of the Arabic letter *g*. In the figure, rectangular frames mark the different forms.

Although context-dependence may seem unusual to people accustomed to Latin scripts, Latin uppercase and lowercase letters are themselves examples of the concept. Just as position information dictates when to choose a specific version of an Arabic letter, grammatical rules dictate when to choose an uppercase Latin letter over its lowercase counterpart. And while an Arabic letter looks very different in its various forms, so too can Latin letters. Consider the differences among 'A,' 'a,' and cursive '*a*.' It takes experience to learn that these are the same letter.

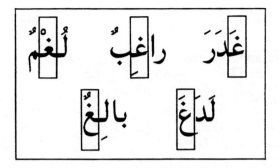

Figure 2.5   Forms of Arabic Letter 'G'

2.5   Ideographic Scripts

Although this chapter has covered a large variety of scripts so far, up to now all of them have been alphabetic or phonetic. That is, the scripts include a specific set of letters, each of which represents a phonetic sound. People combine the finite number of letters in nearly infinite ways to form words.

Other types of scripts exist. Several Asian countries use systems that consist of symbols rather than collections of phonetic letters. This means that, rather than combining letters in different ways to create words, each word consists of its own symbol or set of symbols. These symbols are called *ideographs* or *ideograms*.

2.5.1   The Concept of Ideographs

At first, ideographs were pictographs; that is, pictures of the objects they represented. *Sun* originally was a circle with a dot at its center; *moon* was a crescent with or without a line. Over hundreds of years, however, many characters changed so much that it now is difficult to tell what they depict. In some cases, this is a result of changing writing styles. In others, it reflects the fact that there is no obvious picture for a concept (for example, love, learning, anger, joy) as opposed to an object (a tree, a house, a mountain).

Here are a few ideographs and their English translations:

Ideograph	Meaning
福	Fortune
夢	Dream
空	Sky

Ideographs consist in part of one or more *radicals*. A radical indicates the class of objects to which the word belongs. For example, words like *wood, forest,* and *table* all contain the radical for *wood*.

Although ideographs often seem like an unusual concept to people who are familiar with an alphabetic writing system, they are commonplace in most cultures. Consider Arabic numbers. Each digit (1, 2, 3, etc.) is an ideograph that represents a quantity rather than a sound. Because they are ideographs, Arabic numbers cross language boundaries. The number *42* means the same thing to English, French, and German speakers, although the English speaker pronounces it *forty-two*, the French *quarante-deux*, and the German *zweiundvierzig*.

Ideographs also are common on signs. Those signs can be on roadways or in airports, but the idea is to convey information quickly with a minimum of text. Ideographs also are commonplace on computer screens in the form of icons. Figure 2.6 shows common ideographs meaning no-smoking, do-not-enter, and recycle, respectively.

Figure 2.6   No-smoking, Do-not-enter, Recycle Ideographs

While most languages or cultures use only a few ideographs, some languages use them for the majority of words. Such languages are said to use an *ideographic script*. Examples include Chinese and Japanese, while some Korean words also may be written with ideographs. The ideographs in these systems all are derived from Chinese, and each language has its own name for them. Table 2.4 lists the names. Collectively, these characters are sometimes called *Han*.

Table 2.4   Ideographic Characters' Names

Name	Language(s)
Hanzi	Traditional and Simplified Chinese
Kanji	Japanese
Hanja	Korean

Depending on who is doing the counting, anywhere from 70,000 to 100,000 different ideographs have been identified, although many appear only in scholarly texts. Far fewer are used in everyday life. A Japanese adult might know how to read or write anywhere from 2,000 to 8,000 Kanji characters. This is analogous to English speakers, who typically use only a few thousand words in everyday conversation even though there are approximately 500,000 words in the language.

Although the Han have a common origin, they are used differently in each language.

2.5.2   Chinese

Today's Han ideographs are descended from a set that originated in China several thousand years ago. The characters have evolved considerably over the years, but significant changes in this century have resulted in two separate types of Chinese Hanzi.

In 1955, the government in the People's Republic of China (PRC) launched a campaign to simplify some ideographs and eliminate others all together. Under the plan, characters would be streamlined every five years. Characters have been revised several times now, resulting in a smaller, simpler set called *Simplified Chinese*.

No streamlining has occurred, however, in the Republic of China (ROC) on the island of Taiwan. There, the older, more complex characters still are the norm, and the set needed for everyday use is considerably larger than the PRC set. The ideographs used in the ROC (Taiwan) are called *Traditional Chinese*. Here is a sentence written first in Traditional Chinese, and then with the Simplified characters.

申請人須以正楷填寫中英文資料及香港身份證號碼，否則所得的「管理進修學分」將不會被紀錄。本會將根據表格上之資料頒發證書。

申请人须以正楷填写中英文资料及香港身份证号码，否则所得的‘管理进修学分’将不会被纪录。本会将根据表格上之资料颁发证书。

Computer systems generally process only a subset of all the ideographs in a given language, but the number of characters in that subset gives some indication of what is considered a basic vocabulary. Simplified Chinese systems generally handle about 7,000 ideographs, while current Traditional Chinese versions process up to 15,000. Some future systems are expected to support a 1992 expansion of the standard ROC set to 48,000 characters.

2.5.3 Japanese

Although Japanese is linguistically unrelated to Chinese, it adopted the Chinese ideographs about 1,700 years ago. Over the years, the characters have evolved differently than they did in the PRC. Despite that, a fairly significant percentage of ideographs in the two languages' writing systems are still the same—or close enough that one can easily identify them as expressing the same concept. The result is that although Japanese and Chinese speakers can't understand each others' spoken language, they usually can understand some percentage of each others' written text.

While Chinese text consists almost exclusively of ideographs, Japanese almost always mixes ideographs and phonetic characters. The phonetic characters serve a variety of purposes. Some words tend to be written phonetically, particularly new or foreign words for which no ideograph has been created. In addition, phonetic characters can act as modifiers for some ideographs. This is analogous to the purpose common English word endings (*-ment, -ing, -ed*) serve when appended to a root word. Here is an example of Japanese text:

第30回のテーマは『情報化社会と国際化』です。

コンピューターとその利用技術を通じさまざまな問題解決のお手伝いを致します。

These sentences contain a mixture of Kanji and phonetic characters. In the second sentence, the first seven characters are in one phonetic script, while the next three are in another (see below for details on Japanese phonetic scripts). The following four characters are Kanji. As this example shows, ideographs tend to be more complex than phonetic characters.

Japanese computer systems usually process between 6,000 and 12,000 ideographs. This meets the needs of most everyday text processing.

2.5.4 Korean

South Korea also uses ideographs based on the set invented in China, but to a much lesser degree than does Japan. All Korean text can be written using a phonetic writing system called *Hangul*, which is described in the next section. However, some words (for example, people's names) may be written with Hanja ideographs instead of in Hangul. South Korean computer systems usually process about 4,500 to 6,000 ideographs.

2.5.5 Complementary Phonetic Scripts

Languages that use an ideographic script also often have a phonetic (alphabetic-based) script. Naturally, the phonetic scripts have different characteristics.

- **Japanese**: There are two phonetic systems: *katakana* and *hiragana*. In general, katakana is for words of foreign origin, and hiragana is for writing native Japanese words. Collectively, the two systems are called *kana*. Each set consists of approximately 50 characters.

  Like Latin scripts, which usually include two versions of every letter, katakana and hiragana essentially are two ways of writing the same phonetic characters. Katakana is more angular in appearance, while hiragana is more rounded. The following shows the same five kana characters, first written in katakana and then in hiragana. Commas separate the kana characters.

Katakana:	ア、イ、ウ、エ、オ
Hiragana:	あ、い、う、え、お

The kana characters represent the sounds *a, i, u, e,* and *o,* respectively.

- **Korean:** *Hangul* is the phonetic writing system, and it has 24 characters that each represent a specific sound. You combine between two and seven of the characters to form syllables, and these syllables are the basic units on which most text processing is done. For example, a delete operation usually works on a syllable rather than the individual characters within it. Here is an example of Hangul:

우리나라의 중허리 장산곶은 그 텃셰가 거세기로 유명한 곳이다. 대륙의 묏뿌리가 바다를 향해 미친듯이 냅다 뻗히다가 갑자기 허리가 잘리니, 거기 서부터 깊은 수렁이 생겨 물살이 숨가쁘게 소용돌이친다.

Each printed unit in the Hangul text is a syllable composed of several characters. For example, the final line in the example contains six syllables and a period (.).

- **Simplified Chinese**: *Pinyin* is the most commonly used phonetic system in the PRC. With Pinyin or several other phonetic systems, Latin letters approximate the sounds of Chinese words. However, since the different phonetic systems have varying rules, they render words in a variety of ways. A well-known example of this is the two versions of the name of the PRC's capital city: *Beijing* in Pinyin and *Peking* in an older system called Wade-Giles.

- **Traditional Chinese**: No standard phonetic system exists for Traditional Chinese. Many people use a system called *BoPoMoFo* which, like Japanese kana, has its own set of characters. Others use a form of Pinyin.

In the past, children and foreigners were the ones who tended to use Chinese phonetic systems, while native adults seldom did. However, adults are beginning to use them more often as input mediums on computers. See Appendix B for details.

2.6   Numbers

In addition to the different characters people around the world use to construct words, they also use a variety of characters to represent numbers. However, there is less variety in numbering schemes than there is in alphabetic or ideographic scripts.

Arabic numbers by far are the most commonly used in the world. They are the standard in Europe, North and South America, Australia, and much of Asia and Africa. The familiar *1, 2, 3 . . .* numbers are common even in countries that have indigenous numeric characters. Thai paper money has both Arabic and Thai numbers printed on it. Japanese has Kanji characters for numbers, but it is more common to use the Arabic versions.

Although Arabic numerals are the most common, other numbering systems also are in use. Many Middle Eastern countries (including, ironically, Saudi Arabia) do not use Arabic numbers, but instead use what they call Hindi numbers. Hindi speakers also use a set of what they call Hindi numbers, but the two versions of *Hindi* numbers look considerably different. And, like several Southeast Asia countries, Thailand also has its own digits. All of these numbering systems are decimal-based.

Other, nondecimal systems also are in use around the world. Roman numerals probably are the most common non-Arabic numbers, even though their use these days is fairly rare. Italy still uses them to some extent (as the section on dates later in this chapter shows). Otherwise, they are most common in Hollywood movie sequel titles, building cornerstones, and American Super Bowls.

Han ideographic numbers are another example of a nondecimal numbering system. The PRC, Japan, and the ROC use these numbers to some extent, but Arabic numbers are becoming more and more common. Figure 2.7 shows examples of equivalent quantities using Arabic, Roman, and Han numbers. The Han numbers are written vertically rather than horizontally. Notice that the Han versions of

	1	2	3	4	5	10	20	25	100
Arabic	1	2	3	4	5	10	20	25	100
Roman	I	II	III	IV	V	X	XX	XXV	C
Chinese	一	二	三	四	五	十	二十	二十五	百

Figure 2.7   Equivalent Arabic, Roman, and Han Numeric Quantities

20 and *25* consist of multiple digits, while all other Han quantities include only one digit. For example, *20* consists of the digit *2*, followed by the digit *10*—that is, two-tens.

2.7 Language-Specific Conventions

Knowing the characters necessary to write a language or express numeric quantities is one thing, but that's only the tip of the language iceberg. There are many other characteristics of languages that affect software.

2.8 Character Classification

It often is useful to classify a character, to describe what groups it belongs to. Is it an alphabetic character? Uppercase? A control character? Knowing what groups a character belongs to makes it possible to decide how to process that character.

Some programming languages supply their own set of classifications. C includes classification functions like **isupper( )** (for uppercase) or **ispunct( )** (for punctuation). The set was designed to meet American English needs, and it did so well, but the set often wasn't capable of handling other languages. For example, there is a general assumption that all letters come in two varieties (uppercase and lowercase). Programs may also include a hard-coded definition of uppercase characters—and that definition only includes English letters. Such assumptions are obsolete in an international setting.

2.8.1 Uppercase and Lowercase

Many scripts have no concept of case; there is just one version of each phonetic character or symbolic ideograph. Ideographic scripts such as those used in Japan, the ROC, and the PRC all have only one case, while phonetic scripts such as those used for Arabic, Hindi, and Thai also only have one case.

Even languages that do differentiate between case sometimes make exceptions, or add other rules that don't exist in American English. In German, the Eszett (ß) is a lowercase letter that has no single-letter uppercase equivalent. Instead, it gets converted to two uppercase S's. That means, for example, that the uppercase version of *straße* is *STRASSE*. You therefore cannot assume every lowercase character has a simple uppercase equivalent.

When the French write uppercase letters, most omit diacritics that would appear on equivalent lowercase letters. That means a word like *être* becomes *ETRE*. It might therefore seem logical that when converting the case of French letters, you map any lowercase letter with a diacritic to its plain uppercase counterpart. But when converting from uppercase to lowercase, you need to know how to map now-plain letters to the appropriate versions-with-diacritics. Note that this isn't an issue with Canadian French. In that variety of French, letters keep diacritics in both lowercase and uppercase versions.

There also are situations when letters that used to be inverses of each other no longer are. Turkish has two versions of the letter *I* : one with a dot over it and one without. The uppercase dotless-I is the inverse of the lowercase dotless-i, while the two dotted versions are inverses of each other. That probably seems logical until you remember that most Latin scripts consider the uppercase dotless-I to be the inverse of a lowercase *dotted*-i.

2.8.2 Ligatures

Ligatures are sequences of characters that must be treated as a unit. Sometimes that is easy to do because the ligature gets defined as a letter in the alphabet. Both Danish and Norwegian include the æ character, which really is a combination of the letters *a* and *e*.

It is not so simple, however, with other languages. The *ij* ligature in Dutch is an example. Some Dutch typewriters and computer keyboards have a single key for *ij*, but it also is common for users to enter the ligature as the two separate letters *i* and *j*. Software, however, may need to treat the two letters as a unit. For example, the correct way to write the name for *Iceland* in Dutch is *IJsland*. This characteristic has an effect on routines that capitalize the first "letter" in each word of a string.

Languages that use Latin scripts have only a few ligatures, but context-dependent languages such as Arabic and Hindi have dozens. Each Arabic letter can be written separately, but when certain pairs appear next to each other, they get combined into a ligature. Figure 2.8 shows the process. In the figure, the three letters (from right to left) Lam, Hamza-Fathah, and Hamza-Sukoun generate the Lam-Mad character.

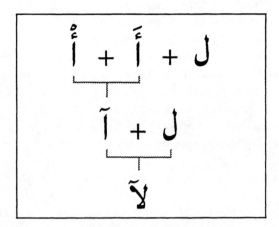

Figure 2.8   Sample Formation of Arabic Ligature

Input routines and editors are among the software packages that may need revising to handle ligatures correctly.

2.8.3 New Character Classifications

Classes like **alpha** or **upper** cover the needs of languages that use Latin scripts fairly well, but they are inadequate to process other languages. Languages that use both phonetic and ideographic scripts find it helpful to be able to differentiate between the characters of those scripts. For example, some Japanese vendors supply Japanese-specific functions like **jkata**, **jkanji**, and **jhira**.

Chinese and Korean need similar classes, though the names obviously differ from the Japanese-specific names. Other languages need additional, but different, classes. Hindi and Thai need to be able to differentiate a vowel from a consonant. That's because some sorting schemes depend on picking out the first vowel in a word while others give vowels different weights than consonants.

Classifications that only cover English- or Latin-based concepts aren't enough to satisfy international needs.

2.9   Putting Things in Order

A common task for computer software is to sort an unordered list of data, or add new data into an already-ordered list. This is fairly easy for English data, since sorting rules usually are very simple: each letter sorts to only one place. For most applications, the only complicated aspect of sorting is whether to separate letters by case. Many computer systems make that decision for users because their default sort order puts all uppercase letters before all lowercase. This is not quite a natural order, but most of their users are accustomed to that anomaly. In fact, many developers of UNIX-like systems depend on the uppercase-first order. Consider README files. Developers often put important information in such files, knowing that when users list the contents of a directory, README appears before all file names that start with lowercase letters. Since most people use only lowercase letters in file names, the chances are good that README is the first in the list.

While English rules are simple, other languages include an enormous variety of collation methods, or combinations of methods. The variety means old assumptions like where README appears are invalid in an international setting.

2.9.1   Handling Additional Characters

What probably is the easiest sorting method beyond typical American English computer sorts involves adding characters to the English set the system handles. In Danish and Norwegian, there are three letters after *z* in the alphabet: *æ, ø,* and *å*. Swedish also has additional letters after *z* : *å, ä,* and *ö*. In Spanish, *ñ* comes between *n* and *o* in the alphabet.

Handling such additions simply involves recognizing that there is more to an alphabet than English A–Z and a–z, and providing a way to include the additional characters.

2.9.2   Multilevel Sorting

In some languages, specific groups of characters sort to one primary location, and then if there is a tie, a secondary sort is applied. To refine the collated order even more, you can apply an additional sort or sorts. A simple example of a multilevel sort is sorting uppercase and lowercase versions of letters together, and then applying a secondary sort to break ties. These lists show a single-level sort that segregates letters by case, and a multilevel sort that ignores case on the first pass, and then uses it to break ties.

Single-Level	Multilevel
Az	a.out
README	Az
a.out	rare
rare	README
temp.c	temp.c

Several European languages use a more complex multilevel sorting method. In French, the versions of the letter *a* (*a, á, à,* and *â*) all sort to the same primary location. If two strings collate to the same primary location, the secondary sort goes into effect. Consider these two orders for the same French words:

Correct	Incorrect
a	a
à	abord
abord	après
âpre	azur
après	court
âpreté	rapport
azur	voyage
court	à
rapport	âpre
voyage	âpreté

The correct output on the left uses a secondary sort, while the output on the right shows how the words sort if all versions of *a* are considered separate, different characters. In the incorrect order, words that begin with *a*'s with diacritics sort after words that begin with other plain letters because the plain letters have a lower encoded value than those with diacritics. (Chapter 4 explains encoded values and Chapter 8 explains how they have been used in collation.)

Arabic also uses a form of multilevel sorting. On a first pass, strings are ordered based on consonants only; any vowels are ignored. On the second pass, if two strings contain identical consonants, vowels are used to break ties.

2.9.3   One-to-Many Character Mappings

Collation systems that use one-to-many character mappings require that certain single characters be treated as if they were multiple characters. In German, ß collates as if it were *ss*. Here are two orders for the same German words:

Correct	Incorrect
laß	lassen
lassen	lässig
lässig	laß
läßig	läßig
laßt	laßt

The incorrect output shows how the words sort if ß is defined as a single character falling between *s* and *t*.

2.9.4 Many-to-One Character Mappings

Some languages treat multiple characters as if they were single elements. That is, when being sorted, these multicharacter strings are treated as if they are single characters. Spanish treats the *ch* and *ll* sequences as individual elements within the alphabet. Spanish dictionaries include separate sections for them; that is, there are entries for *a, b, c, ch, d,* and so on. Given such rules, these words are in correct Spanish order:

    construir
    curioso
    chal
    chocolate
    dama
    líquido
    lugar
    llama
    lloro
    maíz

Notice that, unlike an English sort, *chal* and *chocolate* appear after the words that begin with *co* and *cu*. Likewise, words that begin with *ll* sort after *lugar*.

Vietnamese also uses multicharacter collating elements. This is part of the collation sequence:

    . . . k, kh, l, m, n, ng (and ngh), nh, o, ô . . .

Although multicharacter collating elements most often consist of two characters, as the example above shows (*ngh*), they can include more.

2.9.5 Don't-Care Character Mappings

Some collating methods require that certain characters be ignored during processing. If dash (-) is a don't-care character, the strings *re-locate* and *relocate* sort to the same place. While a dash can be defined as a don't-care character, a space is a more common example. Computer sorts tend to consider spaces significant, but, as the following example illustrates, dictionaries often ignore them. The output on the left is in typical English dictionary order and so ignores spaces, while that on the right uses spaces in determining the order.

Ignore spaces	Don't ignore spaces
natural	natural
natural gas	natural gas
naturalize	natural language
natural language	natural resource
natural resource	naturalize
nature	nature

2.9.6 Collating Ideographs

Words in languages that use ideographic scripts, like Japanese and Chinese, consist of one or more symbols rather than collections of letters, and so collation methods are considerably different from those for phonetic scripts. Among the commonly used sorting schemes are:

- **Stroke count**. Ideographs consist of varying numbers of strokes. Very simple characters may have only two or three strokes, while the most complex have 20 or more. A stroke count collating method counts the strokes in each character and puts those with the fewest strokes first, followed by the increasingly complex characters. This method often is combined with the radical method (described next). When combined, the primary sort is by stroke count and the secondary is by radical.
- **Radical**. Ideographic characters are composed in part of a small number of basic building blocks called radicals. A sort by radical groups together characters that contain the same radical(s). Just as a radical sort often is a secondary sort with the stroke count method, it is common to combine radical sorting with stroke count. In this case, however, the primary sort is by radical and the secondary by stroke count.

- **Pronunciation**. Under this method, ideographs sort according to the way they are pronounced. Implementing such a method is much more difficult than it may seem. There are no letters to compare for like values; two words that collate near each other may look completely different. This means pronunciation information must be associated in some way with each word. Some implementations of this sorting method keep each string in two forms—as ideographs and as the phonetic characters that match its pronunciation.

To illustrate the effect of these collation methods, here is how the same characters sort using each of these methods:

Stroke	Radical	Pronunciation
舟	刊	偉
偉	号	家
刊	舟	霾
能	寿	刊
号	家	号
家	能	寿
寿	偉	舟
霾	霾	能

Notice that the first ideograph on the **Stroke** list moves down to third in the radical order, and to seventh in the pronunciation order. Similarly, the first ideograph on the **Radical** list is third in stroke order and fourth in pronunciation order.

2.9.7 Collation Flexibility

There are many more collation methods than those outlined in this section, but you should now understand that sorting algorithms need much more functionality than tends to exist in American English versions. However, there is another requirement: the ability to choose a sort order. It is common for a single language to use multiple sort orders including dictionary, mixed case, book index, and telephone book. Users require a method for choosing the sort that meets their needs.

2.10 Directionality

The direction in which text is written differs from language to language. Horizontal, left-to-right text probably is the most common direction, with languages that use Latin and Cyrillic scripts being among those written in that direction. Most

Indian languages, including Hindi and Bengali, also run left-to-right as do other languages like Greek and Thai.

Left-to-right text isn't the only way to go, however. Languages that use ideographic scripts, such as Japanese or Chinese, may be written vertically right-to-left. The following shows vertical Japanese text:

今日は良いお天気ですね。ハイキングに出かけませんか。

Here is another example of vertical text using English characters:

This is the direction for some ideographic text: vertical and right to left.

(This example also shows that it is permissible to divide words anywhere. See the section "Hyphenation and Justification" for more information.)

While Japanese and Chinese may be written vertically, they also can appear horizontally left-to-right—that is, they may appear in the same order as the languages mentioned earlier. Horizontal writing has become the norm in the PRC (the norm still is vertical in the ROC), while the direction for Japanese usually depends on the subject of the text and on how many foreign characters appear in it. The more foreign characters, the more likely it is the text appears horizontally. It is common to render newspaper articles and novels vertically (although newspaper headlines often are horizontal). In contrast, the rendering for articles and books on technical subjects is almost always horizontal, while a lot of everyday text such as advertisements also appears horizontally. In any case, it is desirable for users to be able to select the direction in which they want text to appear.

In addition to the horizontal left-to-right, and the vertical right-to-left writing directions, other scripts are written horizontally, right-to-left. Examples include Arabic and Hebrew. For example, if you pretend this is Arabic:

```
.tfel-ot-thgir nettirw si sihT
```

Numbers can add an additional wrinkle to the directionality story. Although text in Hebrew goes right-to-left, numbers go left-to-right, so Hebrew actually is bi-directional. For instance, if this were in Hebrew:

```
.1942 ni desaeler saw acnalbasaC
```

it would be saying that the movie *Casablanca* was released in the year 1942, not 2491. Here is actual Hebrew text that includes letters and numbers. The letters go right-to-left, and the digits go left-to-right.

כידוע לכם, החל מתאריך 30 לספטמבר 1991,
קבוצתנו עוברת להיות תחת ניהולה של יחידת
המיחשוב המרכזית.

בתאריך זה יעברו משרדינו לרחוב הגפן 579,
שדרות הגעתון, נהריה 789 33. לפיכך כל פניה
בכתב תעשה לכתובתנו החדשה.

Numbers in Arabic also appear to be written left-to-right, but they actually go right-to-left. The difference is the way people express quantities. Assume an Arabic text contains the quantity *123* written in Hindi digits. While, for example, an American would read this left-to-right as *one hundred twenty three*, a Saudi Arabian would read it right-to-left as something like *three ones, two twenties, one hundred*. The American expresses the most significant portion of the number first, while the Saudi Arabian expresses the least significant.

2.11   Understanding What's Written

Along with the variety of scripts for writing languages, collation methods, and character classification rules, there also is variety in language-parsing systems. This section looks at common assumptions ranging from methods for identifying works to differing punctuation rules, and shows where those assumptions break down.

2.11.1   Picking Out Words

A common assumption is that white space—usually blanks, tabs, or carriage returns—separates words in text. This assumption gets applied in several ways. It is used to count the number of words in a file, or to figure out how to justify text—especially for editors that don't know how to hyphenate words. An editor might also use the assumption to advance the cursor to the next word in text.

The problem is, this assumption doesn't apply to some languages. Instead of using a space between words, an Ethiopian uses a symbol that looks similar to a colon (:). Other languages use nothing to delimit words. Although some Japanese hiragana-only children's books might use spaces to help young readers pick out words, anything beyond a beginning Japanese reading text does not contain spaces. This example shows the absence of spaces:

人は言葉や文字で意志を表して来ました。中でも文字は言葉を形にし、
意味を知らせる工夫の結晶です。象形・表意・表音など東西でそれぞ
れ異なっても 文字は情報の重要な伝達手段です。

The lack of spaces in languages that use ideographs may seem fairly easy to understand. After all, if many words consist of only one or two ideographs, spaces aren't necessary to delineate them. However, there also are phonetic writing systems—for example, Thai and Burmese—that don't use spaces to separate words. So:

```
AThaisentenceiswrittenlikethis.
```

Spaces do, however, appear between phrases in Thai text. Their use is roughly analogous to commas (,) in English text.

2.11.2   Hyphenation and Justification

The absence of spaces can create new algorithmic challenges for applications like word processors. How do they decide where to break a line when justifying text? For some no-space languages, it actually is relatively easy. Japanese permits

breaks anywhere except at some punctuation. And unlike most languages that use
Latin scripts, there is no need to insert hyphens at a word break. For example:

```
If this were written in Japanese, th
e way these words are broken would b
e acceptable. However, you cannot be
gin a line with some puncutation cha
racters such as a period, close quot
es, comma, etc. Also, you cannot end
a line with a beginning quote charac
ter.
```

Despite the fact that languages like Japanese have simple rules regarding breaks
within words, justification routines must be aware of technology-driven aspects of
these languages. You can break words, but you can't break characters. It takes two
or more bytes to encode most ideographs, and a line break scheme that chops text at,
say, 80-byte boundaries might slice right through the middle of a multiple byte character. To avoid this, the justification algorithm must include some character-
processing logic.

However, the sophistication needed for a Japanese justification algorithm is
small compared to that for many European languages. Justification without hyphenation for European languages is only permissible at word boundaries, but the output
can have excessive space. For example:

```
Justified text in English or other languages that
use the Latin script  can be distracting  to read
if word    breaks force     excessive   space in the
output.
```

The problem is even tougher with Thai. That language only allows breaks at
word boundaries, but since spaces delineate phrases rather than words, software has
to be very sophisticated to find word breaks. One common approach to solving this
problem is to build in rules of character groupings (and perhaps dictionaries of
words), and then to examine each sentence for logical groupings. This is similar to
the algorithms used in word processors that do automatic hyphenation.

Different languages have different hyphenation rules—or, as the Japanese example shows, no hyphenation rules. A word processor that includes a hyphenation
algorithm for English obviously needs to learn new rules if it now needs to hyphenate, say, French or German text. It also may need logic for handling additional

hyphenation requirements, such as revising the spelling of some words. In German, hyphenation changes the string *ck* to *kk*. For example, *Zucker* and *backen* become *Zuk-ker* and *bak-ken*, respectively.

Some languages don't need hyphenation algorithms, but whether that simplifies or complicates word processing depends on other language characteristics. As you have seen, languages that use ideographic scripts do not hyphenate. Instead, words can run across line boundaries almost without restriction. Many Middle Eastern or Indian writing systems, such as Arabic and Hindi, also do not use hyphens, but that is because they disallow breaks within words. This may make it more difficult to produce justified text that doesn't include excessive space between words.

2.11.3 Punctuation

The correct symbols for punctuating text depend on the language in use. Many languages use a question mark (?) at the end of a question, but Spanish adds an inverted question mark (¿) at the beginning. Greek uses a semicolon (;) where other languages use the question mark. This is how to punctuate the question *What time is it?* in a variety of languages:

Text	Language
Quelle heure est-il?	French
¿Qué hora es?	Spanish
Τι ώρα είναι;	Greek

There are other differences in punctuation. Neither Hindi nor Japanese uses a period (.) at the end of a sentence. Instead, Hindi uses a vertical bar and Japanese uses a small circle. Here is an example of a Japanese sentence:

第３０回のテーマは『情報化社会と国際化』です。

Greek and French enclose literal speech in guillemets (« and ») rather than quotation marks ("). Russian and English use the same symbol to end a quote ("), but Russian uses a low double quote at the beginning. Japanese uses symbols that look similar to inverted and backward L's to enclose literal speech. Here is an example of a quoted Japanese sentence:

「今日は、とても良い天気ですね。」

These and other differences in punctuation can be important if your software searches for a particular character for any reason.

2.11.4 Varieties of a Single Language

In addition to the differences that exist *between* languages, there also are differences *within* languages, and those differences need to be factored into software. Americans and the British arguably both speak English, but there are considerable differences in the two versions of the language. Similarly, there are differences between Portuguese as spoken and written in Portugal and Brazil, or in Spanish as used in Spain and Argentina. Other varieties of languages exist throughout the world.

Pronunciation differences are perhaps the most noticeable attribute of language varieties, but most software doesn't care about the spoken word; just about the written. (Voice recognition systems are an obvious exception.) There are other differences, however, that do impact the majority of software.

There may be differences in spelling, which affect spelling checkers and possibly hyphenation systems. Consider these examples of American and British spelling:

American	British
center	centre
color	colour
check	cheque
maneuver	manoeuvre
tire	tyre

Grammatical rules may differ between varieties of languages. In American English, collective nouns such as *company, government,* and *department* are considered singular, and so take a singular verb (*The government has decided ...*). In British English, these nouns are plural, and take a plural verb (*The government have decided ...*).

The vocabulary in branches of a language tends to differ. In some cases, the varieties each have unique words for one concept. Most Spanish speakers use either *tú* or the more formal *usted* for the English *you*, but in Argentina, people use a different word: *vos*. In Spain, the word for *car* is *coche*, but in most other Spanish-speaking countries, it is a *carro*. Similarly, in American English, one might use the terms *mail, gasoline,* and *garbage can*, while in British English, the equivalent words are *post, petrol,* and *dustbin*.

There also are cases when the same word has different meanings in separate varieties of a language. Consider these American and British names for various types of beds:

American	British
cot	camp bed
crib	cot
bassinet	crib

These differences affect the user-visible text that programs produce. Both British and American users expect program prompts and messages to use proper grammar and for all words to be spelled correctly. Similarly, Brazilian and Portuguese users expect software to interact with them in their own version of their language. The issue is that the separate nationalities have different ideas about what is proper and correct.

2.12   Country-Specific Conventions

The somewhat dizzying variety described so far concentrates only on attributes of language—that is, the way people write, the letters or characters they use, and grammatical conventions including sorting and hyphenation. There are separate differences, however, that have little to do with language. Instead, they are features of a culture or country.

2.13   Dates

A date seems like a simple piece of information. You want to express what day of the year it is, and can use either descriptive names (*January, Wednesday*) for months and weekdays, or abbreviations (*Jan, Wed*). Numbers in place of names (1/1/94) make things even simpler. Right?

Not any more. Users around the world express dates using a huge variety of conventions—or they would if their systems would let them. While Americans. might express dates as

Fri, Mar 12, 1993
or
Friday, March 12, 1993

the equivalent dates in French are

ven, 12 mar 1993
or
vendredi, le 12 mars 1993

Notice that not only do the day and month names differ, but the format does as well—American in *month-day-year* order and French in *day-month-year* order. There is much more variety to come.

2.13.1 Abbreviations and Capitalization

Naturally, each language has its own names for the days and months, and software should handle these. American-based software also needs to recognize that there is more to the world than American conventions. Consider capitalization. In English, month and day names are capitalized, but that is not the case in, say, French or Danish. The Danish weekday names are *søndag (Sunday), mandag, tirsdag,* and so on. It is not appropriate to force dates in all languages to use capitalized names. Just as *monday* looks strange to American eyes, *Mandag* looks odd to Danish eyes.

In order to abbreviate month and day names, Americans typically use the first three letters of each name (*Jan, Feb, Mar*). It is common for software to assume that such abbreviations take three—and only the first three—letters.

The three-letter rule doesn't work for all languages. In some cases, two names share the same initial three letters (for example, the French *juin* and *juillet*). In other cases, it is impossible to take the first three letters because there aren't three letters. Japanese month names up to October are written with two characters: one that indicates the number of the month, and a second that is the Kanji for the word *month*. In still other cases, there are no linguistic problems with taking the first three letters, but it is not the accepted convention. When abbreviating weekday names, Germans use only the first two letters of the names (*So, Mo, Di*, etc.).

2.13.2 Month/Day/Year and Other Orders

In addition to differences in day and month names and in abbreviation rules, people around the world also use every order and piece of punctuation you can think of to express dates. Earlier, you saw an example of an American date in this order:

weekday_name, month_name day, year

Table 2.5 shows common methods for formatting dates using only numbers.

Table 2.5   Varieties of Numeric Date Formats

Date	Country and Description
12/3/93	England: day/month/year order
12.3.93	France: day.month.year order
12. 3. '93	Iceland: month. day. 'year order
12-III-93	Italy: day-month-year order; uses the Roman numeral for the month
93.3.12	Japan: year.month.day order
5.3.12	Japan Emperor: same order, but the year is the number of years the current emperor has been reigning, rather than the Gregorian calendar year
3/12/93	USA: month/day/year order

Table 2.6 shows more date-formatting examples, this time using day and month names.

Table 2.6   Varieties of Date Formats

Date	Country
fredag, 12. marts 1993	Denmark
Friday, 12 March 1993	England
vendredi, 12 mars 1993	France
1993 במרץ 12 ,יום שישי	Israel; right-to-left text
平成5年3月１２日 (金曜日)	Japan Emperor
1993년 3월12일 금요일	South Korea
Friday, March 12, 1993	USA

The formats in these tables are not the only way to write the date in the listed country. Just as Americans might use any of these:

3/12/93
3-12-93
Mar 12, 1993

people in other countries also have multiple ways of writing a date.

2.13.3   The Beginning of the Week

The seven-day week is nearly universal throughout the world, even if languages have their own names for the individual days. But when it comes to picking the first

of those seven days, there is a bit of disagreement. To Americans, the week begins
on Sunday and ends on Saturday. Software often reflects this, because the first value
in an array of weekday names tends to be Sunday, the second value Monday, and so
on.

In Europe, however, Monday generally is considered to be the first day of the
week and Sunday is the last day. Calendars are often arranged so that Monday is the
left-most day, and the weekend days of Saturday and Sunday appear together at the
end. It also is common for calendars to appear with a different row-column orienta-
tion than is the standard in the United States. Instead of headings being along the
top and day numbers reading across the rows, headings are along the left side, and
day numbers read down the columns. Here are two examples of a German calendar
for December, 1993:

```
      Dezember 1993                 Dezember 1993

Mo Di Mi Do Fr Sa So        Mo        6 13 20 27
          1  2  3  4  5      Di        7 14 21 28
 6  7  8  9 10 11 12         Mi    1   8 15 22 29
13 14 15 16 17 18 19         Do    2   9 16 23 30
20 21 22 23 24 25 26         Fr    3  10 17 24 31
27 28 29 30 31               Sa    4  11 18 25
                             So    5  12 19 26
```

2.13.4   The Days and Months in the Year

Countries from Brazil to Germany to the United States use the 12-month,
365-day (366 in leap years) Gregorian calendar and define January 1 as the first day
of a new year. This simplifies programming to a degree. However, many predominantly Moslem countries including Saudi Arabia and Egypt use a calendar with 12
months, but only 354 or 355 days. Because this year is shorter than the Gregorian
version, the first day of the year changes year-to-year relative to Gregorian reckon-
ing. If the first day of the Moslem year this year is, say, April 1 on the Gregorian
calendar, next year the first day will be around March 21. This means Moslem
months have no lasting relation to the seasons. While it always is winter during January on the Gregorian calendar (in the northern hemisphere), it may be any of the
four seasons during the first month of the Moslem calendar.

Israelis use the Hebrew calendar that has either 12 or 13 months, depending on
whether it is or isn't a leap year. Similar to the Moslem calendar, non-leap years
have 12 months and between 353 and 355 days. In a leap year, however, there is
an extra thirteenth month. The leap month allows the Hebrew calendar to stay

synchronized with the seasons of the year. Rosh Hashanah (New Year's) is in September or October relative to the Gregorian calendar.

Table 2.7 shows the months of several calendars.

Table 2.7   Months of Gregorian, Hebrew, and Moslem Calendars

Gregorian		Hebrew		Moslem	
Months	**Days**	**Months**	**Days**	**Months**	**Days**
January	31	Tishri	30	Moharram	30
February	28 or 29	Heshvan	29 or 30	Safar	29
March	31	Kislev	29 or 30	Rabi I	30
April	30	Tevet	29	Rabi II	29
May	31	Shevat	30	Jumada I	30
June	30	Adar	29 or 30*	Jumada II	29
July	31	Nisan	30	Rajab	30
August	31	Iyar	29	Shaban	29
September	30	Sivan	30	Ramadan	30
October	31	Tammuz	29	Shawwal	29
November	30	Av	30	Dhu 'l-Qa'da	30
December	31	Elul	29	Dhu 'l-hijjah	29 or 30

*In leap years, the 29-day month Veadar comes after Adar

2.13.5 The Twentieth Century—and Others

If you happen to live in a country that uses the Christian-based Gregorian calendar, this book was written in the 1990s. Under this calendar, counting started in the year Jesus Christ was born—or, at least, that was the idea. Ironically, modern scholars now believe Christ was born about 4 B.C. [Before Christ]. In any event, it is now the latter part of the twentieth century.

Your notion of what year it is, however, depends on the calendar in use. Although Japan uses the Gregorian calendar, it also uses a year-numbering system called Emperor Time. This system is based on the number of years the current emperor has been reigning. When the reigning emperor dies and a new emperor ascends to the throne, a new era begins, and the year count for that era begins. For example, when Hirohito became emperor in 1926 (Gregorian), the Showa era began, and the era year number was set to one (1). Showa continued for the 64 years Hirohito reigned, but when he died in 1989 and Akihito became emperor, the Heisei era began, and the era year number was reset to one (1).

Just as the Gregorian and Japanese emperor calendars begin counting at a significant event, so do most other year-counting systems. The Moslem calendar begins counting from when Mohammed fled from Mecca to Medina on July 16, 622 (Gregorian). The Buddhist calendar used in countries such as India and Thailand dates from the birth of Buddha. The Hebrew calendar dates from the traditional beginning of the world. (According to the Hebrew calendar, the world began approximately 5,750 years ago.) Table 2.8 shows the corresponding year numbers according to various calendars.

Table 2.8   Years According to Various Calendars

Year	Calendar
1992	Gregorian
4 Heisei	Japanese Emperor
1412	Moslem
5753	Hebrew

Note that not all year numbers are valid for an entire Gregorian year because some calendars use a start date other than January 1. The Hebrew year 5753 ran from September 9, 1991 to September 28, 1992. Similarly, the Moslem year of 1412 ran from July 12, 1991 to July 1, 1992.

It is common for countries to use a historic, national calendar and the Gregorian calendar. As noted, both Emperor and Gregorian counting are familiar in Japan. It is not optimal, however, to force countries to use Gregorian dates only. Software that assumes we all use the same calendar assumes too much.

2.14   Time

Just as dates are more variable than you might have thought, so too are time formats, time zones, and daylight savings time conventions.

2.14.1   12-Hour and 24-Hour Clocks

Americans use a 12-hour clock with a.m. and p.m. designations. If Americans think about a 24-hour clock, they tend to think of it as military time (*The attack begins at 0500 hours*). However, a 24-hour clock is common throughout the world. People in Europe, South America, and Asia use it for written times—on airline or railroad timetables, on signs listing a store's hours, and so on. However, people still often use 12-hour conventions in conversation (*I'll meet you at 6 p.m.*).

2.14.2 Formatting Times

In addition to the 12-hour/24-hour time differences, punctuation for written times varies. Table 2.9 shows some common ways of writing times.

Table 2.9   Sample Time Formats

Format	Country
1520	Argentina
15h20	France
15:20 Uhr	Germany
15:20	Japan
15.20	Sweden
3:20 p.m.	USA

As with dates, many countries use multiple formats for writing times.

2.14.3 Time Zones

A good bit of American software knows about the Eastern, Central, Mountain, and Pacific time zones. It may also understand Coordinated Universal Time (UTC), or the zone to which Hawaii and most of Alaska belong, but its knowledge often fails after these few zones. However, there are many more time zones, and the zones may have unexpected characteristics.

First, and most obviously, there are more zones than the American ones. Theoretically, the world is divided into 24 standard time zones—one for every hour of the day and for every 15 degrees of longitude. But it is much messier than that. Countries (or regions within countries) have the freedom to set their own times. Figure 2.9 shows a map of the world's time zones. As the map shows, while many time zones vary from their neighbors by one hour, there are exceptions. Canada, India, and Australia are among the countries with time zones that differ from the next zone by 30 minutes. In South America, Suriname's time is 30 minutes different from that of the next zone, while Guyana's is 45 minutes. It is typical, however, for software to assume that time zones only come in neat, one-hour increments.

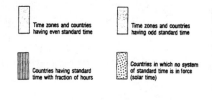

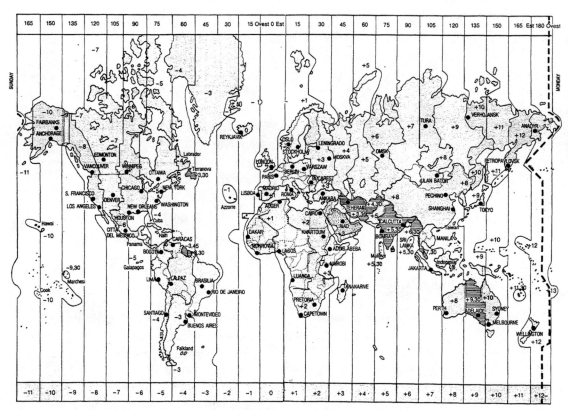

Figure 2.9   Worldwide Time Zones

Single times zones also can have multiple names. Japan and South Korea are both nominally in the same time zone (nine hours ahead of UTC), but in Japan it is called Japan Standard Time (JST) while across the Sea of Japan in South Korea, it is called Korean Standard Time (KST). Also, multiple zones may share an abbreviation. EST stands for Eastern Standard Time in North America, but Eastern Summer Time in Australia.

2.14.4 Daylight Savings Time

The idea of multiple names for a single time zone actually already is familiar to most Americans. The Pacific zone is called Pacific Standard Time (PST) or Pacific Daylight Time (PDT) depending on the time of the year. Daylight Savings Time (DST) is another wrinkle in world time-telling conventions and one that has tripped up some American-based software even when dealing with the United States only.

Some system utilities, including UNIX's **ctime( )** function, were written with hard-coded dates that designated the switchover to or from DST. The idea was that system clocks could make the switch automatically, without intervention from system administrators or users. However, the start and end dates have changed several times, including in 1974 and 1975, forcing existing programs to be recoded. In addition, most programs never were sophisticated enough to handle exceptions, such as some portions of a time zone *not* switching to daylight time. For example, the U.S. state of Arizona remains on Mountain Standard Time all year.

So there have been problems even in dealing with American varieties of DST rules. The world, of course, has more variety to offer. Much of Western Europe goes on what it calls Summer Time in late March, about one week before clocks change in the United States. Most South American countries stay on standard time all year, but Chile adjusts its clocks to save daylight. Japan and South Korea stay on standard time all year long, but South Korea did go on DST in 1988 when it hosted the Summer Olympics.

The southern hemisphere throws one more variable into DST. Since seasons are reversed there relative to the northern hemisphere, DST begins about the same time as it ends in the northern hemisphere. While people in the north are turning their clocks back because it is autumn, residents of the south are turning their clocks ahead because it is spring.

2.14.5 Date and Time Recap

Since dates and times are such an integral part of modern life (when was the last time you went a whole day without looking at a clock or calendar?), software should be able to handle them correctly. A lot has to change, though, before it will.

2.15 Numeric and Monetary Formatting

American conventions for numeric and monetary formats are inadequate for most other countries. The characters used to format such entities vary from place to place. Americans and the British are among those who use a period (.) as the *radix character* (the character that separates whole and fractional quantities), and a comma (,) as a thousands separator. In many European and South American countries, these definitions are reversed. Table 2.10 shows some formatted numeric quantities.

Table 2.10   Sample Numeric Formats

Format	Country and Description
1 234,56	Finland: space as thousands separator; comma as radix character
1.234,56	Germany: period as thousands separator; comma as radix character
1.234 56	Russia: period as thousands separator; space as radix character
1,234.56	United States: comma as thousands separator; period as radix character

Monetary amounts show even more variety. As with numeric quantities, countries use different characters as the thousands separator and radix character. In addition, a plethora of symbols ($, £, ¤, ¥), alphabetic characters (FF, SFrs, kr), or combinations (Cz$) designate the currency in question. There are differing conventions about how many numbers can appear after the radix character. Countries like the United States and Norway allow two digits, but Italy and Japan typically don't use any fractional quantities when expressing amounts in lira and yen, respectively.

There also are many rules about the placement of the currency symbol. Most countries put the symbol at the beginning of the quantity, but some, including Poland, put it at the end. Portugal uses it as the radix character. There are also different meanings for symbols. Many countries use *$* as all or part of their currency symbol, but the name residents attach to that symbol varies. Americans, Canadians, Australians, and others see it as designating dollars (although all these *dollars* actually are different entities), Portuguese as escudos, and Brazilians as cruzados or new cruzados. Table 2.11 shows examples of monetary formats.

In addition to the conventions for formatting amounts in the local currency, there are some special needs when converting between currencies. Although a U.S.

Table 2.11   Sample Monetary Formats

Formatted Amount	Country and Currency
Cz$1.234,50	Brazil; cruzados
¥1,234	Japan; yen
kr1.234,50	Norway; krona
1.234$50	Portugal; escudos
$1,234.50	USA; dollars

dollar amount typically only has two decimal digits, if you needed to convert Italian lira to U.S. dollars, you might well need extra digits.

Many programs that process formatted monetary data are tied to the U.S. dollar as surely as are the world's oil prices. Similarly, anything that formats plain numbers often defines the comma—and only the comma—to separate thousands, and the period—and only the period—for fractional quantities. That means the programs aren't up to the challenge of taking on the world.

2.16   Miscellaneous Differences

In addition to the broad categories of country-specific differences discussed so far (dates, time, numeric, and monetary), there also are a potpourri of other conventions that have a bearing on software design.

2.16.1   People's Names

Americans with mildly unusual names often know first-hand how rigid software can be. You go by your middle name? Too bad. Many computerized forms only accept names of the form *given_name middle_initial surname*. That means someone who is called *Jennifer* Knotts may find herself listed in a database as *Gertrude J. Knotts*.

People without two given names may find similarly inflexible software. A plain John Smith may turn into *John NMI Smith*, where NMI stands for No Middle Initial. Or suppose instead of having "too few" names (from the software's standpoint), you have "too many." A person with three or more given names (like George Herbert Walker Bush) may only be able to enter one and a single initial in computerized forms.

Considering the trouble American programs can have with even American names, it is not surprising that the software fails in other ways when faced with the world's variety. Some Dutch surnames include spaces and use different conventions for capitalization like this:

de Vries

van der Meer

It is not correct in The Netherlands to shove the parts together and capitalize the first letter—*Devries* and *Vandermeer* are wrong—but software often wants to do just that.

These Dutch names aren't written quite like many other European names, but they do follow the same convention of listing given name(s) followed by the surname (family name). That is not the typical order, however, in countries like Japan, the PRC, and South Korea. There, surnames appear first, and the given name appears second. In a Korean name like Kim Soo Jin, *Kim* is the family name and *Soo Jin* is the two-syllable given name. (Note that when working with Westerners, people from these countries often say their names in reverse order. While a person may be known as *Oda Akio* in Japan, he introduces himself as *Akio Oda* in the United States.) These differences show why it is not appropriate to refer to names by position. One culture may consider a "first" name to be a family name, while another thinks of it as the initial given name.

While the absence of a middle name is not unknown in most Western countries, it usually is the exception. Most people have two given names, which is why so much existing software has fields for a surname and two given names (or a given name and initial). For some countries, however, the software is wasteful. In Japan and South Korea, people typically have only one given name (and, of course, a surname). This may affect software design.

2.16.2 Addresses

American applications that include fields for mailing addresses usually assume a format like this:

```
Addressee
Company (Optional)
Number Street-Name
City or Town, State, ZIP Code
```

The format may only allow two-letter abbreviations in the `State` field, and probably restricts the `ZIP Code` field to containing exactly five digits (or nine digits and a hyphen (-), if it allows ZIP+4 codes).

The format accommodates American addresses, but is grossly inadequate for most other countries. Canadian addresses are similar to those in the United States, but in place of a digits-only Zip code, there is a mixed numeric-and-alphabetic postal code (for example, *A1B 2C3*). German addresses typically look something like this:

```
Addressee
Company (Optional)
Street-Name Number

Postal Code, City or Town, District Number
```

Notice that the building number comes after the street name rather than before, as with most American or Canadian addresses. Instead of:

```
24 Fifth Ave.
```

this part of the address looks something like:

```
Arabellastrasse 24
```

Also notice there is a blank line between the street address information and the city and town line, and that addresses typically include both a postal code and a district number.

In Great Britain, addresses generally follow this format:

```
Addressee
House/Building name (if any)
Street Address
Town
County
Post Code
```

British post codes usually follow the format *aan naa*, where *a* is an alphabetic and *n* is a numeric, but they can also include an extra number and thus have the format *aann naa*.

The formats listed so far are similar in that they begin with the most specific data (the individual addressee), and get increasingly less specific (street to town to state or district). Some countries, however, use a mostly opposite format. In South Korea, addresses follow this format:

```
Country
City
District
Number Street-Name
Addressee
Post Code
```

In addition to using a different order, it is common to write a South Korean address on a single line rather than putting fields on separate lines. The format above shows the information on separate lines only to improve readability. Figure 2.10 describes and shows typical South Korean addresses.

The representation of Korean address has two schemes for the central cities and the local areas. The address for the central cities includes the following format where 대한민국 denotes country, 시 denotes city, 구 denotes district, 동 denotes street, and the proper name. And the address for the local areas includes the following format where 대한민 국 denotes country, 도 denotes city, 군 denotes district, 리 denotes street, and the proper name. The post code(zip code) for both schemes is after the address. And in the Korean proper name the family name precedes the personal name.

Examples:

대한민국 서울시 동대문구 청량리동 207-43 홍 길동 130-650
대한민국 경기도 파주군 교하면 와동리 401번지 홍 길동 413-830

Figure 2.10   Sample South Korean Addresses

2.16.3 Telephone Numbers

An individual telephone number is one of the very few pieces of information that is absolutely unique. Other people can have the same name as you, or live on the same street, but no-one outside your household has your exact telephone number. Numbers have to be unique, because there has to be some way to guarantee that when a person dials a certain combination of digits, one—and only one—phone somewhere in the world rings. And if the numbers themselves are all one-of-a-kind, the formatting rules for those numbers seem almost as unique.

American and Canadian telephone numbers follow this format:

```
1 (123) 456-7890
```

where the fields break down as follows:

- The initial 1 is what residents call the long-distance code, and what international callers know as the country code;
- The next three digits make up the area code, which designates a specific region in either of the countries; and
- The final seven digits are the local telephone number.

Every country has its own country code, but it can be anywhere from one to three digits. Table 2.12 shows examples of country codes.

Table 2.12   Sample Telephone Country Codes

Code	Country
1	Canada
56	Chile
20	Egypt
358	Finland
33	France
351	Portugal
7	Russia
1	USA

After a country code, there usually is a city code (area code). These codes usually are one or two digits, but can be three. After the city code comes the local number, which usually has between five and eight digits. Note that local numbers within a country can have different numbers of digits. German local numbers, for example, have anywhere from two to seven digits. Table 2.13 shows examples of phone numbers around the world, including typical formatting conventions. In the table, the plus sign (+) indicates the country code.

Table 2.13   Sample Telephone Numbers

Number	City and Country
+44 71 123 4567	London, England
+33 91–12–34–56	Marseille, France
+39 (6) 1234567	Rome, Italy
+81 3 3123–4567	Tokyo, Japan
+66 221–1234–56	Bangkok, Thailand
+1 (617) 123–4567	Boston, USA

Telephone numbers also can change over time. Until the late 1980s, the city code for London, England was 1. In the early 1990s, that changed to 71 for inner London and 81 for outer London, and in 1995, the codes are scheduled to change again to 171 and 181. This variety matters if your software assumes a telephone number is always *1-area code-number*.

2.16.4 Measurement Systems

Applications such as editors, forms-generating programs, or print drivers typically rely heavily on measurements. An editor may permit users to specify the amount of space that should appear between paragraphs. Likewise, a forms program often includes the ability to set the distance between fields. A print driver may include measurements for overall page margins.

American software usually defines these measurements in terms of inches. Such software might allow you to leave one-quarter (0.25) inch between paragraphs, or to leave one-inch margins at the top and bottom of a page. Most non-American users, however, would prefer to designate sizes in centimeters—if the software would let them.

The metric system, which uses centimeters, meters, and kilometers for distance measurement, liters and deciliters for liquid measurements, and grams and kilograms for weight measurements, is used throughout the world. In contrast, the Imperial system of inches, yards, and miles for distances, quarts and gallons for liquids, and ounces and pounds for weights is widespread in the United States, and used to some degree in England, Canada, and a few other countries. (Canada officially changed to the metric system some years ago, but it still is common for people to discuss things in terms of pounds and yards rather than kilograms or meters. Liters and kilometers have pretty much replaced gallons and miles, however, probably because gasoline is sold in liters and highway signs state distances in kilometers. England has made a similarly mixed adjustment to the metric system. Distances there still are measured in miles, although gas is sold in liters.)

In any event, if your software currently only understands Imperial units, chances are very good there is an international user who would prefer that it handle the metric system.

In addition to the differences between the metric and Imperial systems, there also is the matter of methods for figuring out how hot or cold it is. Despite the best efforts of TV weathercasters and bank thermometers, most Americans still use the Fahrenheit scale for temperatures, while most of the rest of the world uses the Celsius scale.

2.16.5 Standard Paper Sizes

The fact that Americans still use the Imperial system of measurements while most of the rest of the world has long since gone metric is very visible when it comes to paper sizes. In the United States, the standard paper size is 8.5 by 11 inches. In Europe and Asia, the predominant standard size is A4, and it is 210 by 297 millimeters—slightly longer and narrower than the American size.

Differing paper sizes affect print drivers because most assume they know the geometry of a sheet of paper, and so plan line lengths, margins, and the number of lines per page based on that geometry. In addition, while nearly everything discussed in this chapter affects software rather than hardware, the paper size mismatch also impacts hardware. That is because items like paper trays and paper guides often are suitable for only one size.

2.17 Making Order of All This Chaos

This chapter has described a wide array of linguistic and cultural conventions. These are some of the major points:

- **Scripts and writing systems**. Many scripts are used to express words and ideas on paper. Some scripts, including Latin, Arabic, Hebrew, and Hangul, are phonetic, while others are ideographic and so include thousands of characters. Languages like Japanese use writing systems that combine multiple phonetic and ideographic scripts. Some scripts are context-dependent—that is, characters have multiple forms, and the form to use depends on the character's position within a word.
- **Numbers**. Arabic numbers (0, 1, 2, 3, . . .) are the most common, but others also are in use. Not all numbering systems are decimal-based.
- **Language-specific conventions**. Among the variety is:

  — **Character classification**. Languages have varying requirements for character classification. Not all scripts have the concept of case; others can be grouped into classes that don't exist in the Latin script.
  — **Ligatures**. Characters may be combined to form ligatures that must be treated as discrete units.
  — **Collation**. In addition to simple English A–Z sorting, there may be more letters in the alphabet, or the language may require a multilevel sort. Some single characters may sort as more than one, while some multicharacter

strings may sort as a single unit. There are multiple sort orders for ideographs, including stroke count, radical, and pronunciation.

- **Directionality**. The direction in which text is written depends on the script in use and sometimes on user preferences. Horizontal, left-to-right is the most common text direction, but some scripts use horizontal, right-to-left and others use vertical, right-to-left. Text may also have mixed directions—right-to-left for the local language and left-to-right for numbers or foreign text.
- **Parsing**. Some scripts use white space to separate words, while others use it to separate phrases, and still others omit white space completely. Hyphenation and justification methods and requirements differ by language, as do the set of punctuation characters. Spelling and grammar may differ among varieties of a single language.
- **Country-specific conventions**. Some differences are a result of cultural conventions rather than linguistic requirements. Among the variety is:

  - **Dates**. There are many formats for numeric (1/10/94 vs. 10.1.94) and string (January 10, 1994) dates. Each language has its own names for weekdays and months, as well as individual abbreviation and capitalization rules. A variety of calendars exist that count years in alternate ways, or that include different numbers of days or months.
  - **Time**. Times may be expressed with a 12- or 24-hour clock, and use a variety of local formats. Time zones do not always differ from each other in one-hour increments, and such zones go on Daylight Savings Time at different times throughout the year (if they go on Daylight Savings Time at all).
  - **Numeric and monetary**. There are many formats for numeric and monetary quantities, as well as varying currency symbols and rules about the placement of those symbols.

- **Miscellaneous differences**. Nearly every form of textual data people use is subject to unique local requirements. Among the miscellaneous differences are:

  - **People's names**. The order in which names are expressed, as well as the number of given names, and capitalization conventions, may differ from country to country.
  - **Addresses**. The order of information may be from most specific (the individual addressee) to least specific (the country in which he or she lives) or vice versa. Postal/Zip codes include varying numbers of characters and formatting conventions. Building numbers may appear before or after street names.

— **Telephone numbers**. Formats and the number of digits in a telephone number are specific to a country or city.

— **Measurement systems**. Users may want to express quantities or distances in units like quarts, inches, and miles or in units like liters, centimeters, and kilometers.

This list is far from exhaustive. There are local conventions for everything from tax systems to general ledger formats to banking conventions. (See Appendix C for suggestions on how to get specific information about an application area, language, or country.) Knowing that this list is long but not complete may prompt this reaction from an American: *Oh, why can't they just learn English?* A non-American user or maintainer of American software may think: *Who cares about all these other languages; how do I get the software to support* **my** *language?*

These are typical reactions, but, of course, they ignore reality. English can make a claim of being the world's de facto *lingua franca,* but even users who speak English fluently as a second (or third or . . .) language almost always are more comfortable using their native language. And those who understand minimal or no English obviously are stuck when it comes to American English-based software. Such software needs significant changes to handle the variety of linguistic and cultural conventions described in this chapter. Non-American software that handles some other single language is just as limited as its American-only counterpart and needs many of the same changes to become suitable for nonnative users.

Designing for the World 3

In the previous chapter, you learned there are important differences throughout the world in the way people write, speak, and process data. Now you probably want to know what to *do* about these differences. This chapter covers basic design approaches and ways to make the right design work. It covers:

- Why most software (especially a first release) only handles one language.
- The two major design approaches—localization/customization and internationalization—for making a system support more languages and cultures, and the pros and cons of each.
- Ways to provide internationalized systems. This includes sources of appropriate functions, key aspects of the design, and the levels of internationalization support.

3.1   Release 1.0

The first version of most software almost always only understands the language of the developers who wrote it. If the developers happened to be French, the code generally has French error messages, produces dates using French conventions, and features French comments within the source code. If the developers were Japanese, the results probably are a Japanese-speaking package. And, of course, if the developers were American, the code almost always understands only American conventions.

Programmers and users around the world are probably all too familiar with American-only software. A large percentage of commonly used software originated in the United States. Operating systems like UNIX, DEC's VMS, IBM's MVS, and

Microsoft's MS-DOS, as well as other packages like the X Window System and the Apple Macintosh user interface are just a few of the American-born packages or systems that have worldwide audiences. While most of these now handle at least some of the vast spectrum of cultural and linguistic needs, most were firmly tied to American needs in their early years.

Suppose your situation is similar. Assume you are an American and have a software package that works just fine for your users in Dallas, Boston, and Seattle. Trouble is, users in Paris and Tokyo are not interested because the software won't speak to them in their language. Even London users are complaining because the package uses '$' instead of '£' for the currency sign and dates are in the American month/day/year order rather than the British day/month/year format.

What can you do?

3.2   The First Idea — Customization

When first faced with the need to adapt software that handles one language or culture to support another, most developers reopen the code and do one of two things:

- **Remove-Replace**. Delete the current language/cultural support and replace it with the new.
- **Add-On**. Add support for the new language/culture without removing the original.

The following examples show how these approaches might work. First, here is the original code:

```
#include <stdio.h>
#define MAX_ANS 10
/* Given a date, this routine determines what number
 * day of the year it is. Leap years are ignored to
 * simplify the example.
 */
int main (void) {

char answer = 'y';
int i, month, day, num_days;
static int months[12] =
{31, 28, 31, 30, 31, 30, 31, 31, 30, 31, 30, 31};
```

```
do {
/* Error-checking is omitted to simplify the code. */
printf("Enter a date in mm/dd format: ");
scanf("%d/%d", &month, &day);
fflush(stdin);

num_days = 0;
for (i=0; i<month-1; i++)
num_days += months[i];
num_days += day;
printf("%d/%d is day number %d\n", month, day, num_days);

printf("Again? ");
fgets(&answer, MAX_ANS, stdin);
}
while ((answer == 'y') || (answer == 'Y'));
}
```

This brief routine prints English language messages, accepts y or Y (for the word *yes*) in answer to a question, and also accepts dates from the user in the American month/day order. Here's a sample run of the program:

```
Enter a date in mm/dd format: 7/13
7/13 is day number 194
Again? y
Enter a date in mm/dd format: 2/5
2/5 is day number 36
Again? n
```

Now suppose you want to make this code suitable for the French market. Using the Remove-Replace method, this is how you might rewrite it.

```
/* French version; most variable declarations omitted */
. . .
int main (void) {
char answer = 'o';
```

```
do {
  printf("Rentrez une date dans le format jj-mm: ");
  scanf("%d-%d", &day, &month);
  fflush(stdin);
  num_days = 0;
  for (i=0; i<month-1; i++)
    num_days += months[i];
  num_days += day;
  printf("%d-%d est le jour numero %d\n",
    day, month, num_days);

  printf("Encore? ");
  fgets(&answer, MAX_ANS, stdin);
}
while ((answer == 'o') || (answer == 'O'));
}
```

While the code looks similar to the original American version, there are in fact a number of changes. The **printf( )** text is now in French. The variable answer is initialized to *o* (for the French *oui*), and the **do-while** statement now checks for *o* or *O*.

The most significant changes involve user input. While the original code accepts dates in the American month/day order, the revised code takes them in day-month order. This affects these two lines:

Original: scanf("%d/%d", &month, &day);
Revision: scanf("%d-%d", &day, &month);

Original:
printf("%d/%d is day number %d\n", month, day, num_days);
Revision:
printf("%d-%d est le jour numero %d\n",
    day, month, num_days);

Not only are the parameters reordered, but there is also the more subtle change of substituting the hyphen for the slash in the **printf( )** so that the function now produces dates using the more typical French punctuation. Here is a sample run of the French version, using the same data as earlier:

```
Rentrez une date dans le format jj-mm: 13-7
13-7 est le jour numero 194
Encore? o
Rentrez une date dans le format jj-mm: 5-2
5-2 est le jour numero 36
Encore? n
```

An alternative to this design is to retain the American support while adding French; that is, to use the Add-On approach. This requires a more significant rewrite.

```
#include <stdio.h>
#define MAX_ANS 10
/* French and American version */

int main (void) {

char answer;
int month, day, num_days;
int french;

/* This routine follows the French or American path
 * depending on the setting of a system variable.
 * The code for obtaining the variable's value is
 * omitted to save space.
 */
if (french) {
  do {
    printf("Rentrez une date dans le format jj-mm: " );
    scanf("%d-%d", &day, &month);  fflush(stdin);
    num_days = compute_days(day, month);
    printf("%d-%d est le jour numero %d\n",
      day, month, num_days);
    printf("Encore? ");
    fgets(&answer, MAX_ANS, stdin);
  }
  while ((answer == 'o') || (answer == 'O'));
}
```

```
    else { /* american */
      do {
        printf("Enter a date in mm/dd format: ");
        scanf("%d/%d", &month, &day);  fflush(stdin);
        num_days = compute_days(day, month);
        printf("%d/%d is day number %d\n",
                month, day, num_days);
        printf("Again? ");
        fgets(&answer, MAX_ANS, stdin);
      }
      while ((answer == 'y') || (answer == 'Y'));
    }
}               /* end main */

int compute_days(day, month)
int day, month;
{
  int i, total = 0;
  static int months[12] =
    {31, 28, 31, 30, 31, 30, 31, 31, 30, 31, 30, 31};

  for (i=0; i<month-1; i++)
    total += months[i];
  total += day;
  return(total);
}
```

The rewritten code bears only passing resemblance to the original. A variable now determines whether to follow the French or American path. (The logic for determing the value of the variable is omitted to simplify the example.) Since all I/O depends on the language in which the program runs, there are two versions of each **printf( )** and **scanf( )** call. And, of course, there are separate **do-while** loops because the language in use affects the end condition in each. The actual day number computation doesn't change when the language does, so rather than duplicate that code in each branch of the **if**, it has been moved to a function.

There are, of course, other ways to rewrite the code so that it handles both languages, but any Add-On implementation has to duplicate all I/O handling as well as any other culture-specific functionality.

Of the two design choices, Add-On may seem the more technically savvy. Sure, you have to make more significant changes, but the result is software that is twice as smart as it used to be—it's bilingual! However, neither Add-On nor Remove-Replace is the best choice to make, as you shall see.

Both of these approaches are variations on a design called *localization* or *customization*. With this design, you revise existing code to add the specific features, functionality, and text necessary to make it work in the new local environment. Adding the new may also involve subtracting the old, but that choice is up to you.

It is important to draw a distinction between localization of *software* and of *data*. Later sections of this chapter discuss a design alternative that uses localized data. The next sections describe the pros and cons of localized (or customized) software.

3.3   Ways to Localize Software

When companies decide to localize software, they usually follow the Remove-Replace coding model. In doing so, they hire programmers in the new, target country and send them the source code. These new developers make the necessary changes in the code, test it, and produce a shippable version. They then are responsible for supporting the local version. With this approach, there are as many versions of the software as there are programming teams in countries.

Local programmers are the norm because they tend to be most up-to-date on the language and requirements of their country. Technical terms change at lightning speed in every language around the world, so there must be developers in the local environment to ensure that customized products meet current user needs.

Some companies follow another model for doing localization: they do everything from one central location. This model is more typical with companies that are localizing for several languages simultaneously and choosing the Add-On model. The idea here is that instead of having separate versions of the code for every language/culture, the code stays together. Since the code is only being revised once, everyone must get together to make all the needed changes. Companies would never ship a product if they first sent it to a team of programmers in Country A to make the necessary changes, and then sent it to a team in Country B, and then sent it to Country C, and so on.

3.4   Why Customized Software Can Seem Like a Good Idea

As stated, it is most common to choose a localized or customized design when first branching out into foreign markets. You might choose this design for several reasons.

- **Easy to understand.** Your code currently does things one way but you now need it to work a different way. Localizing software allows you to revise the program to satisfy the new set of needs.

- **Usually meets customers' needs.** Assuming you have done your homework, you know what the new customers want, and can customize the software to meet those exact needs. In addition to changing existing software, this may involve writing new routines (for example, adding an input method for Japanese text), but the result should be right for the new markets. Note, however, that localized software doesn't always meet customers' timing needs.
- **Minimal impact on original developers.** Since programmers in the target country usually do the localization, there is little impact on the developers who wrote the original code—and who probably are already deep into development of the next release. Therefore, the original programmers can work full speed on the next generation of code while developers around the world localize the current generation.

These advantages usually are readily apparent when it comes time to do new work, so the Localization Express goes roaring out of the station before anyone notices the problems lurking down the tracks.

3.5   Why Customized Software Really Is a Bad Idea

These are some of the problems you let yourself in for when you choose customization as a software design strategy: late releases, extra expenses, software that is not extensible, and software management and maintenance problems.

3.5.1   Late, Late, Late

Customized products are *always* late. Remember that an advantage of customization is that it doesn't impact the original developers? That's because they have nothing to do with it. They finish their code, release the local language version, and then hand it off to groups in other countries to begin the customization work. Although the length of time between release dates for the original and the customized versions depends on the complexity of the recoding effort, a 6- to 12-month delay is not unusual. Given the nanosecond-like pace of changing technology, such a delay is about as desirable as 300 baud modems.

You may think you can lessen the delay by starting the customization work in parallel with the original development. The problem is that it is only feasible to begin customizing code when the original version is stable. After all, there's no point in translating messages multiple times, recoding functions again and again, and retesting the changes repeatedly.

Most proponents of this approach wait until they feel confident that what they need to change has itself stopped changing. However, despite the best efforts of project management, the reality of most software development is that many things continue changing right up until the time the product ships—and sometimes after.

Certainly, some parts of the code are stable long before the product ships, and you can begin customizing those segments early. But it takes equal measures of intelligence and luck to predict what those pieces are. If you guess wrong, you must repeat work. Even if you guess completely right, some work cannot begin until the very end of the original development cycle. No matter what, localized software is significantly later than the original release.

Depending on how late the customized version is, sales of that version may be adversely affected. If customization teams haven't finished with Release 1.0 by the time the main engineering group announces Release 1.1, customers may not buy the localized 1.0 when it is finally ready. Instead, they may wait for the new features that will be in 1.1.

3.5.2 Extra Programmers, Extra Expenses

When you localize code, by definition, you are rewriting it for a specific culture. In most cases, the original developers can't do the customization. After all, they were the ones who wrote the monolingual software in the first place. Besides, it is highly unlikely that the average developer whose first language is English (or Japanese or German or something else) understands the needs of other cultures well enough to produce a customized product. For example, how many American engineers speak Chinese fluently enough to do a customized Chinese product? Similarly, how many engineers in the ROC can write software customized to Germany? There are always exceptions, but in general, you need local people to produce customized products.

Since customization requires changes to the program logic, you cannot simply hire anyone who is fluent in the target language to make the necessary changes. Rather, you must hire programmers in the target location to change the code. They are the ones who have the appropriate background to revise existing code and create new routines as needed. There are additional cost-related problems associated with customized software. These include:

- **Costs and new markets**. The need to hire programmers hits most companies where it hurts most: in the budget. Programmers generally are much more expensive to hire than translators, so they add a significant cost to getting a product into nonlocal markets. This cost may mean that you cannot go into some new markets, either because you don't have the up-front capital, or because expected additional sales won't cover customization expenses.

American-based computer companies usually have little trouble justifying the expense of moving into major markets such as Germany, Japan, and France, but the amount of added revenue they can get from, say, Finland or Thailand or Hungary might not be enough to cover the customization costs.

• **Finding the Right People.** Even if a company does have the cash to localize for the countries of its choice, it usually is more difficult to find developers than it is to find translators. This problem can be particularly acute if you choose the Add-On customization model. At least when you try to find programmers in another country, the chances are good that they will be fluent in that country's language (or languages). But when you choose the Add-On model, you need a team of programmers in *your* country with the right combination of technical and cultural/linguistic skills.

Assume you are customizing a graphics package. You need engineers with graphics experience who are fluent in the language(s) for which you are customizing. That might be a tough combination to find.

3.5.3 Hard to Extend

A particularly aggravating feature of customized software is the fact that it is not extensible. You can't support, say, Swedish with software that has been customized for Portuguese. Anytime you want to handle a new language or culture, you must reopen the source code, add the new information, recompile, and retest it. The situation is the same regardless of whether you use Remove-Replace or Add-On. The one advantage to localizing a program for the second or third or *n*th time is that it should be easier to find the statements that need to change.

The Add-On design creates some additional problems. As the number of supported languages grows, so does the code size. Imagine you want to customize for Western European markets. The code may look like this:

```
if (french)
    . . .
else if (german)
    . . .
else if (british-english)
    . . .
else if (spanish)
    . . .
```

```
else if (swedish)
   . . .
else if (italian)
   . . .
else /* american-english */
   . . .
```

This example only lists seven possibilities—not even all the major Western European markets—and already it is long and unwieldy. Besides consuming too much process space when running, a program like this would also suffer some performance degradation.

You can reduce the code size to its original, slimmed-down dimensions if you change all the **if-else**s to **#ifdef-#elseif**. This way you conditionally compile the code, and create separate objects for each supported language. Of course, that defeats the purpose of the Add-On model: instead of supporting multiple languages, the software only supports one at a time.

3.5.4   The Dangers of Repetition

Suppose you have a German-based software package that you want to customize for Italian. You have decided to use the Remove-Replace model, and so hire Italian programmers, give them the code, and ship the customized product they produce. Now suppose you want a French version of this product. You hire programmers in France, once again give them the code, and ship the French version of the product. Next time you really branch out. You want British English, American English, Swedish, and Spanish. Now you hire developers in four new locations, and have them all do the right thing.

What a mess! Every time you enter a new market, you essentially do the same thing over again. Besides the obvious expense of revising code repeatedly, this approach has several other major disadvantages:

- **Program management problems**. With localized or customized software, there are developers spread out in multiple countries revising the original code in different ways. It is difficult to keep track of who is doing what coding, what testing it has received, when it will be available, and how to ship it to users.
- **Maintenance headaches**. After solving or ignoring program management issues, you have something to send to users. More accurately, you have several somethings to send, and that's just the problem.

One of the most challenging aspects of the software business is the existence of multiple versions of a package. Users might have any of four or five different releases of a software vendor's product, while that vendor is busy developing yet another new version. Customized versions of products add to this confusion. Now instead of *n* releases to maintain and support, there are *n* releases times *m* language versions to keep track of. The main development group must maintain the original version, while those doing the customization work must merge their changes with each new release.

Suppose an American-based company creates the first version of Product XYZ, and that product only handles American English. Now assume the company creates French, German, Japanese, Spanish, and Swedish localized versions of Product XYZ 1.0. In the first example, there is only one release to track. Now there are six—the original American English version and the five additional customized versions. Figure 3.1 shows the different versions.

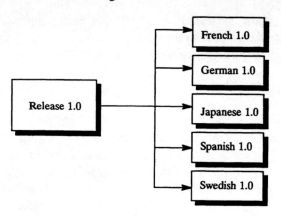

Figure 3.1   One Customized Release Cycle

Now the main software development group puts out Release 1.1. The customization groups must merge the functional changes from Release 1.1 into all five customized versions, as well as customizing the new functionality. Without extra customized versions, there are two releases at this point. With them, there are 12. Figure 3.2 shows the ever-growing number of releases.

Maintaining all these releases consumes more resources than most companies can afford. There also is the additional problem of finding and fixing bugs—is a reported problem in one customized version only, or does it exist (and need to be fixed) in all versions?

• **Inconsistent operations**. Tracking and supporting customized releases would be a hard enough job if there were, say, five or ten versions of the same thing. However, it is not that simple.

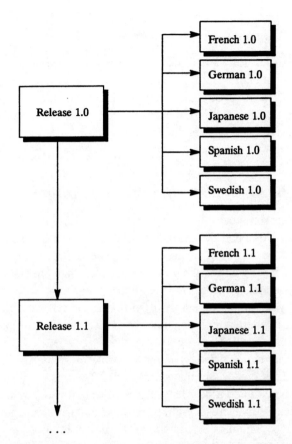

Figure 3.2   Multiple Customized Release Cycles

Whenever you give code to separate groups of programmers, you can be sure they will modify it in different ways. Some of the differences may be because of varying coding styles. Some may be because the local requirements in one country don't match the requirements in another. Still other differences may be because it is hard for local engineers to resist fixing or "improving" parts of the system once they have the source code.

The result is that the various customized versions are inconsistent. A French product may operate in a slightly different way than does the one for Spain, and the two European versions probably are different from the customized versions in Japan and the ROC. That means users (and support personnel) who know one customized version may be stymied when faced with a different one.

3.5.5 There Must Be a Better Way

Localized software is easy to understand and it doesn't impact the original development team. But it has severe disadvantages, ranging from being late to costing too much money to being very difficult to maintain. Given these disadvantages, it should be clear that re-engineering code for separate sets of user needs is not the most efficient way to meet those needs.

There is a better way.

3.6 The Right Approach—Internationalization

The reason most software doesn't work outside its country of origin is because it contains hard-coded dependencies on cultural and linguistic conventions. Localizing software simply replaces one hard-coded set of rules with another. A better approach is to remove the hard-coded rules that prevent software from traveling across borders. Instead of, in essence, translating software from one culture to another, you should generalize it so that it can handle different users' needs. The process of generalizing computer systems to handle multiple cultural and linguistic conventions is called *internationalization*.

An internationalized system is capable of supporting new languages and cultures without changes to the source code. There is no need to rewrite or recompile every time you add a new language to your software's repertoire. Instead, the software includes calls to generalized routines that get language- or culture-specific data at run time. The data still has to be localized, but not the code. Indeed, while the previous sections describe the disadvantages of localized *software*, localized *data* is the fuel that makes internationalized software run.

Internationalization is a good concept, but it's an awful word. Much too long to type, and hard to say as well. So before going any further, the usual abbreviation for the term is *I18N*. That's because the word has 18 letters between the initial *I* and final *N*. It is pronounced *I-eighteen-N* rather than *I-one-eight-N*.

With that bit of housekeeping out of the way, think back to the sample code from the beginning of this chapter. You already have seen two ways to localize it. Here is an example of an internationalized version:

```
/* Internationalized version. */
#include <stdio.h>
#include <locale.h>
#include <nl_types.h>
#include <langinfo.h>
#include "find_date.h"
#define MAX_ANS 20
```

```c
int main (void) {

unsigned char c;
char answer[20], localyes[20], *yes_str;
int i, month, day, num_days;
static int months[12] =
{31, 28, 31, 30, 31, 30, 31, 31, 30, 31, 30, 31};
nl_catd catd;

(void)setlocale(LC_ALL,"");
/* open message catalog */
catd = catopen("find_date.cat", NL_CAT_LOCALE);

/* get the language-appropriate version of "yes"
 * and copy to local storage
 */
yes_str = nl_langinfo(YESSTR);
strcpy(localyes, yes_str);

do {
  printf(catgets(catd, SET_1, DATE_ENTRY,
                 "Enter a date in mm/dd format: "));
  scanf(catgets(catd, SET_1, INPUT_FMT, "%1$d%2$c%3$d"),
                &month, &c, &day);
  fflush(stdin);

  num_days = 0;
  for (i=0; i<month-1; i++)
    num_days += months[i];
  num_days += day;
  printf(catgets(catd, SET_1, RESULT,
                 "%1$d/%2$d is day number %3$d\n"),
                 month, day, num_days);

  printf(catgets(catd, SET_1, AGAIN, "Again? "));
  fgets(&answer, MAX_ANS, stdin);
}
while (strncmp (answer, localyes, 1) == 0);

catclose(catd); /* close message catalog */

}
```

Future chapters describe the new function calls in this example in detail; for now, you only need to look at the conceptual changes. One of the most important is the call to the function **setlocale( )**. This function controls which set of linguistic and cultural rules the program uses when it runs. One user may want the program to run in Spanish; the next may choose Korean. **setlocale( )** finds the appropriate data and rules to fulfill these requests.

A change that probably is more obvious is the new look of the **printf( )** and **scanf( )** statements. They now include a call to **catgets( )**. This call, which is part of a messaging system, gives the program access to one of multiple translations of the program's messages. Instead of translating the program text within the code, you can keep the translations separate, and load the appropriate language at run time. The calls include default text (in this case, the original English message) in case a requested translation is not available.

Changes to I/O format strings (from, say, **%d** to **%1$d**) provide information about the order in which parameters should be filled. That is so the program can accept and print dates in month/day or day-month order. Suppose you want to run this example program using French rules. Consider the **scanf( )** call:

```
scanf(catgets(catd, SET_1, INPUT_FMT, "%1$d%2$c%3$d"),
     &month, &c, &day);
```

The quoted format string is what the program uses if it can't find the requested (in this case, French) message catalog. The numbers in the format instruct the program to plug the first value into the first parameter (month), the second into c, and the third into day. In contrast to the default format string, the French format string that **catgets( )** returns would look like this:

```
"%3$d%2$c%1$d"
```

This instructs the program to plug the first value the user enters into the third parameter (day), the second into c, and the third into the first parameter (month). In other words, it takes the user input in the French day-month order.

The final major change to the program is that instead of hard-coding the answer to the **do-while** condition, the program calls a separate function that returns the equivalent of *yes* for the language in which the program is running. The program allocates 20 bytes for arrays that hold the user's response and for the language-specific version of *yes*. There is no rule for the amount of space to allow; this covers most languages' needs.

Because of these at-this-point sketchily described changes, this one program is capable of working in languages like German, Japanese, French, Polish, and

Chinese—and, of course, English. It still relies on the Gregorian calendar of 12 months and 365 (or 366) days, so it is not suitable for computing dates on systems like the Moslem or Hebrew calendars. But compared to customized code, which yields a result that works in only a small group of hard-coded situations, internationalized code is a great leap forward.

Given this brief glimpse into the methods for internationalizing code, it is time to look at the advantages and disadvantages of I18N.

3.7   I18N Advantages

As you probably have guessed by now (otherwise, there would be no reason for this book), there are many good reasons to choose internationalization when designing software. The advantages include:

- fewer code revisions
- less delay in reaching users
- reduced operational inconsistencies
- simplified extension model
- simplified program management
- cost savings
- potential for expanded markets
- simplified maintenance

3.7.1   Do It Once

Unlike software customization, which requires that you change code every time you go into a new market, internationalization can be done once. Instead of having one release for Germany, a separate one for France, another for Japan, and so on, you can have one release that works in all these countries.

The number of times you revisit code and the amount of changes necessary when you do so depends on the functionality in your I18N tools or routines, and on the design decisions you make along the way. If you assume you will never need to handle Chinese or Japanese, and instead optimize your design for European languages, chances are you will have to revise the code when your company opens offices in Tokyo, Taipei, and Hong Kong. Despite the fact that I18N isn't always a one-time fix, it does significantly reduce the number of times you have to change code and the amount of changes you have to make.

3.7.2 Faster Results

Internationalized software is ready faster. Instead of a two-phase development cycle—one for the main code development, and a second for customization—all development occurs at one time. Culture-specific versions still usually arrive slightly later than the original because it takes some time to translate program messages and the like, but the delay is much shorter than it would be if the software were customized. In a few well-planned, well-engineered cases, there is no delay at all.

3.7.3 Consistent Operations

Since there is only one internationalized program for multiple languages/cultures, an internationalized program works the same way for those multiple possibilities. You don't have to worry about code having been customized in inconsistent ways. You also don't have to worry about varying degrees of customization.

Consider a simple example. Suppose you send copies of a software package to two separate customization teams. Further suppose the code needs 1,000 customization-related changes. (If that number sounds high, consider the number of changes required for the brief example earlier in this chapter. A full product obviously includes much more code and therefore needs many more changes.) It is likely the customization teams will miss a few of the needed changes, so assume they each make 950 of the needed changes. However, there is no guarantee the teams make the *same* 950 changes, or that they make identical changes to the ones they both fix. So some needed changes don't get made at all, and others occur in inconsistent ways. The result is software that may operate differently in different countries and create special headaches for support staff.

Since there is only one version of internationalized software, it operates the same from country to country. Assume now that instead of customizing your software, you internationalize it and that it needs 1,000 I18N-related changes. If you only make 950 of the needed fixes, you know that something that works for, say, French also works for German. Similarly, if it doesn't work for French, it doesn't work for German either.

3.7.4 Easy to Extend

A major, major advantage to internationalization is that the design makes it easy to add new languages/countries. Instead of rewriting and recompiling code, you only have to supply a new set of localized data. This assumes, of course, that the

I18N support in your program can handle the new requirement. Software that has only been internationalized to support alphabetic writing systems like Russian or Spanish won't suddenly handle Chinese correctly just because you load some Chinese files. However, internationalized code supports a range of possibilities; localized software only handles hard-coded facts.

3.7.5 Simplified Program Management

Suppose you want your software to work in five languages. With customization, you probably have programmers in five different sites around the world, each doing something slightly different to that one piece of software. And you have to manage that process.

With internationalization, however, everything except the translation work occurs at the same place as the rest of the development process. It therefore is much easier to track.

3.7.6 Saving Money

When you internationalize code, you reduce the need for programmers in target markets. In general, you can hire translators to produce the localized data that the internationalized code uses. Since translators generally are significantly less expensive to hire than programmers, internationalization saves money. In addition, it takes less time to develop one internationalized version of a software package than it does to develop multiple customized versions, so costs are less.

Even with internationalized code, you still may need a few local programmers. It depends on the users' requirements. Many Asian and Middle Eastern languages require sophisticated software input methods. It doesn't matter how internationalized the base software is; if it doesn't include input software, you may need local developers to write it for you. But this situation is the exception. Localized software always requires local developers; internationalized software usually doesn't.

3.7.7 Expanding Horizons

In addition to saving money on engineering costs, internationalization may also help make more money. Remember that the costs of localizing software sometimes outweigh potential sales in a given market. This is particularly common for small software firms. With an internationalized system, however, you only have to cover the costs of localizing data. Since those costs are considerably lower than localizing the software, it may be economically feasible to expand into new markets.

3.7.8 Maintaining Order Where There Was Chaos

One of the most serious disadvantages of customization is the maintenance problem it creates. With localized software, you must add all bug fixes and new features to every version of the code. In addition, if local features creep into some versions, there may be special integration problems. Internationalized software does away with the need for separate versions of the same release; there's only one version of the code to fix or enhance. The only part that still needs country-by-country care is the localized data. Figure 3.3 shows an internationalized release cycle with multiple localized data kits.

3.8 I18N Drawbacks

Internationalization has many advantages to offer, but like most design decisions, it has drawbacks as well.

You already have learned that software customization almost always happens in the country for which the new version of software is being produced. Developers finish the original release, and then send it off to the target country to be customized. Not so with internationalization. Since it is part of the regular development cycle, the programmers who were writing culture-specific code must be retrained in the New World Order. Many may resist the retraining because they may see I18N as extra work that isn't really necessary. Typical reactions are to complain about the users: *Why can't they just learn English?* or *They've been getting along with the product the way it is so far. Why do we have to change it now?*

Obviously, the first complaint/suggestion is absurd, and the second is uninformed. However, even programmers who understand the importance of internationalization may have problems delivering internationalized software. Developers know how to write software that works in their language and uses their customs. Without realizing it, they often make assumptions that limit the code's usefulness in other areas of the world. They therefore have to unlearn what they think they know. It takes time and effort to get programmers to take a world view.

Another disadvantage to internationalization is that it impacts system performance. The amount of that impact varies greatly from implementation to implementation. I18N still is relatively new to most programmers, and the emphasis so far has focused on getting the functionality up and running. It is inevitable that parts of the recoding include some poor decisions with regard to performance. Because I18N involves generalizing software, the result may be slower than code that is tuned to

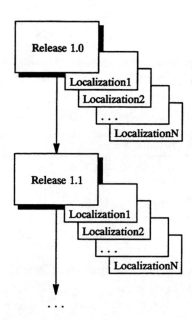

Figure 3.3   Internationalized Releases with Localization Kits

one set of cultural rules. However, intelligent programming can reduce the difference between single-culture and internationalized code.

It may also be necessary to do internationalization work more than once. The truth is that it is extremely difficult to write something so general that it works for all languages or all cultures. Software that has been generalized to handle all European languages probably needs to be revisited when it is being readied for Asian markets. Similarly, a package that works for Europe and Asia may need additional work when faced with Middle Eastern requirements. However, the number of times you need to revisit code and the changes necessary when you do so are significantly less than if you create customized versions for each language or culture.

Under certain conditions, internationalizing software may have one other drawback. If you need to revise single-culture software to handle one more—and only one more—set of cultural conventions, it may be faster to localize rather than internationalize the code. Remember, though, that what you localize this year may need to be ripped out next year when you realize you really should have internationalized.

3.9 Summary: Internationalized versus Customized Software

The previous sections provide an in-depth look at the pros and cons of customizing and internationalizing software. Table 3.1 summarizes the main points.

Table 3.1 Summary of Customization versus Internationalization

Localization/Customization	Internationalization
Repeat for every language/culture	Can internationalize once
Always late	Minimal delay in reaching users
Complicated to manage	Simpler to manage
Hard to extend	Easy to extend
Inconsistent operations worldwide	Minimal operational inconsistencies
Higher costs	Lower costs
May keep you out of some markets	Easier to get into new markets
Huge maintenance burden	Reduced maintenance burden
No impact on original developers	Some retraining required for original developers
Minimal performance impact	Can adversely affect performance

As this table shows, internationalization easily beats customization.

3.10 Providing I18N Functionality

After deciding to internationalize software, the next step is to determine how to introduce it into existing software, or to plan for it in new products. This section covers likely sources of I18N support, and discusses choices that help ensure a successful implementation.

3.10.1 Sources of Internationalization Support

Reader Alert: *This is a boring section. It can't be anything else, because it covers many standards groups and industry consortia, the acronyms they go by, and the acronyms they produce. However, this information really is important because the names and acronyms appear (in less concentrated doses) throughout the remaining chapters.*

Internationalizing software is a daunting task if you have to start from scratch; that is, if you work on a system or in a programming language that has no internationalized capabilities. Fortunately, increasing internationalization support is appearing in software development building blocks. You still may have to write some routines yourself, but many internationalized routines are available.

Programming language standards include some commonly used routines, while international standards bodies and industry consortia create others. Still others are the products of individual computer companies. Table 3.2 lists some of the major groups in the internationalization arena and the acronyms (if any) they go by.

Table 3.2   Groups Working on Internationalization

Organization Name	Acronym
American National Standards Institute	ANSI
European Computer Manufacturers Association	ECMA
International Electrotechnical Commission	IEC
Institute of Electrical and Electronics Engineers	IEEE
International Organization for Standardization	ISO
X Consortium	—
X/Open	—

(Yes, the acronym for ISO is correct, even though the group's name indicates that the abbreviation should be IOS. Also, note that this is not an exhaustive list. It only includes organizations that produce I18N-related documents or products mentioned later in this book.)

ANSI creates American standards for a variety of computer-related topics. These standards sometimes become international (i.e., ISO) standards. The ANSI standard that has the most to do with internationalization is that for the C programming language. ANSI C (ANSI X3.169–1989) contains a variety of interfaces designed for handling international programming needs.

ECMA creates standards for European users. As with ANSI, ISO sometimes promotes the ECMA regional standards into international standards. For example, ISO has adopted several ECMA code sets.

IEC includes many technical committees that produce international standards in a variety of fields. In the area of I18N, IEC often produces joint standards with ISO. See the description of ISO below.

IEEE is another group that sometimes feeds work into ISO. Particularly notable with respect to internationalization is the work of IEEE's 1003 committee on a standard called POSIX (Portable Operating System Interface). POSIX is a UNIX-like operating system specification that includes standard functionality and interfaces that are guaranteed to be on all compliant systems. This allows development of portable code.

IEEE's 1003 committee is divided into several so-called *dot groups*—1003.1, 1003.2, 1003.3, and so on—each of which concentrates on a particular aspect of the system. The two that have the most internationalization-related content are 1003.1 (System Application Program Interface) and 1003.2 (Shells and Utilities). Each dot group produces a specification for its particular area. The specifications—and the dot groups, for that matter—typically are called "POSIX.*n*", where *n* is the number of the dot group. For example, there's POSIX.1, POSIX.2 (pronounced *POSIX-dot-one, POSIX-dot-two*), and so on.

As the standards of POSIX's dot groups near final form, they are sent through ANSI to **ISO** for consideration as international standards. This makes it possible for them to be accepted internationally soon after they are accepted in the United States. ISO is the top of the standards food chain; the place you want to be. ISO also is divided into so many subcommittees, working groups, and informal rapporteur groups, it is nearly impossible to keep them all straight. Fortunately, you only need to know a few of ISO's standards and groups to tackle the internationalization techniques described in this book.

ISO C is the international standard for the C programming language. It is technically equivalent to ANSI C. ISO also creates standard code sets for a variety of natural language groups, as well as defining abbreviations for names of languages, countries, currencies, and so on.

All ISO standards have numbers. For example, in the ISO world, POSIX.1 is known as ISO/IEC 9945–1:1990, while ISO C is known as ISO/IEC 9899:1990. (In both cases, 1990 refers to the year the standard was adopted). Note that while some standards are joint products of ISO and IEC, in common usage, the IEC reference often is omitted. This saves a few letters when typing or speaking, but strictly speaking is incorrect.

The **X Consortium** is an open organization funded by the participants and with a charter of supporting and controlling the development of the X Window system. Development is managed out of the Laboratory for Computer Science at the Massachusetts Institute of Technology (MIT). Most companies use Version 11 of X Windows, also known as X11. Within X11, there are various releases (for example, R4 [Release 4], R5).

X/Open Company is not a standards-making body, but an industry consortium that creates system specifications. Member companies pledge to produce products that adhere to the specifications, meaning that products are portable from one X/Open-compliant system to another. The specifications are published in a series called the **X/Open Portability Guide** (XPG). Numbers designate versions of the specification. For example, the X/Open Portability Guide, Issue 4 is called XPG4.

While work is under way to define internationalization support in other programming languages, standards, or industry specifications, this book concentrates mainly on concepts, types, and functions available in ISO C, POSIX, and the X/Open Portability Guides.

3.10.2   Design Strategies

In order to make internationalization work, you must make several design decisions. Two are relatively generic, while the third has to do with nitty-gritty details.

- **I18N is part of the product.** First and foremost, you must decide that internationalization is an integral part of your product. That is regardless of whether you are starting a new project or revising existing code.

  Under the best circumstances, you will be starting out fresh, and can use internationalized routines and programming practices throughout the initial development cycle. A more likely scenario, however, is that there is existing code to be retro-fitted with internationalization support. In that case, you must change your programming style (or others') to accommodate the new internationalized way of doing things. This can be difficult. You may see I18N as an annoying frill; something that takes up the time you should be devoting to "real" work. You may argue that you could add three great new features to the product if only you didn't have to waste time on internationalization.

  It helps to remember that without internationalization, your software is only suitable for people who speak your language. If you add those three new features to the existing, say, 50 features, the people who already can use your product now have three new possibilities from which to choose. If, instead, you internationalize it, people who can't use it at all have 50 features at their command. Internationalization is a powerful tool for making software accessible to more users.

- **You need a spectrum of experiences**. If you buy a world map in North America, chances are North America is in the middle. If you do your map-buying in Europe, Europe tends to move to center stage. A trip to the Far East often yields a world map with—you guessed it—the Far East in the middle. The point is, people look at the world from their own cultural vantage points. Each person brings his or her own assumptions, biases, and information about the "right" way to do things. When internationalizing a system, you need access to this variety.

  Companies sometimes forget this. They may ship all the I18N work off to one country—call it Exoticland—to be done. They figure *Oh, those Exoticlanders; they know all about that international stuff.* Then they are dismayed when the revised software handles Exoticland's needs flawlessly, and other languages, well, flawfully.

When designing an internationalized system, you must understand various languages' and cultures' requirements. To do so, you either need access to programmers or users from multiple countries, or to someone with I18N experience. You don't need a technical contact for each language or culture you plan to support, but it is best to get a representative sample.

- **You must choose what to support from the world's smorgasbord.** After establishing internationalization as an integral part of your system, and making sure you have access to information about different users' needs, it is time to move to the next step in I18N planning. You must decide exactly what groups of languages and cultures you want to support.

Chapter 2 covers some of the nearly infinite variety that exists in the way people write, sort, tell time, measure, and so on. A purist would say that a system isn't internationalized until it handles the entire spectrum of world needs. But purists never seem to ship a product, do they?

Practically speaking, it is most common to internationalize in phases. North American or European companies tend to get their software to accept the menu of European possibilities first, and then branch out around the world. Asian companies often add English support (if it doesn't already exist) and support for their geographical neighbors' needs. A Middle Eastern or Southeast Asian firm typically is interested in languages from its own part of the world.

When deciding what support to add, keep these questions in mind:

- What do your current users need (in priority order)?
- What do prospective users need (again, in priority order)? These are the ones who can't use your software now, but could if it supported their language or culture.
- How many more copies of your software can you expect to sell if you add a certain level of I18N support?
- Is your current software written in a programming language that includes internationalization features? If not, is it feasible to choose a new programming language?
- What internationalized routines are available to you? Can you use standards-defined routines? What company-specific routines, if any, are available? Do you need to write additional routines from scratch to meet specific requirements?
- If you add support for a relatively small group of languages and cultures now, are there routines you can use or design choices you can make so that it will be easier to expand that support in the future?

After answering these questions, you can decide exactly what groups of languages and cultures you want to support, and create a plan for your development phases. American-based companies often have added European languages first, Asian second, and Middle Eastern/Southeast Asian third. However, as you will learn in future chapters, some internationalized routines available now make it much easier to combine phases. Certainly, you should take advantage of such capabilities and change the code as few times as possible.

3.11   Levels of I18N Support

After deciding what you want your system to do, you actually have to make it happen. That most likely requires a layered approach. That's because internationalization can affect nearly every piece of software, and even have an impact on hardware. If the software layers your code depends on have not been internationalized, all the work you do on your little corner of the code may be for naught.

In other words, your code is only as smart as the stupidest software it uses.

Since internationalization tends to affect nearly all parts of the system, it helps to break the work down into somewhat more manageable chunks. Logical segments include:

- **"Speaking" to the system in many languages**. As you begin internationalizing a system, you must first provide the basics: access to the characters from the languages you are going to support, data types and routines for manipulating them, as well as the ability to input the characters, display, edit, store, and print them. Chapters 4, 6, and 7 cover these topics.
- **Getting the system to understand many languages and cultures**. After teaching the system to accept a wide variety of characters, the next step is handling linguistic and cultural conventions. Just because the system can display, say, *ä* doesn't mean it knows how to sort or classify the letter. Similarly, it doesn't know the way different countries format numeric or monetary quantities, or what rules to use when displaying dates. Users need the ability to tell the system what linguistic or cultural rules they want a program to use, and programs need access to the localized information that makes it possible to meet such user requests. In addition, software needs to use internationalized routines in place of culture-dependent versions. See Chapters 5 and 8 for details on how to provide this support.

- **Getting the system to "speak" in a chosen language**. It is fine for the system to accept your language, but it is likely you want the favor to be returned. That is, you probably want program text to appear in your language. That goal is achievable if you add Chapter 9's internationalization support.
- **Handling multilingual text or distributed computing**. Having the ability to handle different languages is nice, but there may be times you need to mix two or more languages. Alternatively, you may need to distribute a program's processing across several nodes in your network. These seemingly dissimilar tasks face many of the same I18N-related issues. Chapter 12 covers these topics.

Although this list describes the capabilities you must provide, in most cases many people do the work. The job is too big for any single programmer. But even if you don't do all the work single-handedly, it helps to understand what features must exist throughout the system. The remaining chapters cover each of these I18N levels in detail. In addition, there are chapters about documenting internationalized systems (more complicated than you might think) and about the few parts of the system that internationalization doesn't affect.

Encoding Characters 4

The first step in providing an internationalized system is to revise programs so that they allow characters in a variety of languages and scripts. English-only or other single-language software only meets limited user needs. Before you can change programs to handle international characters, however, you need to understand how characters are encoded and what code sets exist. Then you can write programs capable of handling all possibilities or a chosen subset. This chapter covers some of the amazing variety that exists for these topics:

- Encoding characters
- Seven-bit, eight-bit, and multiple-byte code sets
- Encoding methods
- Portable character sets

Note that this chapter concentrates on the characteristics of code sets and encoding methods, and that later chapters describe programming techniques, including the use of multibyte and wide characters, for supporting these encodings.

Before discussing how to encode characters, however, it is important to establish what they are. This is deceptively difficult. Most people have an instinctive, rather than a precise, understanding of characters. Certainly, most would agree that individual letters, ideographs, digits, or symbols in a writing system are characters. The problem comes when something that looks like a unit actually consists of multiple subpieces. Consider the letter *ö*. Some would consider this to be two characters—lowercase *o* and the umlaut diacritic—but most would view this as the single character *o-with-umlaut*. That is because the diacritic has no meaning independent of the base letter, and typical text-processing functions apply to the complete unit of letter plus diacritic.

Contrast the Latin-based *ö*, however, with Arabic text. The base characters in Arabic are consonants, and some marks that appear above or beside consonants are vowels. In this case, although an Arabic consonant-plus-vowel appears similar to a Latin script's letter-plus-diacritic, the Arabic string is generally considered to consist of two characters.

Although there are many ways to define *character*, in this book, it is an independent member of a set of elements used to represent data within a writing system. Examples include a letter, a letter with diacritic, an ideograph, a digit, or a punctuation symbol.

4.1 Character Sets and Code Sets

When handling characters, computer systems treat them as numeric codes rather than as the graphic representation of those characters. If a data stream includes the letter *s*, there is a numeric code that software interprets as meaning *s*. The codes are necessary because computers only handle binary numeric codes, so everything must be reduced to that form.

Before you can assign codes, you must first decide which characters you want to encode. The group may include letters, numbers, symbols, control characters, and others. A group of characters without associated encodings is called a *character set*.

A *code set* is a mapping of a *character set* to specific numeric codes. These are the codes that stand in for the characters when the computer handles them. Some standards groups call this a *coded character set*, but this book uses the simpler term.

4.1.1 Early Code Sets

Many different schemes for encoding characters were used in the early days of computing. Because memory and disk space were far more expensive back in the 1950s, and data transmission was much slower, the emphasis often was on using the smallest amount of space possible. This meant early sets often only had the uppercase English characters—after all, Americans could say anything they needed to say with uppercase. AND IF ALL TEXT LOOKED LIKE YOU WERE SHOUTING, WHO CARED? All the uppercase letters, the digits, and a few punctuation characters could fit in only six bits (64 code positions). With some fancy finagling, it even was possible to encode characters in four or five bits.

This was back in the days when there was no standard size for a byte. The concept of a byte itself wasn't even standard. Many manufacturers handled data in *words*, and those words could be anything from 12 to 60 bits each. Over time, the eight-bit byte became the de facto standard size for handling character data. There also was general agreement on the character set—by this time, thankfully including lowercase English letters—that computer systems would process. The next step was agreeing on the encoding of those characters.

4.2   Standard American Code Sets

In the early days of computing, American computer firms used many code sets, but that group gradually dwindled down. In general, IBM used U.S. EBCDIC, and most others used ASCII (American Standard Code for Information Interchange). As used in the United States, the two sets encode almost the same character set. They both have the following:

- uppercase and lowercase English letters A–Z and a–z
- Arabic digits 0–9
- punctuation characters ! " # $ % & ' ( ) * + , - . / : ; < = > ? @
- some common control characters including NULL, CR (Carriage Return), and DEL (delete)

Table 4.1 shows the way ASCII encodes characters. In the table, shaded entries denote control characters. Also note that the row and column headings in Table 4.1 are hexadecimal digits. To find the encoded value of a character, read the column number followed by the row number. For example, the value of A is 0x41. There are several major differences between ASCII and U.S. EBCDIC. As Table 4.1 shows, ASCII encodes uppercase and lowercase letters in English alphabetic order, although some punctuation characters separate the two groups of letters. In addition, all ASCII codes are in the range 0x00–0x7f, so all ASCII characters fit in seven bits. Consider the binary encodings of A (0x41) and the DEL control character (0x7f):

```
         MSB                    LSB
  A    | 0 | 1 | 0 | 0 | 0 | 0 | 0 | 1 |

DEL    | 0 | 1 | 1 | 1 | 1 | 1 | 1 | 1 |
```

Notice that the Most Significant Bit (MSB) for both is off—that is, set to zero. The MSB for all ASCII characters is always off.

Table 4.1   ASCII Code Set

	0	1	2	3	4	5	6	7
0	NUL	DLE	SP	0	@	P	`	p
1	SOH	DC1	!	1	A	Q	a	q
2	STX	DC2	"	2	B	R	b	r
3	ETX	DC3	#	3	C	S	c	s
4	EOT	DC4	$	4	D	T	d	t
5	ENQ	NAK	%	5	E	U	e	u
6	ACK	SYN	&	6	F	V	f	v
7	BEL	ETB	'	7	G	W	g	w
8	BS	CAN	(	8	H	X	h	x
9	TAB	EM	)	9	I	Y	i	y
A	LF	SUB	*	:	J	Z	j	z
B	VT	ESC	+	;	K	[	k	{
C	FF	FS	,	<	L	\	l	|
D	CR	GS	–	=	M	]	m	}
E	SO	RS		>	N	^	n	~
F	SI	US	/	?	O	_	o	DEL

Not so with U.S. EBCDIC. That set spreads out its characters throughout the range of 0x00–0xff, so it takes up all eight bits of a byte. Lowercase letters come before uppercase in the set, and letters are encoded in subgroups. English letters a–i are encoded together followed by seven code places, then j–r, then eight places, and then s–z.

There are other differences between ASCII and U.S. EBCDIC. Although both continue in wide use, the rest of this chapter (and, indeed, this book) concentrates on ASCII and ASCII-based code sets. That is because the majority of standards-based internationalization activities under way involve ASCII-based code sets and systems.

4.2.1   Hey! There's a Bit Left Over!

As the computer world gradually standardized on eight-bit bytes and the non-EBCDIC world decided on a code set that used only seven of those eight bits, it became inevitable that software developers would find ways to use the "leftover" bit. They used it for parity checking, or to mark sections of data that needed special processing, or for numerous other tasks. Pretty soon, the eighth bit was being used for so many odd jobs that it was impossible to use it the way the other seven bits were being used: to encode characters. *That* was a major problem because, as you shall see, seven bits just aren't enough.

4.2.2   The Problem with ASCII

The fact that ASCII became the most commonly used code set is fine if you happen to want an American English system, but is inadequate for nearly anything else. You learned in Chapter 2 that there are many different alphabets and writing systems in the world. The letters in ASCII are only sufficient for English, Swahili, and Hawaiian. All other languages need characters that ASCII lacks.

Although ASCII has the letters for a few other languages, it still is distinctly American. For example, ASCII includes the dollar sign ($), but no other currency symbol. So although British users have access to all English letters, they have no way to write their currency symbol (£). While Canadians also use the dollar sign for their currency, and can use ASCII if they only need to write English, a significant portion of Canada is French-speaking, and ASCII does not include the accented characters French uses.

4.3   Alternate Seven-Bit Sets

Given that ASCII is so obviously American, developers around the world had two choices: they could accept the limited group of characters encoded in the set, or they could revise or extend ASCII to meet their specific needs. In the past, when a higher percentage of computer users were doing technical and scientific tasks, it was fairly common to choose the first alternative. After all, when computers were mostly crunching numbers, it didn't matter as much that the rest of the system only spoke English. But over time, computer keyboards have moved under the fingertips of people who do general business tasks. That means it is mandatory to choose the second alternative.

System vendors around the world created variations on the traditional ASCII set to include their own specific characters. These variations are codified in ISO 646. ISO 646 defines rules for encoding graphic characters (code values 0x20–0x7e). Different countries or standards bodies apply the rules to create individual versions of ISO 646 sets. The standard defines one particular version that it calls the IRV (International Reference Version). ISO 646 IRV:1991 is exactly the same as traditional ASCII.

ISO 646 specifies a set of characters and their associated code values that are guaranteed to be in every version of 646. These so-called *invariant* characters include most of the entries in the ASCII code set. However, to accommodate other languages' needs, ISO 646 also defines a much smaller group of *variant* characters. Table 4.2 shows that group.

Table 4.2   Variant Characters in ISO 646

Character	Character Name	Code Value
#	number sign	0x23
$	dollar sign	0x24
@	commercial at	0x40
[	left square bracket	0x5b
\	backslash	0x5c
]	right square bracket	0x5d
^	circumflex	0x5e
`	grave accent	0x60
{	left curly bracket	0x7b
|	vertical bar	0x7c
}	right curly bracket	0x7d
~	tilde	0x7e

ISO 646 allows these variant characters to be replaced with those needed for other languages. Many countries used the substitution rules to create individual national versions of ISO 646. Table 4.3 shows the substitutions the French and Danish versions of ISO 646 make.

Notice there is no requirement that a national version of ISO 646 replace all the variant characters. Both Danish and French leave the dollar sign and circumflex in their national sets.

The individual versions of ISO 646 give users access to different characters than are available in the IRV, but they have several limitations. Because the national characters replace some characters in the IRV (that is, some "ASCII" characters), you can no longer see them. As Table 4.3 shows, the French version of 646 replaces the left and right curly brackets ({ }) with the letters é and è. This means that if you use French 646, you can't use real curly brackets. This can create some oddities when writing programs. After all, C uses curly brackets for **begin** and **end** statements, while Pascal uses them as default comment delimiters.

What makes this more confusing is that it is possible to write syntactically correct C or Pascal programs using national variants of ISO 646. Just like the rest of

Table 4.3   Example ISO 646 Substitutions

IRV	Danish	French
#		£
$		
@		à
[	Æ	°
\	Ø	ç
]	Å	§
^		
`		μ
{	æ	é
|	ø	ù
}	å	è
~		..

the system, compilers don't know what character is associated with a particular code value. In general, a C compiler simply knows that code value 0x7b means **begin**. It neither knows nor cares whether your font displays a left curly bracket or an accented *e* for 0x7b. (See more about the difference between code sets and fonts in Chapter 7.) Using French 646, this C fragment is correct:

```
for (i = 0; i < end_num; i++) é
   /* processing */
   è
```

Another problem with the ISO 646 sets is that they are too limited for some languages. You can only make substitutions for the 12 variant characters, but languages like French have more national characters than there are substitution slots. All French vowels can take circumflexes (â, ê, î, ô, û), but there is not enough room for them and all the other French characters. The result is that French 646 really only handles limited French.

Despite the limitations of ISO 646, some national versions are in use today throughout the world. As more systems break free of the seven-bit-only world, however, ISO 646 variations have been replaced with other, eight-bit sets.

4.4 Eight-Bit Sets

Code sets that use all eight bits of a byte can support languages that use Latin, Cyrillic, some Middle Eastern, and other alphabetic scripts. The most popular standard sets are the ISO 8859 series. The first in the series is ISO 8859-1, the second is ISO 8859-2, and so on through ISO 8859-10. Table 4.4 lists each set and the languages it supports.

As the table shows, many ISO 8859 sets share similar nicknames. The first is called **Latin-1**, the second is **Latin-2**, and so on up to **Latin-4**. These

Table 4.4 ISO 8859 Code Sets

Formal Name	Informal Name	Languages Covered
ISO 8859-1	Latin-1	Western European — Danish, Dutch, English, Faeroese, Finnish, French, German, Icelandic, Italian, Norwegian, Portuguese, Spanish, Swedish
ISO 8859-2	Latin-2	Eastern European — Albanian, Czechoslovakian, English, German, Hungarian, Polish, Rumanian, Serbo-Croatian, Slovak, Slovene
ISO 8859-3	Latin-3	Southeastern European — Afrikaans, Catalan, Dutch, English, Esperanto, German, Italian, Maltese, Spanish, Turkish
ISO 8859-4	Latin-4	Northern European — Danish, Estonian, English, Finnish, German, Greenlandic, Lappish, Latvian, Lithuanian, Norwegian, Swedish
ISO/IEC 8859-5	—	English & Cyrillic-Based — Bulgarian, Byelorussian, English, Macedonian, Russian, Serbo-Croatian, Ukrainian
ISO 8859-6	—	English & Arabic
ISO 8859-7	—	English & Greek
ISO 8859-8	—	English & Hebrew
ISO/IEC 8859-9	Latin-5	Western European & Turkish (no Icelandic)
ISO/IEC 8859-10	Latin-6	Danish, English, Estonian, Faeroese, Finnish, German, Greenlandic, Icelandic, Lappish, Latvian, Lithuanian, Norwegian, Swedish

nicknames reflect the fact that the sets contain the characters for the Latin script. Sets 5–8 do not have commonly accepted nicknames, although they sometimes are called **ISO-*script***, where *script* is the name of the additional script it supports. Under this system, ISO 8859-7 sometimes is called **ISO-Greek** because it contains the characters for Greek. ISO/IEC 8859-9 and -10 round out the list. Their non-intuitive nicknames are **Latin-5** and **Latin-6** because they are the fifth and sixth sets that support the Latin script.

Most of the 8859 sets were national or regional standards before ISO adopted them. ISO 8859-1 through -4 all were in the European standard ECMA 94. ISO 8859-6 is based on the Arab standard ASMO 449, and -8 matches the Israeli standard SII 1311.

ISO 8859 defines graphic characters only for each set, and all sets share the same layout. In that layout, the section in the range 0x20–0x7f is called the *lower half* or *left half*, and the 0xa0–0xff section is the *upper half* or *right half*. Figure 4.1 shows the layout.

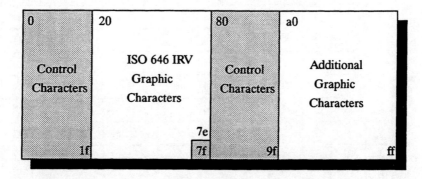

Figure 4.1   Structure of ISO 8859 Code Sets

Because many existing programs rely to some degree on ASCII, these sets and most other sets in common use today include ASCII graphic characters (ISO 646 IRV) in code positions 0x20–0x7e, and then put additional characters in positions 0xa0–0xff. For eight-bit sets like the ISO 8859 series, this allows the addition of up to 96 graphic characters over those already in ASCII. Graphic characters that appear in multiple ISO 8859 sets almost always have the same encoding. For example, Â appears in ISO 8859-1, -2, -3, -4, and -9, and in all sets its encoded value is 0xc2.

The ranges 0x00–0x1f and 0x7f–0x9f are reserved for control characters, but ISO 8859 does not make control character assignments. See Appendix E for information on control characters.

4.4.1 ISO 8859-1 (Latin-1)

The most commonly used of the ISO 8859 sets is Latin-1. As noted above, it contains the characters necessary for Western European languages such as French, German, Italian, and Spanish. Since the computer industries in Western European nations are well developed, there is considerable demand for Latin-1. Table 4.5 shows the set.

Table 4.5   ISO 8859-1 (Latin-1) Code Set

	2	3	4	5	6	7	A	B	C	D	E	F
0	SP	0	@	P	`	p	NBSP	°	À	Ð	à	ð
1	!	1	A	Q	a	q	¡	±	Á	Ñ	á	ñ
2	"	2	B	R	b	r	¢	²	Â	Ò	â	ò
3	#	3	C	S	c	s	£	³	Ã	Ó	ã	ó
4	$	4	D	T	d	t	¤	´	Ä	Ô	ä	ô
5	%	5	E	U	e	u	¥	µ	Å	Õ	å	õ
6	&	6	F	V	f	v	¦	¶	Æ	Ö	æ	ö
7	'	7	G	W	g	w	§	·	Ç	×	ç	÷
8	(	8	H	X	h	x	¨	¸	è	Ø	è	ø
9	)	9	I	Y	i	y	©	¹	É	Ù	é	ù
A	*	:	J	Z	j	z	ª	º	Ê	Ú	ê	ú
B	+	;	K	[	k	{	<<	>>	Ë	Û	ë	û
C	,	<	L	\	l	|	¬	¼	Ì	Ü	ì	ü
D	–	=	M	]	m	}	SHY	½	Í	Ý	í	ý
E	.	>	N	^	n	~	®	¾	Î	Þ	î	þ
F	/	?	O	_	o	DEL	‾	¿	Ï	ß	ï	ÿ

Unlike some national variants of ISO 646, Latin-1 contains all the letters needed to support the languages it covers. Also, since the set supports a range of languages, it is possible to have, say, French, Spanish, and Portuguese text in a single file. With ISO 646 sets, you can have French *or* Spanish *or* Portuguese, but not the combination.

4.4.2   Other ISO 8859 Sets

The remaining ISO 8859 sets are in varying degrees of use, depending on a variety of factors. As Eastern European nations build up their computer industries, Latin-2 is becoming increasingly important. ISO 8859-5 (ISO-Cyrillic) and -8 (ISO-Hebrew) probably will face a similar upswing in use. ISO 8859-3, -4, -9, and -10 address specific language groups' needs, and are likely to experience more limited use. Note that ISO 8859-3 and ISO 8859-4 may be withdrawn in favor of the newer ISO 8859-10. The latter set was approved in 1992.

The other two sets, which cover Arabic and Greek, are in a different category. They fulfill only part of each language's requirements, and so may not be suitable for all text processing. While the sets that cover Latin scripts include individual code positions for all the variations of a given letter (plain and with a range of diacritics), ISO 8859-7 (ISO-Greek) has only the plain Greek letters and then has a few diacritics encoded as separate values. But Modern Greek uses some accented characters, and Ancient Greek allows characters to have an almost-dizzying variety of diacritics. ISO 8859-7 is less than complete because, like all the ISO 8859 code sets, it can only contain 96 additional characters. If you want to write Greek using this set, you cannot use letters with diacritics.

Similarly, while most Arabic consonants have four forms—initial, medial, final, and isolated—ISO 8859-6 (ISO-Arabic) generally contains only one form of these characters. Depending on your text processing requirements, it may or may not be possible to use ISO-Arabic for languages that use the Arabic script.

4.4.3   Other Eight-Bit Sets

In addition to the ISO 8859 standard sets, there also are national standards for other languages or scripts. LTD 37(1610)-1988 is the Indian standard code set, while Thailand has a national standard set called TIS 620-2529:1986 (Thai Industrial Standard for Thai Character Code for Computer). Both encode characters in eight-bit entities.

4.4.4   An Alternate European Set

The ISO 8859 sets assign each character to one eight-bit code value. This means a plain letter gets one code value, and a version of the same letter with a diacritical mark gets a different value. Because there only is room for 96 non-ASCII characters in an ISO 8859 set, it is not possible to fit all variations of Latin letters-with-diacritics in one set.

This restriction results in the family of 8859 sets—with each entry supporting a different group of languages. An alternative approach, implemented in ISO 6937, makes it possible for one group of code values to support a much larger set of languages. ISO 6937 includes the ASCII graphic characters in code positions 0x20–0x7e but the upper half consists of a wide range of diacritics, some symbols, and a few characters or ligatures that don't exist in the English alphabet.

The difference in ISO 6937 is in the way it encodes characters. A plain letter's encoded value is a single eight-bit entity. However, a letter with a diacritic is encoded as a two-byte value: the diacritic followed by the plain letter. For example, here is how to encode ä:

$$\boxed{1\,|\,1\,|\,0\,|\,0\,|\,1\,|\,0\,|\,0\,|\,0} + \boxed{0\,|\,1\,|\,1\,|\,0\,|\,0\,|\,0\,|\,0\,|\,1} = \text{¨} \quad a \quad = \quad ä$$

This approach makes it possible to combine any letter with any diacritic in the set. So while, say, à and ă are in two different 8859 sets (Latin-1 and Latin-2, respectively), both are available within 6937.

Actually, it is only theoretically possible to combine any letter with any diacritic in ISO 6937. Rather than permitting unsuitable pairs, the standard includes a list of acceptable combinations. It allows you, say, to put a grave accent on an *e*, but prohibits you from putting the same accent on an *f*. Given that no European language using a Latin script includes an *f-grave*, the restriction doesn't keep many people awake at night. The fact that 6937 has a list of acceptable combinations means it has a *closed repertoire*. If it allowed combinations without restrictions, it would be said to have an *open repertoire*.

The disadvantage of ISO 6937 is that characters in a data stream no longer are a consistent width. It typically is easier to process characters when they are all one size, so 6937 is most often used only for data interchange (e.g., in mail systems), rather than for text processing. Indeed, the designers of ISO 6937 only intended for it to be used for data interchange. Of course, code sets and standards often are used in ways their designers never intended.

4.4.5 Vendor-Specific Eight-Bit Sets

In addition to standard ISO or national sets, several major computer companies have their own eight-bit code sets. These proprietary sets sometimes predate the creation of the standards, and continue in use today because an existing base of customers depends on them. In many cases, the proprietary sets bear more than a passing resemblance to the standard sets, but there are important differences.

For its PC and UNIX-based lines, IBM has a collection of eight-bit sets that are similar to the ISO 8859 sets. The one that is similar to Latin-1 is called pc850. Like Latin-1, it includes ASCII in code positions 0x00–0x7f, and then has characters for Western European languages assigned to 0x80–0xff. However, while Latin-1 reserves 0x80-0x9f for control characters, pc850 uses those positions for European letters. Also, pc850 includes many graphic characters that PC developers typically use to build boxes. The result is that while many characters are common to Latin-1 and pc850, each set also has unique characters. Even characters that are common to the two sets have differences because they often have different encoded values. For example, õ is at 0xf5 in Latin-1, and 0xe4 in pc850.

Hewlett-Packard also has a collection of eight-bit sets that look very much like the 8859 sets. Examples include ROMAN8, ARABIC8, and GREEK8. ROMAN8 is comparable to Latin-1 in that it also has ASCII in the lower half, and supports the same set of languages. Like pc850, the characters it has in common with Latin-1 are assigned different code values than what Latin-1 uses. ROMAN8 also contains some unique characters and doesn't have some that exist in Latin-1. The ROMAN8-specific characters tend to be seldom-used punctuation or symbols.

Other code sets that are similar to Latin-1 include ones from Apple Computer and Microsoft Corporation. Like the other proprietary sets, Apple's eight-bit Roman code set includes most of the familiar letters for handling Western European languages, but also has some Greek mathematical symbols (for example, Σ, π, Ω) that don't exist in Latin-1, as well as graphic symbols like the Apple logo. Microsoft uses an eight-bit set that is identical to IBM's pc437. In addition to Latin letters-with-diacritics, it contains graphic symbols that PC developers use to draw boxes on the screen, several Greek letters, and other mathematical symbols.

Notice that all of the Latin-1-like sets are designed to support pretty much the same group of languages, and yet all encode slightly different character sets. Table 4.6 shows comparable encoded values of a sampling of characters in these sets. In the table, a dash (—) indicates that the character does not exist in the listed set.

Table 4.6   Comparable Encodings in ISO 8859-1-Like Code Sets

Character	ISO 8859-1	Apple Roman	pc437	pc850	ROMAN8
à	0xe0	0x88	0x85	0x85	0xc8
á	0xe1	0x87	0xa0	0xa0	0xc4
¿	0xbf	0xc0	0xa8	0xa8	0xb9
þ	0xfe	—	—	0xe7	0xf1
Ω	—	0xbd	0xea	—	—

There are other proprietary eight-bit sets around, but this gives you an idea of some of the variety that exists. The good news, though, is that some computer vendors are trying to phase out their unique sets in favor of standard versions.

4.5 Ideographic Code Sets

Languages like Japanese, Chinese, and Korean use writing systems that combine phonetic and ideographic characters, and those systems have literally thousands of characters. Because of this, an eight-bit code set with its maximum of 256 characters obviously is inadequate. These languages need to use 16 bits or more for most characters.

National standards bodies in Japan, South Korea, the PRC, and the ROC have created code sets for the phonetic and selected ideographic (Kanji, Hanja, Hanzi) characters for each of these languages. The way phonetic and ideographic sets are combined along with English characters is covered later in the Encoding Methods section. This section explores only the code sets themselves.

Table 4.7 lists standard sets for ideographs in each of these languages. The two- or three-letter prefix with each standard identifies the organization that registered it—JIS for Japanese Industrial Standard, KS for Korean Standard, GB for Guo Biao, and CNS for Chinese National Standard.

Table 4.7   Asian Standard Code Sets

Language/Writing System	Standard Set	Year Adopted	Number of Chars
Japanese	JIS X0208	1978	6,349
Japanese	JIS X0212	1990	6,067
Korean	KS C5601	1987	8,235
Simplified Chinese (PRC)	GB 2312	1980	6,763
Traditional Chinese (ROC)	CNS 11643	1986	13,735

While most sets in Table 4.7 contain mainly ideographs, the Korean set includes 2,350 Hangul syllables along with Hanja ideographs. Also note that JIS X0208 has been updated twice—in 1983 and 1990—since its adoption in 1978, and that CNS 11643 was revised in 1992 to increase its characters to 48,228.

In all of these sets, only the lower seven bits of an eight-bit byte are used for encoding characters. The MSB of every byte for every character is used independently to allow mixtures of code sets. It is possible, for example, for Japanese JIS X0208 characters to appear in a data stream with the MSB on (set to one) for all bytes, or for the MSB to be off (set to zero) for all bytes. Whether the MSB is on or off depends on the encoding method you are using. (Again, more on this later.)

All sets mentioned here except the 1992 version of CNS 11643 use two bytes per character. There are 65,536 possible code positions in a two-byte code set, but, as noted, these sets all contain less than 15,000 characters. Why? Because of the restriction that only the lower seven bits are available for encoding characters. Given that rule, data bytes that appear different are considered equivalent. The following shows two two-byte characters that differ only with respect to the MSB:

| 1 | 1 | 0 | 0 | 0 | 0 | 1 | 1 | | 1 | 1 | 0 | 0 | 1 | 1 | 0 | 1 |

| 0 | 1 | 0 | 0 | 0 | 0 | 1 | 1 | | 0 | 1 | 0 | 0 | 1 | 1 | 0 | 1 |

Because the MSB is, in effect, ignored, these two are equivalent. Note also that the MSB is either on or off for all bytes in these code sets; that is, it is not permissible for the MSB to be on in one byte of a two-byte character and off in the other. Such restrictions mean that only about 16,000 of the more than 65,000 possible code values in a two-byte space are usable. In addition, some code sets disallow encodings that match the lower seven bits of ASCII control characters. This means no byte can be in the range 0x00–0x1f or 0x7f–0x9f and further reduces the number of allowable encodings to about 8,800.

Although a code set with between 8,000 and 16,000 characters may seem ample, it doesn't fulfill all of a Japanese, Chinese, or Korean user's potential needs. There are thousands of ideographs—and, in the case of Korean, Hangul syllables—that don't appear in the standard sets. In order to expand the repertoire, several countries already have created multiple code sets. As noted in Table 4.7, Japan already has two standard sets that encode completely different groups of ideographic Kanji, while the ROC (Taiwan) revised CNS 11643 in 1992 to add almost 35,000 more ideographs, for a grand total of 48,228 characters. The additional ROC characters consume four bytes each.

4.6   Encoding Methods

Although non-American computer users might prefer to work exclusively in their native language, they almost always need to retain access to English characters while adding support for their own language. After all, the commands that most systems expect are English (or what passes for English). Likewise, programming language keywords are likely to be English-based.

Because some users need to use characters from multiple languages, they need a way to mix code sets. That is where *encoding methods* come in. They provide a predictable way to mix characters from multiple sets. It is most common to use encoding methods for Pacific Rim (Asian) writing systems, but they also exist for other language groups. This section covers:

- an encoding method framework
- stateful encodings
- encoding method implementations

4.6.1   An Encoding Method Framework

Although many encoding method implementations are in use today, most are versions of a system described in ISO 2022 (Code extension techniques). This encoding method permits multiple code sets to be combined in either seven-bit or eight-bit formats and uses escape sequences to identify the various sets in use. The seven-bit form of ISO 2022 is most commonly used when data needs to pass through software that cannot handle full, eight-bit data. Many electronic mail programs fall into this category.

Seven-bit ISO 2022 starts with the basic code set structure shown in Figure 4.2.

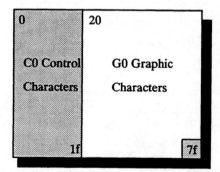

Figure 4.2   Seven-Bit ISO 2022 Structure

ISO 2022 groups characters into one of these elements:

- **C0 set**. A set of 32 control characters assigned to code values 0x00–0x1f.
- **C1 set**. An additional set of 32 control characters.
- **G0 set**. A set of 94 graphic characters assigned to code values 0x21–0x7e. Characters that consume more than one byte may be part of a G0 set.

- **G1, G2, and G3 sets**. Additional sets of 94 graphic characters. Again, these sets can include characters that take up more than one byte.

In practice, the G0 set almost always contains ASCII graphic characters, while C0 usually contains familiar control characters like null, ESC (escape), and carriage return. See Appendix E for a list of the C0 control characters.

A typical ISO 2022 implementation uses several control characters, most of which are in the C0 space. Table 4.8 shows the most commonly used controls.

Table 4.8   Sample ISO 2022 Control Characters

Code Value	Abbreviation	Name	Meaning
0x1b	ESC	Escape	Escape
0x0f	SI	Shift-In	Shift In the G0 set
0x0e	SO	Shift-Out	Replace current graphic set with G1
ESC 0x6e	LS2	Locking shift 2	Replace current graphic set with G2
ESC 0x6f	LS3	Locking shift 3	Replace current graphic set with G3
0x8e	SS2	Single shift 2	The next character only is part of G2
0x8f	SS3	Single shift 3	The next character only is part of G3

Despite the fact that SI, SO, LS2, and LS3 have different sounding names, they actually perform basically the same function: a *locking shift*. That is, they initiate a state that then applies to all following data. The state persists until there is another locking shift in the data stream. A stream that includes locking shifts is called a *stateful encoding*. See the section Stateful Encodings below for more details.

The other type of shift function is a *single shift*, so called because it signals a state that applies only to the single character that follows it. SS2 and SS3 are single shift functions.

By default, the C0 and G0 sets are active at the beginning of a stream of ISO 2022-encoded data. All data is interpreted as if it were a member of one of those sets until one of the control characters mentioned above occurs. For an example, suppose you want to encode the French word *hôtel* in ISO 2022. The *ô* is part of the G1 set, the rest of the letters are in G0. The data stream looks like this:

h	SO	ô	SI	t	e	l

The SO signals the shift out of G0 and into G1 in order to find the *ô*. The SI signals a shift back into G0 for the rest of the characters.

Now suppose you want to encode the string *hièéαε*. In this example, assume:

- *h* and *i* are in G0, where the full G0 set is the ISO 646 IRV (ASCII) graphic characters,
- *è* and *é* are in G1, where the full G1 set is the upper half of ISO 8859-1 (Latin-1),
- α and ε are in G2, where G2 represents the upper half of ISO 8859-7 (ISO-Greek).

Further suppose that you want to use the single-shift function SS2 for the final two Greek characters rather than the locking shift. The data stream looks like this:

h	i	SO	è	é	SS2	α	SS2	ε

At the end of this string, the G1 set—the one with Latin-1—is resident. That is because a single-shift SS2 function only affects the single character that follows it rather than making a full set replacement.

Since the code values for characters in all G sets in the 7-bit ISO 2022 structure must be in the range 0x20–0x7e, code values have different interpretations depending on which set is active at any given time. The value 0x68 is the letter *h* in G0 and *è* in G1. Similarly, 0x69 is the value for *i* in G0 and *é* in G1. Here are the code values in the data stream:

0x68	0x69	0x0e	0x68	0x69	0x8e	0x61	0x8e	0x65

The result is that a code value's interpretation depends on the shift state around it.

ISO 2022 allows you to encode any character in a seven-bit structure, but it also includes techniques for using all eight bits of a byte. Figure 4.3 shows the eight-bit structure. Note that G0 graphic characters must always occupy the left half of the eight-bit structure (code values 0x21–0x7e), while G1, G2, and G3 can reside in either the left or right half.

The seven- and eight-bit structures and all the control characters are only part of the ISO 2022 story. Consider the earlier example of the data stream for the string *hièéαε*. Notice that it assumes you know which code sets G0, G1, and G2 represent, but that it contains no explicit instructions to identify these sets. Obviously, there must be some way to identify sets because one implementation might assign the upper half of Latin-1 characters to G1 and Greek to G2, while another assigns the

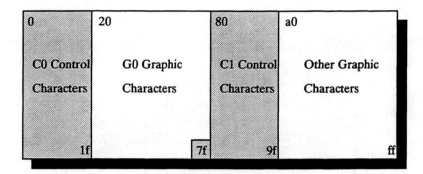

Figure 4.3   Eight-Bit ISO 2022 Structure

upper halves of Latin-2 and Latin-3 to G1 and G2. Without an identification method, an ISO 2022 data stream could be incomprehensible.

Fortunately, there is an identification method. ISO 2022 includes predefined escape sequences that announce specific code sets. The sequences consist of three segments:

1. The **escape** character (ESC, code value 0x1b) to signal announcement information
2. One or more bytes that designate the ISO 2022 set (C0, G0, G1, etc.) to which this escape sequence refers
3. One or more bytes that designate an individual code set (ASCII, Latin-1, JIS X0208, etc.)

ISO registers code values for each of these segments. For example, if the second segment is 0x28 or 0x2c, the full escape sequence designates sets of single-byte characters for G0. A value of 0x24 in the second segment designates sets of multiple-byte characters for G0. The two-byte sequence 0x24 0x29 in the second segment designates sets of multiple-byte characters for G1. All of these values also define SO as the control character that invokes the set.

In addition to identifying code sets, escape sequences specify other characteristics of ISO 2022-encoded text. There are sequences to define the values of ISO 2022 control characters, as well as sequences for identifying code set updates. Table 4.9 shows some ISO-registered escape sequences and their meanings. Note that escape sequences consist of varying numbers of bytes. Table 4.9 shows sequences with between two and four bytes.

Table 4.9   Sample ISO 2022 Escape Sequences

Escape Sequence	Assignment/Meaning
ESC 0x28 0x42	ASCII to G0; SI invokes set
ESC 0x2d 0x41	Right half of Latin-1 to G1; SO invokes set
ESC 0x2d 0x42	Right half of Latin-2 to G1; SO invokes set
ESC 0x24 0x29 0x42	JIS X0208-1983 to G1; SO invokes set
ESC 0x20 0x5a	Use SS2 to invoke G2
ESC 0x20 0x5b	Use SS3 to invoke G3
ESC 0x26	Updated code set

4.6.2 Stateful Encodings and ISO 2022

Fully specified ISO 2022-encoded text begins with several escape sequences that define the characteristics of the data that follows. Assume one of these sequences is:

ESC 0x2d 0x41

As noted in Table 4.9, this defines G1 as containing the right half of Latin-1, so every time you encounter SO in the data stream, you know what set it assigns to G1.

A complete set of escape sequences avoids ambiguity in 2022-encoded data. It also creates a *stateful encoding*, which is an encoding that contains byte sequences embedded in the data that describe how to interpret the data. In the case of 2022, such sequences designate the code set to which the following data belongs, but in other stateful encodings, sequences might designate anything from text direction to the number of bytes per character. Generally, an encoding is only considered stateful if it includes locking shifts. One that uses only single shifts—the control characters that affect only the single character following them—usually is not considered a stateful encoding.

Stateful encodings provide an unambiguous way to designate characteristics about the data they surround. They also provide great flexibility. With simple standard code sets, it is only possible to use characters within the sets. If your code set is, say, Latin-1, you only have access to Western European characters. Using an ISO 2022 stateful encoding, however, it is possible to combine characters from any registered code set. If you need to combine characters from ASCII, Latin-1, JIS X0208, and KS C5601 in a single data stream, and to be able to find the boundaries of each code set, ISO 2022 provides the mechanism for doing so. Such a data stream begins with a series of escape sequences that list the code sets in the data stream, the G-set (G0, G1, G2, or G3) to which they are assigned, and the control sequence that invokes the set further down the stream. Assume a stream contains these code sets and that the listed control character invokes the set:

Code Set	Invoking Control
ASCII	SI
Latin-1	SO
JIS X0208	LS2
JIS X0201	LS3

The data stream might look like this:

ASCII–id	*Latin–1–id*	*JIS X0208–id*	*JIS X0201–id*	SI	b

b	b	SO	b	b	b	b	SI	b	b	b	LS2

b	b	b	b	LS3	b	b	SI	b	b	b	b	. . .

In this example, italicized entries at the beginning are the byte sequences that identify the named code set. A *b* is a data byte, and the control characters (SI, SO, and so on) signal a change from one code set to another.

While stateful encodings provide almost infinite flexibility, they require more sophisticated text processing software than do stateless encodings. Since the interpretation of all data within a stream depends on the state information around it, programs must search for the state and then use it to process data correctly. Instead of being able to seek randomly in a stream, you need to find the most current state information so you know how to interpret the data. Consider a simple stateful data stream. In the following example, *b* designates a data byte and SO and SI are ISO 2022 control characters. Numbers above the data help you count individual bytes. The initial code set identification sequences are omitted.

						1													2	
1	2	3	4	5	6	7	8	9	0	1	2	3	4	5	6	7	8	9	0	1
b	b	b	b	b	b	SO	b	b	b	SI	b	b	b	b	b	b	b	b	b	b

Suppose you begin reading this stream from the end and want to work toward the beginning. There is no way to know the state of the data from looking at the end of the stream and therefore no way to know how to interpret the characters. The only way to determine the state is to scan backward until you encounter a control character. In this example, 10 data bytes appear after the last state information (SI), so a program needs to scan backward 10 times. While that is a relatively small number, it is easy to imagine very large files in which thousands of bytes separate state information and the data it affects. Because state information may appear anywhere in the stream, software that handles such encodings typically avoids backward or random scanning.

Although many text processing packages create and process stateful encodings, commonly used utilities like those on UNIX-based systems assume data is stateless. Because of this assumption, some ISO 2022-based implementations omit some or all of the escape sequences and instead assume certain defaults. This removes the need to teach software to look for and either process or ignore the escape sequences. Removing the sequences works as long as all parties that process the data assume the same defaults, but it naturally breaks down under conflicting definitions.

Now that you know what ISO 2022 and stateful encodings are, it is time to look at some encoding method implementations.

4.6.3 Compound Text/Compound Strings

Compound Text (CT) and Compound Strings (CS) are related implementations that are in broad use. CT is the format the X Consortium defines for interchanging data and is based on ISO 2022, while CS is an internal format that OSF/Motif uses in some cases.

The main difference between CT and CS is defaults. Unless there are escape sequences to the contrary, CT assumes that G0 contains ASCII graphic characters, and G1 contains the right half of Latin-1. In contrast, CS assumes no default state. Each CS data segment has a three-part escape sequence that identifies the data's characteristics as follows:

1. An escape sequence that announces the type of data in the segment
2. A length value that specifies the number of bytes in the segment
3. The actual data

CT and CS both have advantages and disadvantages. Since CT assumes a default state, existing ASCII or Latin-1 text can be exchanged as CT without modification. However, if the data is exchanged with a system that uses different defaults, it is interpreted incorrectly. CS avoids problems with incompatible defaults, but at the cost of requiring changes to existing ASCII or Latin-1 data streams.

CT also includes additional control sequences that specify a text segment's directionality. It currently handles only left-to-right and right-to-left directions. Table 4.10 shows the directionality sequences.

Table 4.10   CT Directionality Sequences

Control Sequence	Meaning
0x9b 0x31 0x5d	begin left-to-right text
0x9b 0x32 0x5d	begin right-to-left text
0x9b 0x5d	end of string

Notice that the sequences do not begin with ESC. ISO 2022 has no provisions for defining directionality, so these sequences are extensions to the basic ISO 2022 methodology.

4.6.4 Pacific Rim Encoding Methods

European users have the luxury of choosing between fixed-width sets like Latin-1 and the mixed-length encodings like ISO 6937. In either case, though, a single code set usually fulfills their needs. Pacific Rim users like those in Japan, South Korea, the PRC, or the ROC don't have quite the same options because they need both single-byte ASCII to enter the commands and other keywords their systems depend on, and multiple-byte phonetic and ideographic characters to write their language. Because of this, it has been common to use encoding methods based on ISO 2022 or other methodologies.

The two most popular methods for encoding data are Extended UNIX Codes (EUC) and Personal Computer (PC) codes. EUC is commonly used for UNIX-based systems, and has been implemented for all Asian writing systems that include ideographs. PC codes tend to be the de facto standards for personal computers in a given country although they also are available on other systems.

Extended UNIX Codes (EUC)

EUC is an ISO 2022-compliant encoding methodology that allows concurrent support of up to four code sets (CSs). Table 4.11 illustrates the encoding layout and shows the relationship between the CSs and ISO 2022's graphic sets. In the figure, the ranges indicate the acceptable values for a given byte. Italics indicate optional bytes.

Table 4.11   EUC Encoding Layout

Set #	ISO 2022 Set	First Byte	Additional Byte(s)
CS0	G0	0x00–0x7f	—
CS1	G1	0xa0–0xff	*0xa0–0xff* . . .
CS2	G2	0x8e	0xa0–0xff *0xa0–0xff* . . .
CS3	G3	0x8f	0xa0–0xff *0xa0–0xff* . . .

The first set, CS0, is always single-byte ASCII. As is always the case with ASCII, the MSB (Most Significant Bit) for each byte is zero (0). The second set, CS1, has characters of one or more bytes, and the MSB of each byte is 1. In most Asian implementations, the characters in the second set are two bytes each and contain ideographs or phonetic syllables (for example, Korean Hangul).

In CS2, each character begins with the one-byte control character SS2 (Single Shift 2; code value 0x8e). One or more bytes follow the SS2. As with CS1, the MSB of each byte is on. In most implementations, the characters in CS2 are two bytes each (the SS2 flag and one more byte), and contain phonetic characters such as Japanese kana.

The final set, CS3, is similar to CS2. Each character begins with the one-byte control character SS3 (Single Shift 3; 0x8f), and is followed by one or more additional bytes. In the past, few EUC implementations used CS3, but that is changing now. In those that do use CS3, the characters are three or four bytes each: one byte for SS3, and then two or three bytes for ideographs that supplement those in CS1.

To reliably identify the set to which a particular character belongs, no byte in CS1 can have the same code value as SS2 or SS3. Likewise, no additional byte in CS2 or CS3 can have the same code value as SS2 or SS3.

Although EUC allows combinations of up to four code sets, you can use fewer. ASCII-only data is the simplest form of EUC, because it uses only CS0. A Latin-1 data stream is a slightly more complex EUC. Despite these simpler implementations, EUC usually is considered an Asian (or Pacific Rim) encoding method. Table 4.12 shows the structure of a typical implementation—Japanese AJEC (Advanced Japanese EUC Code). Note that while AJEC includes characters in CS3, previous Japanese EUC encodings (sometimes called UJIS) either left CS3 empty, or used it for vendor- or user-definable characters.

Models similar to the Japanese are gaining popularity in South Korea, the PRC, and the ROC.

Note that in EUC, every byte of every character other than those in CS0 has the MSB on. The restriction exists to try to make things easier for software that has ASCII dependencies. Since all ASCII characters have the MSB turned off, making

Table 4.12   Definition of Japanese AJEC

Set #	First Byte	Additional Byte(s)	Set Contains
CS0	0x00–0x7f	—	ASCII
CS1	0xa1–0xfe	0xa1–0xfe	JIS X0208; Kanji characters
CS2	0x8e	0xa1–0xfe	JIS X0201; katakana characters
CS3	0x8f	0xa1–0xfe 0xa1–0xfe	JIS X0212; supplemental Kanji

other EUC characters have the MSB on means it is easy to scan for ASCII characters in a data stream. Code sets or encoding methods that permit byte values in the range 0x00–0x7f to contain ASCII characters only are said to be *ASCII-transparent*. A set or method is not ASCII-transparent if it contains bytes with values in the ASCII range that are something other than ASCII.

Although EUC is based on ISO 2022, an EUC data stream omits all escape and control sequences except SS2 and SS3. This means systems must know the EUC in which their data is encoded in order to interpret it correctly. There is nothing in the data to indicate whether the stream contains Japanese EUC, Korean EUC, or another EUC implementation.

Because EUC data streams omit most signaling bytes, they avoid some of the processing problems described in the earlier Stateful Encodings and ISO 2022 section. Instead of having to scan for an unknown number of escape sequences and other control characters, and having to process data with locking shifts, an EUC parser only needs to look for SS2 and SS3.

PC Codes

The encoding methods popular on Asian PCs aren't as accommodating to ASCII characters as is EUC. Unlike EUC, which is ASCII-transparent, the PC codes use different rules.

The Japanese PC code is called Shift-JIS (or SJIS), and it combines ASCII, JIS X0208, and JIS X0201, but it does so differently than EUC. With SJIS, a byte's value determines what kind of character it is. The characteristics associated with a particular value vary from vendor to vendor, but in a typical implementation, if the byte is in the range 0x81–0x9f or 0xe0–0xfc, it is the first of a two-byte character.

The second byte can have any value except an ASCII control character. Some implementations also prohibit second bytes from being in the range 0x20–0x3f. This simplifies parsing of UNIX-style file names, because ASCII dot (.) or slash (/) are in that range (0x2e and 0x2f, respectively). The restriction is not universal, but notice that even the most restrictive SJIS implementations permit second bytes to have values in the range 0x40–0xfc (except 0x7f). This means a second byte can have the same value as any ASCII letter and some ASCII symbols.

Any character sequence that does not begin with a "first of two" byte value is treated as a one-byte character. If the MSB is off, that one-byte character is ASCII; if it is on and in the range 0xa1–0xdf, the character is a single-byte phonetic kana. Table 4.13 shows ranges of a typical SJIS implementation.

Table 4.13   Sample SJIS Implementation

First Byte	Second Byte	Character Is
0x00–0x7f	—	ASCII
0xa1–0xdf	—	single-byte JIS X0201
0x81–0x9f, 0xe0–0xfc	0x40–0xfc*	two-byte JIS X0208

* excluding 0x7f

Notice that unlike AJEC, SJIS does not support the JIS X0212 code set.

The ROC's PC Code, which is called Big 5, is similar to Japan's SJIS. It, too, varies from implementation to implementation, but it permits second bytes with values that match ASCII characters.

Built-In Differences

EUC and PC encodings leave some space for *vendor-definable* and *user-definable characters* (VDCs and UDCs). The standard ideographic code sets include only a subset of the vast number of ideographs that exist in various Asian writing systems. As noted in Chapter 2, there are tens of thousands of ideographs, and most standard code sets include between 6,000 and 8,000 of the most commonly used of those characters.

Suppose, however, that your business uses ideographs the standard sets do not contain. For example, a hospital uses vocabulary that differs from what a publishing firm uses. Both businesses probably need ideographs that don't appear in the standards, but each needs different ones. Likewise, the vendor that supplies the computer system typically wants to add characters that don't exist in the standard sets. That is where UDCs and VDCs come in.

Standard encoding methods set aside specific code ranges for UDCs and VDCs so that developers know both where to put the characters they need, and that they can't predict what characters are assigned to those values. In a typical SJIS implementation, a value in the range 0xf0–0xfc is considered the first byte of a two-byte UDC/VDC. Japanese AJEC reserves several areas for UDC/VDCs including the area in CS1 in which the first byte is in the range 0xf5–0xfe.

4.6.5 ASN.1

In addition to the ISO 2022 encoding methodology, example implementations like EUC and CT, and alternate encoding methods like PC Codes, there is still another encoding method. ASN.1 (Abstract Syntax Notation 1) is a wide-ranging specification that includes the rules for defining complicated types and also for specifying the values for these types. ASN.1 includes specifications for many data types, but in the area of characters, it defines a general character string type syntax. It also includes several predefined types including one called PrintableString. PrintableString contains the English letters A–Z and a–z, digits (0–9), space, and 11 punctuation symbols: apostrophe, left and right parentheses, plus sign, comma, hyphen, period, slash, colon, equal sign, and question mark.

Once an ASN.1 type is defined, programmers can use it to build data structures. They might decide, for example, that file names on the system must be of type PrintableString and therefore can only contain a limited set of characters. Some European standards designate that certain fields must take PrintableString values.

ISO 8824 and 8825 describe ASN.1 and its uses in excruciating detail.

4.7 Universal Code Sets

Most of the code sets and encoding methods discussed so far each support one language or a group of related languages. This is fine if you want to process groups of languages that are part of a typical mix, but not so fine if you want a more exotic blend. English plus Japanese is okay (for that matter, English and just about any single language works), but something like German and Japanese is not. Likewise, French plus Spanish is fine (Latin-1 supports both), but French plus Arabic—a common mix in Northern Africa—is not because one requires Latin-1, the other ISO 8859-6.

One potential solution is to give software the wherewithal to handle arbitrary mixtures of code sets. That takes considerable effort, as you will learn in Chapter 12. Another partial solution is to combine all characters into a *universal code set*. A universal set is supposed to combine every character for all commonly used scripts and languages, as well as all the symbols you could ever need, in one large code set.

Until 1991, there were two very different proposals for universal code sets: Unicode and ISO DIS 10646 (DIS stands for Draft International Standard). However, the two proposals were merged into a new set called ISO/IEC 10646-1. Despite the name, the merged proposal had much more in common with Unicode than with the original 10646 and it was accepted as an ISO standard in 1993. (For brevity, the set is referred to as ISO 10646.) The approved version does, however, contain features that do not exist in Unicode.

4.7.1 ISO/IEC 10646-1

Characters in ISO 10646 are encoded in multiple octets, where *octet* is an eight-bit byte. Code space is divided into four units—group, plane, row, and cell—like this:

Group-octet	Plane-octet	Row-octet	Cell-octet

In their canonical form, code values consume four octets each. This form is called UCS-4 (Universal Coded Character Set-4). However, the most commonly used portion of the set is expected to be the BMP (Basic Multilingual Plane), and in it, code values take up the lower two octets (row and cell) each. This form is called UCS-2 (Universal Coded Character Set-2). This is the encoding of an *A* in UCS-2 and UCS-4:

UCS-2:
```
Binary: 00000000 01000001
Hex:    0x00     0x41
```

UCS-4:
```
Binary: 00000000 00000000 00000000 01000001
Hex:    0x00     0x00     0x00     0x41
```

Currently, UCS-2 and UCS-4 encode exactly the same characters. The four-octet space is reserved for possible future expansion. Also note that Unicode only allows the two-octet (16-bit) form for code values. Unicode Version 1.1 contains the same entries as are in UCS-2.

Unlike most other code sets or encoding methods previously described, 10646 does not reserve code values to avoid confusion with all or part of ASCII. All of the 65,536 code positions possible in the two octets of UCS-2 are valid, as are the more than 4 billion possibilities in UCS-4. Even ASCII characters change from their previous single-octet encodings to being two or four octets each.

The initial version of 10646 contains approximately 33,000 assigned code values covering a long list of scripts including European, Asian, Middle Eastern, Indian, and others. It also sets aside 6,000 code positions for private use. The set covers such a wide array of scripts and languages in relatively few encoded values in part because of two techniques: Han unification and combining characters.

- **Han unification**. The Han ideographs that various Asian writing systems use all are descended from the set invented in China. Because they share a common ancestor, it is common for, say, Japanese people to be able to read some Chinese text, even if they do not speak Chinese. Not all of the ideographs look familiar, but some portion are. The idea of Han unification is to combine similar ideographs from Japanese, Korean, Traditional Chinese, and Simplified Chinese into one code value. For example, the ideograph for *sun* exists in all four writing systems and looks similar, so in 10646 these ideographs are unified into one code value.

  There are many logical arguments for unifying similar Han characters. After all, if characters are the "same," why repeat them in a set? Similar characters in other languages already are unified in many code sets. Sets from Latin-1 to ISO 10646 have just one Latin *A*, rather than having one for English, one for French, one for German, and so on. Imagine the text processing difficulties if there *were* dozens of *A*s. However, it is true that not all instances of letters that look similar are unified in 10646 or other sets. Uppercase *A*'s look the same in the Latin, Greek, and Cyrillic scripts, and yet are not unified because they come from different scripts. The Latin and Cyrillic *A*s, for instance, have separate code values both in ISO 8859-5 and 10646. Similarly, uppercase and lowercase English letters are not unified in 10646, although one could argue that they are the same.

  So the problem is to define sameness. Scholars around the world disagree about whether a given group of Han ideographs are alike enough to be combined, and have varying opinions about the way 10646 has done the job.

  In addition to this controversy, some developers in the local countries oppose Han unification because it means that ideographs no longer are encoded in the same order as they are in individual national standards. It is convenient to have one's own language grouped together, and since the national standards provide that convenience, some don't want to give it up.

- **Combining characters**. ISO 10646 includes all the letters-with-diacritics that appear in the ISO 8859 family of code sets, which means there are individual code positions for *à*, *Ñ*, and others. But languages like Greek and Thai allow base letters to take a huge variety of diacritics or tone marks. Similarly, some users want the freedom to create new combinations of characters-with-diacritics that are not predefined in 10646 or other code sets. Instead of encoding all combinations separately, 10646 uses an ISO 6937-like encoding.

  Under the ISO 6937 technique, you may remember, a single diacritic may be combined with a base letter. The resulting character encoding consumes two octets. In the 10646 version of this technique, you can combine any number of *combining characters* with a base character. The resulting unit—called a *composite sequence*—is encoded like this (italics indicate optional combining characters):

base	combining_char1	*combining_char2*	. . .	*combining_charN*

Notice that while diacritics precede base characters in an ISO 6937 encoding, combining characters follow the base in ISO 10646.

The use of combining characters to create composite sequences is an effective way to increase a code set's repertoire, but it adds new text processing requirements to software. Since characters have no uniform length, software must examine individual UCS entities to determine the correct thing to do. Suppose you want to delete a character. It no longer is enough to remove two or four octets. Now you have to keep parsing for an end condition that will come after an unspecified number of octets.

Because not all software wants to deal with the complexity of combining characters, ISO 10646 defines three conformance levels:

- **Level 1**. Combining characters are not allowed.
- **Level 2**. Combining characters are permitted for this group of scripts only: Arabic, Hebrew, Indic, and Thai.
- **Level 3**. Combining characters are permitted without restrictions. At this level, ISO 10646 has an open repertoire.

Unicode is equivalent to a UCS-2, Level 3 implementation of 10646.

When describing Unicode and ISO 10646, it is common to hear them referred to as fixed-width character encodings. Given the definition this book uses for *character*, and the presence of combining characters in the two sets, such a description seems inaccurate. After all, if some characters consist of a base character plus multiple combining characters, while others are only a single base character, then characters are not fixed-width; they are variable.

The confusion comes from varying definitions. Unicode defines every two-octet entry in the code set as being a *character*. Since all code values are two octets, Unicode characters are indeed fixed-width. The unit that a base and zero or more combining characters forms is a *text element* (what this book calls a *character*). A text element also can be more than this book's definition of *character* covers. Some collation methods require two or more characters to be treated as a unit (for example, *ch* and *ll* in Spanish). These are considered text elements for collation.

In addition to the official forms of ISO 10646, one of the standard's informative annexes defines an unofficial form called UTF (UCS Transformation Format). Informative annexes are not part of official ISO standards, so there is no requirement to support UTF, or any assurance that it will remain in the standard. However, support for some form of UTF is considered likely because it provides compatibility between UCS-2 or UCS-4 and ASCII. In fact, there already are definitions for two UTF forms—the one in the ISO 10646 annex, and another called FSS-UTF (File System Safe UCS Transformation Format). These two forms are sometimes called UTF-1 and UTF-2, respectively.

In UTF-1 form, characters that are common to 10646 and ASCII shrink back from being two or four octets to being a single octet (that is, they are encoded exactly the same as traditional ASCII). In addition, no octet of any UTF-1 character can be in the range 0x00–0x20 or 0x7f–0x9f, so no UTF-1 octets have the same values as control characters. UTF-1 does, however, allow octets to be in the range 0x21–0x7e. That creates problems for UNIX-like file systems because the range includes the ASCII value for slash (/, code value 0x2f), and those systems assume that 0x2f equals slash. That's where UTF-2 (FSS-UTF) comes in. In part to provide greater compatibility between existing file systems and ISO 10646, UTF-2 maps all characters that don't appear in ASCII such that the MSB of all octets is on. As with UTF-1, characters that do appear in ASCII get mapped to a single octet with the MSB off. Table 4.14 shows examples of encoded values for several characters in international or national code sets, UTF-1, UTF-2, and UCS-2.

Table 4.14   Comparable Encodings

Character	Code Set	Code Value
A	ASCII	0x41
	UTF-1	0x41
	UTF-2	0x41
	UCS-2	0x00 0x41
á	ISO 8859-1	0xe1
	UTF-1	0xa0 0xe1
	UTF-2	0xc3 0xa1
	UCS-2	0x00 0xe1
Ideograph "one"	JIS X0208	0x30 0x6c
	UTF-1	0xf6 0x21 0xd0
	UTF-2	0xe4 0xb8 0x80
	UCS-2	0x4e 0x00

Notice that ASCII and the UTF values are identical, but that encodings of characters in other code sets consume more octets in the UTF forms than do those same characters in other existing standards—two octets in each UTF form versus one in ISO 8859-1; three octets in each UTF form versus two in JIS X0208.

ISO 10646 has considerable advantages and disadvantages. A main advantage is that it allows mixtures of languages not possible in other existing code sets. A major disadvantage is that the UCS-2 and UCS-4 forms are not compatible with ASCII or ASCII-based code sets. This means programs with ASCII dependencies must be revised to handle UCS-encoded data.

Since ISO 10646 was new when this book was written, there were few systems that support it, but that was expected to change over time. Also note that a universal code set is only one piece in the puzzle of processing multilingual data. Chapter 12 discusses this in more detail.

4.8   Summarizing Code Sets

If, when you began reading this chapter, you only knew about ASCII and perhaps one or two other code sets, you may be feeling overwhelmed with all the variety that exists. The following tables summarize the names and main attributes of the code sets and encoding methods covered earlier.

In Table 4.15, the column **Bits Per Code Element** lists the number of bits that each unit in the set consumes. In some sets, it takes multiple elements to encode a character. The last column tells whether the set is ASCII-transparent. Although fully internationalized code should not have dependencies on ASCII, much existing software does. Knowing which sets are ASCII-transparent has an effect on some character-processing tasks. If you currently parse data a byte at a time looking for one or more ASCII characters, and your software only needs to handle ASCII-transparent sets, this parsing does not need to change. However, byte-oriented searches for ASCII characters must change if your software supports sets that aren't ASCII-transparent. Note that while some dependencies can remain in software that handles ASCII-transparent sets only, others must go. See Chapters 6 and 8 for more information.

Table 4.16 summarizes encoding methods, listing the number of code sets each method supports, and also the number of bits per character. Bit counts include single-shift control characters, where they exist. For example, a 24-bit Japanese AJEC character consists of an eight-bit control character plus 16 bits for the ideograph.

Table 4.15   Summary of Code Sets

Code Set	Bits Per Code Element	Bits Per Character	Scripts / Languages	ASCII-Transparent?
ASCII	7	7	American English	yes
CNS 11643	16 or 32	16 or 32	Traditional Chinese	yes
GB 2312	16	16	Simplified Chinese	yes
ISO 646 IRV	7	7	American English	yes
ISO 646 national variants	7	7	varies	yes
ISO 6937	8	8 or 16	European	yes
ISO 8859-1	8	8	Western European	yes
ISO 8859-2	8	8	Eastern European	yes
ISO 8859-3	8	8	Southeastern European	yes
ISO 8859-4	8	8	Northern European	yes
ISO 8859-5	8	8	English and Cyrillic	yes
ISO 8859-6	8	8	English and Arabic	yes
ISO 8859-7	8	8	English and Greek	yes
ISO 8859-8	8	8	English and Hebrew	yes
ISO 8859-9	8	8	W. European (and Turkish)	yes
ISO 8859-10	8	8	Northern European	yes
ISO 10646:				
UCS-2, Level 1	16	16	universal	no
UCS-2, Level 2	16	varies	universal	no
UCS-2, Level 3	16	varies	universal	no
UCS-4, Level 1	32	32	universal	no
UCS-4, Level 2	32	varies	universal	no
UCS-4, Level 3	32	varies	universal	no
UTF-1*	8, 16, or 24	varies	universal	no
UTF-2*	8, 16, or 24	varies	universal	yes
JIS X0201	8	8	Japanese katakana	both
JIS X0208	16	16	Japanese Kanji	both
JIS X0212	16	16	Japanese Kanji	both
KS C5601	16	16	Korean	yes
Unicode (R1.1)	16	varies	universal	no
U.S. EBCDIC	8	8	American English	no

* currently assigned ranges

Table 4.16   Summary of Encoding Methods

Name	Number of Code Sets	Bits Per Character	Scripts/ Languages	ASCII-Transparent?
Japanese EUC (AJEC)	4	8, 16, and 24	Japanese	yes
SJIS	3	8 and 16	Japanese	no
Japanese EUC (UJIS)*	3	8 and 16	Japanese	yes
Korean EUC (eucKR)	2	8 and 16	Korean	yes
Taiwanese EUC (eucTW)	2	8, 16, and 32	Traditional Chinese	yes
Big 5	2	8 and 16	Traditional Chinese	no
Compound Text	varies	varies	varies	no
Compound Strings	varies	varies	varies	no
ASN.1	varies	varies	varies	no
ISO 2022	varies	varies	varies	no

* becoming obsolete

4.9   Converting Between Encodings

The fact that many code sets exist means that characters can be encoded many different ways. French text may be encoded in Latin-1, the French version of ISO 646, the universal set ISO 10646, or a proprietary set like IBM's pc850 or HP's ROMAN8. Consider these encodings for the string *côté*:

Latin-1	0x63 0xf4 0x74 0xe9
ISO 10646 (UCS-2)	0x00 0x63 0x00 0xf4 0x00 0x74 0x00 0xe9
pc850	0x63 0x93 0x74 0x82

Similarly, Japanese text may be encoded in AJEC or SJIS. Traditional Chinese may be encoded in Taiwanese EUC or Big 5. It is probably true that every character appears in multiple code sets, but most systems are only capable of handling a finite group of sets. For example, a system may handle Latin-1 but not pc850, or it may understand UCS-2 but not Latin-1. That means you may receive data encoded in ways your system doesn't handle, or that you may need to convert data from your local encoding before sending it to another system.

The X/Open Portability Guide defines the **iconv** utility for converting data from one encoding to another. You specify the way the source file is encoded (its *from-code*), and the way you want the destination file encoded (the *to-code*). The command has this syntax:

iconv -f *from-code* **-t** *to-code source-file*

By default, the result goes to standard output, but you can redirect it to a file. This example converts `ajec.file` from Japanese AJEC to SJIS and stores the output in `sjis.file`:

```
iconv -f AJEC -t SJIS ajec.file > sjis.file
```

Supported conversions are implementation-dependent. Companies naturally include converters to and from their own proprietary code sets or encodings, but they usually do not have converters for other companies' proprietary sets. In addition, some sites may support newer standards and so include converters to and from ISO 10646 forms, while other sites may not. Check your system's **iconv** man page for information about supported conversions.

4.10   Portable Characters

The many code sets available for encoding the world's characters make it possible for your company's software to handle groups of languages. They make the same thing possible for other companies' software. Of course, there is no guarantee that the group your company picks to support and the group others pick are the same. You may write software that handles European languages. Another developer may target Asian languages. Another may stay in the computer stone age and stubbornly cling to ASCII-only products.

This diversity becomes a problem when you need to exchange information. The Asian and ASCII-only packages won't understand your European characters, and your software surely won't be able to decipher Asian ideographs.

It is not feasible to expect every system to understand every existing character or code set, but software does need to count on some characters being understood. This need has led to the creation of *portable character sets*. The product of standards bodies or industry consortia, they represent a minimum set of characters guaranteed to exist on a given compliant system. For example, if your system supports POSIX.1, it must handle all entries in the POSIX.1 Portable Filename Character Set.

A portable set has these characteristics:

- **Minimum set of characters.** Implementations can (and most likely do) handle more than this minimum set, but software can only count on the characters in the set being supported on a compliant system.

- **Encodings are not specified.** These are character sets rather than code sets, which means that the encodings of characters within the sets are not defined. If a portable set includes the English letters A–Z and a–z, one compliant implementation can encode them in ASCII, while another encodes them in U.S. EBCDIC.

Portable sets define a restricted set of available characters. A major goal of internationalization, however, is to make *more* characters available, so you should think carefully before deciding that a given string must only contain portable characters. Some systems restrict file names to containing characters in a portable set, while the contents of the files can be in any language. Similarly, compilers usually restrict variable names to a small character set, but allow strings or comments to contain any character. This code fragment is acceptable for most compilers:

```
char        buff[BUFSIZ];
time_t      ct;
char        *dt_fmt;                   /* strftime用日時のフォーマット    */
struct tm   *local;                    /* ローカル・タイム              */
(void) setlocale(LC_ALL, "");          /* ロケールの設定                */

ct   = time(NULL);                     /* 秒による現在時刻の取得          */
local = localtime(&ct);                /* tmフォーマットへの時刻の変換     */
dt_fmt= nl_langinfo(D_T_FMT);          /* ロケールにあるD_T_FMT値を得る    */
if (strftime(buff,BUFSIZ, dt_fmt, local)) /* 現在時刻をD_T_FMTフォ  */
  printf("%s¥n", buff);                /* ーマットに変換し印刷    */
```

The fragment contains Japanese comments, but uses the Latin characters for the actual source code statements and for all variable names.

If you are concerned about portability, restrict yourself to a portable character set when naming variables or other fields. Unfortunately, this is not as simple as it may seem. Instead of there being a single portable set, there are many. All commonly used sets include the English letters A–Z and a–z and also Arabic digits 0–9, but they mandate different sets of symbols. Table 4.17 shows some commonly used portable sets of graphic (printable) characters.

The strategy under which some portable sets were created was to define as small a group as possible. The POSIX.1 set and ISO's PrintableString are sets of this type. Over time, though, it has been more common to allow more characters in the sets. A system that only supports the POSIX.1 set, for instance, can't handle slashes in file names, colons as pathname separators, or the syntax of most programming languages. More recent portable sets therefore have more entries.

Notice that the last set in Table 4.17 includes all the graphic characters in ASCII. POSIX.2 defines this set (along with some control characters) as its *Portable Character Set*. The differences between the POSIX.1 Portable Filename

Table 4.17   Standard Portable Character Sets

Set Name	Issuing Group	Number of Characters	Additional Characters*
Portable Filename Character Set	POSIX.1	65	-._
PrintableString	ISO 8824	74	' ()+,-./:=?
ASN.1 Character Set	ISO 8824	76	"'(),-.:<=[]{}
International Alphabet 5 Unique Graphic Char Set	CCITT T.50	82	!"%&'()*+,-./:;<=>?_
Unique Graphic Character Set	ISO 646	84	!"%&'()*+,-./:;<=>?^_'
International Reference Version (IRV) Graphic Char Set (1991)	ISO 646	94	!"#%$&'()*+,-./:;<=>?@[\]^_'{|}~

* all sets contain English letters A–Z, a–z and digits 0–9

Character Set and the POSIX.2 Portable Character Set confuse many users, but reflect differing objectives in the various standards.

4.11   Obsolete Code Set Assumptions

Given all the code sets and encoding methods in use around the world, it is obvious that some "facts" programmers have used to write code now are as out of date as the horse-and-buggy. Following are some internationalized rules about code sets.

- **Character does not equal byte.** The C and Pascal programming languages use the data type **char** as the name for byte storage. FORTRAN's **character** data type performs much the same function. It is little wonder then that in most people's minds, characters and bytes are the same thing.

  This is no longer the case. EUC, ISO 10646, ISO 6937 and other code sets or encoding methods prove that characters and bytes are two distinctly different entities. Characters can, and often do, span multiple bytes. *Character does not equal byte anymore!*

- **A code value can encode many characters.** Since so many programs have relied on ASCII encodings, it has been typical to assume that a particular code value is assigned to one and only one character. Under this assumption, if you find, say, a 0x61, you know it is a lowercase *a* and nothing else.

No such exclusivity exists anymore. While many code sets and encoding methods make it easy to find the 0x00–0x7f range of ASCII characters, others do not give ASCII special treatment. And the 128 code values from 0x80 through 0xff can represent anything from a European letter-with-diacritic to one part of an Asian ideograph. For example, the code value 0xe3 is *ã* in Latin-1, *ă* in Latin-2, and *y* (lowercase Cyrillic u) in ISO 8859-5.

- **Sort order may be unrelated to encoded order.** In ASCII, letters are arranged in English alphabetical order (even though they are segregated by case). Because of this, programmers since the time of vacuum tubes have compared characters' encoded values to determine collation order. But characters in sets like Latin-1 and Latin-2 are not in any language's order. Instead of comparing encoded values, you have to build tables or use routines that describe a character's collation position independent of its encoded value.

- **Code sets may sort multiple ways.** It is typical to assume that a code set can be sorted one, and only one, way. This isn't surprising given that computer sorts have typically relied on a character's encoded value. But the characters in many code sets can be sorted in a variety of ways. It is possible to sort Latin-1 using French collation rules, or Danish, or other Western European language, and the results differ depending on the rules in effect when the sort runs.

  Consider this example. Both German and Swedish include the character *ä* (Latin-1 code value 0xe4). In German, *ä* sorts with plain a's, while in Swedish, it is considered a separate letter and appears after *z* in the alphabet. If you sort Latin-1 text using German rules, *ä* sorts one place, and if you sort that same text using Swedish rules, *ä* sorts to a different place.

Future chapters describe routines you can use in place of obsolete logic, as well as introducing techniques for handling more-than-single-byte characters.

4.12   Choosing Code Sets—and More

Although data can take forms ranging from seven-bit ASCII to multiple-byte EUC to ISO 10646, most current implementations handle only some of the code sets and encoding methods described in this chapter. If you are an application developer, you must decide which sets and methods you want your software to support and then make the appropriate revisions in the software.

The next chapter describes how users designate the code set or encoding method they are using and how programs get access to users' choices. Such a choice is one part of a *locale*.

Locales

5

Individual languages and countries have varying requirements for the way data should be processed or presented, and an internationalized system is capable of handling this variety. ISO C defines both the concept of a *locale* for holding the collection of rules and text specific to a language and geographical area, and several functions that set and use locales. Other standards or industry specifications define additional commands and functions that use locales.

A locale includes information such as collation rules, date and time formats, and character classification data for a language or culture. It thus provides part of the localized data that an internationalized program uses.

This chapter covers locales in detail as it describes:

- Using locales, including naming conventions, selecting locales, locale categories, and setting a locale within a program
- Locale-specific information, including storage strategies and access functions
- Character maps (*charmaps*) and locale definitions (**localedef**s)

5.1 Using Locales

An internationalized system lets users decide at program run time how culture-specific tasks will be done. One user may want to use a Hebrew locale while another wants German and still another wants American English.

Since most internationalized systems support many locales, there has to be a way for individual sites or users to declare which one they want to use. The method is a series of environment variables to which you assign locale names. These variables announce to the system how you want it to work.

125

5.1.1 Locale Name Segments

A locale name often consists of between one and three parts: *language, terri-tory,* and *codeset.* Each segment provides important—and different—information about how you want the system to work for you.

- **Language**. As the name implies, the *language* segment refers to the natural language you want the system to process. You may want to interact with the system in Portuguese, while a colleague wants to use Korean. By setting the language appropriately, each of you can have your wish. The language setting affects a variety of system functions, including collation rules, character classifi-cation, the names of weekdays and months, and the appropriate answers to yes/no questions.
- **Territory**. The *territory* piece of a locale generally refers to a country, although it can refer to a region within a country, or to a collection of countries. Typical examples of territories are Argentina, Great Britain, Japan, or Kenya. The terri-tory of a given locale affects culture-specific information such as date and time formats, numeric formatting, and what to use as a currency symbol. The terri-tory can also further refine the language field because it specifies the way the language is used in a particular geographic region.
- **Code set**. You learned in Chapter 4 that there are nearly as many code sets in the world as there are standards committees. The third segment that may appear in a locale name lets you specify which one to use. You may choose ISO 8859-1 (Latin-1), or Japanese AJEC, or plain ASCII. Note that *codeset* in this case can refer to a true code set, or—as with AJEC—to an encoding method implementation.

When selecting a locale, some standards only require you to specify the lan-guage segment, while others make no requirements at all about what to specify. However, most implementations at least encourage you to include all three parts in order to reduce ambiguity. Suppose you decide to specify only the language when setting a locale. Further suppose you set it to English. English is spoken in the United States, Australia, Great Britain and other countries, but these places each have unique date, time, and monetary formats. A simple English locale setting doesn't tell the system how to handle these culture-specific chores.

Just as a language-only locale name is unspecific, so too is a territory-only name. In the previous example, the value of the territory field implies the value the language would have—that is, with the United States, Australia, or Great Britain as the territory, the language almost certainly is English. But numerous countries have multiple official languages. Switzerland has four: French, German, Italian, and Romansh. Canada has two: English and French. Designating a locale as `Switzerland` or `Canada` doesn't provide software with enough information to do locale-specific tasks such as sorting data or determining which letters are upper-case.

Finally, the code set segment of the locale also gives important information. This is because there is an implicit tie between the language and the code set. A code set includes a particular set of characters, and those characters cover some sub-set of the world's languages. By choosing a particular code set in your locale, you are in effect choosing a language or group of languages to which you want access. In the United States, a user might prefer ASCII, U.S. EBCDIC, or Latin-1. In Japan, a user might prefer SJIS or AJEC.

5.1.2   Locale Naming Conventions

As noted, a locale name generally includes language, territory, and code set. Naturally, there are exceptions to that rule. ISO C specifies that there be a locale named `C`. This locale produces the same results as an uninternationalized American-based system produces. IEEE's POSIX committee also specifies a locale name called (appropriately enough) `POSIX`. It currently is exactly the same as the `C` locale.

`C` and `POSIX` are exceptions. Beyond those, there are no standards for locale names, although work was under way when this book was written to create such standards. The lack of existing standards meant, however, that there was an astounding variety of naming schemes. Here is a small sample:

- **Complete words versus abbreviations.** Some companies use complete words for locale name segments (for example, `English, French`), while others use abbreviations (`En, Fr`).
- **Country versus nationality.** When filling in the territory, some use the name of the country (`Canada, Switzerland`), while others use the nationality of the people who live there (`Canadian, Swiss`).
- **English versus native language.** Some always use English-based names (`Germany`), while others use the local-language name (`Deutschland`).
- **Predictability versus chaos.** Some have predictable naming methods, while others don't (`c-french` for Canadian French, or `chinese-t` for Traditional Chinese).

Despite the variety, more companies are moving toward a predictable locale-naming system. It is based on this outline from the X/Open Portability Guide:

ll_TT.CODESET

where:

ll   is a two-lowercase-letter abbreviation for the language name. The abbreviations come from ISO 639 (Code for the Representation of Names of Languages). Examples:

        `en` English
        `fr` French
        `ja` Japanese
        `de` German (from the German name for the language: Deutsch)

TT   is a two-uppercase-letter abbreviation for the territory name. The abbreviations come from ISO 3166 (Codes for the Representation of Names of Countries). Examples:

        `JP` Japan
        `NL` The Netherlands
        `US` United States
        `ES` Spain (from the Spanish name for the country: España)

CODESET is the name of the code set or encoding method. Currently, there are no international standards for names of code sets or encoding methods, but some countries have chosen names for their local implementations. Examples:

        `ASCII`   7-bit ASCII
        `ISO8859-1` ISO 8859-1
        `AJEC`   Advanced Japanese EUC Code

Given these conventions, Table 5.1 shows some complete locale names.

Table 5.1   Sample Locale Names

Name	Meaning
`en_US.ASCII`	English, USA, ASCII
`fr_FR.ISO8859-1`	French, France, ISO 8859-1
`fr_CH.ISO8859-1`	French, Switzerland, ISO 8859-1
`ja_JP.AJEC`	Japanese, Japan, AJEC

While this naming scheme is highly predictable, it is not a model of user-friendliness. Most people don't know the ISO abbreviations for the language and territory of their choice, and they may be hard-pressed to remember the sequence of field separators (*Does the period come before or after the country name?*). Therefore, it is a good idea to allow sites to define more mnemonic names as symbolic links to the standard names. A site in France, for instance, might equate français with fr_FR.ISO8859-1, while a French-Canadian site might choose the same mnemonic as the match for fr_CA.ISO8859-1. Providing flexibility is the key.

5.1.3 Selecting a Locale

Either an individual user or a system administrator can select a locale. When system administrators do the work, it is likely they are selecting the default locale for an entire site. Depending on the implementation, users may or may not have the freedom to override the default.

To select a locale, you must assign a locale name to one or more environment variables. The simplest case is to assign a value to a variable called LANG. This environment variable covers an entire instance of a locale. Here are examples of setting LANG:

```
% setenv LANG fr_FR.ISO8859-1          /* C shell */
$ LANG=fr_FR.ISO8859-1; export LANG  /* Bourne/Korn shell */
```

These examples set the locale to French for the shells in which they are invoked and all child processes of those shells. If you want another shell to have a different locale, assign a different value to LANG in that particular shell.

Because separate processes can have different locales, it is possible for a single user to work in multiple locales on a single display. Figure 5.1 shows a display that includes shells running in French, German, English, and Japanese.

Assigning a value to LANG is the most common way to select a locale because it names an entire locale. If you set only LANG, the system performs all locale-specific tasks according to the rules associated with that LANG setting. If LANG is set to a Japanese locale, and you run a program that sorts data, the program sorts it using Japanese rules. If you reset LANG to a French locale and rerun the same program, the program uses French sort rules on the data.

In addition to selecting a locale in a shell, there are other ways to set it. Some applications allow locale specification at program start-up. For example:

```
% my_app -lang fr_FR.ISO8859-1
```

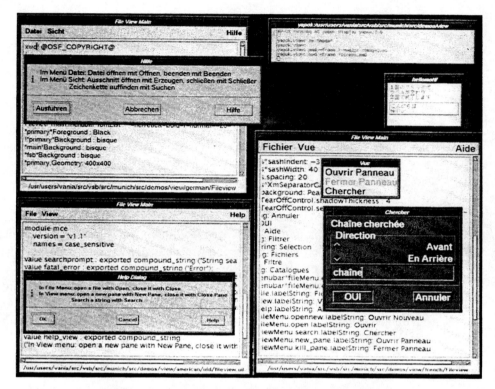

Figure 5.1   Multiple Locales in Separate Processes

5.1.4 Locale Categories and LC_ALL

While LANG applies to an entire locale, there may be times when you want the system to perform some locale-related tasks according to one locale and other tasks according to a different locale. The standards provide locale categories that apply to different pieces of a locale. Table 5.2 shows the standards-defined categories.

As with LANG, all category names are environment variables to which you can assign locale values. This allows you to mix-and-match pieces as appropriate for your needs. Suppose you are a Miami businessperson who works closely with Spanish-speaking Latin America customers. Since you are in the United States, you may choose to set LC_NUMERIC and LC_MONETARY to an American locale, but set LANG to an appropriate Latin American locale in order to sort data correctly and properly process Spanish letters.

The LC_ variables differ from LANG in that the values you assign to them can include an additional segment. This field (**@***modifier*) allows you to select a specific version of locale-specific data. Suppose there are two ways to sort data in a given

Table 5.2   Locale Categories

Category	Purpose
LC_COLLATE	Collation (sorting) rules
LC_CTYPE	Character classification (ctype functions)
LC_MESSAGES	The values for affirmative (*yes*) and negative (*no*) answers, and the language in which program messages should be displayed
LC_MONETARY	Monetary formatting
LC_NUMERIC	Numeric formatting
LC_TIME	Date and time information

language: dictionary and telephone-book order. Further suppose the locale's standard setup uses dictionary rules, but you need telephone-book. You might assign your environment variables this way:

```
% setenv LC_COLLATE fr_FR.ISO8859-1@phone
% setenv LANG fr_FR.ISO8859-1
```

The explicit value of LC_COLLATE overrides LANG's implicit value for that portion of the locale.

In addition to the smaller LC_* categories, there also is one other environment variable. It is LC_ALL, and like LANG, it designates the overall locale. However, there is an important difference. Although individual LC_* category settings override LANG, they do not override LC_ALL. LC_ALL has the highest precedence and so overrides all other LC_* variables and the value of LANG. Table 5.3 shows the locale-related environment variables and their order of precedence.

Table 5.3   Locale Categories by Precedence

Category	Precedence
LC_ALL	highest
LC_COLLATE LC_CTYPE LC_MESSAGES LC_MONETARY LC_NUMERIC LC_TIME	equal precedence
LANG	lowest

Given these precedence rules, consider some examples.

Example 1:
```
% setenv LC_ALL en_US.ASCII
% setenv LC_COLLATE fr_FR.ISO8859-1
```

Example 2:
```
% setenv LANG en_US.ASCII
% setenv LC_COLLATE fr_FR.ISO8859-1
```

In the first example, the value of the entire locale is en_US.ASCII and the lower precedence value of LC_COLLATE is ignored. In the second example, assuming no other locale-related variables are set, the system performs collation according to fr_FR.ISO8859-1 rules, but does all other locale-related tasks according to en_US.ASCII rules.

5.1.5 Setting or Querying a Locale in a Program

An internationalized program needs to know the locale in which it should run, so there is a function called **setlocale( )** that either:

- explicitly sets the locale for the program, or
- returns the current value of a named locale category.

setlocale( ) makes available the appropriate locale-related data and possibly additional functions for the named locale. The function has this syntax:

#include <locale.h>
char *setlocale(int *category,* **const char** **locale);*

category is one of the LC_* categories named earlier. *locale* is a pointer to a string containing a hard-coded locale (for example, setlocale(LC_ALL, "fr_FR.ISO8859-1")) or one of:

C   Specifies the minimal, uninternationalized environment. If a program does not call **setlocale( )**, it runs as if this locale had been selected.

POSIX   Same as C.

" "   Specifies an implementation-defined environment. In essence, this tells the program to use the value assigned to the environment variable with *category*'s name, or, if *category* is not set, the value of LANG.

NULL   Directs **setlocale( )** to return the current value of *category* without changing it.

When internationalizing software, you must decide whether your program does anything that is locale-dependent. If so, and the program is application-level as opposed to being a library function, you must add a **setlocale( )** call. Among the locale-specific tasks are sorting, parsing, character classification, string manipulation, numeric or monetary formatting, and date and time handling. If your application does any of these, add the **setlocale( )** call.

You should analyze your code, however. Depending on how it is implemented, **setlocale( )** can impact performance. There is no point in paying the performance price if your program never does anything with a locale. But while you shouldn't waste a **setlocale( )** call, be aware that cultural-specific data crops up in unexpected places. If you are conservative, you might want to add the call by default and then remove it if you have good evidence it is not needed.

Here are other hints for using the function:

- **Which category?** It is safest to call **setlocale( )** with the category LC_ALL rather than a specific category. That is because it often is difficult to determine what locale-specific information a program (and the library functions it accesses) will use. While it probably is obvious that a utility like **sort** uses collation information, and so would be affected by LC_COLLATE, you might not realize that **sort** also needs the information associated with LC_CTYPE. (The LC_CTYPE setting affects **sort**'s -d and -i options.)

  The disadvantage of using LC_ALL is that it may impact performance. The amount of performance loss depends on the way **setlocale( )** is implemented.
- **Which locale string?** In nearly all cases, you will want the program to use the user's locale as defined in LANG or one of the other environment variables. In that case, *locale* must be the empty string rather than a pointer to a hard-coded locale. The empty string allows the program's behavior to change depending on the value of the environment variables. A hard-coded locale limits your program's run-time behavior to what is defined in that one locale. Since internationalized software handles a variety of locales, using a hard-coded locale defeats the purpose of using **setlocale( )**. However, this might be the correct choice if your software has only been partially internationalized, and you want to ensure that it runs in a supported locale until all work is complete.
- **Where to put the call?** Assuming you determine that your program does locale-specific processing, **setlocale( )** should be one of the first statements in **main( )**. **setlocale( )** should only appear in application programs—not in library functions.

Given these hints, here is a typical call to **setlocale( )**:

```
#include <locale.h>
main() {
    (void)setlocale(LC_ALL, "");
    /* program processing */
}
```

Although many implementations do not check **setlocale()**'s return value, you can use it for error checking, as this example shows:

```
#include <locale.h>
main() {
    char *locale;

    locale = setlocale(LC_ALL, "");

    /* setlocale returns NULL pointer if error occurs */
    if (!locale)
        printf("Cannot operate in the requested locale.\n
            Continuing in the C locale.\n");
    /* program processing */
}
```

A typical **setlocale()** call checks the value of the locale-related environment variables and then looks for the current locale among the set of those available on the system. Figure 5.2 shows part of this process.

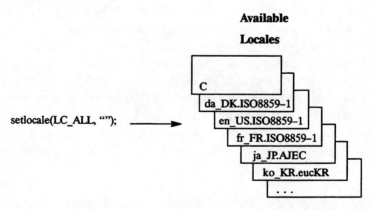

Figure 5.2   Finding the Appropriate Locale

Since an internationalized system usually includes multiple locales, **setlocale( )** makes it possible for a single program to produce a range of locale-specific results.

5.2 Locale-Specific Information

When you call **setlocale( )**, it generally looks for the current value of LANG or the LC_* variables. Then, armed with those values, it goes off to find the appropriate locale's data and routines. It is the data that spells out information such as collation rules or month names or the proper characters for formatting numbers. The following sections describe where to find locale-specific data, what it looks like, and functions for accessing specific pieces of it.

5.2.1 Finding the Information

Before you can use a locale's data or functions, you first have to find them. There are no standards for data locations, so individual implementations put the information in different places. For example:

1. `/usr/lib/nls/loc/`*locale*
2. `/usr/lib/nls/`*locale*
3. `/usr/lpp/nls/`*locale* and `/usr/lpp/nls/`*locale*`.en`
4. `/usr/lib/nls/`*language*/*territory*/*codeset*
5. `/lib/locale/`*locale*/*category*

Besides the obvious difference in the directories, there also is considerable variety in the number of files associated with each locale. For the first two examples listed above, all information is in the single, *locale* file. In the third example, the two files listed form a locale. The plain *locale* file contains character classification and collation information, while *locale*`.en` holds date and time information, numeric and monetary formats, and yes/no responses.

In the fourth example, all information is in one file, but there are separate directories for each of the three pieces of a locale name. In the last example, there are separate files for each LC_* category. The full structure for this example looks like this:

```
/lib/locale/locale/LC_COLLATE
          "       /LC_CTYPE
          "       /LC_MESSAGES
          "       /LC_MONETARY
          "       /LC_NUMERIC
          "       /LC_TIME
```

Using the directory structure in the first example, here are some sample locale pathnames:

```
/usr/lib/nls/loc/da_DK.ISO8859-1      /* Danish */
/usr/lib/nls/loc/en_US.ISO8859-1      /* English */
/usr/lib/nls/loc/fr_FR.ISO8859-1      /* French */
/usr/lib/nls/loc/hu_HU.ISO8859-2      /* Hungarian */
/usr/lib/nls/loc/ja_JP.AJEC           /* Japanese */
/usr/lib/nls/loc/zh_TW.eucTW          /* Taiwanese Chinese */
. . .
```

Although system-supplied locale information usually is in one place, do not hard-code that location into application programs or library routines. (Some early internationalized systems included hard-coded default paths.) As you have seen, the information's location is implementation-dependent, and if you hard-code in a path, your programs work only for that one path. In these days of heterogeneous networks, such exclusivity almost guarantees that you will have problems.

Some implementations provide an additional environment variable (for example, LOCPATH) for specifying the location of locale-related data. In addition to helping out with heterogeneous issues, such a variable also allows you to supply private locale data in a separate directory. For instance, you might set up the variable like this:

```
LOCPATH=/my_dir/my_localeinfo:/usr/lib/nls/loc
```

Under this setting, the system searches /my_dir/my_localeinfo first for the current locale's data. If that search fails, the operation looks in the standard system directory (/usr/lib/nls/loc).

5.2.2 Accessing Locale-Specific Information

It is important to know where locale-specific information resides on a system, but it is even more important to know how to access that information. There are two standard functions for accessing parts of locale-specific data: **nl_langinfo( )** and **localeconv( )**.

The two are specified in different documents—the former in XPG, the latter in ISO C. They have some overlapping fields, but neither is a complete subset of the other, so you may need to use both. Table 5.4 shows the information the two calls return.

Table 5.4   Information Available From localeconv( ) and nl_langinfo( )

Type of Data	localeconv	nl_langinfo
Code set name		•
Day/time formats		•
Weekday names		•
Month names		•
Abbreviated day names		•
Abbreviated month names		•
Era name and year		•
Radix character	•	•
Thousands separator	•	•
Local currency symbol	•	•
International currency symbol	•	
Currency symbol placement	•	•
Numeric grouping rules	•	
Monetary grouping rules	•	
Number of fractional digits	•	
Positive/negative signs	•	
Negative quantity formats	•	
Yes/No responses		•

As Table 5.4 shows, **nl_langinfo( )** provides access to parts of the information associated with the LC_MESSAGES, LC_MONETARY, LC_NUMERIC, and LC_TIME categories. It has this syntax:

> **#include <nl_types.h>**
> **#include <langinfo.h>**
> **char *nl_langinfo (nl_item** *item*);

where *item* is a constant that names a particular property of a locale. The function returns a pointer to a string containing the value of *item* as defined in the current locale. The header file **<langinfo.h>** contains the constants you can supply as the *item* argument. Table 5.5 shows a sample of the available constants. Check your system's **<langinfo.h>** man page for the full set of available constants.

Here is an example of how to use **nl_langinfo( )** to get different pieces of information:

Table 5.5   Sample nl_langinfo( ) Constants

Constant	Meaning
YESSTR	affirmative response for yes/no questions
RADIXCHAR	radix character
THOUSEP	thousands separator
D_T_FMT	format string for date and time
D_FMT	format string for date only
DAY_1	name of the first day in week (Sunday equivalent)
DAY_2	name of second day in week
. . .	. . .
DAY_7	name of seventh day in week
ABDAY_1	abbreviated name of first day in week
. . .	. . .
ABDAY_7	abbreviated name of seventh day in week
MON_1	name of first month in year (January equivalent)

```c
#include <stdio.h>
#include <langinfo.h>
#include <locale.h>
#include <nl_types.h>

int main(void) {
  char *radix;
  int i;
  nl_item months[12] = {MON_1, MON_2, MON_3, MON_4,
          MON_5, MON_6, MON_7, MON_8, MON_9, MON_10,
          MON_11, MON_12};

  (void)setlocale(LC_ALL, "");

  /* Find the radix character for the current locale */
  radix = nl_langinfo(RADIXCHAR);

  /* Print the month names for the current locale.
   * Current standards support 12-month calendars only.
   */
  for (i = 0; i < 12; i++)
    puts(nl_langinfo(months[i]));
}
```

Table 5.6 shows the output this program produces when run under the C locale and typical Finnish and Italian locales.

Table 5.6   nl_langinfo( ) Sample Output by Locale

C	Finnish	Italian
January	tammikuu	gennaio
February	helmikuu	febbraio
March	maaliskuu	marzo
April	huhtikuu	aprile
May	tuokokuu	maggio
June	kesäkuu	guigno
July	heinäkuu	luglio
August	elokuu	agosto
September	syyskuu	settembre
October	lokakuu	ottobre
November	marraskuu	novembre
December	joulukuu	dicembre

While **nl_langinfo( )** provides access to some pieces of information available through various LC_* categories, **localeconv( )** obtains all of the data defined in LC_MONETARY and LC_NUMERIC. It has this syntax:

#include <locale.h>
struct lconv *localeconv(void);

The function returns a pointer to a struct of type **lconv** which contains the values of the numeric and monetary formatting strings defined by LC_MONETARY and LC_NUMERIC. The following example shows how you might use the call:

```
#include <locale.h>
main() {
  struct lconv *p;
  char *currency, *thous;

  (void)setlocale(LC_ALL, "");
  p = localeconv();
```

```
/* Obtain the currency character and the
 * thousands separator for the current locale.
 */
currency = p->currency_symbol;
thous = p->thousands_sep;

/* further processing */
}
```

While **nl_langinfo( )** and **localeconv( )** give easy access to part of a locale's data, there are no standard functions for getting at the information specified in LC_CTYPE and LC_COLLATE. That is because the data in these categories are not strings, as they are in the other categories. You must write your own function if you want to see this data. However, there is not much you can do with the data if you do obtain it.

5.3 Supplying a Locale's Data

After locating your system's locale data and possibly using **nl_langinfo( )** or **localeconv( )** to access parts of it, you can decide whether the data fits your needs. System vendors generally supply a group of locales with their software, and in many cases, that group is all you will need. However, you may choose to add your own locale if:

- Your vendor does not supply a locale you need. For example, it is common for vendors to ship many Western European locales, but that won't help much if you want to break into Eastern European markets.
- A vendor-supplied locale doesn't meet local users' requirements. This can happen if there are multiple acceptable ways to perform a task. As noted earlier, many countries have both dictionary and telephone book sort orders, and users may need one or the other at different times. If the vendor's locale has instructions for dictionary sort order, you may need to add a second locale with telephone book sorting.

Along with adding new locales, you may also be able to modify existing ones. Before you can add or modify them, however, you need to understand how to create a locale. Locale data can be supplied in several source formats, but the most common probably will be the format defined in POSIX.2. It specifies a complete syntax for **localedef** (*locale def*inition) input files. These source files contain the information necessary for the various LC_* categories. After completing a source file, you feed it to the **localedef** command and it creates an object file from that source.

setlocale( ) and other functions access locale object files rather than source to improve performance.

5.3.1   Character Maps (charmaps)

When writing **localedef** input files, you can tie them to a specific code set, or write them so that they are independent of an individual set. Locale definitions that work with one code set use actual characters in the source file, while the more flexible input files use *symbolic names* to represent the actual characters. Angle brackets (<>) enclose symbolic names, as these examples of corresponding actual characters and symbolic names show:

Actual	Symbolic Name
A	\<A\>
2	\<two\>
;	\<semicolon\>

Actual characters have the encoded value that they had when you built your locale object file. If you build a locale using an ASCII-based code set, *A* has the value 0x41; if you build it on top of an EBCDIC-based set, it is 0xc1.

In contrast to actual characters, symbolic names have no specific encoding associated with them. Instead, they get their encoded values from entries in a POSIX.2-defined entity called a *charmap* (*char*acter *map*). Suppose you want the symbolic characters listed above to have ASCII code values. Your charmap would include these lines:

Symbolic Name	Encoding
\<A\>	\x41
\<two\>	\x32
\<semicolon\>	\x3b

Under POSIX syntax, the prefix **\x** precedes hexadecimal numbers, **\d** precedes decimal numbers, and a plain \ precedes octal. A charmap may use numbers in any of these three forms. To indicate a multiple-byte character, you simply list the byte values in sequence. These are some typical symbolic names for characters in Japanese JIS X0208, and their EUC-based code values:

Symbolic Name	Encoding
\<j0501\>	\xa5\xa1
\<j0502\>	\xa5\xa2
\<j0503\>	\xa5\xa3

Because many code sets contain thousands of characters, and because it would be extremely tedious to list each in a charmap, POSIX.2 allows you to use ellipses to indicate ranges of characters. The line:

```
<j0201>...<j0205>      \xa2\xa1
```

is interpreted as:

```
<j0201>              \xa2\xa1
<j0202>              \xa2\xa2
<j0203>              \xa2\xa3
<j0204>              \xa2\xa4
<j0205>              \xa2\xa5
```

POSIX.2 defines standard symbolic names for the members of its Portable Character Set. In addition, some national standards groups have created names for their characters, and the universal code set ISO 10646 includes a set of long symbolic names. All other names currently are implementation-defined. Table 5.7 shows the POSIX.2 symbolic names. Notice that several characters have two standard symbolic names (for example, period/full-stop, slash/solidus). This accommodates the fact that characters often have been known by multiple names.

Among the other important declarations in a charmap are `<mb_cur_max>` and `<mb_cur_min>`. The former takes a value equal to the maximum number of bytes per character in the charmap, while the latter gets the value of the minimum number of bytes per character. By default, `<mb_cur_max>` equals one, while `<mb_cur_min>` must be less than or equal to `<mb_cur_max>`. The header file **<stdlib.h>** contains the macro MB_CUR_MAX that gets the current locale's value of `<mb_cur_max>`.

See Appendix A for a complete charmap example.

5.3.2   Pros and Cons of Symbolic Names

Since symbolic names require charmaps and actual characters do not, you may be wondering why you should bother with symbolic names rather than using actual characters in **localedef** files. The answer is flexibility.

As noted, actual characters tie a **localedef** to one particular encoding. Suppose you write a Japanese locale. There are two common Japanese encoding methods—EUC and SJIS—and dozens of specific implementations of those general methods.

Table 5.7   POSIX.2 Symbolic Names

Symbolic Name	Glyph	Symbolic Name	Glyph	Symbolic Name	Glyph
\<NUL>		\<colon>	:	\<circumflex>	^
\<alert>		\<semicolon>	;	\<circumflex-accent>	^
\<backspace>		\<less-than-sign>	<	\<underscore>	_
\<tab>		\<equals-sign>	=	\<low-line>	_
\<newline>		\<greater-than-sign>	>	\<grave-accent>	`
\<vertical-tab>		\<question-mark>	?	\<a>	a
\<form-feed>		\<commercial-at>	@	\<b>	b
\<carriage-return>		\<A>	A	\<c>	c
\<space>		\<B>	B	\<d>	d
\<exclamation-mark>	!	\<C>	C	\<e>	e
\<quotation-mark>	"	\<D>	D	\<f>	f
\<number-sign>	#	\<E>	E	\<g>	g
\<dollar-sign>	$	\<F>	F	\<h>	h
\<percent-sign>	%	\<G>	G	\<i>	i
\<ampersand>	&	\<H>	H	\<j>	j
\<apostrophe>	'	\<I>	I	\<k>	k
\<left-parenthesis>	(	\<J>	J	\<l>	l
\<right-parenthesis>	)	\<K>	K	\<m>	m
\<asterisk>	*	\<L>	L	\<n>	n
\<plus-sign>	+	\<M>	M	\<o>	o
\<comma>	,	\<N>	N	\<p>	p
\<hyphen>	-	\<O>	O	\<q>	q
\<hyphen-minus>	-	\<P>	P	\<r>	r
\<period>	.	\<Q>	Q	\<s>	s
\<full-stop>	.	\<R>	R	\<t>	t
\<slash>	/	\<S>	S	\<u>	u
\<solidus>	/	\<T>	T	\<v>	v
\<zero>	0	\<U>	U	\<w>	w
\<one>	1	\<V>	V	\<x>	x
\<two>	2	\<W>	W	\<y>	y
\<three>	3	\<X>	X	\<z>	z
\<four>	4	\<Y>	Y	\<left-brace>	{
\<five>	5	\<Z>	Z	\<left-curly-bracket>	{
\<six>	6	\<left-square-bracket>	[	\<vertical-line>		
\<seven>	7	\<backslash>	\	\<right-brace>	}
\<eight>	8	\<reverse-solidus>	\	\<right-curly-bracket>	}
\<nine>	9	\<right-square-bracket>	]	\<tilde>	~

If you use actual characters in a **localedef,** that file works for only one of those implementations. If you use symbolic names, your **localedef** source file probably works across many implementations. (You may need to make some minor revisions.) You must supply a charmap for each specific encoding, but it is easier to write a charmap than a locale definition.

Despite the functional advantages to using symbolic names, there is an aesthetic disadvantage to them. **localedef** source files are supposed to be human-readable, but when they include symbolic names, they quickly become very hard on the eyes. Compare three brief excerpts of the LC_TIME section of a sample French locale. This one uses actual characters:

```
# abbreviated month names
abmon     "jan";"fév";"mar";"avr";"jun";"jul";\
          "aoû";"sep";"oct";"nov";"déc"
#
# full month names
mon       "janvier";"février";"mars";"avril";\
          "juin";"juillet";"août";"septembre";\
          "octobre";"novembre";"décembre"
. . .


# date/time format
d_t_fmt   "%a %d %b %Y %H:%M:%S"
```

This second example uses short symbolic names:

```
# example using short symbolic names
#
# abbreviated month names
abmon     "<j><a><n>";"<f><e-acute><v>";\
          "<m><a><r>";"<a><v><r>";"<m><a><i>";\
          "<j><u><n>";"<j><u><l>";\
          "<a><o><u-circumflex>";\
          "<s><e><p>";"<o><c><t>";\
          "<n><o><v>";"<d><e-acute><c>"
```

```
#
# full month names
mon        "<j><a><n><v><i><e><r>";\
           "<f><e-acute><v><r><i><e><r>";\
           "<m><a><r><s>";\
           "<a><v><r><i><l>";\
           "<m><a><i>";\
           "<j><u><i><n>";\
           "<j><u><i><l><l><e><t>";\
           "<a><o><u-circumflex><t>";\
           "<s><e><p><t><e><m><b><r><e>";\
           "<o><c><t><o><b><r><e>";\
           "<n><o><v><e><m><b><r><e>";\
           "<d><e-acute><c><e><m><b><r><e>"
. . .

# date/time format; The following designates this format:
#          "%a %d %b %Y %H:%M:%S"
d_t_fmt    "<percent-sign><a><space><percent-sign>\
<d><space><percent-sign><b><space><percent-sign><Y>\
<space><percent-sign><H><colon><percent-sign><M>\
<colon><percent-sign><S>"
```

This third example uses slightly modified ISO 10646 symbolic names (10646 names use spaces to separate words rather than hyphens, but spaces are invalid in POSIX.2 symbolic names):

```
# example using ISO 10646 long symbolic names
#
# abbreviated month names
abmon      "<LATIN-SMALL-LETTER-J>\
           <LATIN-SMALL-LETTER-A>\
           <LATIN-SMALL-LETTER-N>";\
           "<LATIN-SMALL-LETTER-F>\
           <LATIN-SMALL-LETTER-E-WITH-ACUTE>\
           <LATIN-SMALL-LETTER-V>";\
           "<LATIN-SMALL-LETTER-M>\
           <LATIN-SMALL-LETTER-A>\
           <LATIN-SMALL-LETTER-R>";\
           "<LATIN-SMALL-LETTER-A>\
           <LATIN-SMALL-LETTER-V>\
           <LATIN-SMALL-LETTER-R>";\
           "<LATIN-SMALL-LETTER-M>\
```

```
                      <LATIN-SMALL-LETTER-A>\
                      <LATIN-SMALL-LETTER-I>";\
                     "<LATIN-SMALL-LETTER-J>\
                      <LATIN-SMALL-LETTER-U>\
                      <LATIN-SMALL-LETTER-N>";\
                     "<LATIN-SMALL-LETTER-J>\
                      <LATIN-SMALL-LETTER-U>\
                      <LATIN-SMALL-LETTER-L>";\
                     "<LATIN-SMALL-LETTER-A>\
                      <LATIN-SMALL-LETTER-O>\
                      <LATIN-SMALL-LETTER-U-WITH-CIRCUMFLEX>";\
                     "<LATIN-SMALL-LETTER-S>\
                      <LATIN-SMALL-LETTER-E>\
                      <LATIN-SMALL-LETTER-P>";\
                     "<LATIN-SMALL-LETTER-O>\
                      <LATIN-SMALL-LETTER-C>\
                      <LATIN-SMALL-LETTER-T>";\
                     "<LATIN-SMALL-LETTER-N>\
                      <LATIN-SMALL-LETTER-O>\
                      <LATIN-SMALL-LETTER-V>";\
                     "<LATIN-SMALL-LETTER-D>\
                      <LATIN-SMALL-LETTER-E-WITH-ACUTE>\
                      <LATIN-SMALL-LETTER-C>"
#
# remainder deleted to save space and eyesight
#
```

Human-readable? The second example is far from what most people saw in their reading texts in school. The third is even farther away. And that is true whether school happened to be in Boston, Paris, Tokyo, or anyplace else.

In order to improve readability, most of the remaining examples in this section use actual characters rather than symbolic names. However, think carefully about which form you want to use if you write **localedef** source files. If you want one source to work for multiple code sets, symbolic names are the right choice.

5.3.3 localedef Source Files

After deciding whether to use symbolic names or actual characters, you can begin writing a new locale or modifying an existing one. Depending on the linguistic and cultural conventions of your locale, the **localedef** source syntax is very

simple or somewhat complex. There is a section for each LC_* category except
LC_ALL. Each section includes keywords followed by the syntax or data associated with that keyword. A pound sign (#) in the first column of a line is the default
comment character, and the backslash (\) is the default line continuation character.
The source file structure looks like this:

LC_CTYPE
 # character classification definitions
END LC_CTYPE
#
LC_COLLATE
 # collation information
END LC_COLLATE
...
 # other locale category definitions
...

Before continuing with the description, note that this section describes the
basics of a **localedef** source file, but it does not cover every keyword or every syntax
detail. See your system's locale file format man page [usually **locale(4)**] or
POSIX.2 for a complete list of available keywords and the instructions associated
with each. See also Appendix A for a complete **localedef** source file example.

With that caveat out of the way, consider a simple example. Suppose you want
to define uppercase characters for your locale. The keyword **upper** designates the
character class you are defining, and following that are the characters that are uppercase for the locale. Here is a sample **upper** definition for a German locale:

```
LC_CTYPE
#
upper     A;Ä;B;C;D;E;F;G;H;I;J;K;L;M;N;O;Ö;\
          P;Q;R;S;T;U;Ü;V;W;X;Y;Z
  . . .
END LC_CTYPE
```

You can use a shortcut in the definition. Instead of listing each character individually, you can use ellipses to indicate a range of characters like this:

```
upper     A;Ä;B;...;O;Ö;P;...;U;Ü;V;W;X;Y;Z
```

Be careful when using ellipses! **localedef** uses characters' encoded values to
decide what falls within a range. If you run **localedef** on the example above and the

underlying system is ASCII-based, **localedef** decides that everything between 0x42 (ASCII letter *B*) and 0x4f (letter *O*) is an uppercase letter. That means your input file is tied to one specific encoding.

You may assume that you are only going to support ASCII-based code sets, and so don't have to worry about the fact that your **upper** definition is now cemented to ASCII. But ellipses also make it very easy to make mistakes. You might just list A;...;Z for the German uppercase characters, because, after all, the alphabet does begin with *A* and end with *Z*. That range, however, goes only from the encoded value of *A* (0x41) to *Z* (0x5a) and omits *Ä*, *Ö*, and *Ü* (Latin-1 encoded values 0xc4, 0xd6, and 0xdc, respectively).

Now you know how to list the members of a keyword in a locale definition file, and have been warned about the dangers of seductively convenient ellipses. But there is much more to **localedef** source files. Some keywords take string values—for instance, the currency symbol in a given locale, or the names of the months. Double quotes (") enclose strings, as this German example shows:

```
LC_NUMERIC

decimal_point        ","
thousands_sep        "."
#. . .

END LC_NUMERIC

LC_TIME

# abbreviated weekday names
#
abday      "So";"Mo";"Di";"Mi";"Do";"Fr";"Sa"
#
# full month names
#
day        "Sonntag";"Montag";"Dienstag";"Mittwoch";\
           "Donnerstag";"Freitag";"Samstag"
# . . .
END LC_TIME
```

A somewhat more complicated part of specifying a locale is that of defining the proper behavior for classes like **toupper** and **tolower**. Even this, though, is relatively simple. The syntax calls for pairs of comma-separated characters enclosed in parentheses. For example:

```
toupper    (a,A);(ä,Ä);(b,B);(c,C);(d,D);(e,E); . . .
```

Note that the first character in a pair is the one on which the conversion is to be done, and the result of that conversion is the second in the pair. In this example, the lowercase characters come first, and their uppercase equivalents follow. Definitions of the **tolower** class are reversed; that is, (A, a) ; (Ä, ä) ; and so on.

You must list all case-conversion pairs in your locale. If you omit a pair, the functions **toupper( )** and **tolower( )** return the input character unchanged. For example, suppose you accidentally left the (ä, Ä) pair out of the locale definition. A **toupper( )** call on *ä* then returns *ä*. Note, however, that you can omit the entire **tolower** specification. If you do so, character mappings are the reverse of what you specify in **toupper**.

The least intuitively obvious part of a locale definition is the collation section. That is because collation itself often is complicated. If your locale has simple sort rules, this section is simple, too. If not, it isn't.

In its simplest form, the section looks something like this:

```
LC_COLLATE
order_start        forward
# omitting ASCII control chars and symbols to save space
A
B
C
D
E
F
G

. . .
# omitting rest of sequence to save space
order_end
END LC_COLLATE
```

The keywords **order_start** and **order_end** designate the beginning and ending of the collation sequence. The keyword **forward** says that sorting operations should start at the beginning of an input string and proceed to the end. (The converse keyword **backward** indicates that comparisons start at the end and work toward the beginning.) The characters (A, B, C, . . .) appear in the order in which they should be collated. This sequence designates that *A* comes before *B* which comes before *C*, and so on.

Suppose your collation rules are more complicated than simply putting one character after another. Suppose they include some of the collation models described in Chapter 2; for example:

- Multilevel sorting (multiple characters sort to the same primary location, and additional sorts break ties).
- Multicharacter collating symbols (such as *ch* and *ll* in Spanish).
- Single characters that sort as if they were two (like the German *ß* [Eszett], which sorts as if it were *ss*).

Given these requirements, here is a sample collation section:

```
# This is just an excerpt! It is not a complete
# collation definition.
LC_COLLATE
collating-element <ch> from <c><h>
collating-element <Ch> from <C><h>
order_start            forward;forward;forward
. . .
<a>                    <a>;<a>;<a>
<A>                    <a>;<a>;<A>
<a-acute>              <a>;<a-acute>;<a-acute>
<A-acute>              <a>;<a-acute>;<A-acute>
<a-grave>              <a>;<a-grave>;<a-grave>
<A-grave>              <a>;<a-grave>;<A-grave>
<a-circumflex>         <a>;<a-circumflex>;<a-circumflex>
<A-circumflex>         <a>;<a-circumflex>;<A-circumflex>
<b>                    <b>;<b>;<b>
<B>                    <b>;<b>;<B>
<c>                    <c>;<c>;<c>
<C>                    <c>;<c>;<C>
<ch>                   <ch>;<ch>;<ch>
<Ch>                   <ch>;<ch>;<Ch>
<d>                    <d>;<d>;<d>
<D>                    <d>;<d>;<D>
. . .
<s>                    <s>;<s>;<s>
<S>                    <s>;<s>;<S>
<Eszett>               <s><s>;<s><s>;<s><s>
. . .
```

```
# omitting rest of sequence to save space
order_end
END LC_COLLATE
```

The **collating-element** clauses let you define which characters make up a multi-character collating element. In the first example clause, the letters *c* and *h* make up the *ch* collating element. Given this definition, the string *ch* collates as a single element rather than as two separate letters.

After the **order_start** directive, the first column lists each character for which collation information is being specified. The second column lists collation weights for each character. The first operand specifies the primary weight, the second is the secondary weight, and so on. In this example, *A*, *á*, *Á*, *à*, *À*, *â*, and *Â* all sort to the same primary location as a plain *a*, so the first operand is the symbolic name <a> for all these letters.

The secondary sort is by diacritic, while the tertiary is by case. Since uppercase *A* has no diacritic, in the secondary sort it still is treated as if it were a lowercase *a*. The same is true for other uppercase letters without diacritics. In the secondary sort, *B* is treated as if it were a *b*, *C* as if it were a *c*, and so on. In the tertiary sort, the collation definition distinguishes uppercase from lowercase.

When a **localedef** omits sort information, characters are ordered according to their encoded values. This can result in significantly different output than what users may expect. Assuming the encoding is Latin-1, consider the difference in output between a sort that uses multilevel rules and one that orders data by encoded value only.

Multilevel Results	Encoded Value Results
acre	Acre
Acre	acre
âcre	aprés
Âcre	bague
âpre	Âcre
aprés	âcre
bague	âpre

See Chapter 8 for a detailed description of multilevel sorting.

This collation example shows that all sorts are forward sorts; that is:

```
order_start            forward;forward;forward
```

There are cases, however, when this isn't appropriate. When sorting by diacritic, Canadian French uses a backward sort. That is, it examines strings from the end and works toward the beginning of the string. Here is the difference between forward and backward versions of a sort by diacritics:

Forward	Backward
cote	cote
coté	côte
côte	coté
côté	côté

In the forward sort, *coté* sorts before *côte* because a plain *o* comes before *ô*. In the backward sort, comparisons start at the end of the string. Therefore, *côte* sorts before *coté* because the plain *e* comes before *é*.

5.3.4 Locale Contents

When building a locale definition, you obviously have to decide what goes in it. This is harder than it seems. You probably can choose a single set of month names fairly easily, and most likely you won't have much trouble figuring out what currency symbol to include. But deciding what to include in various character classes or collation sequences may stir up a hornet's nest of possibilities.

If a system only had to support ASCII, there would be no doubts. Every one of the 128 characters in the set is defined in one or more classes, and all traditionally collate according to their encoded value. Clean and simple. But now suppose you want to list the members of the class **lower** for a French locale.

Some choices are still simple. You definitely include the letters *a–z* because French uses all of them. There also is no doubt about listing common French letters like *á, ç,* and *ê*. But what about *ß* or *ø*? Neither is part of French—the former appears only in German, while the latter is valid in several Scandinavian languages. Should you designate letters like these as being lowercase in a French locale?

It depends. From a purist's standpoint, it seems logical not to include the non-French letters. After all, they are not part of the language, so they have no business being in the locale definition. This kind of thinking can lead to unexpected results. It is not uncommon for text that is written in one language to include words from another. This book is a primary example. It is written in English, but has text from many other languages. Some system functions decide whether a character is valid based on the classes to which it belongs. If this text were run against a locale that

only included English letters, such functions would assume all non-English characters in this text are mistakes. The functions would be mistaken.

In order to avoid considering commonly used characters as mistakes, some
argue that the source file should include all characters in the code sets to which the
localedef source is likely to be applied. Using this strategy, you might include all
characters in Western European code sets (Latin-1, ROMAN8, pc850, and others) in
one or more of the French locale's character classes. You also would define a sort
order for each.

You don't have to think very long to realize this approach isn't always suitable.
Suppose the French locale will be combined with an ISO 10646 charmap. You
probably wouldn't want to include each of the over 33,000 characters in 10646 in
the locale. Besides the work involved in building such a locale, it also would consume excessive disk space and run-time memory. A smaller, trimmer locale would
run rings around a bulky one.

Instead of taking either the *my-language-only* or the *throw-in-everything* view,
the best solution is to find a happy medium. For single-byte code sets, it probably is
best to include all of that set's possible characters in your locale. For larger sets, you
should do some intelligent pruning. You may decide, for example, to include all
Latin characters in any locale that uses a Latin script, but to exclude everything
else—Chinese, Arabic, Hindi, and others—from the locale. Of course, the locale
should fit your specific needs. If you know you need to mix Latin scripts and Chinese, you should keep Chinese in your locale definition.

Further localedef Refinements

There are other ways to refine a locale. You might specify that only the characters that are part of your locale's language can be in classes like **lower** and **upper**,
but include characters outside the language in more general classes like **print**. This
lets programs pass through the characters without implying they are part of the language.

Suppose you are running in a German locale and want to list a directory that
includes file names like leçon, instrução, and Maß (French, Portuguese, and
German words, respectively). Most implementations of the **ls** utility use **isprint( )** to
decide whether a character is printable. If **isprint( )** says it isn't, **ls** lists a substitute
character (usually space or question mark) instead. If your locale definition includes
only German characters in **print**, **ls** produces a listing like this:

% ls
```
instru??o    le?on    Maß
```

A locale definition that includes a wider selection of European characters for the **print** class more accurately produces:

```
% ls
instrução      leçon      Maß
```

While the example above includes a broad definition of characters that belong to a **print** class, it is up to you to decide whether to try to devise sensible sort definitions for these characters, or just collate them by their encoded value.

There are many other ways to tailor locales, and **localedef** gives you the power to choose which one you like. In the best case, that is as simple as accepting the locales already available on your system.

5.4 Locale-Sensitive Programming

This chapter has described what locales are, the information they include, and how programs use **setlocale( )** to access them. However, internationalized programs need to do much more than to get access to locale-related information; they need to use it. The next chapters describe data types for handling international data, standard functions that use locale-specific information, and techniques for writing locale-sensitive programs.

Supporting Multiple Encodings   6

Since there are many more characters than seven-bit ASCII can accommodate, and since many existing programs rely to some degree on ASCII, these programs need to change in order to be capable of handling international requirements. That means revising software to use new data types or use old types in new ways. It also means removing assumptions about character sizes or encodings. This chapter describes some of the changes necessary to internationalize programs as it covers these topics:

- Multibyte characters
- Wide characters
- Providing data transparent programs
- Standard functions for processing multibyte and wide characters and techniques for using them

6.1   Character Types

As Chapter 4 shows, characters have grown beyond simply being one-byte entities. In current implementations, they often are anything from one to four bytes each, and there are circumstances (such as an ISO 10646-based composite sequence) when they consume even more bytes.

In addition to the traditional single-byte character data types that most programming languages support, there are two major types of not-necessarily-one-byte characters in C: *multibyte characters* and *wide characters*.

6.1.1 Multibyte Characters

Multibyte characters are sequences of one or more bytes that can be represented within C's **char** data type. Multibyte strings typically consist of characters encoded in defined code sets. The defined sets may be broadly used standards like Latin-1 and JIS X0208, or vendor-defined sets like Hewlett-Packard's ROMAN8 or IBM's pc850. Multibyte strings also can contain mixtures of code sets and characters of varying widths. The EUC and PC encoding methods described in Chapter 4 both are multibyte because they combine single-byte ASCII with multiple-byte ideographic and phonetic characters. However, even something as simple as ASCII or any other single-byte-only code set is a multibyte encoding.

Figure 6.1 shows a multibyte data stream. In the figure, *a* indicates a single-byte character, while *B* designates a byte of a multiple-byte character. Note that although there are 12 bytes in the data stream, there are only eight characters.

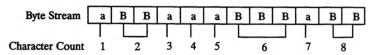

Figure 6.1   Multibyte Data Stream

Multibyte characters are processed with the familiar **char** data type. **char** allows you to examine individual bytes of multibyte data to find character boundaries, or do other general processing. It also allows you to process byte streams efficiently when there is no need to handle individual characters.

ISO C requires that within a multibyte encoding, a byte with all bits zero be interpreted as the null character. This means that no byte of a multibyte character can have the same encoding as null, and it also means that a single null byte terminates any multibyte string. All of the code sets and encoding methods described in Chapter 4 can fit the ISO C definition of multibyte characters, but Unicode and the UCS forms of ISO 10646 do not fit within common implementations of the standard. The difference between the standard and common practice is the definition of byte.

ISO C does not define the size of a byte, but in most existing implementations, it is eight bits (or one octet). On such implementations, the UCS forms and Unicode are not valid as multibyte encodings because they contain all-zeroes octets that the implementations interpret as being nulls. It would be possible to create an ISO C-compliant system with a 16-bit byte, and in that case, UCS-2 and Unicode would be valid multibyte encodings. Note, however, that such a system would probably have significant interoperability problems with existing, eight-bit byte implementations. Instead of redefining the size of a byte, planned or existing systems with ISO 10646 support use one of the UTF forms as the multibyte encoding rather than UCS.

Multibyte data streams that may include mixed-width characters create processing challenges that don't exist for software that handles only single-byte characters. See Handling **wchar_t** and Multibyte Characters later in this chapter for more information.

6.1.2   Wide Characters

Multibyte characters work well for many text processing tasks, but there are times when it is easier to process data in consistent, fixed-width chunks. Therefore, ISO C includes the integral type **wchar_t**. Usually implemented as a typedef, it is supposed to be as wide as is necessary to hold the largest character in the code sets your implementation supports. This somewhat-mushy definition allows individual vendors to define **wchar_t** to fit their needs. Most implementations define **wchar_t** as either 16 or 32 bits but there are cases when you might choose to define **wchar_t** as a synonym for **char**. (See the section on File and Process Codes below for details.) An obvious result of **wchar_t**'s flexible definition is that you cannot assume anything about its size.

wchar_t's size is set at compile time. If defined to be 32 bits, all wide character data is handled in 32-bit chunks. Figure 6.2 shows the multibyte data stream from Figure 6.1 in wide character *(wc)* form, including how many bytes of original data get mapped into each *wc*.

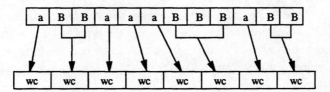

Figure 6.2   Wide Character Data Stream

Since each wide character holds a character, there are eight wide characters in the data stream. In an implementation that defines **wchar_t** to be 32 bits, the eight characters therefore consume 32 bytes.

Wide characters are intended for internal processing only. When starting a program, character data should be in multibyte form. If necessary, you convert it to wide characters, process it, and convert it back to multibyte before the program exits. **wchar_t** data is not meant to persist between program invocations. There are no standards for the size or contents of **wchar_t**, so results are unpredictable if you read wide character data in from disk. That is because the process that wrote the wide characters might have made different assumptions about **wchar_t** than does your system. A distributed application could be particularly prone to wide character definition mismatches since separate parts of that application could run on different nodes in a heterogeneous network.

Since there are no standards for the contents of **wchar_t**, vendors implement different algorithms for converting data from multibyte to wide character form. While multibyte characters get their encodings from defined code sets or encoding methods, making their values predictable, that is not the case with wide characters. Consider Japanese AJEC. All implementations that support this multibyte encoding interpret code values the same way—0x41 is always *A*, 0x8ea1 is always the Japanese period, 0xa1a1 is a double-byte space character, and so on. However, implementations are free to write their own algorithms for converting the multibyte characters to **wchar_t** form. Here are the corresponding wide character values using two common conversion algorithms and assuming **wchar_t** is 32 bits:

Multibyte	Wide Char 1	Wide Char 2
0x41	0x00000041	0x00000041
0xa1a1	0x300010a1	0x0000015e
0x8ea1	0x10000021	0x00000100
0x8fa1a1	0x200010a1	0x0000303c

Clearly, if programs make assumptions about wide character values, those assumptions may prove false.

The header file **<stddef.h>** contains the **wchar_t** definition, while **<stdlib.h>** and **<wchar.h>** declare functions that use the typedef. The **wchar_t** definition also often appears in the latter two header files to reduce the number of files that need to be included. Future examples in this chapter assume **wchar_t** also appears in these headers.

6.1.3   File and Process Codes

Given that characters can take at least two forms—multibyte and wide character—it is common to use the forms for different tasks. The **char**-based multibyte format in which data is stored is called the *file code* (or, sometimes, the *external code*). The format data has when programs are manipulating it is the *process code* (or *internal code*).

File and process codes can be identical, and they usually are if an implementation supports single-byte code sets only, or if it passes multibyte data through without interpreting it as characters. In these cases, the data usually stays in multibyte file code form. However, file and process codes may also be different. This may occur when you need to process (for example, sort or edit) characters. In that case, it may be easier to process the data entities when they all are the same size, so programs will convert **char**-based file code data to a **wchar_t**-based process code. See Deciding When to Use Wide Characters later in this chapter for details. Remember, however, that although multibyte **char** data can be both file and process code, **wchar_t** is only intended to be a process code. In most cases, you should not write wide characters to disk or exchange them with other running processes.

6.2   Data Transparency

A crucial consequence of the existence of new code sets, wide characters, and multibyte characters is that programs can no longer use any bit in a data byte for their own purposes. Unlike seven-bit ASCII, which only uses the lower seven bits of a data byte, nearly every other code set uses all eight bits. That means an internationalized program must not tamper with any of those bits. It also must look at all eight bits of every data byte instead of assuming that it is safe to ignore one or more bits. A program that avoids changing any data bits and that examines all eight bits of any data byte is said to be *data transparent* or *eight-bit clean*.

Providing data transparent programs is one of the first and most basic steps in providing an internationalized system. It is the foundation on which all other I18N support builds; without it your software cannot hope to meet international needs. The following sections describe techniques for writing data transparent code.

6.2.1   Removing Obsolete Restrictions

When programs only had to deal with ASCII data, it was common to add simple error-checking to make sure the data was indeed ASCII. Programs often either called the **isascii** macro or included lines like:

```
if (c > 127) {
    printf ("Invalid character %d\n", c);
    /* additional error processing */
}
```

After all, since ASCII characters are in the range 0–127 (or 0x00–0x7f), it was obvious that anything beyond that range had to be a mistake. However, single- and multiple-byte code sets allow characters to occupy a much broader range, so it isn't a mistake in an internationalized program to find a character with an encoded value greater than 127. To allow a program to handle a wider range of characters, simply remove the error checking.

Most ASCII-only restrictions like this are obsolete and can be removed. However, you do have to think before routinely deleting an error trap. Many programming languages place restrictions on the characters that can be used in variable or identifier names. For example, an ISO C-conformant program can have variables with names such as a, b, and c, but it is not legal to use names like á, ñ, and ö. Likewise, many systems restrict electronic mail names to including only ASCII characters because some mail protocols only accept seven-bit data. Do not remove logic that enforces such restrictions.

6.2.2 Deleting Bit Masks

Some older programs use the MSB to save information about a character. An editor might set the MSB to mark a text area that is going to be processed, or a driver might set the bit to mark characters where a delayed write can be done. Most of the standard utilities that exhibit this behavior already have been cleaned up, but you can check for either a bitwise & (and) or bitwise ! (or) with bit masks equivalent to the values 0x7f or 0x80. Also look in **#include** files to see whether there are any **#define**s set to these bit masks.

6.2.3 Data Types for Single-Byte Data

When seven-bit ASCII was the only supported code set, it frequently didn't matter whether a program used **signed char**s, **unsigned char**s, or **int**s to store character data. Now, however, you must be careful about which data type you use.

It is always correct to put single-byte data strings into arrays of **char**. However, you may need to use **unsigned char** or **int** if you want to process single characters (which may or may not be part of an array). It depends on what processing you need to do. If you are copying data from one array to another, comparing entities for equality, or performing other simple tasks, it still is okay to leave data as **char**s.

On the other hand, if you are doing any arithmetic-based operations on characters, such as indexing into an array, you probably should change your data type to **unsigned char**. Suppose you use a character as an index into an array (e.g., my_array[c]). If you declare c as a **signed char** (or as just **char**, if your compiler by default considers **char**s to be signed), your code does not work properly for characters in the upper half of a single-byte set. That is because a **signed char** has a range from –0x7f to +0x7f, while characters in the upper half of the set are in the range +0x80 to +0xff. Figure 6.3 shows the range of both **char** types.

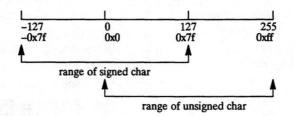

Figure 6.3   Ranges of Signed and Unsigned Chars

Suppose c is a **signed char**, and you assign the Latin-1 character *Ï* (0xcf or decimal 207) to it. The character is incorrectly interpreted as –0x4f (decimal –79). (Note, also, that negative array indices are not legal in C.)

While indexing into an array usually requires an **unsigned char** for single-byte data, there are other conditions under which you need to change the type to **int**. Suppose you compare character data against integer quantities, as in this code fragment:

```
char c;
extern int getchar();
. . .
if ((c = getchar()) == EOF) . . .
```

Now suppose **getchar()** finds a *ÿ*. In its Latin-1 encoding, *ÿ* equals 0xff. The **int** that **getchar()** returns is narrowed to a **char** for the assignment to c. However, before comparing c to EOF (–1 on most systems), it is widened to an **int** using sign extension. Assuming your system's **int** is four bytes long, that means the character turns into 0xffffffff. That's –1, so the comparison to EOF returns true. But *ÿ* clearly is not EOF.

To fix the problem, change the declaration of c from a **char** to an **int**. In that case, there is no need to narrow the **int** that **getchar()** returns to a **char**, or to do any sign extension because c already is the right data type. This time around, though, its value is 0x000000ff, and the comparison to EOF correctly returns false.

6.3   Handling wchar_t and Multibyte Characters

Taking steps to make code eight-bit clean or to use appropriate single-byte data types is a good foundation for handling international character-processing requirements. But additional steps in the form of specific wide character and multibyte support also are usually necessary. In the case of wide characters, you must use the **wchar_t** type as appropriate, and also use **wchar_t**-based functions. Logic that handles multibyte characters needs to be prepared for the possibility that characters may span multiple bytes. This section describes functions available for this purpose, describes other changes you may need to make to process the characters correctly, and then discusses criteria for choosing the appropriate data format.

Note that the value of the current locale affects the behavior of the standard functions. Therefore, if you use these functions in an application program, that program must include a prior call to **setlocale( )**.

6.3.1   ISO C wchar_t and Multibyte Functions

Support for multibyte and wide characters has been or is being added to many de facto and formal standards. Table 6.1 shows the functions ISO C contains for this purpose.

Table 6.1   ISO C Multibyte and Wide Character Functions

Function	Purpose
mblen	Determine the length of a multibyte character in bytes
mbstowcs	Convert a multibyte string to a wide character string
mbtowc	Convert a multibyte character to a wide character
wcstombs	Convert a wide character string to a multibyte string
wctomb	Convert a wide character to a multibyte character

Here is the syntax for these functions:

```
#include <stdlib.h>
int mblen(const char *s, size_t n);
size_t mbstowcs(wchar_t *pwcs, const char *s, size_t n);
int mbtowc(wchar_t *pwc, const char *s, size_t n);
size_t wcstombs(char *s, const wchar_t *pwcs, size_t n);
int wctomb(char *s, wchar_t wchar);
```

In these functions, *s* is a string, *pwcs* is a wide character string, and *pwc* a wide character. In addition, in **mblen( )** and **mbtowc( )**, *n* is a maximum number of bytes the function examines, while in **mbstowcs( )** it is the maximum number of wide characters to be stored in *pwcs*, and in **wcstombs( )** it is the maximum number of bytes to be stored in *s*.

The functions perform conversions based on the current locale. For example, when **mblen( )** determines the number of bytes in a character, the answer obviously depends on how the data is encoded. **mblen( )** uses the current locale to determine whether to apply, say, ISO 8859-1 or ISO-Arabic or Korean EUC rules, or something else, to the data.

The standard functions are straightforward to use. Suppose you want to convert a multibyte string to wide character form. Here's how:

```
#include <stdlib.h>
#include <locale.h>
. . .
char *s;
wchar_t *pwcs;
size_t return_val, n;
(void) setlocale(LC_ALL,"");

. . .
/* compute number of bytes in input string,
 * including terminating null
 */
n = strlen(s) + 1;

/* allocate space for wchar array */
pwcs = (wchar_t *)malloc(n * sizeof(wchar_t));

return_val = mbstowcs(pwcs, s, n);
if (return_val == -1) {
    /* error processing */
}
else {
    /* pwcs contains wide character string and
     * return_val equals the number of wide
     * characters stored (less null)
     */;
}
. . .
```

mbstowcs( ) converts the characters in the array pointed to by *s* into their corresponding wide character codes. It stores no more than *n* wide characters in the array *pwcs* points to. The function returns either the number of wide character codes in *pwcs* or (size_t)-1 if it encounters an invalid character in *s*.

Note that this example allocates the largest buffer that could be needed to hold the wide character array because it counts the number of bytes in the input string and creates an array with that many wide characters. Since there may be fewer characters in the input than there are bytes, and since each **wchar_t** holds one character, *pwcs* may be larger than is necessary. However, it is faster to allocate more space than may be necessary than it is to count the number of characters in the input string and create a *pwcs* with exactly that number of **wchar_t**s.

6.3.2 Wide Character Constants

Previously existing syntax for single-byte character constants also works for multibyte characters, but does not for wide characters. Therefore, ISO C defines additional syntax for wide character constants. The letter **L** must precede any such constant; for example:

```
L' '
```

is the wide character space, while

```
L'\n'
```

is the wide character new-line. You might use this syntax when processing wide characters. For example:

```
    . . .
/* get character, wc, from input file in wchar_t form */
if (wc == L'\n')
   /* end-of-line processing */
else if (wc == L'\t')
   /* tab processing */
else if (wc == L' ')
   /* space processing */
else
    . . .
```

6.3.3   Additional wchar_t Functions

Along with the small number of multibyte and wide character functions in ISO C, X/Open includes other **wchar_t**-based functions in XPG4. The functions also are likely to be added to ISO C in a section called Multibyte Support Extensions (MSE). Like the ISO C functions, the XPG versions also use the current locale to determine how to process a data stream. Table 6.2 shows the **char**-based string handling functions and their **wchar_t** equivalents. The strings that the **wchar_t** functions process are all wide character strings.

Table 6.2   char- and wchar_t-Based String Handling Functions

char-Based	wchar_t-Based	Purpose
strcpy	**wcscpy**	copy a string
strncpy	**wcsncpy**	copy part of a string
strcat	**wcscat**	concatenate two strings
strncat	**wcsncat**	concatenate two substrings
strchr	**wcschr**	scan a string
strrchr	**wcsrchr**	scan a string
strcspn	**wcscspn**	get length of complementary substring
strlen	**wcslen**	get string length
strpbrk	**wcspbrk**	scan string for [byte | wide character]
strspn	**wcsspn**	get length of substring
strstr	**wcswcs**	find substring
strtok	**wcstok**	split string into tokens

The header files that declare the **wchar_t** versions of these functions differ depending on the implementation. For most, **<wchar.h>** declares the functions, while for others, **<string.h>** holds the declarations. Examples in this section use **<wchar.h>**.

<wchar.h> also contains two other important definitions:

- The constant **WEOF**. This is the wide character end-of-file (EOF).
- The typedef **wint_t**. This is a data object type that can hold any wide character and the end-of-file value. (There may not be a unique value in the **wchar_t**'s domain to represent EOF. For example, if **wchar_t**'s size is eight bits, and its internal encoding matches ISO 8859-1, there is no value in ISO 8859-1 that can be used for EOF—all values have other assignments.) While many **char**-based I/O functions return an **int**, the **wchar_t** versions return a **wint_t**.

In addition to the functions listed in Table 6.2, there also are **wchar_t** versions of I/O, character classification, collation, and date and time functions. See Chapter 7 for details of the I/O functions, and Chapter 8 for information on the rest.

Most **wchar_t**-based functions are similar to their **char**-based counterparts. The data types of parameters differ, but the purpose of those parameters generally doesn't. For example:

#include <string.h>
char *strcpy(char *s1, **const char ***s2**);**

#include <wchar.h>
wchar_t *wcscpy(wchar_t *ws1, **const wchar_t ***ws2**);**

strcpy( ) copies the string that *s2* points to (including the terminating null byte) into the array pointed to by *s1*. The corresponding **wcscpy( )** copies the wide character string that *ws2* points to (including the terminating null wide character) into the array pointed to by *ws1*. This fragment shows how to use **wcslen( )** and **wcscpy( )** to copy a wide character string into a wide character array:

```
#include <wchar.h>
. . .
wchar_t *pwcs1, *pwcs2;
. . .
/* compute number of wide characters in input string
 * (including null) and allocate space for the wide
 * character array
 */
pwcs1 = (wchar_t *)malloc
    ((wcslen(pwcs2) + 1) * sizeof(wchar_t));
wcscpy(pwcs1, pwcs2);
```

This fragment also uses **wcslen( )** and shows how to convert a wide character string back to multibyte form:

```
#include <stdlib.h>    /* includes MB_CUR_MAX */
#include <locale.h>
#include <wchar.h>
. . .
wchar_t *pwcs;
char *s;
```

```
size_t len, return_val;
(void)setlocale(LC_ALL, "");


. . .

/* Compute the number of wide character codes (len) in
 * pwcs and malloc the space for the multibyte version.
 * The current locale provides the value of MB_CUR_MAX.
 */
s = (char *)malloc (len = (wcslen(pwcs) * MB_CUR_MAX) + 1);
if (s == NULL)
   /* error processing */;

return_val = wcstombs(s, pwcs, len);
if (return_val == -1) {
   /* error processing */
}
else {
   /* s contains multibyte string and return_val
    * equals the number of bytes stored (less null)
    */;
}
```

See your system's man pages or XPG4 for details on these **wchar_t**-based functions.

6.3.4 Parsing Multibyte and Wide Character Strings

Just as certain changes are necessary to make software data transparent and pass through all eight bits of every data byte, other changes are necessary when characters can span multiple bytes or are in wide character form. The standard functions provide some of the needed functionality for handling such characters, while you may have to write other routines or logic yourself.

The first step is to remove assumptions that one byte equals one character. Suppose a C compiler searches a source program a byte at a time for curly brackets ({ }). The curly brackets have ASCII-encoded values of 0x7b and 0x7d, respectively. In a Japanese SJIS encoding, those byte values may appear as the second byte of many two-byte characters. The second byte of each of these SJIS characters has the same value as one of the curly brackets:

Character	Encoded Value
笠	0x8A 0x7D
旬	0x8F 0x7B
府	0x95 0x7B
±	0x81 0x7D

If the compiler parses source programs a byte at a time, it incorrectly assumes it has found a curly bracket if the data stream includes one of these SJIS-encoded characters. To fix this problem, the compiler might use **mbstowcs( )** to convert the source to wide character format, and then parse the source program a wide character at a time. While individual bytes within a multibyte stream can have multiple interpretations, each wide character code has a single meaning.

Instead of converting to wide character, the compiler might use **mblen( )** to find character boundaries. Since the characters most compilers look for are encoded as single bytes, it could skip over any character for which **mblen( )** returned a value of more than one. Consider this fragment:

```
#include <stdlib.h>   /* includes mblen and MB_CUR_MAX */
#include <locale.h>
. . .
char *s;
int return_val;
. . .
(void)setlocale(LC_ALL, "");

return_val = mblen(s, MB_CUR_MAX);
if (return_val == -1) {
   /* error processing */
}
else {
   /* return_val contains the number of bytes in s */;
}
```

mblen( ) returns the number of bytes in the character pointed to by *s*. This implicitly allows you to find the beginning of the next character in a string;

```
ptr + (mblen(s, MB_CUR_MAX))
```

advances a pointer to the next character.

While byte-by-byte parsing of data often needs to change when adding multi-byte support to software, some such parsing may still work. It depends on the code sets and encoding methods your software supports and the characters for which you are parsing. A simple, but not very internationalized, scenario is if your software supports single-byte code sets only. In that case, since all characters fit in one byte, all byte-by-byte parsing is permissible.

A more interesting scenario is if your software supports a variety of encodings—some single-byte, others multiple-byte. However, even in this case, some byte-oriented parsing is acceptable. As noted earlier, ISO C requires that all multi-byte encodings include an all-zeroes byte that is interpreted as null. This means software can scan a byte at a time for null; an all-zeroes byte will never be part of a multiple-byte character.

Most code sets and encoding methods also prohibit bytes of multiple-byte characters from having the same values as common control characters—that is, from being in the range 0x00–0x1f. Suppose you have decided to support these code sets or encoding methods:

ISO 8859-1 through ISO 8859-10
Asian EUC implementations (Japanese, Korean, Simplified Chinese,
    Traditional Chinese)
Japanese PC Code (SJIS)

These encodings all require that all bytes with values in the range 0x00–0x1f can only be control characters, so parsing like this is permissible:

```
char c;
. . .
c = getchar();
if (c == '\n')
    /* new-line processing */
else if (c == '\t')
    /* tab processing */
else
    /* other control-oriented processing */
    . . .
```

To determine which byte-oriented parsing is permissible and which must change, you must decide what encodings you are supporting, and then adjust your software to meet those encodings' characteristics.

6.3.5 Truncation and Multibyte Characters

In addition to changing parsing routines, you may need to change other code to avoid truncating characters. Truncation isn't a consideration when processing single-byte-only characters because a program can't stop processing in the middle of a byte. It can, however, stop *after* a byte, and that byte may or may not mark the boundary of a multibyte character. That means you must rewrite software to make sure it processes complete characters. This code fragment uses **mblen**() to avoid truncating characters:

```c
#include <stdlib.h>
#include <stdio.h>
#include <locale.h>
. . .
/* MB_LEN_MAX is a system-wide value for the maximum
 * number of bytes in a multibyte character
 */
char *out_buffer, s[MB_LEN_MAX];
int len1, len2, i, c;
. . .

(void)setlocale(LC_ALL, "");
c = getchar();
. . .
len2 = 1;
s[0] = c;

/* Use mblen to determine if the current byte of s[i]
 * is a character boundary. If not, get the next byte and
 * try again. Continue until you find a complete character
 * or len1 exceeds the current locale's MB_CUR_MAX.
 */
if ((len1 = mblen(s, MB_CUR_MAX)) < 0)
  /* invalid input character; process error */
else {
  while (len1 != len2)
    if (++len2 > MB_CUR_MAX)
      /* error */;
    s[len1-1] = getchar();
}
```

```
/* Copy len1 bytes to out_buffer */
for (i=0; i<len1; i++)
    *out_buffer++ = s[i];
. . .
```

In addition to taking in all bytes of a multibyte character, you also need to make sure you put them all back out. This fragment uses **mbtowc( )**'s return value as the upper bound in the output **for** loop:

```
. . .
int len, i;
char *s;
wchar_t wc;
(void)setlocale(LC_ALL, "");
. . .

/* If len <= 0, the next character is null or invalid;
 * otherwise, len equals the number of bytes in next
 * multibyte character
 */
while ((len = mbtowc(&wc, s, MB_CUR_MAX)) > 0) {
    /* if wc is not printable, do non-printable
     * wide character processing
     */
    else
        for (i=0; i<len; i++)
            putc(*s++, stdout);
}
```

As an alternative to using **mbtowc( )**, you could use **mblen( )** like this:

```
while ((len = mblen(s, MB_CUR_MAX)) > 0) {
. . .
```

Using **mblen( )** is more efficient if you don't need to do anything with the wide character **mbtowc( )** produces because **mblen( )** only counts the bytes in s rather than also converting it to wide character form.

6.3.6 Implementation Details

While the multibyte and **wchar_t** functions are easy to use, the underlying implementations may be fairly complex because they require detailed knowledge of supported code sets and encoding methods. Only with such knowledge can the functions find character boundaries and figure out either how to convert between multibyte and wide character form, or how to process the individual characters.

Consider a simple **mblen( )** implementation. Suppose your system supports only single-byte code sets and Japanese AJEC. The single-byte support in **mblen( )** is easy; every character's length is one byte. AJEC, however, requires more processing. When the current locale indicates that the data is encoded in AJEC, **mblen( )** looks at the first byte of a character (s[0]) and computes the number of bytes using this algorithm:

```
/* pseudo-code; 0x8e is SS2; 0x8f is SS3 */

if s[0] >= 0x00 and s[0] <= 0x9f
   (except 0x8e and 0x8f)
   single-byte ASCII or extended controls
else if s[0] == 0x8e
   double-byte JIS X0201 (katakana)
else if s[0] == 0x8f
   triple-byte JIS X0212 characters
else if s[0] >= 0xa1 and s[0] <= 0xfe
   double-byte JIS X0208 characters
else
   error
```

Now expand the example. Suppose the system supports many code sets and encoding methods. As the group of supported sets grows, so too does **mblen( )**. Consider this pseudocode:

```
if single-byte code set
   characters equal bytes, so length is always 1
else if EUC-style encoding
   determine which EUC it is and apply
   appropriate rules
else if PC-code encoding
   determine which PC code it is and apply
   appropriate rules
```

```
else if ISO 10646
   determine which form of 10646 it is and
   apply appropriate rules
else if . . .
   . . .
else
   error
```

Note that you can convert this pseudocode into real code in a variety of ways. There might be an extended **if** or **case** (switch) statement with all the appropriate details, or there might be separate subroutines for each code set. Usually, an implementation starts out with everything in one subroutine, but as the number of supported code sets grows, it becomes more practical to break it up.

Still, while implementations of multibyte and **wchar_t** functions may be complex, these differences usually are invisible to application programmers because the standard interfaces do not change. Suppose you use **mbstowcs( )** in a program and bind with an implementation that supports single-byte code sets and SJIS only. If the implementation later adds support for EUC varieties, your **mbstowcs( )** gains the ability to convert the multibyte EUC varieties to wide characters without any programmatic changes on your part. Of course, depending on the level of I18N support in your overall program, you may or may not need to make other changes to support EUC encodings.

6.3.7   Deciding When to Use Wide Characters

Wide characters add a nagging question to internationalization efforts: when should you use them? Given that there are wide character versions of most existing functions, should you replace all **char**-based functions with calls to the equivalent **wchar_t** functions?

No.

It takes time to convert data between multibyte and wide character form. The specific amount differs by implementation and by code set, but there is no point in spending it at all if you don't need to. However, the only way to determine whether to convert is to analyze your program logic. The choice between multibyte and wide characters depends on a variety of factors including the task to be performed, the code sets and encoding methods your implementation supports, the current state of the data, and the amount of data that needs to be converted.

For some operations, multibyte is a clear win. These include:

- **Copying or moving data**. A program that copies a text file into another file doesn't need to distinguish individual multibyte characters; it only needs to copy bytes. Similarly, a program that pushes bytes from one location to another doesn't need to parse characters. Such programs can keep data in multibyte form.
- **Comparing for equality**. It is faster to compare two multibyte strings or characters for equality than it is to convert them to wide characters and then do the comparison. Of course, if the data already is in wide character form, there is no need to convert it back to multibyte before doing the comparison.
- **Searching for control characters**. No byte of a multibyte character in most commonly used code sets and encoding methods can be in the range of control characters (0x00–0x1f, 0x7f). This means you can scan a byte at a time for nulls, newlines, ESC, and other control characters because it is impossible for a byte of a multiple-byte character to have the same code value as one of the controls. An exception to this is if the data is encoded in UCS-2 or UCS-4. Octets in these forms of ISO 10646 can and often do match the values of common control characters.
- **Single-byte data**. If your program is processing single-byte data only, there is no reason to convert it to wide character form. Therefore, you may choose to write an application that checks the value of MB_CUR_MAX. If it equals 1 (one), the application does not convert to **wchar_t**; if it is more than 1, the application may do other analysis to determine whether to convert.

While multibyte typically is the right choice for some tasks, **wchar_t** may work better for others. These include:

- **Collation**. Sorting is a very character-specific operation. The order in which strings should appear depends on the characters within them. It therefore usually is more efficient to collate strings when they are uniform widths (wide characters) than it is to process potentially variable-width multibyte strings.
- **Parsing**. Parsing a data stream often involves breaking the stream into characters or words. A compiler may need to search for characters like curly brackets, parentheses, or semicolons. A spell checker needs to find word boundaries so that it can check for mistakes in those words. Software that supports more than single-byte characters cannot parse such strings a byte at a time because a byte with the same encoding as, say, a curly bracket, may be part of a multiple-byte character. And while it is possible to use **mblen( )** to find character boundaries, it may be inefficient to do so if your program parses large files, or searches for many different characters, or makes many passes through the same data. Many

parsing tasks become easy, however, if the data is in **wchar_t** form. Now a compiler looking for, say, a left curly bracket can parse the stream a wide character at a time. No two characters have the same wide character code value, so when the compiler finds the wide character representation of the left curly bracket, it doesn't have to worry that it may have found part of another character.

- **String editing**. Typical editing operations involve many changes to a data stream. When editing a file, you probably insert characters or delete lines or press backspace to delete ill-chosen words. It is more efficient to do these operations on wide characters than on multibyte versions. A backspace-delete operation on multibytes needs to search backward for character boundaries to determine how many bytes to remove from the data stream, and this may be very difficult in a **char**-based stream. That is because standard functions like **mblen( )** only work forward in a stream; there is no standard function for identifying a character boundary when moving backward. In contrast, the same operation on wide characters simply involves removing one **wchar_t**. For most editing operations, process data in wide character form.

- **Random offsets**. When processing multibyte data streams that include characters with varying widths, it may be difficult or inefficient to find character boundaries unless you begin processing at the start of the stream and move linearly through it. When making random searches into the data, there is no simple way to determine whether a given byte is at a character boundary. If you need to move to random offsets within the stream, it is most efficient to convert the data to wide character form; each **wchar_t** then is a character boundary.

- **Truncation**. Since a multibyte character can span multiple bytes in a data stream, it is important for programs to make sure they get all the bytes in a character. A truncated character is corrupted data. As demonstrated earlier, it is possible to use **mblen( )** or **mbtowc( )** to find character boundaries, but the job may be simpler if the data is in wide character form. In that case, the program can process wide characters, secure in the knowledge that each wide character equals one character.

There are caveats, however. Suppose your program searches a file for a specific string and then writes that string to another file. It might seem logical to convert the data to wide character form so that you can be sure to copy complete characters to the destination file. However, the original file could be anything from a few hundred bytes to many megabytes. If the file is very large, the program uses significant time converting all data to wide character form before performing the search and copy. If your program is only making limited access on an input file, it may be faster to leave the input in multibyte form and use **mblen( )** to find character boundaries.

Another caveat is if you are writing software that supports ISO 10646's combining characters. In that case, characters may span multiple **wchar_t**'s, making truncation possible despite the fact that data is in wide character form. When this book was written, there were no standard functions for handling combining characters. That means you would need to write such functions yourself.

It is clear there is no easy answer to the question of whether to convert data from multibyte to wide character form. Generally, if you keep data in multibyte form, you may need to use **mblen( )** or **mbtowc( )** to find individual characters in the data stream. If you use wide characters, you must convert the data, process the **wchar_t**'s, and convert them back to multibyte form. Use wide characters if it takes less time to complete the *convert-process-reconvert* cycle than it does to handle the multibyte data. Use multibyte if you don't need to process individual characters, or if it is faster to process a few multibyte characters than it would be to convert all input to wide character form.

6.3.8 Code Set Independence

The wide character interfaces are designed in part to promote *code set independence* (CSI) in programs. This is a programming methodology that involves removing dependencies on specific code sets or encoding methods from programs and replacing them with general functions that theoretically are capable of handling any encoding. CSI grew out of a realization that since many older programs had hardcoded dependencies on ASCII, they could not meet international needs. CSI is an attempt to write programs that do not have the same restrictions. You can consider CSI as the encoding-specific part of overall internationalization. While internationalizing programs involves removing dependencies on languages or cultures or encodings, CSI addresses only the encoding-specific part of I18N.

There is some controversy about whether CSI is the right design to use in writing programs. Some advocates of Unicode or ISO 10646 believe it is easier and more efficient to write programs that support a single universal encoding. Others reason that users want continued support for their existing encodings as well as expanded support for newer encodings, and so conclude that CSI is the proper design. They also reason that requirements often change over time, and software that has built-in dependencies on one code set may not be able to meet the changing requirements.

Although the **wchar_t** interfaces are capable of handling many code sets and encoding methods, they are not completely code set independent because they implicitly assume that one **wchar_t** equals one complete character. For code sets like ISO 10646, that may not always be the case. With combining characters, one composite sequence spans several wide characters. In that case, while the interfaces do not fail, they may not return the correct answer. Consider two possible UCS encodings for the French word *côté*:

UCS-2, Level 1 (four wchar_t's)	c	ô	t	é		
UCS-2, Level 3 (six wchar_t's)	c	o	^	t	e	′

Note that it is possible to encode *côté* exactly the same way in Level 3 as it is encoded in Level 1. However, the possibility exists that it could be encoded using combining characters as shown here.

The **wchar_t** interfaces assume each **wchar_t** is a character, so in the first example, they process ô and é, but in the second, they process the o and ^ (circumflex) and the e and ′ (acute accent) separately. While the results in the first example are correct, that may not be the case for the second example.

When this book was written, there were proposals to add support for combining characters to the **wchar_t** interfaces. Until that happens, the interfaces are not completely code set independent, but they are capable of handling most other code sets or encoding methods—including Level 1 UCS-2 or UCS-4.

6.4   Taking the Next Steps

You have learned in this chapter about programming basics for handling single-byte, multibyte, and wide characters. If you revise software to accept more code sets and to process the characters, you will have made the first step toward internationalizing your software. The next chapter covers aspects of allowing input and output of international characters.

Input and Output   7

Previous chapters describe the internal representation of many of the world's characters, and some functions you can use to process them. However, for a system to be able to process such characters implies that it has access to them; that there is a way to input them. The ability to input international characters also implies that there is (or needs to be) the converse ability to output them. This chapter describes rendering, editing, input, and output considerations as it covers these topics:

- Fonts. These allow you to see the characters you use on the screen or on printed output.
- Display and editing considerations. Display software and editors need to know how to maneuver around international text.
- I/O in programs. Internationalization affects formatted and unformatted I/O functions and techniques for using them.
- Printers. There must be some way to print the characters you use.

While the need to provide internationalized systems means some changes in most application developer's programming techniques—for example, most need to use **setlocale( )** and to understand techniques for handling multibyte and wide characters—most input and output is different. Relatively few developers create fonts or editors or rendering routines; most of us simply use what those few create. However, it is very helpful to understand what internationalized I/O tools must be available on a system, and this chapter describes the functionality those tools must provide. (Appendix B also describes software-based input methods, and hardware changes for enabling input of many languages.)

If you are an application developer who just wants to understand the changes likely to be necessary in *your* programs, you can skip to the section on I/O in programs. This covers the internationalized capabilities of frequently used I/O functions like **printf( )**, **fgetc( )**, **fgetwc( )**, and others.

7.1   Fonts for International Characters

The wide range of characters available in today's code sets means you should have no trouble finding sets that include the characters you want to see. But the code sets only provide the internal encoding of these new characters. In order to see them, you need fonts that include these characters.

7.1.1   Fonts and Code Sets

In thinking about fonts, the first thing to realize is that they are distinct from code sets. A code set defines the internal representation of characters; a font contains the visual representation. A single character may have differing visual representations in different fonts. For example, **a,** a, and *a* all are the same character in different fonts. While they appear different, they all have the same internal representation within a data stream. In the case of ASCII, that internal encoding is 0x61. Figure 7.1 shows the relationship.

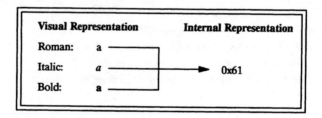

Figure 7.1   Visual and Internal Character Representation

A *glyph* is the graphic representation of a character; that is, how that character looks in a particular font. The glyph *S* obviously looks different from the glyph S, even though both are the same character. A *font* is an ordered set of glyphs that share visual characteristics such as size or typeface. For example, a set of bold glyphs (**a b c d** ... **à á â** ...) makes up a **bold** font.

Glyph characteristics differ depending on the characters being represented. Glyphs in a proportional font can take up different amounts of space on a screen or on paper (for example, consider the different space that *i* and *W* consume), while in a monospaced font, all glyphs consume the same space (for example, i and W). With some scripts, such as Latin, both proportional and monospace fonts are common. With others, however, monospace fonts are most common. This is the case for glyphs of ideographs—each takes up a consistent, square space. Names for fonts of ideographs often indicate the size of the square that font uses—for example, a Japanese *24x24* font consists of glyphs that are 24 pixels wide by 24 pixels tall.

Ideographic glyphs generally are larger than glyphs of letters or punctuation because many ideographs are more complex than letters and so require more space to display the strokes within them. Usually, the smallest acceptable size for glyphs of ideographs is 16x16.

While a given code set (ASCII, Latin-1, JIS X0208, and so on) has a one-to-one relationship between characters and code values, there usually are many different fonts to represent those characters. Suppose your system only supports ASCII. It still may have italic and bold fonts, or fonts in multiple typefaces, and in different sizes. So there usually is a one-to-many relationship between code sets and fonts.

Unlike characters in a code set, however, individual glyphs do not have any inherent code values associated with them. Those values must be explicitly assigned. The explicit assignments are where fonts and code sets get tied together. Often, font glyphs are stored in an array with a given glyph's index being equal to the encoded value of the character it represents. In this scenario, the *a* glyph in an ASCII-based italic font is assigned to array index 0x61 because 0x61 is the ASCII value of lowercase 'a.' Similarly, when the bold font needs assignments for its glyphs, the **a** glyph gets the value 0x61. Note that there is no requirement that glyph indexes equal characters' encoded values, but such equality tends to simplify font processing.

However, the fact that glyphs have no inherent code values means you can use one set of glyphs for multiple encodings. The Japanese AJEC and SJIS encoding methods both include the ideographs in the JIS X0208 code set, but they assign different code values to the JIS X0208 characters. Despite the differences in the internal representation, the glyphs for the ideographs remain constant. That means a font-maker could create a font with the glyphs arranged in JIS X0208 order, and then rendering software could perform the mapping between the glyphs' X0208-based indexes and the characters' AJEC or SJIS encoded values.

7.1.2 Identifying a Font's Code Set

Since one code set can have many fonts, and one set of glyphs may be the basis of fonts in multiple code sets, there needs to be some way to tie fonts to a particular set. In the ASCII-only days, it was simple: all fonts were ASCII fonts, and they generally were all grouped together in a system directory. They had names like *Times-roman12, f9x12,* or *italic10.* The names tell something about a font's size and typeface, but nothing about the characters it contains.

This is not adequate on an internationalized system because such a system may include fonts for a variety of code sets and languages. It might have ASCII, Latin-1, Latin-2, Japanese, Traditional Chinese, Simplified Chinese, and Arabic fonts. Faced with such a potpourri of possibilities, a name like *Times-roman12* is plainly lacking in precision.

There are two common ways to solve fonts' identity crises. There may be individual directories for code sets, with all fonts for a given set grouped in the appropriate directory, or each font name may include its code set. Under the directory approach, fonts might have names like this:

```
/sys/lib/fonts/ASCII/Times-bold10
                     Times-roman10
                     Times-roman12
                         . . .
/sys/lib/fonts/ISO8859-1/Times-bold10
                         Times-roman10
                         Times-roman12
                             . . .
/sys/lib/fonts/JISX0208/16x16
                        24x24
                         . . .
/sys/lib/fonts/JISX0212/16x16
                        24x24
                         . . .
```

With the directory approach of tying code sets to fonts, there can be several, say, *Times-roman12* fonts on the system. That is not the case if the font name includes the code set. Under that alternative, the fonts might be stored like this:

```
/sys/lib/fonts/Times-bold10.ISO8859-1
               Times-bold10.ISO8859-2
               Times-roman10.ISO8859-1
               Times-roman10.ISO8859-2
                   . . .
```

The X Window System from MIT's X Consortium uses this second kind of approach. X font names specify many characteristics about the font—from typeface to point size to code set. Although you can use wild cards in place of the various fields, here is an example of a full X font name:

```
-adobe-helvetica-bold-r-normal-10-100-75-75-m-60-iso8859-1
```

The important part of the name from an I18N perspective is the last part—`iso8859-1`. This defines the indexes of the glyphs in this font. For a font with Japanese glyphs arranged in JIS X0208 order, the value of the field would be `jisx0208.1983-0`.

7.1.3 Managing Fonts

A system that handles only one code set doesn't need to worry much about strategies for managing fonts. In a single-font application, the user or application picks one, the system loads it, and the proper glyphs appear on the screen. That one font contains all the glyphs the user needs. A more sophisticated program, like a modern word processor, allows users to mix many fonts, including those in different typefaces—**bold**, *italic*, and roman—as well as different sizes in text. If that program only supports one code set, however, there still is not much to manage, because the set of supported characters is small.

It is not so simple with an internationalized system. Suppose you have only supported ASCII so far and now want to broaden your horizons to encompass Western Europe. Should you modify existing seven-bit ASCII-based fonts to become Latin-1 fonts (or your company's proprietary equivalent)? Or should you maintain two groups of fonts—one set with the ASCII characters and the other with the European characters? Now what happens if you expand again into Eastern Europe or Japan or some other market?

In most implementations, the old, 128-glyph ASCII-based fonts double their size to 256 to include new glyphs. The contents of those glyphs depends on the languages the implementation supports. If you are handling Western European languages, the fonts include characters like those defined in the upper half of Latin-1. If you are supporting Eastern Europe, the glyphs for the characters in the upper half of Latin-2 may join the fonts.

Oftentimes, the set of glyphs available in a given font is the same as the characters in a code set. Since many code sets include ASCII characters (ISO 8859-1 through -10, IBM's pc850, and so on), many fonts also include ASCII glyphs. For example, a font based on ISO 8859-1 includes the ASCII glyphs, and so does a font based on ISO 8859-2, and a font based on ISO 8859-3, and so on.

7.1.4 Combining Multiple Fonts

Stretching font boundaries beyond ASCII is one thing, but there is more to managing fonts than adding new glyphs. Since the contents of fonts tend to match code sets, and since encoding methods like Compound Text and EUC let you combine code sets, there must be a way to combine fonts.

Among the strategies for handling the combination is the one the X Window System uses. It allows you to define a *font set*. Suppose a data stream contains Japanese AJEC-encoded text. That includes ASCII, JIS X0208 (Kanji ideographs), JIS X0201 (katakana), and JIS X0212 (more Kanji). Typically, there are several fonts for each code set. For example, you may have ASCII fonts in several typefaces or point sizes. To render the AJEC text, you need one font for each code set. In X, here is a way to designate that you need multiple fonts:

```
*fontSet :
-adobe-helvetica-bold-r-normal-10-100-75-75-m-60-*,\
-JIS-Fixed-Medium-R-Normal--26-180-100-100-C-240-*,\
-JIS-Fixed-Medium-R-Normal--26-180-100-100-C-120-*
```

While this example shows very specific designations of the requested fonts, it also is possible to use wild cards in place of many of the fields. See X Window System documentation for more details. In addition, X also includes functions that determine which font in a set to use for rendering a string. See the section Rendering Text later in this chapter for more information.

Although fonts tend to match code sets, there are exceptions. It may be impractical to create one giant font for use with a universal set like ISO 10646; such a font would consume significant system resources. Even if you had more megabytes than you knew what to do with, it wouldn't be smart to use them on a massive font. A universal set is designed to cover all possibilities, but any given file probably contains less than 10 percent of the characters in that set's universe. It doesn't make sense to use up the space a universal font needs when most users stay comfortably within their own galaxy. A better solution may be to maintain separate fonts for logical chunks of characters and use something like X's font set syntax.

7.2 Displaying and Editing International Text

Once you have fonts that include glyphs of the characters your language uses, you probably want to display that text on a screen, and have the ability to manipulate it properly. Assuming your system already handles English text, displaying and editing some languages is easy. For others, software needs to learn new tricks. If you are an application developer, the changes you can make depend very strongly on the capabilities or limitations of the software on which you build your application. If that software is unable to render or edit international text, there may be little you can do in your application to enable such functionality. However, if your application depends on software with an appropriate level of internationalization support, it can take advantage of those I18N capabilities. The following describes some problems that need to be addressed, and some potential methods for handling them.

7.2.1   Where to Begin and Where to Move

Assume you use some sort of windowing software and want to create a new file. You open a new window and want to enter text. Okay, where should input begin?

No, this is not a trick question. While it may seem obvious to start in the upper left corner and for the cursor to move left-to-right as you enter text, that start point and cursor direction only works for some languages. It is great for languages that use Latin and Cyrillic scripts, and also for other left-to-right languages such as Hindi and Thai. But other languages pick a different start point.

When entering a language like Arabic, Hebrew, or Urdu, the display software needs to allow the upper *right* corner to be defined as home. Then, the cursor needs to move horizontally right-to-left as you enter letters, and switch to left-to-right when you enter numbers or some foreign text. Users working in languages such as Chinese and Japanese benefit if the software lets them choose text direction. Figure 7.2 shows samples of the same Japanese text written horizontally and vertically. In the figure, the first example shows text written horizontally, left-to-right, while the second shows vertical, right-to-left text.

To support multiple directions for entering text, you must remove hard-coded assumptions about directionality from display software, and instead build in flexibility. For example, a cursor movement routine needs to support the models shown in Figure 7.3. The small box in each sample shows the location of the first character, while the arrows show the direction of additional text.

Table 7.1 gives a textual description of the cursor movement models. In addition to these basics of cursor movement, there are other display considerations. Horizontal text typically scrolls off the top of a screen or window, but vertical text requires a different type of scrolling action. Text needs to roll off the right side of the screen. This also means that to redisplay text that has rolled off the right side of the screen, the text should roll across from that same side.

Software that controls cursor movement within a file needs additional logic to

Figure 7.2   Horizontal and Vertical Japanese Text

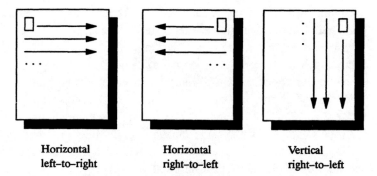

Horizontal	Horizontal	Vertical
left–to–right	right–to–left	right–to–left

Figure 7.3   Cursor Movement Models

handle mixed-width text correctly. Uninternationalized software often moves the cursor in single-byte increments, but since characters can span multiple bytes, such software is inadequate. When handling a two-byte character, such byte-oriented software may put the cursor in the middle of that character. Instead of moving byte-by-byte, the cursor needs to move to character boundaries only. Cursor movement software might therefore use a function like **mblen( )** to find character boundaries, or might convert all text to **wchar_t** form to make it easier to find those boundaries. Figure 7.4 illustrates correct and incorrect cursor movement in mixed-width text two different ways. In the figure, *a* designates a single-byte character, while *B* is a byte of a multiple-byte character.

| | Horizontal Text | | Vertical Text |
	Left–to–right	Right–to–left	Right–to–left
Beginning of file	upper left corner	upper right corner	upper right corner
Cursor moves	right	left (usually)	down
At end–of–line	down and to the left	down and to the right	top of window and to the left

Table 7.1   Summary of Cursor Movement Models

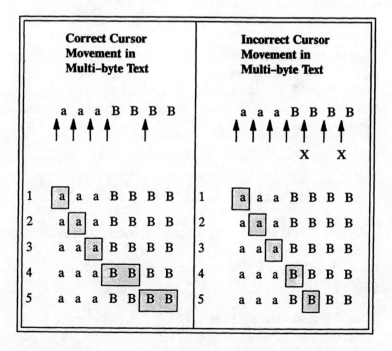

Figure 7.4   Cursor Movement in Mixed-Width Text

When the cursor moves correctly, it moves by character boundaries, as the left half of Figure 7.4 shows. Byte-oriented processing results in cursor movement like that shown on the right. As lines four and five show, the cursor incorrectly moves to one half of the first two-byte character in the stream.

7.2.2 Rendering Text

The ability to move a cursor around mixed-width text implies that the characters have been rendered on the screen. Rendering requires access to the appropriate fonts, and the logic to determine which fonts are appropriate. One implementation for rendering international text is in the internationalized release of the X Window System (X11R5). It uses the current locale and font sets to determine how to draw characters to a display.

The function **XCreateFontSet( )** checks the code set portion of the current locale and determines whether it is an encoding method like AJEC, and so needs multiple fonts, or a simple code set like ISO 8859-1 that needs a single font. It then opens the appropriate font or fonts, places that information into a font set structure, and returns it to the application.

When an X application calls a rendering function (for example, **XmbDrawString( )** for drawing multibyte strings, or **XwcDrawString( )** for drawing wide character strings), the function examines the font set information it received and uses locale-specific information to parse the input string down to single-font segments. Figure 7.5 shows how an AJEC string in **wchar_t** form might be divided into four substrings. The first substring includes four wide characters, the second has two, and so on.

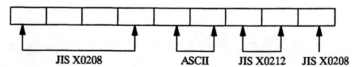

JIS X0208   ASCII   JIS X0212   JIS X0208

Figure 7.5   X's Locale-Dependent Rendering Model

The rendering function then draws each segment with an appropriate font from the specified font set.

7.2.3 Layout Orientation

Just as most input and display software assumes horizontal, left-to-right text, so too does the whole layout of the screen. An application's menu choices, if they exist, usually start on the left, and submenus cascade left-to-right. In windowing systems, an individual window's title usually appears horizontally at the top left or the top center.

Consider, however, the requirements of other languages. For vertical Chinese text, it may be most appropriate for the window title to appear vertically on the right side of the window instead of centered horizontally on top. In addition to vertical text requirements, Figure 7.6 shows the appropriate layout for an application with Hebrew text running in a windowing system.

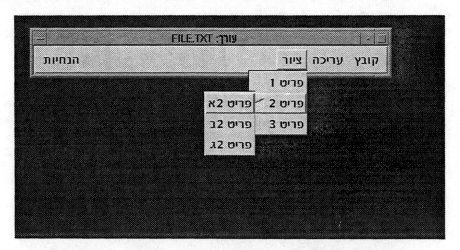

Figure 7.6   Hebrew Window with Right-to-Left Menu Cascades

As the figure shows, Hebrew menu choices begin on the right, and cascading menus fall to the left. In addition, the text in the window's title includes a mixture of right-to-left Hebrew and left-to-right Latin letters.

In order for software that handles the screen layout to be fully internationalized, it must support a variety of text directions. When this book was written, standards did not yet exist for this functionality. If you need this support, you may have to write the appropriate functions yourself.

7.2.4 Mixed-Direction Text

While display software must change if it is to handle text that reads in a direction other than left-to-right, it isn't enough simply to teach the cursor to move in a new direction or to make sure that menus cascade appropriately. Adding such functionality is relatively easy, because it only involves a finite set of new directions.

Once you know where to begin, and the direction in which to point the cursor, the hard part is over.

But, of course, there is more to text handling than just moving in a single direction. Most languages that are written right-to-left revert to left-to-right for numbers or foreign text. To handle such languages, there must be a way to indicate a change in direction—and the software smarts to handle the change.

There are two fairly common ways to store mixed-direction text: in *keyboard* or *display* order. With keyboard order (also known as *logical order*), characters are stored internally in the order in which they were entered from the keyboard. With display order (sometimes called *presentation order*), characters are stored in discrete units (usually one-line chunks) in the left-to-right order in which they appear when rendered on the screen or on paper. For languages that are written left-to-right, keyboard and display order are identical, but that is not the case with languages written right-to-left.

Take an example. Suppose you have a string of Hebrew letters, which go right-to-left, and Latin letters, which go left-to-right. In the following examples, lowercase Latin letters stand in for Hebrew letters. Consider this string:

```
ABCD dcba
```

Here are the contents of the internal data stream for the two orders:

Keyboard Order   **Display Order**

```
a b c d <SPACE> A B C D     A B C D <SPACE> d c b a
```

The most common use for display order is printing, not for on-line files. Text changes frequently as users edit it; two lines can be appended to become one, or one line can be broken apart in multiple ways. When data is stored in display order, software constantly has to reshuffle the data as that display changes. Storing data in keyboard order therefore is a common implementation choice.

Explicit and Implicit Directionality

In addition to deciding the order in which to store data, there is the matter of deciding how to handle directionality information: using an *explicit* or *implicit* method. With the explicit method, a data stream includes signal bytes (sometimes called *tags*) that denote a change in direction, while in an implicit approach, software examines the characters within the data stream to determine direction.

Consider the earlier text example. Assuming the data is stored in keyboard order and uses an explicit method to handle directionality, the data stream might look something like this:

RtoL a b c d <SPACE> **LtoR** A B C D

The **RtoL** and **LtoR** tags explicitly signal the direction changes. Display software uses this information to print the characters correctly like this:

ABCD dcba

While tags provide clear direction information, they create, in essence, a stateful encoding. As discussed in Chapter 4, the tags provide information about their accompanying data, and interpretation of all data depends on the state information around it. That means programs must search for the tags (state) and use them to process data correctly. If existing software assumes data is stateless, significant changes are necessary to add the appropriate support.

Even if you are willing to change software to handle explicit directionality tags, it may not be practical to do so. If you want or need to continue using software that assumes data is stateless, you may choose the implicit directionality scheme. Suppose you have the same text string as earlier and still store it in keyboard order, but use implicit directionality. In this case, the data stream looks like this:

a b c d <SPACE> A B C D

Since there are no explicit directionality tags, software examines the contents of the data stream to determine the order in which to display the characters. It can do so in a variety of ways. In the past, it has been most common for such software to look at the letters' encoded values—all those in the "ASCII" range are Latin left-to-right letters, and all those in the upper half of the ISO-Hebrew set are right-to-left Hebrew—but this method clearly ties the software to a particular code set. Another way might be to create a new character class and then to use a locale's character class definitions to determine the group to which each character belongs. In this case, all Latin letters might be defined in the **alpha** class, while all Hebrew letters might be defined in a **national** (for national characters) class. (See Chapter 8 for details on creating new character classes and using all classes in internationalized software.)

The problem comes with characters that have multiple directions. The example earlier includes a <SPACE>. Does it move right or left? There is no single correct answer, and that is exactly the problem. Implicit directionality works well for characters that have a single direction, but may fail with characters whose direction depends on context. A space goes left-to-right if it is within a left-to-right string, and the opposite direction if it is within a right-to-left string. This example is ambiguous, however, because the space is at the boundary of right-to-left and left-to-right substrings.

Other characters have multiple directions. A left parenthesis [(] may mark the beginning of a parenthetical phrase, meaning that the character to the right is the first in the phrase, but it also may mark the end of a right-to-left substring. In that case, the character to the right is the last in the phrase. In this example:

```
(ABCD) (dcba)
```

A is the first letter in the left-to-right parenthetical phrase, while d is the last letter in the right-to-left counterpart.

An implicit directionality model uses rules that define a character's direction in a given context. The software may define, for example, that if there are right-to-left characters before and after a space, the space moves right-to-left. Likewise, if punctuation characters such as a period or comma immediately follow a left parenthesis, the parenthesis marks the end of a right-to-left parenthetical phrase. Consider this keyboard-ordered data stream:

```
) a b c d ( . A B C D
```

Since a period follows the left parenthesis, the parenthesis is the end of a right-to-left parenthetical phrase. The display software thus renders the input like this:

```
ABCD.(dcba)
```

If the left parenthesis were assumed to move left-to-right, this same data stream could be rendered as:

```
(.ABCDdcba)
```

Although implicit directionality co-exists much more easily with common stateless code sets and with software that assumes stateless data, it does not provide a complete solution. Explicit directionality provides the mechanism for a complete solution, but probably at a higher implementation and processing cost. In addition, data with explicit tags is not compatible with routines that assume data is stateless. When this was written, there were no standards for handling mixed-direction text.

7.2.5 Editing Text

Although many languages share the need for similar editing features—the ability to delete or insert characters, to search for specific strings, to cut and paste within a file and between files—most implementations of editors can only perform such functions one way. Most commonly, an editor can handle English or another single language, but copes with other languages with varying degrees of success. Internationalized editors need enhanced functionality.

Character versus Byte Handling

One of the first and most basic changes most editors need to make is away from processing bytes and toward processing characters instead. When ASCII was the only supported code set, byte and characters were, for all practical purposes, synonyms, but this no longer is the case. Since characters may span multiple bytes, old-style byte processing may result in characters being truncated, or incompletely deleted, or being otherwise mangled.

Although it is possible for an editor to use the standard function **mblen( )** to find character boundaries, it usually is more efficient to convert text to **wchar_t** form and then use wide character processing functions. Consider a simple operation like deleting the previous character in the stream. Uninternationalized editors usually remove one byte from the data stream. However, since characters no longer always fit in one byte, a more worldly editor may need to erase more than just a single byte. But **mblen( )** only works when scanning forward in a multibyte data stream; there is no standard function for finding character boundaries when scanning backward. Finding character boundaries is simple for most code sets, however, when the data is in wide character form, because one **wchar_t** equals one character. (Note that this approach does not work for Unicode or forms of ISO 10646 that include combining characters; you may have to write your own routines to handle these sequences.)

In general, the software logic in an internationalized editor is simpler if the editor processes wide, rather than multibyte, characters. The disadvantage to this approach is that it may waste memory. If, for example, **wchar_t** is 32 bits in your system, and the text being processed consists of single-byte English or European characters only, the text consumes four times more space in wide character form than it does in single-byte.

Cutting and Pasting

When cutting and pasting text to another location in the same file, an editor needs to follow character-handling techniques already mentioned. It must ensure that the region to be cut includes complete characters and so must process text on a character, rather than byte, basis. As with other editing tasks, it usually is easier to handle characters in **wchar_t** form during cut and paste operations instead of processing them in multibyte form. This removes the possibility of cutting a character in mid-byte.

Cut and paste becomes more complicated when it is between processes. Separate processes introduce the possibility of different locales—one could be in French while the other is in Greek, or one could be Japanese AJEC while the other is Japanese SJIS. The results of a cut-and-paste between processes using mismatched locales depends on what software you are using. In many cases, the locale of the source text is ignored, and it is treated as if it were in the destination's locale. If you paste French Latin-1-encoded text into a process running a Greek ISO 8859-7-based locale, the Latin-1 text appears as garbled Greek. The code values in the data do not change; only their interpretation does. Suppose the French input includes this string:

	c	ô	t	é
String				
Encoding	0x63	0xf4	0x74	0xe9

When the string gets displayed in the Greek process, it looks like this:

	c	τ	t	ι
String				

The difference is because in Latin-1, 0xf4 and 0xe9 are the code values of ô (o-circumflex) and é (e-acute), respectively, while in ISO 8859-7, the same code values are τ (tau) and ι (iota). Since most cut-and-paste functions ignore locale information, there is nothing to indicate how code values within the stream should be interpreted.

OSF/Motif uses an alternate cut-and-paste model. It checks the code set portion of the source and destination locales; if they match, characters are moved over without modification. However, if they don't match, Motif converts the source data to Compound Text (CT). The receiving process then converts the CT to the encoding of its current locale.

Data can be lost during this conversion if the source and destination code sets encode different characters. If you apply this model to the French-to-Greek cut-and-paste, ô and é get mapped to a substitute character (usually, question mark or space), because these characters do not exist in ISO 8859-7. This model works best when two processes use different encodings of the same characters. For example, if the source is SJIS and the destination is AJEC, little data is likely to be lost, and the result is ungarbled, ready-to-use text.

When this book was written, there were no standard functions for preventing data loss when exchanging data between processes. However, Chapter 12 discusses some possible models, including the use of data tags.

7.3   General I/O in Programs

While only a few developers need to be aware of the requirements that internationalization adds to software tools described so far in this chapter, most developers write programs that perform formatted or unformatted input and output. Indeed, calls to functions like **printf( )**, **fgets( )**, and **scanf( )** are almost as common in C programs as are curly brackets. In addition, many application programs try to determine the display characteristics of the data they are processing. This section describes new or revised functions for handling such familiar tasks.

7.3.1   Formatted I/O

XPG4 defines enhanced functionality in formatted I/O functions for handling internationalized requirements. (This functionality is likely to be added to ISO C.) Table 7.2 lists the familiar functions and their purpose.

Table 7.2   Formatted I/O Functions

Function	Purpose
fprintf	print formatted output on named *stream*
printf	print formatted output to *stdout*
sprintf	print formatted output in string **s*
fscanf	convert formatted input from named *stream*
scanf	convert formatted input from *stdin*
sscanf	convert formatted input from string *s*

Although the functions are familiar, you may need to change the way you use **char**-based format descriptors. In addition, there are two new **wchar_t**-based descriptors. First, consider the familiar **s** and **c** format descriptors as used in calls like these:

```
printf ("%s\n", my_array);
printf ("%c\n", my_char);
```

The **s** string descriptor works on arrays of **char**. The contents of those arrays may include ASCII, single-byte European, multiple-byte Asian, or other language text. As long as the code set or encoding method allows a single null byte to terminate a string, the **s** descriptor can handle it correctly. Nearly all commonly used code sets or encoding methods fit this description. Exceptions are Unicode and the

UCS forms of ISO 10646 because their coded characters may include all-zero octets that most existing systems interpret as a string-terminating null. However, a simple call like

```
printf("%s\n", weekday);
```

is capable of printing any of these values and encodings:

String	Language	Encoding
søndag	Danish	ISO 8859-1
Sunday	English	ASCII
Κυριακή	Greek	ISO 8859-7
vasárnap	Hungarian	ISO 8859-2

If the s descriptor is capable of handling common single- or multiple-byte encodings, the c descriptor is more limited. Although it usually is thought of as referring to a character, it actually refers to an **unsigned char**. That means it is capable of holding data that fits in an **unsigned char**, but it cannot hold characters that span multiple bytes. Thus, a call like

```
scanf("%c\n", my_char);
```

inputs one **unsigned char**, and works for single-byte input. If applied to a multiple-byte character, this call inputs only the first byte of that character. Similarly, `scanf("%3c\n", my_chars)` inputs three bytes, not three characters.

Along with the previously familiar s and c format descriptors, XPG4 defines two additional descriptors for handling **wchar_t** data: S for wide character strings and C for wide characters. An argument to S must be a pointer to an array of type **wchar_t**. In the **printf( )** functions, the wide characters in the array are converted to a sequence of bytes and printed. The conversion must yield the same results as if **wcstombs( )** had been performed on the data. This **printf( )** prints the wide characters in the string *pwcs*:

```
wchar_t *pwcs;
.  .  .
printf("%S\n", pwcs);
```

The C descriptor matches the specified number of wide characters and converts them to their multibyte form as if **wcstombs( )** had been called.

In the **scanf( )** functions, the input characters to which **S** applies are converted to a sequence of wide characters as they would be if **mbstowcs( )** had been called. The **C** descriptor matches the specified number of characters and converts them to their corresponding wide character codes as if **mbstowcs( )** had been called. For example, %3C matches three input characters and converts them to **wchar_t** form.

It is up to you as an application programmer to decide whether to use wide characters and their descriptors in **printf( )** and **scanf( )** calls. The current state of your data may have an effect on your decision. If you already have converted data to **wchar_t** form and now need to print it, it may be more efficient to use the **S** or **C** descriptors.

See your system's man pages for the **printf( )** and **scanf( )** functions or XPG4 for details on formatted I/O on an internationalized system. In addition, see Chapter 9 for syntax you can use in these functions to enable parameters to be input or output in varying orders.

7.3.2 Unformatted I/O

While internationalized functionality has been added to existing formatted I/O functions, the situation is different with unformatted I/O calls. XPG4 adds wide character-based versions to the older **char**-based functions. (As with all the **wchar_t** functions, these are likely to be added to ISO C.) Table 7.3 shows the complementary functions. The wide character functions are declared in **<wchar.h>**.

Table 7.3   char and wchar_t Unformatted I/O Functions

char-Based	wchar_t-Based	Purpose
fgetc	fgetwc	get [byte I wide char] from stream
fgets	fgetws	get [string I wide char string] from stream
fputc	fputwc	put [byte I wide char] on stream
fputs	fputws	put [string I wide char string] on stream
getc	getwc	get [byte I wide char] from stream
getchar	getwchar	get [byte I wide char] from *stdin*
gets	getws	get [string I wide char string] from *stdin*
putc	putwc	put [byte I wide char] on stream
putchar	putwchar	put [byte I wide char] on *stdout*
puts	putws	put [byte I wide char string] on *stdout*
ungetc	ungetwc	push [byte I wide char] into input stream

As with the string-handling functions described in Chapter 6, the **wchar_t**- and **char**-based I/O functions are very similar. The data types of arguments differ for functions that perform similar functions, but the purpose of those arguments generally doesn't. For example:

#include <stdio.h>
int fgetc(FILE * *stream***);**

#include <wchar.h>
wint_t fgetwc(FILE * *stream***);**

fgetc( ) gets the next byte from the input stream pointed to by *stream* and converts it to an **int. fgetwc( )** gets the next character, which consists of one or more bytes, from the input stream and converts it to the corresponding wide character code. This code fragment shows how to read a file using **fgetwc( )**:

```
#include <stdio.h>
#include <locale.h>
#include <wchar.h>
 . . .
wint_t wc;
FILE *fp;
wchar_t *pwcs;
 . . .
(void)setlocale(LC_ALL, "");

fp = fopen(argv[1], "r");
/* error handling if fp == null omitted */

while ((wc = fgetwc(fp)) != WEOF) {
    *pwcs++ = (wchar_t)wc;
    /* continue till buffer is full */
}
 . . .
```

Because **fgetwc( )** automatically converts multibyte characters to wide character form, using it is an alternative to reading the input stream a byte at a time, using **mblen( )** to find character boundaries, and then converting data to **wchar_t** form using **mbtowc( )** or **mbstowcs( )**. Both alternatives are for use when it is more efficient for your application to process data in wide character, rather than multibyte, form. Chapter 6 discusses circumstances under which you might choose one form over the other.

This example uses **fgetwc( )** to read wide characters from a file and **fputwc( )** to write wide characters to an output file:

```
#include <stdio.h>
#include <locale.h>
#include <wchar.h>

main (int argc, char *argv[]) {
  wint_t wc;
  FILE *fp, *fp2;

  (void) setlocale(LC_ALL,"");

  /* omit error handling for fp == null case */
  fp = fopen(argv[1], "r");
  fp2 = fopen(argv[2], "w");

  /* copy wide characters from input file to output file */
  while ((wc = fgetwc(fp)) != WEOF)
    fputwc(wc, fp2);

}
```

This fragment uses **fputws( )** to write a wide character string to an output file:

```
#include <stdio.h>
#include <locale.h>
#include <wchar.h>

main (int argc, char *argv[]) {
  wchar_t *pwcs;
  int return_val;
  FILE *fp;
  . . .
  (void) setlocale(LC_ALL,"");
  fp = fopen(argv[1], "w");
```

```
/* pwcs points to a wide character string */
return_val = fputws(pwcs, fp);

if (return_val == -1)
    /* error handling */
else
    /* output file contains contents of pwcs */

    . . .


}
```

See your system's man pages or XPG4 for full details on the **wchar_t**-based versions of unformatted I/O functions.

7.3.3 Display Width

Although modern word processors often provide users with a dizzying variety of proportional fonts in different typefaces, many other software packages continue to take a simpler approach to displaying characters. When I/O goes through a typical terminal driver like a **tty** or **pty**, display software usually only provides access to a single font or font set, and the glyphs are monospaced as opposed to being proportional.

With some languages, including those that use the Latin or Cyrillic script, each glyph in a monospaced font consumes one display column. In other languages, however, specific groups of characters may consume two display columns. When rendering Japanese text, for example, ASCII and JIS X0201 (katakana) characters consume one display column, while Kanji ideographs as well as the kana characters in JIS X0208 consume two columns. It often is helpful to be able to determine how much space a given string will consume when rendered, so XPG4 contains the functions **wcwidth( )** and **wcswidth( )** for this purpose. They have this syntax:

#include <wchar.h>
int wcwidth (wint_t *wc***);**

int wcswidth(const wchar_t **pwcs*, **size_t** *n***);**

wcwidth( ) returns the number of columns for the wide character *wc*, while **wcswidth( )** returns the number of display columns required for *n* wide characters in the string pointed to by *pwcs*. Note that the number of display columns a character consumes often differs from the number of bytes it contains. For example, many Hanzi ideographs in the 1992 version of the Taiwanese code set CNS 11643 consume four bytes each, but use only two display columns. Similarly, Table 7.4 shows the bytes and corresponding display widths of characters in Japanese AJEC.

Table 7.4   AJEC Bytes-per-Character versus Display Width

Set #	Contains	Bytes per Character	Display Width
CS0	ASCII	1	1
CS1	Kanji	2	2
CS2	katakana	2	1
CS3	more Kanji	3	2

Software that displays data to a device may use the display width functions to determine how much space the data stream will consume and thus how many characters can fit on a given line. Consider the AJEC data stream in Figure 7.7, where a indicates a single-byte ASCII character, b is a byte of a two-byte Kanji, c is a byte of a two-byte katakana, and d is a byte of a three-byte Kanji.

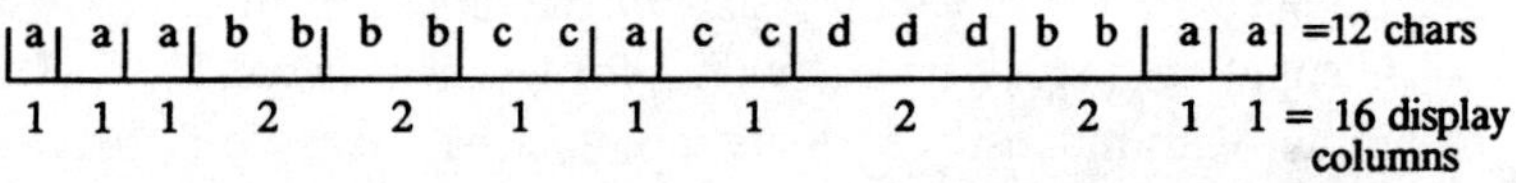

Figure 7.7   Bytes, Characters, and Display Columns

The 19 bytes in the stream encode 12 characters and consume 16 display columns.

When processing input data to determine its display requirements, you might choose to read each character from the input file, call **wcwidth( )**, and store the result in an array like this:

```
. . .
wint_t wc;
int     display_widths[LINE_MAX];
int     i = 0;
. . .
(void) setlocale(LC_ALL,"");
. . .
while ((wc = fgetwc(fp)) != WEOF) {
    display_widths[i++] = wcwidth(wc);
    /* other input processing */
    }
```

The program then can use the display widths to determine how many characters it can display on a given line, and so avoid display truncation. For example, if the program assumes the American de facto standard of 80 columns of display space, and there is a one-column character at column 80, the program can display that character. However, if there is a two-column character at the 80-column boundary, the program must move that character down to the next line. In that case, the program might include a call like this:

```
ungetwc((wint_t)wc, infile);
```

to push the current character wc back on the input stream.

Computing display widths works for terminal-based I/O of languages that can be written with monospaced fonts, and that have simple display rules. Languages that use the Latin script are good candidates, because all glyphs occupy a single display column in monospaced fonts. Languages that use ideographs also are good candidates because all ideographic glyphs occupy a fixed-width space. The concept of display columns is less useful, however, for scripts like Arabic, because the variable width characters are rarely rendered with monospaced fonts.

In addition to the XPG4 display width functions, other software packages may have alternate ways to determine width. Some window-based systems have "width of character" functions that are more sophisticated than the XPG4 functions. If you have access to such functions, use them.

7.4 Printing

When computer systems began poking their way into everyday business, promoters and pundits predicted they would lead to a paperless office. Which just goes to show how wrong the experts can be. Offices probably are more awash in paper than at any time in history.

Since everyone seems to want hard-copy of everything, and since international-ized files can include any number of not-just-English characters, printers need to be taught to reproduce a wide repertoire of characters. The ease with which you can print the repertoire depends on the type of printer available to you and the software that controls it. Two of the most common printer types are *intelligent* and *character* printers.

7.4.1 Intelligent Printers

An intelligent printer is one that understands a page description language such as PostScript. The description language includes methods for interpreting characters and code sets and may also include functionality for handling mixed-direction text.

Most laser printers are intelligent printers. The page description language such printers use issues commands that perform functions like choosing a character, map-ping it to a specific glyph, and printing it at a specific position on the page. Map-pings of character codes to font glyphs are where intelligent printers shine in terms of internationalization. That is because it is relatively easy to add new fonts that include the characters you want to a laser printer.

Some manufacturers provide fonts in a cartridge that you physically plug into the printer. To add fonts with characters that are not in the current fonts, you plug in an appropriate cartridge. Such fonts are said to be *resident* because they are physi-cally tied to the machine.

An advantage of resident fonts is that they are fairly easy to use. When you need new characters, you don't have to rewrite lots of software; you just supply a new cartridge. A disadvantage, though, is that users get their expected output only if the printer has the right cartridge loaded. Suppose your file is encoded in Latin-1 and your printer has a ROMAN8 cartridge. What gets printed on paper looks con-siderably different from what is in the file. For example, if the Latin-1 data contains an ñ (code value 0xf1), the ROMAN8 printer produces a þ because the latter charac-ter has that same 0xf1 value in ROMAN8.

An alternative to resident fonts is *downloaded* fonts. Such fonts are maintained somewhere on the system, and sent to the printer at different times. The printer may specifically request a given font, or a document may carry along its own fonts when it goes to the printer. The downloaded fonts can either supplement or replace the resident fonts.

Downloaded fonts can solve the problem of resident fonts not matching the data they are supposed to reproduce, but print drivers need new logic to determine which fonts a given document needs and to send them along as needed. There were no standards for this functionality when this book was written, but one possibility is to use the value of the user's locale in preparing print requests. In this scenario, if the user is running a Latin-1-based locale, the print software checks whether the target printer has fonts with the Latin-1 characters, and if not, sends along the appropriate set; if the user is running a Japanese AJEC-based locale, the software checks for resident AJEC fonts and sends them along if needed. While this may make it possible to overcome the limitations of resident fonts, there are problems with this approach. Depending on the number of fonts and the number of glyphs in an individual font, it may be very inefficient to download fonts repeatedly. In addition, there is no guarantee that the code set portion of the current locale matches the encoding of the file being sent to the printer. Finally, as this book was written, there was no accepted way to pass all or partial locale information between processes.

7.4.2 Character Printers

A character printer works much the way a typewriter works—a physical object strikes an inked ribbon to produce a character on paper. Some impact printers can produce several characters—or even a whole line—simultaneously, but the repertoire of what they can print is tied tightly to the characters molded in metal or plastic. To produce a character that isn't on the printer's molds (sometimes called *daisy wheels* or *print thimbles*), there are few alternatives. The easiest way is to provide a new mold that has the characters you need. This is similar to laser printers that rely on resident fonts.

Another option is to use software to teach an impact printer to produce letters that aren't exactly on the mold. Suppose your mold only has ASCII characters on it, and you need to print an *ô*. The print driver can send instructions to use multiple keystrokes to create the character. Using these instructions, the printer stamps the *o*, backspaces, and then stamps the ^ over the *o*. The result of this approach sometimes looks as contrived as the escape sequences that produce it, so this isn't a perfect solution, but it can address some printing needs.

7.4.3 Printers and Paper

Along with adding the capability of printing new characters, an internationalized printer also needs to learn about paper. Printers may only know about one size of paper, such as the 8.5 by 11 inch American standard, when the world offers more variety. Much of the world uses the ISO A4 size, which is slightly longer and narrower than the American standard. To accommodate multiple sizes, a system vendor may need to offer new paper trays, or make existing trays more flexible.

In addition to hardware changes for different sizes of paper trays, internationalized print software also must be flexible enough to handle the varying page layouts the different paper sizes dictate. That means it should remove hard-coded rules. For an American locale, the software may by default leave a one-inch margin on the left and right of the page, and print 62 6.5-inch lines per page. For locales that use A4 paper, on the other hand, the rules might define a three-centimeter margin on the left and right, and 70 lines per page. (Note that standard locales do not include information about measurement units or paper sizes, so this functionality would be an extension to the standard.) Individual users might have different ideas about how they want the text to appear, so the print software should allow them to spell out their preferences—using their choice of measurement units.

7.5   The System Speaks

You have learned in this chapter about fonts and font-managing strategies, about the varying display, editing, and printing requirements of some of the world's writing systems, and about existing functions for inputting or outputting multibyte and wide character text. A system that provides internationalized fonts, rendering software, editors, and so on, along with programs that handle multibyte and wide character I/O, makes it possible for users to enter and edit many languages. However, most users need far more than simply to input and output their characters; they want the system to process those characters correctly.

The next chapter covers techniques and functions for meeting those user requirements.

Processing International Data   8

At this point (assuming you have read the previous chapters), you know a lot more about code sets and internationalized I/O and display issues than most people. And what has all that knowledge gotten you? To the point of being able to teach your system how to enter, edit, and print text in many languages. But it still hasn't a clue about how to *process* that text correctly.

Just because your system can display, say, French or Chinese text doesn't mean it can sort the data appropriately, or determine which characters are uppercase, or spell-check the words, or hyphenate-and-justify them. Or do any of the other myriad text-processing tasks that an average system can do on American English text.

Furthermore, the software may still exhibit distinctly American behavior (or the country of origin, if it isn't the United States). Dates typically appear in the American month/day/year format and use the English words for day and month names. Numbers are formatted using American conventions. Monetary amounts assume the dollar sign ($) is the only currency symbol. And on and on.

Internationalization that only goes as far as teaching the system to accept other languages is akin to an Olympic hurdler who stops after clearing the first two hurdles. Yes, it is better than just standing on the starting line, but it is not going to win the race.

This chapter teaches you how to clear the next few hurdles. It covers internationalized functions and techniques for these topics:

- Character classification
- Sorting/collation
- Language parsing
- Dates and time
- Numeric and monetary formatting

It also introduces some of the limitations associated with the locale model.

8.1   Character Classification

It is common for software to process characters based on the groups to which they belong. Numerics may be handled one way, punctuation another, and alphabetics still another. It is so common to need to determine characteristics that C's traditional ctype macros were created. These functions have provided a handy way to classify a character with a simple call. Is the current character uppercase? No need to write your own test; just call **isupper( )**. Is it a white-space character? Call **isspace( )**. Need to convert uppercase to lowercase? **tolower( )** does the trick.

Not surprisingly, the ctype macros were designed to meet the needs of English. For UNIX systems, they also were implemented with the assumption that data was encoded in ASCII. Naturally, a few changes are in order for an internationalized system.

8.1.1   New Ways to Classify

Since many more code sets than ASCII are in use, there are new ways of looking at the old classes and a need for classes that the original ctype developers never considered. One old assumption is that every letter has an inverse case. Under this assumption, if `islower(c)` returns true, `toupper(c)` returns c's alter ego. But the German ß is a lowercase character that has no single uppercase equivalent.

Likewise, the **toupper( )** and **tolower( )** macros assumed that all conversions are a one-to-one affair—one letter is the uppercase version of one and only one lowercase letter. However, it is most common in France for lowercase letters to lose their diacritics when converted to uppercase. So *e, è, é, ê,* and *ë* may all convert to *E,* and the single letter *E* might convert to any one of the plain or diacritical forms.

The old classes need to handle characters beyond those in ASCII, and they also need to accommodate behavior that ASCII characters never displayed. In addition to these two changes, there also is a need for completely new classes. Languages such as Hindi and Thai need to be able to distinguish vowels from consonants. Japanese, Chinese, and Korean need to differentiate phonetic and ideographic characters.

8.1.2   Classification Approaches

In ISO C and XPG, the ctype macros have changed so that they can recognize more than just ASCII. For one thing, in most implementations, they are functions instead of macros. And instead of hard-coding in the characters that belong to a given class, they now look in tables (like the **localedef** information) or use algorithms to decide a character's features. The range of acceptable data has also expanded from the old –0x01 to 0x7f (decimal –1 to 127) to the fuller –0x01 to 0xff (–1 to 255).

If you used the old macros in your programs and now have access to internationalized ctype functions, these changes are invisible. The only change necessary to get the internationalized behavior is to call **setlocale( )** at the beginning of your program. The value LC_CTYPE (or, if it is not set, LC_ALL or LANG) has when your program runs determines what character classification rules are used. Suppose your existing program includes this:

```
#include <ctype.h>
int c;
. . .
if (islower(c))
    /* processing */;
```

Here is the internationalized version:

```
#include <ctype.h>
#include <locale.h>
int c;
. . .
(void)setlocale(LC_ALL, "");
if (islower(c))
    /* processing */;
```

Adding a **setlocale( )** call is the easiest way to put your program on the road to internationalized character classification, but it only works if you are using the standard ctype calls. If you currently use your own routines instead of system-supplied calls, remove your routines and replace them with calls to the ctype functions.

Suppose you currently convert an uppercase letter to lowercase this way:

```
char down, c;
. . .
if ('A' <= c && c <= 'Z')
    down = c - 'A' + 'a';
```

This works if c's value is uppercase ASCII, but fails for most other code sets. Assume your program has to process ISO 8859-2 (Latin-2) data and that c gets the values of two letters: 'G' and 'Š'. Here are the code values of the letters in the equation:

Letter	Hexadecimal	Decimal
A	0x41	65
G	0x47	71
Z	0x5a	90
a	0x61	97
g	0x67	103
Š	0xa9	169
š	0xb9	185

Given these values, here is how the equation gets filled in:

c equals 'G'

| **Hexadecimal:** | `0x67 = 0x47 - 0x41 + 0x61` |
| **Decimal:** | `103 = 71 - 65 + 97` |

c equals 'Š'

| **Hexadecimal:** | `0xc9 = 0xa9 - 0x41 + 0x61` |
| **Decimal:** | `201 = 169 - 65 + 97` |

The first example correctly returns lowercase 'g.' The second example actually wouldn't get as far as filling in the equation because the code value for 'Š' is not in the range of 'A' through 'Z.' However, even if you could rewrite the **if** clause so that 'Š' passes, the formula itself fails. Instead of returning 0xb9, it returns 0xc9, which is the encoding of 'É.'

Since this converter code is not internationalized, you should replace it with a call to **tolower( )**. The revised code looks like this:

```
int c;
unsigned char down;
. . .
(void) setlocale (LC_ALL, "");
if (isupper(c))
    down = tolower(c);
```

As with the example of converting a character's case, many other attribute tests are simple in the ASCII case. In fact, they may only involve a line or two of code, and so may appear frequently in your programs. Here is a common way of finding white-space characters:

```
if (c == ' ' || c == '\t')
    /* processing */;
```

Utilities that parse text looking for word boundaries or that count words may use this kind of test. However, there are other white-space characters beyond the ASCII space and tab in other code sets. You should replace this explicit test with a call to **isspace( )** to find the white-space characters appropriate to each locale.

8.1.3   Classifying More than a Byte

The expanded ctype functions can handle twice as many possibilities—256 versus the original 128—as the old ASCII-based macros. Surely that is enough, isn't it?

No. The functions can't go beyond 256 possibilities because they are restricted to taking a value that can be represented as an **unsigned char** as input. This is despite the fact that the functions actually take and return an **int**, which is always at least 16 bits, and often is 32 bits. The result of this anomaly is that the functions are limited to single-byte code sets. Such sets only satisfy part of the world, and if you want your code to meet more than just some customers' needs, you need different functions.

New functions are available in XPG4 that take as input a character that can be represented as a **wchar_t**. (These functions also will probably be included in a future revision of ISO C.) Table 8.1 shows the equivalent **char-** and **wchar_t**-based functions.

Table 8.1   char- and wchar_t-Based Class Functions

char Function	wchar_t Function	Purpose
isalnum	iswalnum	alphanumeric
isalpha	iswalpha	alphabetic
iscntrl	iswcntrl	control character
isdigit	iswdigit	decimal digit
isgraph	iswgraph	character with visible representation
islower	iswlower	lowercase
isprint	iswprint	printable
ispunct	iswpunct	punctuation
isspace	iswspace	character producing white space
isupper	iswupper	uppercase
isxdigit	iswxdigit	hexadecimal digit
tolower	towlower	convert to lowercase
toupper	towupper	convert to uppercase

The **wchar_t** functions work exactly like their **char** counterparts except that since they process **wchar_t**'s, they have a much wider range than the original **unsigned char**-restricted functions. Unlike the **char** functions, they usually are defined in **<wchar.h>**. A typical definition looks like this:

> **#include <wchar.h>**
> **int iswupper(wint_t** *wc*);

where *wc* is the wide character input value, and **wint_t** is a type definition that can hold any wide character or WEOF (wide character end-of-file).

The following example gets a character from an input stream, converts it to wide character form, and then tests to see if it is an **alpha** character:

```
#include <stdio.h>
#include <locale.h>
#include <wchar.h>

main(int argc, char *argv[]) {
  wint_t next_char;
  FILE *fp;

  (void)setlocale(LC_ALL, "");
  fp = fopen(argv[1], "r");
  /* omit error handling for fp == null case */

  while ((next_char = fgetwc(fp)) != WEOF) {
    if (iswalpha(next_char))
      /* alpha processing */
    else
      /* non-alpha processing */;
  }
}
```

Note that **char**-based and **wchar_t**-based functions for the same character class (for example, **isalpha( )** and **iswalpha( )**) may return differing results. Since the **char** functions are only defined to accept characters that fit in an **unsigned char**, they may return false for alphabetic characters that consume multiple bytes. The **wchar_t** functions return true, however, for the wide character representation of such multibyte values as long as the current locale definition includes them. For example, Japan's JIS X0208 code set includes two-byte versions of English letters A–Z and a–z, as well as Greek and Cyrillic letters. The Japanese national standard locale designates these letters as being part of the **alpha** class. That means **iswalpha( )** returns true if given one of these characters as input, while **isalpha( )**'s results are undefined.

8.1.4   New Classes

Once you add a **setlocale( )** call and replace private routines with standard ctype calls, your code can handle character classification chores for most languages using Latin scripts and (probably) those that use Greek and Cyrillic scripts. The **wchar_t**-based functions add the ability to classify characters that are bigger than a byte. But as noted earlier, many languages need to classify characters in ways that **lower, punct,** and the other standard classes don't cover.

POSIX.2 requires that you support the 11 standard classes that the existing functions cover, and allows you to add new classes. However, it currently does not define how to add classes, or how to access them once you set them up. XPG4 contains two new functions to handle these tasks. The functions take an implementation-defined property name as a parameter using this syntax:

#include <wchar.h>
wctype_t wctype (const char **charclass**);**

int iswctype(wint_t *wc*, **wctype_t** *charclass*);

The first function—**wctype( )**—tests whether the value of *charclass* is valid for the current locale. If it is, it returns a value of type **wctype_t** for use in the second function. **iswctype( )** tests the wide character value *wc* to determine if it has the named *charclass*.

You can use the new functions to mimic the behavior of existing ctype functions. The following:

```
iswctype(wc, wctype("alpha"));
```

is equivalent to an **iswalpha( )** function call. Of course, it doesn't make much sense to use the general **wctype( )/iswctype( )** calls for classes that already have their own specialized functions. The general calls are most useful when you need to test a wide character against a new class.

Suppose you need to find and process vowels. You could define a **vowel** class and use it as the *charclass* parameter to the new functions. The following example shows how to do this:

```
#include <locale.h>
#include <wchar.h>

main() {
  wint_t wc;
  int is_vowel;
  wctype_t class_name;

  (void)setlocale(LC_ALL, "");
  class_name = wctype("vowel");
  if (class_name == (wctype)-1)
    /* class_name is invalid for this locale.
     * Process the error.
     */;
  . . .
  is_vowel = iswctype(wc, class_name);
  if (!is_vowel)
    /* the character wc is not part of the class "vowel" */
  else
    /* the character wc is part of the class "vowel" */;
}
```

These general functions offer a great deal of flexibility. Instead of requiring you to implement a new function call for each class you add, they are capable of handling all new classification chores.

8.1.5 Naming Classes

When adding new classes, think carefully before naming them. It is common for developers in a given country to choose names that are specific to their language, even though the classes cover concepts that exist in several locales. For example, the Japanese might create a **kanji** class while the Koreans create **hanja** and the Chinese invent **hanzi**. All three designate the same thing: Han ideographs. The members of the classes differ from language to language (as the members of **alpha** differ from, say, French to Hungarian to English), but the idea is the same.

Having country-specific names makes it difficult to write internationalized code. If you use the **wctype( )/iswctype( )** functions, you may have to decide among these calls:

```
class_name = wctype("hanja");
class_name = wctype("hanzi");
class_name = wctype("kanji");
```

Similarly, if you create individual functions for each class, you might have to choose among **ishanja( )**, **ishanzi( )**, and **iskanji( )**. You can set up aliases to mask the inconsistencies, but a better solution is to choose one name that covers all similar cases. In this case, you might name the class **ideograph**. Then a single call like:

```
class_name = wctype("ideograph");
```

is sufficient to find and process ideographs for all locales with that class.

8.1.6   Why Classify?

As you look through code to determine what classification changes are necessary, you also should analyze *why* you are classifying or converting characters. It may be possible to remove some tests without adversely affecting functionality. Compilers often convert names to uppercase before putting them in error messages like this:

```
Variable FOO not declared in subroutine BAR
```

There is no functional requirement to convert case; it simply makes the names stand out. But case conversion is a bit slower in an internationalized environment, so you might choose to remove the conversion and enclose the names in quotes like this:

```
Variable "foo" not declared in subroutine "bar"
```

You get the same functionality without impacting I18N needs, and you probably pick up a small performance gain as well.

8.2   Collation

Putting data in order is one of the fundamental tasks of many programs. A database application needs to be able to sort data on a variety of keys. A file system needs to present the current directory's file names in order. A spell-checker may build a list of misspelled words and then sort them so that a user can easily scan the output.

Because sorting data is so common, most computer science students spend a good bit of time on sorting algorithms. They learn which algorithms have the best overall performance, and which are suited for particular types of data. Given this background, they try to match the right method with the data their program will be manipulating. Most of this fine-tuning, however, is invalid on an internationalized system. While sorting used to be a many-to-one problem—there were many algorithms you could use to sort data into (basically) one order—the stakes have changed. Now data needs to be sorted in many different ways.

8.2.1   Sorting Varieties

English collation rules are among the simplest in the world. Each letter sorts to its own unique place so *a* comes before *b* which comes before ... About the only monkey wrench in this otherwise simple scheme is how to handle case. Should *A* and *a* sort together or separately? That is, which of the following is correct?

Mixed-Case	Case-Segregated
aardvark	April
April	July
July	September
monkey	aardvark
September	monkey
zebra	zebra

An average person probably would say the mixed-case order is correct. Computer-literate people might lean toward the case-segregated order because they know that ASCII separates letters by case and because many computer sorts have depended on a character's ASCII value. Whatever the answer, case is one of the few debatable or complicated aspects of sorting English.

Enter other languages. And code sets.

Chapter 2 describes sorting methods in use around the world. Here is a brief review of some of those methods:

- **Multilevel.** A group of characters all sort to the same primary location, but have different secondary (or tertiary or ...) locations. The extra sort levels break ties. French and German are examples of languages that use multilevel sorting.
- **One-to-many.** One character sorts as if it were a multicharacter string. The German ß, which sorts as if it were *ss*, is an example.
- **Many-to-one.** A multicharacter string sorts as if it were one character. The Spanish *ch*, which sorts between *c* and *d*, and *ll*, which falls between *l* and *m*, are examples.

See Chapter 2 for more details and examples.

8.2.2   Sorting Out Collation Practices

Because internationalized programs need to support the various sorting rules, they need to unlearn some old and familiar tricks. One of the most widespread is the reliance on a character's code value to determine where it belongs in an ordered list. Once all the setup is done, most sorts rely on a statement like this to determine a character's collation location:

```
char first_char, second_char;
   . . .
if (second_char < first_char)
    /* swap characters */;
```

Functions like **strcmp( )** and **strncmp( )** use this kind of logic. This code works for ASCII-only sorts because the letters are encoded so that *a* is less than *b* which is less than *c*. But many code sets are not organized with letters or characters in ascending order. That is usually because so much code relies on ASCII that there is no way to pry those characters out of their 0x0-0x7f encodings. New characters almost always are assigned elsewhere. This means that although, for example, a French *à* (Latin-1 code value 0xe0) sorts before *b* (0x62), a simple look at the values of the two letters reports otherwise.

In addition to failing for characters that aren't encoded in sorted order, the example above has other problems. It doesn't work at all if the data includes more-than-single-byte characters, because it processes bytes rather than characters.

Clearly, you no longer can rely on a character's encoded value to decide where it falls in an ordered sequence. You also can't assume all characters are a single byte. But if you are tempted to grumble about the efficiency you lose when removing sorts that only work for ASCII, remember that many of the old algorithms can't produce the right answer. In the trade-off between fast-but-wrong and slightly-slower-but-right results, the latter is the clear winner.

While a character's encoded value no longer determines where it collates, you also need to realize that the members of a code set can sort in multiple ways. Sets like Latin-1 support multiple languages (French, Italian, Spanish, and others), and each language has its own collation rules. You can sort Latin-1 data using French rules or Italian rules or whatever, and the results differ each time.

Consider the letter *ä*. In Swedish, it comes near the end of the alphabet (after *z*). In German, the same letter sorts at the beginning of the alphabet with the plain *a*. The place *ä* falls in a given set of Latin-1 data therefore depends on whether the sort runs under a Swedish or German locale. (If you still want to use a letter's encoded value to decide where it goes, this example should sweep the last bit of ASCII stardust from your eyes.)

There are standard functions for handling some international collation needs, but many problems are yet to be solved. The following describes the standard functions, how some can be used in conjunction with older functions, and discusses some of what you may have to invent yourself.

8.2.3 Internationalized Sort Functions

There are four functions for handling international sorting: **strcoll( )** and **strxfrm( )** for **char**-based collation, and **wcscoll( )** and **wcsxfrm( )** for **wchar_t** sorting. They differ from the traditional **strcmp( )** and **strncmp( )** in that they use locale-specific sorting rather than collating by a character's encoded value. The value LC_COLLATE has when your program runs determines the sorting rules these functions use.

strcoll( ) is similar to **strcmp( )**, with the same number, type, and order of parameters. It has this syntax:

```
#include <string.h>
int strcoll(const char *s1, const char *s2);
```

The function compares the string pointed to by *s1* to the string pointed to by *s2*, and, depending on what collation rules are in effect, decides whether *s1* sorts before, after, or to the same place as *s2*.

wcscoll( ) is the wide character version of **strcoll( )**. It, too, resembles **strcmp( )** closely but its parameters are wide characters. It has this syntax:

#include <wchar.h>

int wcscoll(const wchar_t *ws1, const wchar_t *ws2);

The simplest way to internationalize existing collation-based **strcmp( )** calls is to replace them with calls to **strcoll( )** or **wcscoll( )**. However, there is a disadvantage. The ***coll( )** functions typically are slower than **strcmp( )** because they often rely on tables of collation information.

If you can't (or don't want to) pay the performance price, consider using **strxfrm( )** or **wcsxfrm( )** instead. These two functions transform data and return strings of characters that can be given to **strcmp( )** and **wcscmp( )** to be sorted. In effect, they assign numeric values to characters using the current locale's sorting rules so that **strcmp( )** and **wcscmp( )** can do numeric comparisons. They have this syntax:

#include <string.h>

size_t strxfrm(char *s1, char *s2, size_t n);

#include <wchar.h>

size_t wcsxfrm(wchar_t *ws1, wchar_t *ws2, size_t n);

The functions transform the strings pointed to by *s2/ws2* and put the result in *s1/ws1*. No more than *n* characters are put in the array that *s1/ws1* points to including the terminating null.

Suppose you need to sort Danish text. The Danish alphabet, you may remember, has three letters after *z: æ, ø,* and *å.* Assume **strxfrm( )** assigns values this way:

a	100
b	101
c	102
. . .	
z	125
æ	126
ø	127
å	128

Given these assignments, suppose your program compares the strings *præst* and *prøve.* After running them through **strxfrm( )**, they look like this:

p	r	æ	s	t
115	117	126	118	119

p	r	ø	v	e
115	117	127	121	104

Now, when **strcmp( )** looks at these transformed strings, it finds them equal up to the third letter, where it correctly determines that *æ* sorts before *ø*.

strxfrm( ) and **wcsxfrm( )** are useful for efficient sorting when you have to compare the same set of data several times. Instead of including multiple calls to the slower, table-driven **strcoll( )/wcscoll( )** functions, you can transform characters once and then use **strcmp( )/wcscmp( )** multiple times.

The disadvantage of **strxfrm( )** and **wcsxfrm( )** is that there is no way to do the inverse operation (that is, taking the transformed string and converting it back to the original string), so you may need to keep two versions of the string—original and transformed.

Multilevel Sorting

Just as the internationalized sort functions can handle languages that include more characters than English A–Z, they also support those that use multilevel sorting. French, Spanish, and Italian all are examples of languages that include multilevel sort conventions. In a multilevel sort, groups of characters sort to the same primary location, and then additional sorts break ties.

The collation section of a sample **localedef** in Chapter 5 included this information:

```
 . . .
<a>                     <a>;<a>;<a>
<A>                     <a>;<a>;<A>
<a-acute>               <a>;<a-acute>;<a-acute>
<A-acute>               <a>;<a-acute>;<A-acute>
<a-grave>               <a>;<a-grave>;<a-grave>
<A-grave>               <a>;<a-grave>;<A-grave>
<a-circumflex>          <a>;<a-circumflex>;<a-circumflex>
<A-circumflex>          <a>;<a-circumflex>;<A-circumflex>
<b>                     <b>;<b>;<b>
<B>                     <b>;<b>;<B>
 . . .
```

Assume you run **strcoll( )** under a locale with this LC_COLLATE definition and the input is:

Bague
Âcre
âpre
bague
âcre
acre
aprés
Acre

On the first pass of the sort, all words are treated first as if the letters have no diacritics and no case. All forms of *a* (*a*, *A*, *á*, *Á*, *à*, *À*, *â*, and *Â*) sort as if they were *a*. Similarly, lowercase *b* and uppercase *B* sort as if they were *b*. The results of the first pass might be something like:

Âcre
âcre
acre
Acre
âpre
aprés
Bague
bague

If strings sort to the same location on the first pass (as in the case of the first four strings), the secondary sort differentiates by diacritics. In this case, *a* and *A* sort the same, as do *â* and *Â*. After the second pass, the first four words are in this order: *acre*, *Acre*, *Âcre*, and *âcre*. There is no change to the remaining words on the list; any form of a string that begins with *ac* continues to sort before the strings that begin with any form of *ap* or *b*.

The last pass of the sort differentiates by case, which means that *âcre* moves ahead of *Âcre* and *bague* jumps ahead of *Bague*. The final results are:

acre
Acre
âcre
Âcre

âpre
aprés
bague
Bague

Although it is nice to know how multilevel collation works, the good news is that you don't really have to worry about the details. If you have a **localedef** that defines multilevel sorting, and a program that calls **setlocale( )** and **strcoll( )**, your program produces these results.

8.2.4 Searching versus Sorting

The fact that internationalized collation functions exist means you have to draw a distinction between searching and sorting. In the abstract, it is easy to remember that the two are different operations—a search compares two strings for equality, while a sort puts strings in a specific order. The two operations have been confused, however, because it was possible on ASCII-only systems to use functions like **strcmp( )** and **strncmp( )** to perform both tasks.

That no longer is the case. Since many code sets do not encode characters in a language's order, **strcmp( )** and **strncmp( )** are not suitable for international collation. However, they and their wide character counterparts (**wcscmp( )** and **wcsncmp( )**) are still the right functions to use if you need to compare two strings for equality. Before changing all **str[n]cmp( )** calls to use internationalized collation functions, analyze your code. If the purpose of a **str[n]cmp( )** call is an equality comparison, there is no need to change it.

8.2.5 Using Internationalized Sort Functions

Internationalized sort functions make it possible for a single program to collate data correctly for many languages. Here is an example using **strcoll( )**:

```
#include <stdio.h>
#include <locale.h>
#include <string.h>
#define SIZE 256

main() {
  int j, k;
```

```
/* The array "words" contains the strings to be sorted. */
unsigned char *words[SIZE], *temp;
. . .
(void)setlocale(LC_ALL, "");
/* Array-parsing logic omitted to simplify the example. */
. . .
/* use strcoll instead of strcmp for the comparison */
if (strcoll((const char *)words[j],
        (const char *)words[k]) < 0)
  j = -1;     /* quit */
else {        /* do the exchange */
  temp = words[j];
  words[j] = words[k];
  words[k] = temp;
  }
. . .
}
```

Although the **strcoll( )** call looks simple, it, together with the call to **setlocale( )**, makes this program capable of handling most collation requirements for single-byte data. Suppose you have this input:

à
laß
lassen
âpre
a
après
âpreté
llama
luna
être
lase
azur

Given typical locale definitions for Spanish, German, and the C locale, Table 8.2 shows the results the program produces by locale.

Table 8.2   Collation Results by Locale

Spanish	German	C
a	a	a
à	à	après
âpre	âpre	azur
après	après	lase
âpreté	âpreté	lassen
azur	azur	laß
être	être	llama
lase	lase	luna
lassen	laß	à
laß	lassen	âpre
luna	llama	âpreté
llama	luna	être

As Table 8.2 shows, the results can differ dramatically depending on the locale. First, consider the German and Spanish results. The Spanish results take into account the fact that in Spanish, *ll* sorts between *l* and *m*, so *llama* shows up after *luna*. German collation, on the other hand, has no special rule for *ll*, so *llama* sorts before *luna*.

That is not the only difference. Notice that *laß* comes before *lassen* in the German results, but the order is reversed in the Spanish list. German collation treats *ß* as if it were the two letters *ss*. Spanish, however, doesn't include *ß*, so the locale definition simply sorts the character by its encoded value.

Speaking of encoded values, that is exactly what the C locale uses, and that's why its order is so completely different from the other two results. It simply collates the characters according to their (in this case) Latin-1 encodings. That means, for example, *à* sorts after *luna* because *à*'s encoding is 0xe0, while *l*'s is 0x6c.

8.2.6   Collation Freedom of Choice

A side effect of locale-sensitive collation functions is that they give you much more control over the way data sorts. In the past, system-supplied sort functions generally gave two main options: use the ASCII collation order, in which case all uppercase letters sorted before all lowercase, or use a sort that ignored case.

Although these options met most English requirements, they weren't perfect. Most dictionaries ignore spaces or punctuation like apostrophes (') or hyphens (-) in collation, but computer sorts didn't leave them alone. This resulted in some differences between dictionary and computer orders. Consider these differences:

Dictionary Order	ASCII Order
cant	Cantonese
can't	Halloween
Cantonese	can't
halfback	cant
half-baked	half brother
half brother	half-baked
halfhearted	halfback
Halloween	halfhearted

It also is true that sorting rules vary by application. It is common for telephone directories to use collation rules that are quite different from a dictionary sort. Telephone book collation sometimes ignores parts of names, or sorts one substring as if it were another. American telephone books occasionally sort the string *Mac* as if it were *Mc*. Dutch phone books typically ignore lowercase prefixes so that names like *van der Meer* and *van der Bilt* sort with the *M*'s and *B*'s, respectively.

Since **localedef** source files give the ability to define the collation rules for a locale, it is possible to build locales that meet different users' needs. There is no need to force them all to use the few orders the system knows.

8.3   Parsing a Language

In working with text, there are many times when a program needs to break it down into recognizable chunks, or scan through it for certain patterns, or even add specific patterns to certain pieces. These jobs, and others like them, involve the ability to parse text intelligently. The routines which do these jobs include everything from regular expression (RE) parsers to help systems to word counters. Like most software, many had their English rules down pat, but often were befuddled when asked to be more worldly. This section covers these language-parsing topics:

- Regular expressions
- Character and word parsing
- Word processing tasks including capitalization, spelling checkers, hyphenation, and word expansion

8.3.1 Regular Expressions

Using REs is a common way to parse text. Fortunately, just as collation and character classification behavior has been expanded to accommodate international needs, so too have REs. This makes sense since many RE tasks involve sorting or pattern matching. The biggest changes over traditional ASCII-based REs involve the addition of three concepts and a lot of square brackets ([ ]).

First, the brackets. To avoid breaking code and scripts created under the old syntax, the additions to the RE syntax are only valid inside square brackets. Consider these expressions:

```
[=e=]
[[=e=]]
```

The first is valid for ASCII-Only REs. It matches e and = *(equals sign).* (The second equals sign here is redundant.) The second example follows the expanded, internationalized syntax. The extra set of brackets around the expression tells the RE parser to treat the enclosed characters as an expression rather than as individual characters to be matched. The expression matches all versions of a lowercase *e.* If your language were French, the expression might match *e, è, é, ê,* and *ë.*

Don't worry about the details just yet; the important thing to remember is that internationalized REs often come with bundles of brackets. So you might want to acquaint yourself with the location of the bracket keys on your keyboard. After expanding your touch-typing repertoire to include brackets, you are ready to tackle the functionality the brackets enclose. There are three main concepts that didn't exist in earlier versions of REs: *collating symbols, equivalence classes,* and *character classes.*

Collating Symbols

A *collating symbol* (sometimes called a *collating element*) is a character or group of characters that must be treated as a unit for collation purposes. In the past, collation functions worked only on individual single-byte characters. Such functions determined, for example, that *a* came before *b* which came before *c,* and so forth.

This works for ASCII or English-only systems, but not for languages that include multicharacter collating symbols. For example, Spanish collates the string *ch* between the letters *c* and *d.* Internationalized REs enclose collating symbols within *bracket-period* delimiters ([..]). This syntax distinguishes multi-character collating symbols from a list of the individual characters that make up the symbol. Table 8.3 shows several REs and what they match in a Spanish locale.

Table 8.3   Multi-Character Collating Symbols in Spanish REs

RE	Matches
`[ch]`	*c* or *h*
`[[.ch.]]`	the sequence *ch*
`[c[.ch.]]`	*c* or *ch*
`^[a-[.ch.]]`	any word beginning with *a, à, b, c, ch*
`^[a-c]`	any word beginning with *a, à, b, c*

Note the difference in the results of Table 8.3's last two examples. The final example does not match words that begin with *ch* because the collating symbol *ch* follows *c* in a Spanish sort. The next-to-last example does match such words, however, because the RE defines `[.ch.]` as the termination of the range.

Equivalence Classes

An *equivalence class* is a group of characters or collating symbols that sort to the same primary location. They are designed to handle multilevel sorting—that is, for languages like French that define groups of characters as sorting to the same primary location, and then having additional tie-breaking sort or sorts. In an RE, an *equivalence class expression* represents the set of collating elements in an equivalence class. *Bracket-equal* delimiters (`[==]`) enclose these expressions.

Suppose that *a, A, à, À, â,* and *Â* sort to the same primary location in the current locale and therefore make up an equivalence class. The RE `[[=a=]b]` is equivalent to `[aAàÀâÂb]`.

There is no requirement that you use one particular member of an equivalence class when writing REs that include the class. The example above takes the somewhat lazy way out because it uses the plain *a* to stand in for the class. But these:

```
[[=à=]b]
[[=Â=]b]
```

or expressions that use any other class member are acceptable, and indeed, equivalent, to `[[=a=]b]`.

Character Classes

The third and final major addition to RE syntax is a *character class expression*. Instead of listing a group or range of characters to be matched, these expressions list the name of a character class, such as **alpha** or **digit**. All characters that are part of the named class for the current locale return true for this type of RE. POSIX.2 and

XPG require compliant systems to support the standard classes **alnum, alpha, blank, cntrl, digit, graph, lower, print, punct, space, upper,** and **xdigit.**

Bracket-colon delimiters ([: :]) enclose character class expressions. For example, this RE matches all uppercase characters in the current locale:

```
[[:upper:]]
```

You probably need to rewrite existing scripts to use character class expressions. Consider these two ways of matching lowercase letters:

```
[a-z]
[[:lower:]]
```

The first may be the way your existing code does the job. Assuming your underlying sort functions have been internationalized, this example may work for languages like English, French, and German—that is, languages with alphabets that begin with *a* and end with *z*. It depends on your system's locale definitions. If your locales use mixed-case sorts (*aAáÁbBcC* . . .), the RE matches more than just lowercase letters.

While this example may work for some locales, it definitely doesn't for the Scandinavian languages, which have several letters after *z*. It also isn't adequate for languages that are not written with the Latin script, including languages like Greek or Russian.

The second example ([[:lower:]]) uses a character class to provide internationalized RE handling. Since it consults the current locale to determine which characters are lowercase, it handles any locale. Table 8.4 shows other changes you should make in REs to get internationalized behavior for character classes.

Table 8.4   Character Classes in REs

Old Syntax	New Syntax	Matches
[A-Z]	[[:upper:]]	Uppercase letters
[A-Z,a-z]	[[:alpha:]]	Alphabetic letters
[0-9]	[[:digit:]]	Decimal digits
[0-9,A-F,a-f]	[[:xdigit:]]	Hexadecimal digits

Character class expressions probably are the most useful I18N-related addition to RE syntax; they make it very easy to write one RE that covers much of the world. Of course, the standard classes don't meet all language needs, but it is possible to add new classes that do address those requirements.

8.3.2   Words and Other Vague Things

Another common task that includes language parsing knowledge is that of rec-ognizing units of text. Sometimes, the job involves units like words. You may need a word count, or to compare groups of words so you can eliminate duplicates. Other times, the units you are looking for may be more complex—something like para-graphs or bulleted lists. You may need to identify such structures so you can apply specific formatting rules.

Ironically, identifying complex units can be easier than picking out the simpler ones. Text formatting tools such as **troff** or Interleaf all have conventions for desig-nating units like paragraphs, tables, and lists. The conventions vary from tool to tool, but once you know how to designate a paragraph in **troff**, it is easy to pick out any paragraph from **troff** source.

Picking out words or even characters is a completely different matter. Take the simpler of the two: characters. You learned in Chapter 4 that characters and bytes are two different things, and Chapter 6 described data types for handling more-than-single-byte characters. Knowing the number of bytes in a text file doesn't mean you know how many characters it holds. Generally, you need to know the language and the code set of the text to count characters accurately. Languages such as Japanese and Chinese require at least two bytes per ideograph, and the UCS forms of ISO 10646 use more than one byte for even the English letters A–Z and a–z.

ISO C provides several ways to find individual characters. **mblen( )** returns the number of bytes in a character. Once you know how many bytes there are, you can easily advance to the next character in a data stream. An alternative to **mblen( )** is to use **mbtowc( )** or **mbstowcs( )**. These two functions convert multibyte data to **wchar_t** form. Each wide character then equals one character. (See Chapter 6 for more details on these functions.)

While international characters are much more varied than was true in the days of ASCII-only text, character boundaries are much easier to find than word bound-aries. At least there are standard functions for characters. There is no such support for words.

Word recognition can require considerable sophistication. While it is easy for languages that use spaces to delimit words (including those that use Latin, Cyrillic, and Greek scripts), it is potentially CPU-boggling for languages that don't (Japanese, Chinese, Thai, and others). Quick-and-dirty solutions exist, but they only find some boundaries. A Japanese quick-and-dirty routine might define these as word boundaries:

- Spaces or other punctuation. Although spaces are relatively rare in Japanese text, they may separate English-based words. In addition, punctuation characters like commas, quotes, and periods occur only at word boundaries. Note that such punctuation may be single-byte versions familiar in ASCII, or double-byte Japanese versions.

- A single-byte character followed by a multiple-byte character. For example, a kana followed by a Kanji occurs only at a word boundary.
- A Kanji character followed by any ASCII character.

These limited rules find some words, but they can not correctly count the number of words in a string. Words often consist of multiple ideographs or of a combination of phonetic and ideographic characters, so there is no simple way to determine where one word ends and another begins. Consider this Japanese sentence:

スキーが紀元前2500年頃に存在したのは、獣を追う生活に迫られたからです。

The simple rules find only four words in this sentence—the string before *2500*, the number itself, the string after *2500* to the Japanese comma, and the remainder of the string. Here are the four "words" and the two punctuation characters:

1）スキーが紀元前
2）2500
3）年頃に存在したのは
4）、
5）獣を追う生活に迫られたからです
6）。

However, this sentence actually contains 17 words and the two punctuation characters. Here is a breakdown of the words and punctuation:

1）	スキー	11）	獣
2）	が	12）	を
3）	紀元前	13）	追う
4）	2500	14）	生活
5）	年	15）	に
6）	頃	16）	迫られた
7）	に	17）	から
8）	存在した	18）	です
9）	のは	19）	。
10）	、		

The only way to count words accurately in many languages is to use a dictionary lookup together with a context analyzer. Even then you have to be careful to avoid identifying, say, a compound word as two separate words. While it certainly is possible to write the appropriate software—if people can recognize word boundaries, software can be taught to do so as well—it involves considerably more sophistication than exists in standard utilities like **wc** (word count).

8.3.3 Processing Words

Having the ability to recognize words is fine, but you generally want to *do* something with them once you find them. Common tasks include:

- Capitalization
- Spell checking
- Hyphenation and justification
- Substitution and expansion

The following briefly describes the internationalization implications associated with each.

Capitalization

Capitalizing words involves more than simply converting case of characters. If that was all it were, you could simply call functions like **toupper( )** or **towupper( )** and be done with the job. But suppose you want to capitalize the first character In Every Word In A String Like This. First, you need to find word boundaries, as discussed in the section Words and Other Vague Things. Once you find them, you must apply language-specific rules to do the job correctly.

For some languages, capitalization is very easy. While it is difficult to *find* the beginning of a word in, say, Japanese or Chinese, the ideographic and phonetic characters in these languages' writing systems have no case. All you have to do is scan for words in Latin-based or other alphabetic scripts and convert the first character with a simple **to[w]upper( )** call.

In languages that use Latin scripts, it generally is simple to find word boundaries—just look for white-space characters—but there may be other rules that complicate capitalization. When capitalizing Dutch words, you must treat the *ij* ligature as a unit. The correct capitalization of the word *ijs* (ice), for example, is *IJs*, not *Ijs*.

As you already have learned, standard collation facilities exist for handling multicharacter collating symbols like the Spanish *ch*. However, there presently is no support for multicharacter classification, so you would need to write your own code

to handle such tasks. In the case of Dutch *ij*, an obvious way to do this is to capitalize the first letter in a word, and then check to see if it is *I*. If it is, check the next letter. If it is *j*, convert it to uppercase; otherwise, do nothing.

Spelling Checkers

Spelling checkers usually need extensive rewriting to meet international needs.
That is because most rely on hard-coded algorithmic rules for forming plurals, varying tenses, and other forms of words. Such rules are highly language-specific.

Consider rules for forming plurals. The plural form of most English nouns
includes a terminating *s*, (*car, cars; house, houses*), but nouns that end with *o, s, x, z,*
or *sh* take *es* in the plural form (*potato, potatoes; box, boxes*), and some that end
with *y* change to *ies* (*directory, directories*). There are other aspects of plural-
forming rules for English, but now consider French rules. Like English, many plural
nouns take a terminating *s*, and, like English, there are exceptions to the rule. However, the French exceptions are different from those for English. Most nouns that
end in *au, eau,* or *eu* take a terminating *x* (*jeu, jeux*), while most that end in *al*
change to *aux* (*cheval, chevaux*). Again, there are more rules for forming plurals,
but this gives you some idea of how language-specific this task is and why spelling
checkers that use algorithms for word forms typically are tied tightly to a single language. Therefore, adding support for new languages involves removing hard-coded
assumptions about the currently supported language, and writing the program to find
locale-specific versions of routines. Note that there are no standards for such functions.

Other changes are necessary in order for a spelling checker to support multiple
languages. Naturally, the checker must be eight-bit clean before it can hope to go
beyond ASCII and English. In addition, before a checker can verify a word's
spelling, it has to be able to find the word. If the checker assumes a word is always
a space-delimited string, that assumption must be replaced with calls to language-
appropriate routines. Since no standard routines for finding word boundaries exist,
you would have to write such routines yourself.

Hyphenation and Justification

Algorithms that hyphenate and justify text are extremely language-dependent.
Some languages only allow breaks at word boundaries. Others permit breaks at syl-
lables, and others are even more liberal, allowing breaks at nearly any character.
The following illustrates these methods on some sentences from this chapter:

Word boundaries only:

```
Spelling checkers usually need extensive rewriting to
meet international needs. That is because most rely on
hard-coded algorithmic rules for forming plurals, varying
tenses, and other forms of words. Such rules are highly
language-specific.
```

Breaks at syllables:

```
Spelling checkers usually need extensive re-
writing to meet international needs. That is be-
cause most rely on hard-coded algorithmic rules
for forming plurals, varying tenses, and other
forms of words. Such rules are highly language-
specific.
```

Almost anywhere:

```
Spelling checkers usually need extensive rewr
iting to meet international needs. That is be
cause most rely on hard-coded algorithmic rul
es for forming plurals, varying tenses, and o
ther forms of words. Such rules are highly la
nguage-specific.
```

After learning general rules like whether a language allows breaks within words, hyphenation and justification algorithms need to learn the details. Languages that allow breaks at syllable boundaries (including most languages that use Latin scripts) are complex because the letter combinations that constitute syllables differ from language-to-language. There may be other conventions to learn, such as spelling changes. In German, the hyphenated forms of *Zucker* and *backen* are *Zuk-ker* and *bak-ken*, respectively. Before a software package can hyphenate, say, French, English, and Spanish, it needs detailed information about each language.

Even languages that have simple rules need special care. You can break Japanese and Chinese words anywhere, but it is not permissible to break a line such that punctuation like comma, period, or close quotes are the first character on the new line. In addition, you can't break Japanese or Chinese characters. Since ideographs consume at least two bytes, a justification algorithm that chops text at, say, 80-byte boundaries might truncate a multibyte character. To avoid this, the algorithm must use a function like **mblen( )** to find—and justify on—character boundaries only.

Like the issue of finding word boundaries, no standard routines exist for hyphenation or justification. You're on your own.

Word Expansion

One nice feature of some modern help systems is the ability to recognize several forms of a given word or key phrase. An older system might give help on, say, link operations if and only if a user enters the specific string **link**. Newer systems accept multiple versions of the string—say, **links, linking, linked**—and find the correct help entry. In addition to handling letters appended to the end of a word, the help system may also support some grammatical substitutions. For example, the system may be able to match **director***ies* with **director***y*.

All this functionality is very nice, but it usually is geared toward English word endings and grammar, and the built-in substitutions obviously are wrong for other languages. Imagine a help system adding an English *ed* or *ing* to the end of a French verb. French words take their own set of endings, as this partial example of *effacer* (to delete) shows:

> efface*e*
> efface*s*
> effaç*ons*
> efface*z*
> effac*ent*

To internationalize an application that processes forms of a word, you must isolate the language-specific rules and endings so that you can load the appropriate information at program run time. There are no standards for this behavior, but a logical approach is for the software to choose rules and data based on the current locale. Chapter 9 describes methods for isolating and accessing catalogs of language-specific text.

8.4   Date and Time Formatting

Sorting, word parsing, character classification, and other topics covered so far in this chapter are primarily language-dependent. But there is other data that is—or should be—influenced primarily by the country or territory in which it is presented. Date and time values are one such set of data.

8.4.1 Worlds Beyond ctime

On an uninternationalized system, when programs need to produce a formatted date or time string, it is most common to use the **ctime( )** or **asctime( )** functions. **ctime( )** presents information like this:

```
Tue Jul 13 13:48:12 EDT 1993
```

English weekday and month names are hard-coded into the function, and the information is presented in a somewhat odd, but essentially American format:

weekday month day time time_zone year

(It is odd for two reasons: it uses a 24-hour clock, while Americans usually are only comfortable with the 12-hour system, and the *year* value appears at the end instead of next to the *day*.)

The world needs much more variety than the old functions were ever designed to handle. Chapter 2 describes the variety in detail. Briefly, there are differing rules and text for (among others):

1. The names of weekdays and months
2. The order in which data should be presented (*month-day-year, year-month-day, day-month-year*)
3. Field separators (dashes, dots, slashes, colons, etc.)
4. Whether to use a 12- or 24-hour clock
5. The difference between time zones—it is not always one hour
6. The number of the current year
7. The existence of daylight savings time, and if it does exist, the start and end dates
8. The first day of the week (for example, Sunday vs. Monday)
9. The day on which a new year begins
10. The number of days in a year or month, or the number of months in a year

ISO C includes the function **strftime( )** and XPG4 provides the wide character equivalent **wcsftime( )** to handle the first six issues listed above. Actually, that is a bit of an over-simplification. **strftime( )** and **wcsftime( )** have some facilities for handling year-numbering systems other than the Gregorian, but those facilities don't accommodate every possibility. But if the functions don't quite know every way to number years, they do understand that locales each have their own names for months and weekdays, and that there are many different ways to format dates and times.

In addition, **strftime( )/wcsftime( )** use information from the **TZ** (time zone) environment variable to determine what time it is in the current time zone, and when (if at all) daylight savings time begins and ends.

Although **strftime( )/wcsftime( )** can't handle all the date and time issues mentioned above, they are worlds ahead of **ctime( )** and **asctime( )**. You should use the newer functions in place of the old, uninternationalized calls. However, be aware that they take different parameters than do the older functions, so replacing the old with the new takes some thought. They have this format:

```
#include <time.h>
size_t strftime (char *s, size_t maxsize,
     const char *format, const struct tm *timeptr);


#include <wchar.h>
size_t wcsftime (wchar_t *wcs, size_t maxsize,
     const char *format, const struct tm *timeptr);
```

strftime( ) places characters into the array that *s* points to in the format specified by *format*. For **wcsftime( )**, characters are placed into the array that *wcs* points to. No more than *maxsize* bytes or wide character codes can be placed in the arrays. The *format* string is where **strftime( )/wcsftime( )** get their I18N power, because the string can include a wide variety of locale-sensitive field specifiers. Consider this sample *format*:

```
%A, %d %B %Y %T
```

Here is how to decipher *format*:

Specifier	Description
%A	full weekday name (locale-specific version of *Sunday* to *Saturday*)
%d	day of the month [0-31]
%B	full month name (locale-specific version of *January* to *December*)
%Y	Gregorian year including century
%T	24-hour time as hour:minute:second

With this one format, **strftime( )** can produce output appropriate to many locales, as Table 8.5 shows.

Table 8.5   strftime( ) Output in Different Locales

strftime output	Locale
mercredi, 10 août 1994 14:30:15	French
Mittwoch, 10 August 1994 14:30:15	German
Τετάρτη, 10 Αύγουστος 1994 14:30:15	Greek
quarta-feira, 10 agosto 1994 14:30:15	Portuguese

strftime( ) and **wcsftime( )** use the current value of LC_TIME to decide which output to produce. The functions also accept a much longer list of field specifiers than those shown here. See your system's **date** or **strftime( )** man pages or XPG4 for the full list of the available field specifiers.

The most variable part of **strftime( )/wcsftime( )** is *format*. Once you have defined that—sometimes in your locale definition, but always (if you are writing good, internationalized code) in a separate file instead of having hard-coded it in—using the call is straightforward. For example:

```
#include <locale.h>
#include <langinfo.h>
#include <time.h>
. . .
main ( ) {
  char *dtbuf[MAXSIZE];
  time_t clock;
  struct tm *timeptr;

  (void)setlocale(LC_ALL, "");
  clock = time ((long*)NULL);
  timeptr = localtime (&clock);

  strftime(dtbuf, MAXSIZE, nl_langinfo(D_T_FMT), timeptr);
  printf("%s\n", dtbuf);
}
```

This example sets up the appropriate time structures and then calls **setlocale( )** to establish the current locale. **strftime( )** calls **nl_langinfo( )** to get the date-and-time format (D_T_FMT) appropriate for this locale and places the appropriately formatted date and time string in dtbuf.

While **strftime( )** and **wcsftime( )** convert the internal date and time value into a string, there is another function called **strptime( )** which does the reverse—it converts a date/time string to the form used for internal values. It has this syntax:

#include <time.h>
char *strptime (const char **buf***, const char ****format***, struct tm ****tm***);**

strptime( ) uses the format specified by *format* to convert the character string that *buf* points to into values that are stored in the **tm** structure pointed to by *tm*. The *format* may include the same field specifiers as in calls to **strftime( )** and **wcsftime( )**.

8.4.2 Date and Time Designs

As with so many other aspects of internationalizing software, always remember that dates and times are variable; their formats and contents aren't chiseled in stone. The previous section shows a small amount of the possible variety, and Chapter 2 gives even more possibilities. To handle this variety, you must:

- Remove hard-coded assumptions about items such as formats, weekday and month names, and the start and end of daylight savings time.
- Obtain formats and strings from locale definitions.
- Use functions like **strftime( )** rather than **ctime( )** or **asctime( )** to print date and time strings.

Software that follows these guidelines can easily handle many international date and time conventions. However, there are parts of the puzzle for which there are no standard solutions. If you want to address these needs, you must write the code yourself.

Take, for example, the question of the first day of the week. Standard software "knows" it is Sunday—or dimanche or søntag or whatever that day is called in the current locale. However, in many parts of the world, Monday is considered the first day in the week. This means people expect the calendar to be arranged like the example on the right rather than the one on the left:

```
      July 1993                        July 1993
 Su Mo Tu We Th Fr Sa           Mo Tu We Th Fr Sa Su
              1  2  3                       1  2  3  4
  4  5  6  7  8  9 10            5  6  7  8  9 10 11
 11 12 13 14 15 16 17           12 13 14 15 16 17 18
 18 19 20 21 22 23 24           19 20 21 22 23 24 25
 25 26 27 28 29 30 31           26 27 28 29 30 31
```
Sunday-First Calendar   **Monday-First Calendar**

An average calendar-printing routine might print the Sunday-Saturday abbreviation headings, determine what weekday a month begins on (for instance, that the 1st in this example falls on a Thursday), blank-fill unused spaces in the first week, and then print the numbers. It would issue a carriage return after printing any Saturday's number.

Few changes are necessary to produce a Monday-first calendar. The headings code must print the Monday-equivalent abbreviation string through the Sunday string. Blank-filling is from the Monday equivalent to the first day of the month. A carriage return comes not after printing a Saturday's number, but a Sunday's.

Just as you must write code if you want the first day of the week to be something other than Sunday, you also need to supply routines to handle many non-Gregorian calendars. **strftime( )** supports calendars that use a different year-counting system but otherwise match the Gregorian model. For example, Japan and the ROC (Taiwan) both number years based on local events—in Japan, the number of years the current emperor has been reigning; in the ROC, the number of years since the Republic of China was founded—but they otherwise use the Gregorian system of 12 months and 365 (or 366) days. **strftime( )** handles both these variations. However, it does not support calendars like the Moslem or Hebrew systems that have fewer days, more months, or years that start on something other than January 1.

8.5   Numeric and Monetary Information

Just as date and time formatting depend on the rules or customs of a particular country, so too do numeric and monetary formatting. The variable parts of these quantities include:

- The radix character. This is the character that separates whole and decimal quantities. Uninternationalized programs usually use only the period (.), but in many countries, it is more common to use a comma (,) or other character.
- The thousands separator. This is the character that separates groups of thousands. In some countries, it is a comma (e.g., 1,000), while in others, it is a period (1.000).
- The local and international currency symbols and the placement of those symbols. Local symbols are what people use in their own country for monetary amounts. Examples include $, £, ¥, and NT$ (dollar, pound, yen, and New Taiwan dollar, respectively). The international currency symbol is a three-letter string as defined in ISO 4217 (Codes for the Representation of Currencies and Funds). Examples include:

Symbol	Designates
FRF	French franc
JPY	Japanese yen
SEK	Swedish krona
USD	U.S. dollar

Currency symbols may appear at the beginning of a quantity, at the end, or somewhere in the middle. Portugal uses its currency symbol as the radix character (1.234$50).

- The symbols for positive and negative quantities and the rules for formatting such quantities.
- Grouping rules. Grouping may be by thousands (123,456,789), ten thousands (1,2345,6789), or something else.
- Fractional digits. This controls the number of digits that appear in a fractional monetary amount. Many countries use two ($12.34), but there are other conventions as well. Japan has no fractional monetary amounts (¥1234).

Standard I/O functions like the **printf( )** and **scanf( )** families accept input and produce output of numeric quantities using locale-specific rules. The setting that LC_NUMERIC has when a program runs determines how quantities are formatted.

The following example program demonstrates how the I/O functions work when you add a simple **setlocale( )** call to your code. Because all examples in this book should show good internationalized coding practices, this program also includes calls like **catopen( )** and **catgets( )** that are part of a messaging system. See Chapter 9 for details on those calls. Briefly, the calls make the program able to produce messages in a variety of languages.

```
/* This program finds the circumference and area of a
 * circle given a user-supplied radius. Formatting of
 * floating point numbers on input and output depends
 * on the locale.
 */
#include <stdio.h>
#include <locale.h>
#include <nl_types.h>
#include "circles.msg"

#define PI 3.14159
```

```
int main(void) {
  float cir, radius, area;
  nl_catd catd;

  (void)setlocale(LC_ALL, "");
  catd = catopen("circles.cat", NL_CAT_LOCALE);

  printf (catgets(catd, SET_1, INPUT,
    "Enter the circle's radius in inches: "));
  scanf ("%f", &radius);
  cir = 2*PI*radius;
  area = PI*(radius*radius);

  printf (catgets(catd, SET_1, CIRC,
    "The circle's circumference is %6.3f inches\n"), cir);
  printf (catgets(catd, SET_1, RAD,
    "Its area is %6.3f inches\n"), area);
  catclose(catd);
}
```

Here is a sample run of the program under the C locale:

```
Enter the circle's radius in inches: 3.5
The circle's circumference is 21.991 inches
Its area is 38.484 inches
```

Here is what the program produces if you use a typical French locale:

```
Entrez le rayon du cercle dans centimètres: 3,5
La circonference du cercle est 21,991 cm
Sa surface est 38,484 cm
```

Notice that in the first sample run, the input and output values include a period as the radix character, while in the second, they include a comma. Also notice the difference in units of measure. Americans usually use the imperial system (inches, feet, yards), while the French use the metric system (centimeters, meters). The formulas for computing circumference and area remain constant regardless of units of measure, so it is easy to accommodate multiple locales' measurement preferences.

When run in the C locale, it asks for input in inches and produces output in them. When run in a French locale, the program uses centimeters.

Most programs need few changes to produce internationalized numeric quantities. As long as you use standard functions like **printf( )** and **scanf( )** for formatting, a **setlocale( )** call at the beginning of the program is all you need to add. However, if you are using hard-coded format strings for numeric *or* monetary amounts, you must remove these strings and look for the proper formats and strings in locale tables.

Although almost no standard functions use the information associated with the LC_MONETARY category, XPG4 includes **strfmon( )** for converting a monetary value to a string. The function has this syntax:

#include <monetary.h>

size_t strfmon (char *s, size_t *maxsize***, const char ****format***);**

strfmon( ) places characters into the array that *s* points to in the format specified by *format*. No more than *maxsize* bytes are placed in the array. **strfmon( )** uses the current value of LC_MONETARY to determine information including the monetary radix character, the grouping separator, currency symbols, and formats. See your system's **strfmon( )** man page or XPG4 for details.

8.5.1 Number Conversion Functions

In addition to numeric formatting capabilities in **printf( )** and **scanf( )** functions, there also are functions for converting strings to various numeric formats. Table 8.6 shows the functions.

Table 8.6   Number Conversion Functions

char-Based	wchar_t-Based	Purpose
strtod	wcstod	Convert to **double**
strtol	wcstol	Convert to **long int**
strtoul	wcstoul	Convert to **unsigned long int**

<stdlib.h> contains declarations for the **char**-based functions, while **<wchar.h>** contains the XPG4-defined **wchar_t** versions. Both **strtod( )** and **wcstod( )** use locale information to determine the radix character in the current locale. See these functions' man pages for more details.

8.6   Locale-Based Internationalization

Making software suitable for processing international text involves removing culture- or code-set-specific logic from programs and replacing it with international-ized functions. Standard internationalized functions use locales to determine at run time the way to process the data for such tasks as character classification, collation, date/time handling, and numeric/monetary formatting. While there aren't standard routines for all language- or culture-specific operations (for example, hyphenation, word expansion, some calendar systems), existing standard functions do cover many international needs. Where they exist, use the functions. Be aware, however, that while locales provide freedoms that leave ASCII-only or single-language systems tongue-tied, they do have some significant limitations.

* **Locales are independent of data.** Locales are said to apply globally to a pro-cess and its subprocesses; they are not tied to data. This means there is no way to determine the locale under which data was created. This is in part because UNIX text files traditionally have been typeless streams of bytes that contain no identification information. The I18N support makes no changes to data; it only changes the way data is interpreted.

   Since the system has no way of knowing what locale you had set when you created a file, it won't prevent you from processing that data in inappropriate ways. Suppose LANG was set to a German locale when you created file **foo**. Now suppose you reset LANG to a Japanese locale and then **grep** for something in **foo**. Because locales are global, **grep** uses Japanese rules on the German data in the file. There is nothing to prevent you from doing this, or even to warn you that this probably isn't what you intend.

   You might assume this is not a problem because you know you won't change between German and Japanese locales. But what about other users? They may use other locales, and be unaware of your environment. When other users access your file there is nothing to indicate when locales don't match—except perhaps the results themselves.

* **Multilingual support.** The global locale model allows only one locale to be in use at a time. This creates more problems than just processing a file using the wrong locale. It means there is no way to mix languages in a file and have the system recognize that the mixture exists. Suppose you have French, Spanish, and Italian text in a single file. The system interprets it as if it were in the cur-rent locale, which could be one of the three languages, or something entirely different. There is no way to apply French rules to the French section while simultaneously applying Spanish and Italian rules to the other sections.

Windowing systems face related problems with multilingual support. It is quite likely that a single window manager program could be required to handle windows running several different locales. Such multilingual support is beyond the ability of the global locale model.

- **Locale names and contents.** The **localedef** source file format in POSIX.2 is adding order to what used to be a chaos of locale-specific information. But while the format of locale-related information is becoming more predictable, there are no standards for the contents of locales. Standard locales do not exist for most countries, so vendors provide their own (probably unique) versions of locales. Even for the countries that do have standard locales (including Denmark and Japan), the standards are relatively new, so nonstandard definitions are much more common in the marketplace.

  Another problem with locales is the lack of standard naming conventions. Names differ among system providers, making it difficult to identify versions of the "same" locale.

  Efforts were under way when this book was written to standardize or register locale names and contents. If such efforts are successful, locale management will be much simpler.

Many locale model limitations become most apparent when you distribute computing across multiple nodes, or when you want to process multilingual text. See Chapter 12 for detailed discussions of these issues and potential ways to address them.

Program Messages   9

One of the most obvious needs an internationalized system must fill is that of allowing a user to interact with the computer in his or her own language. This means it must be possible to supply program messages in a variety of languages, because while you may want to see Chinese messages when running a given software product, your colleague may prefer that the package produce Spanish, and another user may want French.

However, uninternationalized code typically can produce messages in only one language because the messages are hard-coded into the program logic. It is most common for that language to be English—or what passes for English—because so much software originates in or is designed for English-speaking users. However, English hasn't cornered the market on program text. There are many software packages that "speak" only Japanese, French, Thai, Arabic, or some other single language.

Market requirements demand that internationalized software do better. This chapter describes the changes necessary to make that possible. It covers:

- Single-language software
- Messaging systems and techniques for using them
- Message catalogs
- Default messages
- Translation issues
- Handling yes/no queries in programs

9.1   Single-Language Software

When computers appear in movies or television shows, the common images are
of large machines with lights flashing and tape drives whirring furiously. Such
systems always seem to be isolated somewhere doing "important things" like
crunching numbers. They are seldom seen interacting with users.

While there certainly are number-crunching behemoths, most computing tasks
consist of mundane input and output operations. A user feeds information into the
system and gets back a result. Think of airline ticket agents using a reservation system. Or of a bank customer getting cash from an automatic teller machine. Or of a
would-be author using a word processing package. In all these cases, the emphasis
is on *interacting* with the computer, rather than having it sit in splendid isolation
working on differential equations.

In order for programs to interact with users, they must produce human-readable
instructions or output. An automatic bank teller may display instructions like these:

```
Please choose a transaction:
Withdrawal from checking
Withdrawal from savings
Transfer from checking to savings
Transfer from savings to checking
Balance inquiry
Other
```

Once the customer chooses an option, the software displays text appropriate to
that choice. The textual interaction continues throughout the transaction, finishing
up with something like:

```
Thank you for using our automatic teller
Please take your card and receipt
```

Routine tasks like these are the stuff of which millions of lines of software are
made. Millions of uninternationalized lines.

The code is uninternationalized because it almost always hard codes in any text
the user will see and be expected to respond to. That means the program can
"speak" only one language—the one that's in the I/O statements. However, imagine
how helpful it would be if the program could handle a group. An automatic teller
that could interact with users in the language of their choice would be extremely
helpful in airports, hotels, and conference centers. Before that's possible, however,
software has to change. Consider this simple example:

```
/* Given user-supplied test scores, this English-only
 * program computes and reports the average. Error
 * checking is omitted to simplify the example.
 */
#include <stdio.h>
#define MAX_ANS 100

main () {

  int i, num, grade, total;
  float average;
  char answer;

  printf("How many tests? ");
  scanf ("%d", &num); fflush (stdin);
  do {
    total = 0; printf ("\n");
    for (i=0; i<num; i++) {
      printf("Enter test score number %d: ", (i+1));
      scanf ("%d", &grade); fflush (stdin);
      total += grade;
    }

    average = total/num;
    printf ("\nAverage test score: %4.1f\n", average);

    printf("Again? ");
    fgets(&answer, MAX_ANS, stdin);
  }
  while ((answer == 'y') || (answer == 'Y'));
}
```

The **printf( )** statements, which are about as common in C programs as curly brackets, feature English words between the double quotes, while the **do-while** condition understands the English abbreviation for *yes* (*y* or *Y*). Therefore, this program routine is only suitable for English-speaking users.

As covered in Chapter 3, when first faced with the need for single-language software to speak another language, it is typical to localize (or customize) the affected statements. To write a localized German version of this routine, you would make these changes:

Original: `printf("How many tests? ");`
Revision: `printf("Wieviele Pruefungen?");`
Original: `printf("Enter test score number %d: ", (i+1));`
Revision: `printf`
`("Pruefungsergebnis Nummer %d eingeben: ", (i+1));`
Original: `printf ("\nAverage test score: %4.1f\n", average);`
Revision: `printf ("\nDurchschnittliches Pruefungsergebnis:`
`%4.1f\n", average);`
Original: `printf("Again? ");`
Revision: `printf("Noch einmal? ");`
Original: `while ((answer == 'y') || (answer == 'Y'));`
Revision: `while ((answer == 'j') || (answer == 'J'));`

However, customizing programs creates more problems than it solves. (Again, see Chapter 3 for the details.) The correct solution is to make it possible for a single program to interact with users in their choice of languages. To make such requested diversity a programmed reality, you must remove text from the program and fetch it at run time. The most common way to do this is to use a *messaging system*.

9.2 Messaging Systems

Messaging systems consist of routines for creating, storing, accessing, and updating user-visible program text in a variety of languages. Instead of hard-coding the text into the program, it is stored in a separate message catalog. You then can translate the text into the languages of your choice.

The result is multiple versions of the messages for a given program—one version per language and code set combination. There might be, for example, French, German, Japanese AJEC, Japanese SJIS, Spanish, and American English message catalogs for a program. The program then can interact with a user in any of these languages/encodings. Adding new languages is as easy as supplying a new catalog; you don't have to change the program code.

Although there are a variety of messaging systems in use, the most commonly used one on UNIX-like systems is the collection of interfaces defined in the X/Open Portability Guide (XPG).

9.2.1 Basic Messaging Calls

The XPG messaging system consists of three basic calls for use in application programs:

- **catopen( )** for opening a version of a named message catalog as determined by the current locale,
- **catgets( )** for retrieving a specific message string from that catalog, and
- **catclose( )** for closing the named catalog.

For most implementations, **catopen( )**, like the standard **open( )** call, opens a particular file. The file just happens to be a message catalog. The function has this syntax:

#include <nl_types.h>
nl_catd catopen(const char *name, int oflag);

The function attempts to open the locale-appropriate version of the *name* catalog. It decides which version to look for based on the value of the current locale. If, for example, LC_MESSAGES is set to a Korean locale, **catopen( )** searches for the Korean language version of the *name* catalog. (Note that LC_MESSAGES does not exist prior to XPG4; earlier versions of XPG depend only on the value of LANG.) While the locale environment variables tell **catopen( )** what it should look for, another variable called NLSPATH tells the function where in the directory structure it should look.

If **catopen( )** successfully finds and opens the catalog, it returns a message catalog descriptor that then gets used in later calls to **catgets( )** and **catclose( )**. (**catopen( )** also may return one of several error values. See your system's man page for details.) In many implementations, **catopen( )** does no file type checking, and so will attempt to open a directory if that is the name it gets. You therefore need to be careful to supply a real file name.

The *oflag* parameter designates whether the program uses XPG4 or pre-XPG4 semantics. If *oflag* is set to 0 (zero), the messaging call follows pre-XPG4 behavior and only checks the value of LANG. If *oflag* is set to NL_CAT_LOCALE, **catopen( )** follows XPG4 and later semantics and first checks the value of LC_MESSAGES. If LC_MESSAGES is not set, **catopen( )** checks LANG. Examples in this chapter use the newer XPG4 value.

Just as **catopen( )** closely mimics the already familiar system call **open( )**, **catclose( )** also is very similar to the **close( )** call. It has this syntax:

#include <nl_types.h>
int catclose(nl_catd catd);

catclose( ) closes the catalog that *catd* identifies. In some sense, this call is optional.

If you omit it, the system closes all catalogs when your program terminates. However, it is best to close catalogs explicitly when you no longer need them because it helps free up potentially scarce system resources.

Most internationalized programs only contain one call per catalog to **catopen( )** and **catclose( )**. This is not the case with **catgets( )**. The real workhorse of the XPG messaging system, it retrieves individual program messages. It has this syntax:

#include <nl_types.h>
char *catgets(nl_catd *catd,* **int** *set_id,* **int** *msg_id,* **const char** *s);

where:

- *catd* is the catalog descriptor that **catopen( )** returned.
- *set_id* identifies a set within the catalog from which the string should be retrieved. *set_id* is an integer, but many implementations allow you to use a mnemonic label in its place.
- *msg_id* is an integer that defines which message within the specified set should be retrieved. As with *set_id*, many implementations allow a mnemonic label to stand in for *msg_id*'s integer value.
- *s* is the default string (or a pointer to that string) that is used if the **catopen( )** call failed, or if *msg_id* doesn't exist in the catalog.

Here is a very simple example that shows how to use the messaging calls. The example assumes the message to be retrieved is message 10 in set 1.

```
#include <stdio.h>
#include <locale.h>
#include <nl_types.h>

main() {
  nl_catd catd;
  /* set the program's locale and open the appropriate
   * language message catalog */
  (void)setlocale(LC_ALL, "");
  catd = catopen("hello.cat", NL_CAT_LOCALE);

  /* Retrieve and print the message. The default text
   * is included in case the message is unavailable.
   */
  printf(catgets(catd, 1, 10, "hello, world\n"));
  catclose(catd);
}
```

After establishing the current locale, **catopen( )** uses that locale to determine which version of the message catalog `hello.cat` to attempt to open. If **catopen( )** is successful, **catgets( )** retrieves message number 10 and returns a pointer to the string to **printf( )**, which then prints it. If **catopen( )** fails, or if message 10 does not exist, **printf( )** prints the default string. If you run this program in a French locale and there are no errors, the output is:

```
bonjour, le monde
```

If the French text is not available at run time, the output is:

```
hello, world
```

There are several reasons why translated message text may be unavailable at run time. See Unavailable Catalogs later in this chapter for details.

9.2.2   Mnemonic Labels for Message Identifiers

For many developers, **catgets**' *msg_id* and *set_id* parameters are the most annoying aspect of the XPG messaging system. The parameters must be integers, but the explicit integers are just (to a programmer) meaningless numbers. **catgets( )** needs the numbers so it can find the right set and fetch the right message, but there is no good way for humans to assign or remember them.

A common solution in many implementations is to use mnemonic labels for *set_id* or *msg_id* rather than integers. The labels (for example, FILE_NOT_FOUND) take the place of the integer in the **catgets( )** call. **#define**s associate a mnemonic *set_id* or *msg_id* with an integer. Consider the uninternationalized example program from earlier in this chapter. You could create a file called **test_avg.h** that includes the following:

```
#define SET_1        1
#define HOW_MANY     1
#define INPUT        2
#define OUTPUT       3
#define AGAIN        4
```

Here is the internationalized version of that program. It demonstrates how to use these labels.

```
/* Given user-supplied test scores, this program computes
 * and reports the average. This internationalized
 * program uses message catalogs, so it can handle I/O
 * in a variety of languages.
 * Error checking is omitted to simplify the example.
 */
#include <stdio.h>
#include <locale.h>     /* setlocale declaration */
#include <nl_types.h>   /* messaging calls */
#include <langinfo.h>   /* locale-specific data */
#include "test_avg.h"   /* labels file */
#define MAX_ANS 100

main () {

    int i, num, grade, total;
    float average;
    char answer[10], localyes[10], *yes_str;
    nl_catd catd;

    /* set the program's locale and open the appropriate
     * message catalog */
    (void)setlocale(LC_ALL, "");
    catd = catopen("test_avg.cat", NL_CAT_LOCALE);

    /* get the locale-appropriate version of "yes"
     * and copy to local storage
     */
    yes_str = nl_langinfo(YESSTR);
    strcpy(localyes, yes_str);

    printf(catgets(catd, SET_1, HOW_MANY,
        "How many tests? "));
    scanf ("%d", &num); fflush (stdin);
```

```
    do {
      total = 0; printf ("\n");
      for (i=0; i<num; i++) {
        printf(catgets(catd, SET_1, INPUT,
               "Enter test score number %d: "), (i+1));
        scanf ("%d", &grade); fflush (stdin);
        total += grade;
      }

      average = total/num;
      printf(catgets(catd, SET_1, OUTPUT,
             "\nAverage test score: %4.1f\n"), average);

      printf(catgets(catd, SET_1, AGAIN, "Again? "));
      fgets(&answer, MAX_ANS, stdin);
    } /* end do */
    while (strncmp (answer, localyes, 1) == 0);
    catclose(catd);     /* close the message catalog */
}
```

Because this example uses mnemonic labels in place of integers for the *msg_id*, the messaging calls are easier to read. Don't forget, though, that mnemonics merely stand in for integers—that is, you must assign each mnemonic to an integer. Some implementations include tools that automatically create **#define**s. See the section Building a Message Catalog later in this chapter for details.

Here is a sample run of the program using a German locale:

```
Wieviele Pruefungen? 5

Pruefungsergebnis Nummer 1 eingeben: 87
Pruefungsergebnis Nummer 2 eingeben: 91
Pruefungsergebnis Nummer 3 eingeben: 88
Pruefungsergebnis Nummer 4 eingeben: 100
Pruefungsergebnis Nummer 5 eingeben: 75

Durchschnittliches Pruefungsergebnis: 87,8
Noch einmal? j

Pruefungsergebnis Nummer 1 eingeben: 73
. . .
```

This sample run uses the same data but an English locale:

```
How many tests? 5

Enter test score number 1: 87
Enter test score number 2: 91
Enter test score number 3: 88
Enter test score number 4: 100
Enter test score number 5: 75

Average test score: 87.8
Again? y

Enter test score number 1: 73
. . .
```

Notice that in addition to the program text changing languages, the format for the computed average changes in a locale-appropriate manner. That's because of the I18N support **setlocale( )** and **printf( )** provide. For the German run, the output uses a comma as the radix character (87,8), while for the English version, the radix character is a period (87.8).

9.2.3 Variable Ordering for Message Parameters

The examples so far show how to handle simple cases: message strings with no parameters or only one parameter. Many messages, however, are more complicated than that because they include multiple parameters. That situation requires additional programmatic changes.

When text gets translated, the words often end up in a different order than they were in the original. For example, in English, adjectives generally precede nouns (*the white house*), while in French, they usually follow nouns (*la maison blanche*). The sample program in the previous section shows how parameter placement differs in the English and German versions of a string; that is

```
Enter grade number %d:
Pruefungsergebnis Nummer %d eingeben:
```

When a message contains less than two parameters, differences in word order between languages have no programmatic impact. This is not the case with two or more parameters. When translating such messages, it is very possible parameters will need to be reordered to accommodate the target language's sentence structure or other local conventions. To take a simple example, suppose you want to print a date. Here is how two locales might expect to see such information:

Sun, Apr 11, 1993   American; *weekday, month day, year* order
dom, 11 abr 1993   Spanish; *weekday, day month year* order

There are four parameters in this message, with the order of the second and third differing by locale. Without I18N support, the only way to accommodate these differences is to create separate **printf( )** calls—one for each locale. The two calls might look like this:

```
printf(catgets(catd, SET_1, DATE_FMT, "%s, %s %d, %d"),
       weekday, mon, day, year);
printf(catgets(catd, SET_1, DATE_FMT, "%s, %d %s %d"),
       weekday, day, mon, year);
```

It is impractical (not to mention uninternationalized) to have separate I/O calls for every possible ordering of locale-sensitive data. Fortunately, there is a better way. The **printf( )** and **scanf( )** families of functions include additional functionality for handling variable parameter ordering. Instead of using simple format descriptors like %s or %d, you can expand the % indicator like this:

%n$

where *n* is an integer that denotes a parameter's position in the list. Now you can rewrite the date formatting statement this way:

```
printf(catgets(catd, SET_1, DATE_FMT,
       "%1$s, %2$s %3$d, %4$d"),
       weekday, mon, day, year);
```

The default string syntax instructs **printf( )** to fill in the first format descriptor (%1$s) with the value of the first variable listed (*weekday*), the second descriptor (%2$s) with the second variable (*mon*), the third with the value of *day*, and the fourth with *year*. For a Spanish locale, the DATE_FMT message would have a different format. It might look like this:

```
%1$s, %3$d %2$s %4$d
```

This syntax instructs **printf( )** to fill in the second format descriptor (%3$d) with the value of the third variable listed (*day*), and the third descriptor (%2$s) with the second variable (*mon*). There are no changes to the first and fourth descriptors.

Adding the placement indicators allows translators to change the order of parameters without making changes to the source code.

Note that while the %*n*$ syntax is required in message catalogs, it is not required in default strings, as the example in this section shows. The fact that the **printf( )** call above has both the string and the variables to be substituted into it makes it a handy way to show the new syntax, but using position indicators does slow down variable substitution slightly. In addition, format descriptors in a default string should always be in the same order as the parameters in the associated **printf( )/scanf( )** statements, making variable ordering syntax unnecessary. However, since messages in catalogs often do require reordered parameters, you should always use the %*n*$ syntax for catalog entries with multiple parameters.

9.3 Message Catalogs

When revising **printf( )**, **scanf( )**, and other similar statements to include calls to a messaging system, you need to put the program's message strings into a source file that then gets compiled into a message catalog object. That means you need to be aware of:

- Message source file syntax
- Techniques for building catalogs
- Storage options
- Location strategies

9.3.1 Creating Message Source Files

As you revise software to use messaging calls, you must create a source file that contains all the program's messages. In most cases, the text in this source file duplicates the default strings in the messaging calls. So why create a separate file? Because that's what a translator uses. Theoretically, the translator can look through your source code for all messages, but this is *extremely* undesirable because:

- It is a security breach. Companies usually don't want to give their source code to outside translation firms.

- The result is highly likely to have errors. Most translators are not experienced programmers, so they may not find all the messages within a program. Alternatively, they may inadvertently delete important formatting information when creating a source file.
- It adds to the cost. If you require translators to find the text they are going to translate, instead of simply giving it to them, you will pay more.

You should create the initial source file and give just that to a translator. Several vendors have tools that help automate the process of creating this file.

The source file for the XPG messaging system is straightforward. You list the message's *msg_id* (either an integer or a mnemonic label), follow it with a single ASCII space or tab, and then list the message text. These are typical source lines:

```
25 This is message number 25\n
MNE_TAG This message has a mnemonic tag\n
NOT_DECLARED Variable %s not declared\n
36      This message has four leading spaces\n
```

Note that these example lines do not make up a single, valid message source file. A source file can contain either mnemonic tags or integers as *msg_id*s, but it cannot contain both. Also, if you use integers, they must be in ascending order, but they don't need to be consecutive. A source file that includes messages numbered 1–10, 100–120, and 200–210 is valid.

Message text within a source file can be in any language, and can contain any valid multibyte character. The messaging calls work exactly the same regardless of the language, so you don't have to do anything different to create, say, a Japanese source file than you would do to create the equivalent English file. However, mnemonic labels can only contain characters from your system's portable character set. See Chapter 4 for a description of these sets.

There are several additional setup options, but the body of the message source file is just this simple. Some of the more commonly used options are:

- **Comments**. Any line that begins with a dollar sign ($) followed by a space or tab is treated as a comment. For example:

```
$ This is a comment
```

- **Quoting mechanism**. You can surround message text with a quote character of your choice. Quoting the text makes it easy to see leading or trailing spaces in a string or even empty strings. To designate a quote character, the source file must include a line like this:

$quote "

where the double-quote (") is the designated character. If you want a different character, replace the double-quote with your choice. This sample message uses the quoting mechanism:

```
36 "    This message has four leading spaces\n"
```

- **Continuation character.** Not all message text fits neatly on one line. Use a backslash (\) to continue a message across multiple lines. For example:

```
LONG_MSG This message is so long that it continues \
over two lines in the source file\n
```

- **Message Sets.** Message files may be divided into sets. Sets allow you to put messages in logical groups—for example, you might put all messages related to memory management into one set, all I/O messages in another, and so on. Such grouping may make message source files easier to read, but there is no technical requirement to use sets. To designate a set within a source file, include a line like:

$set *n*

where *n* is the mnemonic or integer value of your set. If it is an integer, it must be 1 (one) or higher.

There are additional details regarding the source file syntax; see your system's **gencat** man page for that information. But even without the last few rules, you now have enough information to write a fairly realistic message source file. This brief example pulls these directives together:

```
$ Messages for program foo
$
$quote "
$set SET_1
NOT_FOUND "File not found\n"
NOT_DECLARED "Variable %1$s not declared in routine %2$s\n"
```

```
LONG_MSG "This message is so long that it continues \
over two lines in the source file\n"
COMPLEX "This message has embedded \n newlines and \
\t tabs as well as a line continuation\n"
```

9.3.2   Building a Message Catalog

The fact that the file described in the previous section is a source file implies that you must use it to produce a corresponding object file. It would be too inefficient for programs to access the plain text source files, so the XPG system includes the command **gencat** (*gen*erate *cat*alog) for creating a binary message catalog from source input.

But **gencat** needs for the source to be in an acceptable format, and what it considers acceptable may not be ideal to you. Rather than accepting mnemonic labels for *msg_id*s and *set_id*s, it only accepts source files with integers. That's because **gencat** needs the actual integer values when it constructs the binary object catalog.

So you may have a problem. You may have chosen to use mnemonics because they make program code and message source files easier to understand, but now **gencat** won't take them. What to do? There is no standard solution for this problem, but some vendors provide utilities that do tackle it. Such nonstandard utilities usually preprocess source files and automatically generate:

- an include file of **#define**s for associating mnemonic labels with integers, and
- a second version of the message source file that has integers instead of mnemonics.

Consider a message source file named **foo.msg** that contains the following:

```
NO_WHILE "while" expected in "do" statement; %s found\n
LEFT_BRACE Left brace ({) expected; %s found\n
TOO_LONG Line exceeds max length of %1$d by %2$d bytes\n
```

A preprocessor might generate these two files:

File 1; include file associating mnemonics and integers
```
#include <limits.h>
#include <nl_types.h>
/* The following was generated from foo.msg. */
#define NO_WHILE 1
#define LEFT_BRACE 2
#define TOO_LONG 3
```

File 2; input file for gencat

```
1 "while" expected in "do" statement; %s found\n
2 Left brace ({) expected; %s found\n
3 Line exceeds max length of %1$d by %2$d bytes\n
```

A preprocessing utility provides a handy way to turn the mnemonics that pro-grammers usually prefer into the integers that **gencat** wants. If such a utility doesn't exist on your system, you can create **gencat**-acceptable files manually, write a script to do the work for you, or simply avoid using mnemonics.

9.3.3 Generating Object Catalogs

Regardless of whether you build a source-file-with-integers manually or have a tool to do the job, once you do have the appropriate input, you need to run **gencat**. This utility takes one or more message source files and produces either a new mes-sage catalog, or merges new message text into an existing catalog. It has this syn-tax:

    gencat *catfile msgfile* . . .

where *catfile* is the target object catalog and *msgfile* is the message source file. You can specify multiple *msgfile*s.

If *catfile* exists, **gencat** adds the messages and sets defined in *msgfile* to *catfile*. If set and message numbers collide, the text in *msgfile* replaces the existing text in *catfile*. (Depending on the implementation, you may or may not be notified about the replacement.) If *catfile* does not exist, **gencat** creates it.

In most implementations, **gencat**'s output is a file with a name of the form *product_name*.**cat** (for example, **ls.cat** or **my_application.cat**). However, you can choose your own naming conventions.

Here is a typical **gencat** command line:

```
% gencat foo.cat foo.msg
```

This example creates the **foo.cat** object catalog from the **foo.msg** input file. Later, when a user runs the **foo** command, the command accesses **foo.cat**.

9.3.4   What Are All Those Files Again?

Messaging systems make it possible for software to speak with many voices, but you may feel lost in the noise of all the files it takes to do so. Table 9.1 shows which files you need if you use integers as message and set identifiers. If you use mnemonic labels in place of integers, you may need two additional files—an **#include** file that associates mnemonics and integers, and an input file for **gencat**.

Table 9.1   Message Files When Using Integer Identifiers

Type	Sample Name	Purpose
Source program	foo.c	Contains program source code with messaging calls
Message source file	foo.msg	Contains source text for messages used in **foo.c**. Source to **gencat**.
Object catalog	foo.cat	Created by **gencat**, this is an object file that **foo** accesses at run time

9.3.5   Storing Catalogs

Binary message catalogs obviously must be available to programs at run time. There are two basic catalog storage models: one that doesn't really work, but that typically is the first solution proposed, and a second that works much better.

Under the first model, catalogs appear in the same directory as the programs they serve. That means a directory might contain something like the following:

```
/usr/bin/fgrep
/usr/bin/fgrep.cat
/usr/bin/file
/usr/bin/file.cat
/usr/bin/find
/usr/bin/find.cat
/usr/bin/finger
/usr/bin/finger.cat
 . . .
```

At first glance, this seems easy, neat, and logical. The problem is, it assumes there
only is one copy of each catalog. In reality, there are multiple copies—one for each
language you support. Suppose you translate American English program messages
into British English, Chinese, French, German, and Japanese. That means there are
six copies of each catalog. If you put all versions in the same directory as the commands, each must have a unique name so you can tell one from another. A logical
choice is to append the name of the locale with which the file is associated. That
quickly gets very messy, as the following shows. (Assume all files are in **/usr/bin**.)

```
fgrep                          /* command name */
fgrep.cat.de_DE.ISO8859-1      /* German */
fgrep.cat.en_GB.ISO8859-1      /* British English */
fgrep.cat.en_US.ISO8859-1      /* American English */
fgrep.cat.fr_FR.ISO8859-1      /* French */
fgrep.cat.ja_JP.AJEC           /* Japanese */
fgrep.cat.zh_TW.eucTW          /* Taiwanese Chinese */
file                           /* command name */
file.cat.de_DE.ISO8859-1       /* German */
file.cat.en_GB.ISO8859-1       /* British English */
file.cat.en_US.ISO8859-1       /* American English */
file.cat.fr_FR.ISO8859-1       /* French */
file.cat.ja_JP.AJEC            /* Japanese */
file.cat.zh_TW.eucTW           /* Taiwanese Chinese */
. . .                          . . .
```

This example shows the files for only two commands, and already the directory is
unwieldy. Imagine if every command in the directory had the same six message catalogs.

Once they see the results of this storage model, most people quickly decide that
it is not such a good idea to store the catalogs along with the programs that use them.
But then where? The most common solution is to create a separate directory structure for message catalogs. Generally, the structure is similar to that in Figure 9.1.

Just as there are no standards for the location of other locale-specific data, there
are no standards for where to put the message catalogs. That means the "I18N directory" in Figure 9.1 can be just about anything. Typical examples include:

1. /usr/lib/nls/msg/*locale*/*name*
2. /lib/locale/*locale*/LC_MESSAGES/*name*
3. /usr/lib/nls/*locale*/*name*.cat

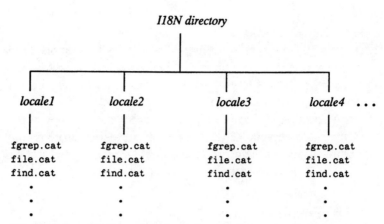

Figure 9.1   Common Message Catalog Directory Structure

Taking the first example, the complete message catalog structure is:

```
/usr/lib/nls/msg/en_US.ISO8859-1/fgrep.cat
                "               /file.cat
                "               /find.cat
                        . . .
/usr/lib/nls/msg/fr_FR.ISO8859-1/fgrep.cat
                "               /file.cat
                        . . .
/usr/lib/nls/msg/ja_JP.AJEC/fgrep.cat
                        . . .
```

In addition to deciding the location of catalogs within the file system, you also need to decide where the physical files should reside in your network. For uninternationalized programs that embed all text within the source logic, this isn't an issue; the programs contain the messages. Typically, program binaries appear on multiple. disks throughout the network, so there are as many copies of a program's messages as there are copies of that program.

This simple storage model doesn't work well in an internationalized environment. Such a system may offer 10 or more translated versions of program messages. It is very likely you don't have the disk space necessary to duplicate all versions of all messages on every disk. Even if you do have the space, there is no point in wasting it on unneeded catalogs. Although there may be demand at your site for messages in 10 languages, most individual users only want one or two. It's just that one user may want Japanese messages, while another wants Spanish and Portuguese, and still another prefers English. Why give users all 10 languages if they will never use them?

A common physical storage technique is to put a copy of each translation on one or more file servers. Then, instead of accessing catalogs directly on their disks, multiple users get them from the central location(s). In most cases, the fact that the catalogs are not on local disks is invisible to users.

9.3.6 Finding Catalogs

After you store object catalogs somewhere, you need to be able to find them again. As part of its messaging system, XPG has an environment variable named NLSPATH for defining the location of catalogs. NLSPATH works much the same as other PATH-like variables. You assign one or more partial pathnames to the variable, and when a program needs to find a catalog, it builds a full path from:

1. the next value in the list assigned to NLSPATH,
2. the current locale name, and
3. the *name* parameter to **catopen( )**.

It keeps constructing and trying full paths until it finds a match or runs out of possibilities.

NLSPATH does have a few extras that most other PATH-like variables don't have. It allows substitution characters within the path that stand in for elements of a locale name. Table 9.2 shows the acceptable substitution characters.

Table 9.2   Elements of an NLSPATH Value

Keyword	Meaning
%N	The value of the *name* parameter passed to **catopen( )**
%L	The value of the full locale name
%l	The *language* part of the locale
%t	The *territory* part of the locale
%c	The *codeset* part of the locale
%%	A single % character

Given these rules, here is a simple example NLSPATH value:

```
NLSPATH=/usr/lib/nls/msg/%L/%N
```

This one-value assignment says to search the current locale's (*%L*) branch of the system directory `/usr/lib/nls/msg` for the *name (%N)* catalog. If the catalog exists, the calling program uses the messages in it. If the catalog is not found using NLSPATH, there may be an additional implementation-defined search path. If the catalog still is not found, the calling program uses default messages.

Although NLSPATH may have only one path assigned to it, it is quite common for it to have multiple values. System-supplied message catalogs may be in one location, while local catalogs are in another. You may divide catalogs along broad product lines, with OS-related catalogs going in one directory, and application programs' catalogs in another. To define multiple catalog locations, assign NLSPATH a list of colon-separated (:) values. For example:

```
NLSPATH=/my_msgs/%l/%N:/site_msgs/%L/%N:/usr/lib/nls/msg/%L/%N
```

This three-level assignment designates a location for personal message catalogs (`my_msgs`), for site-specific catalogs (`site_msgs`), and then for system-wide data. Notice that the first path uses just the language portion (%l) of a locale name rather than the full locale (%L).

At most sites, the system administrator sets a system-wide value for NLSPATH. Users may or may not have the freedom to change or add to that system-wide value.

9.4   Default Messages

A messaging system allows a single program to produce messages in a variety of languages. However, since messages are kept in separate catalogs rather than being embedded in the program logic, the possibility exists that the catalog a user wants will not be available at program run time. Therefore, programs should be designed such that they have access to default messages. This section covers why message catalogs may be unavailable and techniques for supplying default messages.

9.4.1   Unavailable Catalogs

Several times this chapter has referred to the possibility of a catalog being unavailable at run time and therefore forcing a program to use default message strings. This is not just a theoretical possibility. Common reasons for messages being unavailable include:

- **Network problems**. Suppose that, as at most sites, copies of all message catalogs are not stored on each user's local disk, and instead are on centralized file servers. Now suppose there is a network glitch. If you can't reach the appropriate file server, **catopen( )** fails, and the program has to use the defaults.

  Note that while this certainly can and does happen, the disk space you save by *not* duplicating all catalogs almost always far outweighs the inconvience of a user occasionally seeing default strings. Of course, if the catalog includes critical messages, you should include a copy of that catalog on all local disks. For example, the local language version of

  ```
  DANGER—NUCLEAR MELTDOWN IMMINENT!!
  ```

  certainly qualifies as a critical message.
- **Locale not available**. No error-checking or other validation occurs when you set a locale; you can set it however you like. Problems are only uncovered when a program tries to use a locale setting. Suppose you set LANG to `french`, but your system only understands a more formal name like `fr_FR.ISO8859-1`. In this case, there really may be French message catalogs available on your system, but **catopen( )** won't find them because your locale name and the system's name don't match.

  You also may ask for messages in a locale that your site doesn't support. For instance, you may carefully use the right naming conventions to set LANG or LC_MESSAGES to a Hungarian locale. But if catalogs haven't been translated into Hungarian yet, it doesn't matter how correct your locale name is; **catopen( )** can't open the catalogs because they don't exist.
- **Bad NLSPATH**. **catopen( )** can't open the right catalog if NLSPATH is set incorrectly, or isn't set at all. The latter case assumes that your site does not have a system-wide default value for NLSPATH.
- **Incomplete translations**. The bits may be flowing faultlessly through your network, your locale name may be perfect and supported, and your NLSPATH may be flawless. And still you may get default messages. This happens when translation occurs in phases. It is very rare for all system and layered software messages to be translated at one time. Rather, translation tends to occur over time: common user utilities first, then a software package or two, then less frequently used utilities, and so on. The result is that your site may have translations for some parts of the system in, say, Japanese, but not for other parts. In this case, some messages appear in Japanese and others in the default language (usually English).

Since there are several reasons catalogs may be unavailable, it is important to supply default messages rather than leave users with a blank screen. The next section describes the pros and cons of default strings, and strategies for storing those strings.

9.4.2 Storing Default Text

The final parameter of **catgets( )** is the default message string. This is the string that appears if **catgets( )** can't retrieve a requested message for any reason. All examples in this chapter show this parameter being filled in with a hard-coded default, but there are other ways to supply default text.

Before describing alternate methods for supplying defaults, it is important to examine the question of *if* you should include them. Some argue against including default strings because having strings embedded in a program makes object code larger than it would be if the defaults were removed. Therefore, they propose that the original language messages be put in a catalog, and the final parameter to **catgets( )** be a NULL string. That means message calls look like one of these:

With mnemonic tags:
```
printf(catgets(catd, SET_1, NOT_FOUND, ""), name);
```

With integer set and message numbers:
```
printf(catgets(catd, 1, 20, ""), name);
```

Another argument against including default text in messaging calls is that some people feel any program that has to use a default is broken. The lack of default messages, the reasoning goes, lets users know immediately that the program has failed.

While the reduction in object code size that a no-defaults approach produces is an advantage, the approach has significant disadvantages. Without defaults, programs have to rely on message catalogs always being available. As the previous section shows, there is no guarantee of that consistency. A program that can't reach a catalog isn't broken just because there is a network failure or because a requested translation is not available.

Even if you believe a program is broken because of problems elsewhere in the system, the failure to supply default messages can leave users baffled. They get no feedback that tells them there is a problem, and so may not be aware the program has failed. Default strings in an unexpected language are a good clue that something is wrong. Suppose a program is running in a French locale and the user does something that should trigger the message:

```
% Le fichier foo n'existe pas
```

If the French messages are not available, a program without defaults produces:

```
%
```

while a program with defaults probably produces:

```
% File foo not found
```

Of the two possibilities, only the latter gives users a chance to recover from the error. And, of course, some users may be familiar with the language in which the default messages appears, and so be able to continue the program run in that default language.

Programs may also be harder to maintain if there are no default messages. Having messages sprinkled through the program logic makes the code more readable and so tends to help the programmers who maintain it. Compare these messaging calls:

```
printf(catgets(catd, 1, 50,
    "Invalid character in %s; can only contain A-Za-z\n"),
    name);
```

```
printf(catgets(catd, 1, 50, ""), name);
```

With the first example, you can see at a glance what problem the **printf( )** reports. With the second, you have no clue.

Hard-coded defaults do add to the size of object code, but they also tell users when a problem exists, give them a way to continue a program run, and simplify program maintenance. Therefore, it seems clear that it is best to supply defaults. If you decide against including them, however, you probably should always check **catopen( )**'s return value. If it reports that it couldn't find the requested catalog, you might choose to try another version (presumably, the C locale's catalog), or to stop the program run.

While there are considerable advantages to supplying default text, there is more than one way to make it available. Instead of hard-coding the default text into the messaging call, you can replace it with a reference to a constant. To ensure that the default text is available when the program runs, add constant definitions at the beginning of the program, or in a separate module that you bind with the program. Using this approach, the software might look like this:

```
/* Note: the leading "D" stands for "Default" */
#define D_INVALID_CHAR
    "Invalid character in %s; can only contain A-Za-z\n"
#define D_NOT_FOUND "File not found\n"

#define D_CANT_OPEN "Can't open file %s\n"
. . .
printf(catgets(catd, SET_1, INVALID_CHAR, D_INVALID_CHAR),
    name);
. . .
printf(catgets(catd, SET_1, NOT_FOUND, D_NOT_FOUND));
. . .
```

An alternate approach is to create a constant for an entire **catgets( )** call. As
with the previous example, the constants usually appear at the beginning of a program like this:

```
/* The leading "FOO" stands for the utility/product name. */
#define FOO_INVALID_CHAR    catgets (catd, 1, 1,
    "Invalid character in %s; can only contain A-Za-z\n")
#define FOO_NOT_FOUND        catgets (catd, 1, 2,
    "File not found\n")
#define FOO_CANT_OPEN        catgets (catd, 1, 3,
    "Can't open file %s\n")
. . .
printf(FOO_INVALID_CHAR, name);
. . .
printf(FOO_NOT_FOUND);
. . .
```

Some like these models for aesthetic reasons—the messaging calls are less clut-
tered without the actual text being present—but the main advantage becomes apparent if you reuse messages. Suppose several places in the code trigger the
*_INVALID_CHAR message. Rather than retyping the formatted string several
times, you can use the shorter constant name. Having the actual string in only one
place also is helpful if you ever change the text. Instead of searching for and revising each occurrence of the string, you can change it once in the constant declaration.
The disadvantage to defining constants is that the message text no longer appears
with the messaging call, making it more difficult to determine the purpose of the
call.

The way you choose to supply default text depends on your application. If you never reuse messages, it probably is easier to leave the default text in the messaging call. If you do reuse messages, or like an uncluttered look, you may decide to use constants.

One other point—defaults should contain real messages rather than an all-purpose message like `Failure`. Defaults really do get used, so they should be designed to help the user.

9.5   Translation Issues

The fact that program messages can be translated into many languages creates new topics to consider as you write the messages and the program statements that use them. These include:

- Textual clarity
- Differing message lengths and their impact on buffers
- Fragmented messages
- Recycled messages

This section describes these in more detail.

9.5.1   Unclear Messages

When writing software and composing the messages that a given program produces, programmers of course know what a message means and how it fits into the overall program. Because of their detailed knowledge of the software, they may not think much about what a message says (or fails to say). After all, the most important thing is to get the program working. Program text definitely is a secondary priority—higher than spending time on comments within the code, but still in the "I'll do it if I have time" category.

Given such an attitude, a programmer may write minimalist-style messages. On a UNIX-like system, any number of conditions may trigger the spare `Segmentation fault` message, or the popular `Core dump`. Alternatively, the developer may write simply bad messages. Something like:

```
Cannot grok
```

may make sense to the person who wrote it, but not to the rest of us.

Messages frustrate users if they are too terse to provide adequate information, or if they are incomprehensible. The situation gets worse, though, when it comes time to translate such text. Now you give a message source file to a translator, and that translator has to make sense of the words. There is no code surrounding the text to give clues about what a phrase really means. Even if there were, most translators are not experienced programmers, so they probably wouldn't glean much from the actual code.

The combination of poor original text and perhaps technically unsophisticated translators can result in a translated message that is even more muddled than the original. While all translations should be reviewed for accuracy, it can be difficult to find someone who is competent in a given technology *and* fluent in the target language to do such a review. Suppose your company decides to translate messages into Swedish. You may have a sales office in Sweden, but have no programmers working in it. In such a (common) case, the local sales staff is responsible for reviewing translations. They do their best, but may miss problems that an expert in the software package would not.

You can avoid or at least diminish translation problems if you put effort up-front into ensuring that all program text is clear, accurate, and informative. (Users of the original language version will probably thank you, too.) This includes avoiding abbreviations, most acronyms, and slang in text. Consider these examples:

```
%s max pkt bytes required
:-( heap trashed
```

The first example includes two abbreviations (*max* for maximum and *pkt* for packet). While translators may know that *max* is a common abbreviation for maximum, *pkt* may be mystifying. The second example includes the slang graphic :-(which is a sideways frowning face. In informal text, this graphic accompanies unpleasant information (the converse :-) is a sideways smiling face that denotes humor). Such slang should not appear in program messages.

Program text can be very clear and still create problems. Suppose your source file includes this message:

```
INVALID_CHAR "Invalid character in %s;\
can only contain letters or digits\n"
```

This example is easy to translate; it is just that it probably isn't correct. When software limits the characters that can be in a string, it usually restricts them to a subset of ASCII characters. Programming language keywords or variables often can contain only ASCII letters and digits; user and node names may be similarly restricted. Assuming this message describes such a software package, the text is incorrect for an internationalized system. Characters like *é, Æ,* and *ñ* definitely are letters, but they are not ASCII letters. In this case, you should revise the original message like this:

```
INVALID_CHAR "Invalid character in %s;\
can only contain ASCII letters A-Za-z or digits\n"
```

The revised message clearly describes exactly what characters are permissible in the string. It also is easy to translate and provides the correct information.

In addition to seemingly clear, but incorrect messages, there is another type that seems clear and yet creates problems for translators. Consider this message:

```
ERR_READ "The read system call failed. Cannot read %s\n"
```

Function names usually do not change when a system is internationalized, so the system call **read** should not be translated. But there is no way for translators to know that—unless you tell them. Another potential translation problem is the value that goes in *%s*. Given the current text, there are a number of possible substitutions. If translators have to guess, they easily could guess wrong. To avoid these problems, you should add comments like these to the message source:

```
$ Do not translate "read" in the phrase "read system call".
$ %s is a filename.
ERR_READ "The read system call failed. Cannot read %s\n"
```

Consider another example. Suppose a message source file includes a format string like this:

```
FORMAT "%1$s\t%2$s\t%3$s"
```

Without any explanation, there is no way for translators to determine what, if any, changes they need to make to this message. Comments make proper translation possible. For example:

```
$ This is an output format string. The first field
$ holds a user's login name, the second is the user's
$ node name, and the third is the user's full name.
FORMAT "%1$s\t%2$s\t%3$s"
```

With these comments, a translator can determine whether it is necessary to reorder parameters to fit local conventions.

In addition to these instructions, it also helps translators if you provide comments describing the circumstances under which a message occurs and the action(s) a user can take after seeing it. Quite frankly, ordinary users also benefit from such information, and yet, many software vendors don't provide it—usually because of time or budget constraints or because they simply don't think about it.

In an ideal development environment, every facet of the system would be documented clearly and completely. But in the real world of most software development, you do what you think is important and what you have time to complete. In that real world, painstakingly complete documentation usually falls off the To-Do list. The failure to document messages completely, however, has potentially more serious consequences for translators and the users of translated messages than it does for the people who see the original (usually English) messages.

That's because of the difference between users' and translators' roles. Suppose a user does something that causes the message `File not found` to appear. The user knows the context under which the message showed up on the screen. It might have appeared when the user was trying to delete a file, or when trying to open one. However, translators don't have this context. They simply receive message source files that list all program messages.

Without context, it can be difficult to decide on the appropriate translation. That's why comments are so helpful. If there are comments in the file that describe the circumstances under which the message occurs, the translator has a much better chance of writing an accurate translation.

You *should* change programs to improve unclear messages, and you *should* add translation comments to source message catalogs. If you don't, though, and translated messages are not what they could be, your programs still continue to work. There are situations, however, that may *require* changes to existing code.

9.5.2 Buffers and Message Lengths

It should come as no surprise that the number of words or characters it takes to convey a thought differs from language to language. Table 9.3 shows an example of those differences with multiple versions of a brief phrase.

Table 9.3   Equivalent Strings, Unequivalent Lengths

Language	Phrase	Characters	Bytes*
Dutch	A.u.b. persoonlijk berzorgen	28	28
English	Please hand deliver	19	19
French	Veuillez livrer immédiatement	29	29
German	Bitte sofort dem Empfänger überbringen	39	39

* assume code set is ISO8859-1 (Latin 1)

This phrase requires between 19 and 39 bytes—a more than 100 percent differ-ence—to write in these sample languages. Such differences can cause problems in software that has been tuned to only one language. It is typical to do such tuning when messages are in one language. This usually happens unconsciously. You may create an 80-byte buffer, and then make sure no individual message exceeds that length. Similarly, your program may produce formatted output, where the data lines up in neat columns under, say, hard-coded English column names.

Translations often wreak havoc with such hard-coded assumptions. On average, French and German consume 10 to 30 percent more space than does the equivalent English. For short phrases, the difference may be even greater, as the example in Table 9.3 demonstrates. Buffers and formats that readily accommodate English may overflow when faced with French and German.

Similarly, languages that use ideographic scripts (like Chinese and Japanese) may tend to require fewer characters per string than phonetically written languages, but still may consume more bytes for those same strings. That's because Asian characters usually consume multiple bytes—Japanese strings often include double- or triple-byte kana and Kanji along with single-byte ASCII characters.

Software that fails to accommodate different languages' characteristics may truncate messages in mid-word, or even worse, in mid-character. Take a simple example. Suppose you build a software package that has a graphical user interface (GUI). Among the features of your GUI is an error status field, which you define to be 40 bytes long. All of your messages fit within 40 bytes. Now suppose one of your messages is:

```
File exists
```

This string is 11 bytes long in Latin-1-encoded English, but with one possible trans-lation into German, it expands to 41 bytes (Datei oder Dateikatalog existiert bereits). The following shows the byte count and the translated message:

```
          1         2         3         4
1234567890123456789012345678901234567890 1
Datei oder Dateikatalog existiert bereits
```

Because the translation exceeds the carefully-designed-for-English buffer, the last letter of the message gets chopped off. The situation could be worse, however. Here is an example of a Japanese string (the byte count appears above the string):

```
            1             2             3             4
12345678901234567890123456789012345678901234567890012345678
```
無効なオプション "options" が指定されました。

Assuming this is an EUC-encoded string, each of the ASCII letters consumes one byte while the kana and Kanji take up two bytes each. The arrow shows the boundary of the 40-byte buffer, but notice that the string is in mid-character at that point. Instead of a word being truncated (as in the German example), the too-small buffer truncates a Japanese character.

Internationalized software needs to remove or relax as many hard-coded linguistic dependencies as possible. Instead of creating a buffer that is as small as can accommodate the original language message text, be more generous with space. While an 80-byte buffer may have been appropriate when you were supporting one language, you now should expand that to 128 bytes or even 256. It is common for messaging systems to define an even larger maximum message length—say, 1,024 or 8,192 or more bytes—to ensure that all languages' and encodings' needs can be met. Sure, the spacious new buffers will probably have a fair percentage of unused bytes, but they help avoid future problems with wordier languages. In addition to expanding buffer sizes, you also must ensure that you don't truncate characters. See Chapter 6 for information about avoiding character truncation.

While a roomier buffer solves some space problems, it doesn't take care of the problem of meticulously formatted output. Suppose a program prints a list of American names and telephone numbers. It might produce output like this:

Name	Telephone
Wendy Knotts	404-123-4567
Alice Paulsen	909-700-1234
Brian Richards	508-555-2222
Franklin Stewart	212-555-1111

Because you "know" phone numbers have the format *nnn-nnn-nnnn*, you write a **printf( )** statement like this:

```
printf("%s\t%3d-%3d-%4d\n", name, area, exchange, num);
```

The problem is that your format accommodates American and Canadian telephone numbers, but doesn't handle most other countries' rules. There may be more or fewer digits in a given country's numbers. Those digits probably are formatted differently than the one rigid way your **printf( )** statement knows.

Since display formats are locale-specific, instead of hard-coding them in, you should use messaging calls. They can fetch the rules that are appropriate for the current locale.

9.5.3 The Problem with Message Fragments

The examples in this chapter all show complete messages, rather than messages constructed from two or more substrings. That's not an accident. The differing characteristics of languages mean that if you build messages from fragments, there is a very good chance you will create unusable software.

It is quite common for something that appears to be a single message string to be a collection of parts. Consider this typical compiler message:

```
ERROR: Left brace ({) expected; "[" found. [0167]
```

This message actually has three parts: the severity level (in this case, ERROR), the message text, and the message number [0167]. The compiler builds the complete message from three substrings. An internationalized compiler would call **catgets( )** three times for this one message.

Producing a single message that consists of separate and distinct fields is fine. The problem comes when you try to build up one segment from different pieces—for example, if you concatenate several substrings to produce the text segment of the compiler message above. Suppose you have the following English messages:

```
1                    No rights to
2                    open
3                    delete
4                    modify
5                    file %s
6                    user %s
7                    device %s
```

With this group of substrings, you can build a variety of messages including:

```
1 + 2 + 5 = No rights to open file %s
1 + 3 + 5 = No rights to delete file %s
1 + 3 + 6 = No rights to delete user %s
1 + 5 = No rights to file %s
```

This kind of message building may seem attractive—after all, you store frequently used strings like `No rights to`, `delete`, and `file %s` once rather than multiple times—but it is wrong in an internationalized environment. Notice that in the first three cases, *to* is the first part of a verb infinitive (to open, to delete), while in the last example, it is a preposition that refers to the noun phrase `file %s`. It is difficult or impossible in most languages to make one translation of the message `No rights to` that is correct for both cases.

Here is another example that builds singular or plural versions of an English string from several fragments:

```
printf("site%s zero max site parameter%s\n,"
    (result ? " has a" : "s have"),
    (result ? "" : "s"));
```

This **printf( )** can produce either `site has a zero max site parameter` or `sites have zero max site parameters`. However, the multiple dependencies on English make it impossible to translate. The correct way to write this is:

```
if (result != 0)
    printf (catgets(catd, SET_NUM, SITE,
    "site has a zero maximum site parameter\n"));
else
    printf (catgets(catd, SET_NUM, SITES,
    "sites have zero maximum site parameters\n"));
```

In addition to differences in the way singular and plural phrases are formed, other grammatical differences exist. Many languages have both masculine and feminine versions of some words (for example, *old* in French is *ancien* in the masculine form and *ancienne* in the feminine) and the correct form depends on the rest of the phrase in which the word appears. If you use message fragments, you force a translator to pick one form, which may mean some of the resulting translations are incorrect.

Do not use message fragments unless the substrings from which they are built are independent of each other.

9.5.4 Recycled Messages

The previous section describes some problems associated with reusing pieces of messages. You also may create translation problems if you reuse entire messages in inappropriate ways. Suppose a program takes user input and attempts to find specific files or directories or even system resources such as printers. If any of these attempts fails, there is a single error message:

```
%s not found
```

Although the single message isn't a shining example of clarity, it more or less covers all three situations. It wouldn't stun many American users to get a message like this for any of the three cases.

Now suppose you want to create a German message catalog. German text tends to be more precise than does the "equivalent" English version. German users might expect three different versions of the single English message, as Table 9.4 shows.

Table 9.4   German Translations of a Single English Message

Original Message	German Message	English Meaning
file not found	*file* nicht gefunden	*file* not found
directory not found	*directory* existiert nicht	*directory* does not exist
resource not found	*resource* ist nicht erreichbar	*resource* is not reachable

Rather than lumping somewhat-similar situations together under one message, the three separate German messages give precise information about specific situations. Such specificity meets German users' expectations more completely, but it is impossible to deliver if you reuse a single message repeatedly. Translators can not add new messages to a catalog; they can only translate the ones that already exist. This means you should think carefully before reusing messages. Consider whether you are overloading one string with too many meanings. If the circumstances that trigger a message one time differ significantly from those that trigger it another time, it is better to create two separate messages.

9.5.5   Translation Summary

Translated messages have a much better chance of providing meaningful information to users if you follow the guidelines in this section. The original source should be clear and contain notes to translators; you should avoid making assumptions about message lengths or formats in your program code; in most cases, you should avoid building messages from fragments; and you should even think carefully before reusing full messages.

9.6   Yes and No Responses

Messaging systems make it possible for a system to accept input or produce output in the user's chosen language. For almost all possible messages, it is up to a translator or software developer to provide the proper text. However, there is one class of messages that appear so often in software they have special support: yes/no strings.

While it is common for a program to include yes/no queries, naturally, the words for *yes* and *no* differ from language to language. POSIX.2 defines two keywords—**yesexpr** and **noexpr**—to hold the expression(s) for giving an affirmative or negative answer for the current locale. For Spanish, they might be defined this way in a **localedef** source file:

```
# yes expression. The following designates:
# "^([sS]|[sS][ií])"
#
yesexpr "<circumflex><left-parenthesis><left-square-bracket>\
<s><S><right-square-bracket><vertical-line>\
<left-square-bracket><s><S><right-square-bracket>\
<left-square-bracket><i-acute><I-acute>\
<right-square-bracket><right-parenthesis>"


# no expression. The following designates:
# "^([nN]|[nN][oO])"
#
noexpr "<circumflex><left-parenthesis><left-square-bracket>\
<n><N><right-square-bracket><vertical-line>\
<left-square-bracket><n><N><right-square-bracket>\
<left-square-bracket><o><O><right-square-bracket>\
<right-parenthesis>"
```

The setting LC_MESSAGES (or LC_ALL or LANG) has when your program runs determines the values **yesexpr** and **noexpr** return.

In addition to POSIX.2's yes/no expressions, XPG defines simpler yes/no strings. **YESSTR** and **NOSTR** hold locale-specific strings for answering yes/no queries. Again, using a Spanish locale as an example, here is how the strings might be defined in a **localedef** source:

```
YESSTR "<s><i-acute><colon><s><colon><S>"
NOSTR "<n><o><colon><n><colon><N>"
```

Use the XPG function **nl_langinfo( )** to retrieve the values of these strings.
Here is a short example:

```
#include <stdio.h>
#include <langinfo.h>
#include <locale.h>
#include <nl_types.h>
#include <wchar.h>
#include "yes_no.h"
#define MAX_ANS 10

int main(void) {
  char *yes_str;
  wchar_t answer[10];
  wchar_t *wideyes;
  size_t n;
  nl_catd catd;

  (void)setlocale(LC_ALL, "");
  catd = catopen("yes_no.cat", NL_CAT_LOCALE);

  /* get the locale-appropriate version of "yes", allocate
   * a wchar_t buffer, and convert to wide character
   */
  yes_str = nl_langinfo(YESSTR);
  n = strlen(yes_str) + 1;
  wideyes = (wchar_t *)malloc(n * sizeof(wchar_t));
  mbstowcs(wideyes, yes_str, n);

  do {
    /* program processing */
    printf(catgets(catd, SET_1, AGAIN,
             "Do you want to continue? (y or n): "));
    fgetws(&answer, MAX_ANS, stdin);
  }
  while (wcsncmp(answer, wideyes, 1) == 0);

  catclose(catd);
}
```

This example loops until `answer` equals **YESSTR** as defined in the current locale. The example converts the value of **YESSTR** and the user's input to wide character form before using **wcsncmp( )** to compare the first character in each string. Because it uses wide characters, the example works for values of **YESSTR** that include multiple-byte characters.

9.7   Do It

When internationalizing code, you probably will revise more lines to add messaging support than you will for any other I18N-related change. Nearly every program has some amount of program text, and it all must change in order to provide a properly internationalized system. Fortunately, most of the messagizing work is relatively easy, and the result is that otherwise-baffled users everywhere benefit. Can't ask much more than that.

What Doesn't Change

10

Although internationalization affects nearly all software and a smaller percentage of hardware, there are a few items that almost always remain unchanged. This chapter describes what remains constant, why certain things do not change, and discusses the very limited circumstances under which you might choose to break the rules.

10.1 The Constants

As the previous chapters show, internationalized software looks different from single-language software. The changes might include a few previously unfamiliar routines such as **setlocale( )** and **catgets( )**, or they might be more extensive, as this Japanese example shows:

```
char        buff[BUFSIZ];
time_t      ct;
char        *dt_fmt;          /* strftime用日時のフォーマット   */
struct tm   *local;           /* ローカル・タイム               */
(void) setlocale(LC_ALL, "");  /* ロケールの設定                 */

ct   = time(NULL);            /* 秒による現在時刻の取得         */
local = localtime(&ct);       /* tmフォーマットへの時刻の変換   */
dt_fmt= nl_langinfo(D_T_FMT);  /* ロケールにあるD_T_FMT値を得る  */
if (strftime(buff,BUFSIZ, dt_fmt, local)) /* 現在時刻をD_T_FMTフォ */
  printf("%s¥n", buff);         /*   ーマットに変換し印刷       */
```

Just as source code may look different, internationalized commands produce output that differs significantly from that on ASCII-only, or other limited systems. However, you may have noticed that some aspects of the code and commands are reassuringly familiar. On standards-compliant systems, these names or keywords remain constant:

- **Programming language keywords and data types.** C source code includes only the English-based versions of keywords and predefined data types rather than translations of those words. In the Japanese example above, the comments are in Japanese, but the source includes keywords **if** and **struct**, and the standard type **char**. Such keywords and names do not get translated on an internationalized system.
- **Command names and options.** Internationalized commands are capable of performing operations depending on the locale in use. This means that an internationalized **sort** can collate data according to, say, French or Danish or Chinese rules. While the results vary, the command name does not—it is always the English-based string **sort**. Similarly, command options also stay the same. Therefore, **sort** always has an option like **-o**, which is used to designate an output file. Regardless of the locale in which you run, command names and the options they support remain constant. This improves usability, because it means you do not have to learn an entire new set of command names and options for every new locale you want to use.

Suppose command names did change according to the current locale. In that case, instead of typing a standard, familiar name to perform a task, you would type the locale-specific command name. Table 10.1 shows possible locale-specific names for two common commands.

Table 10.1   Locale-Specific Command Names

English	French	German	Italian	Spanish
sort	tri	sortiere	ordinamento	clasificar
date	date	Datum	data	fecha

If command names and options were localized, you would have to remember to enter, say, **clasificar** when sorting data in a Spanish locale, and **sortiere** in a German locale, and so on. In a French locale, if you wanted to direct output to a specific file, you might use localized strings for the command name and option and enter this

```
tri -s sortiefichier
```

rather than

```
sort -o outfile
```

However, names on standards-compliant systems do *not* change according to locale, so you can always use the **sort** command and any of its options.

- **Library functions**. Just as command names remain constant on standards-compliant systems, so too do library function names. Application programmers can use functions like **strcoll( )**, **printf( )**, and **setlocale( )** regardless of the locale in which their programs ultimately run. Although the functions' behavior changes according to the run-time locale, the names do not.

- **System environment variables**. Environment variable names such as PATH, LANG, TERM, and DISPLAY remain the same regardless of locale. Assume you want to run in a French locale. You set LANG to the name of the French locale on your system (say, fr_FR.ISO8859-1 or français) rather than assigning a value to a French translation of that environment variable name (for example, LANGUE).

In addition to names that do not change on an internationalized system, other pieces of software may also remain constant. It depends on what the software does. Obviously, software that does no locale-specific processing does not need to change when you internationalize the system. For example, in many cases, locale-related operations take place in user applications and in user level commands and library routines, but do not touch an operating system's kernel. Internationalization functionality in user space, then, often has no impact on many kernels. This is particularly the case on many UNIX-like kernels. Most are completely unaware of any locale-specific processing. They simply push bytes along without attempting to interpret the contents of those bytes. Naturally, whether I18N impacts your OS kernel depends on the way it has been implemented.

If some software remains constant because it does no locale-specific processing, other software may stay the same because it is *too* locale-specific. Applications that process federal, provincial, or state taxes often contain so many location-specific rules that it would be inefficient to internationalize the code. Instead, customized or localized software might be the right choice. Note that writing customized code is only recommended if most subroutines and algorithms are specific to a single site. However, in the rare cases when localized code is the correct choice, it obviously remains constant regardless of whatever internationalized functionality exists on the system.

10.2   Why Some Things Stay the Same

There are good reasons why keywords and other names remain constant on an internationalized system. Of course, given the myriad other changes necessary to provide such a system, you may not care *why* some things remain constant; you may simply be thankful that something—anything—does stay the same. However, understanding why certain things don't change makes it easier to remember what you can count on now, and to predict what will remain constant in the future. Among the most important reasons are improved portability, usability, and maintainability.

10.2.1   Portability

Source code that contains a single set of familiar keywords and library routines can be used throughout the world. All that is necessary is a standards-compliant compiler, and the appropriate set of library routines. The compiler can parse the source code because it knows the standard set of keywords. On the other hand, if source code includes locale-specific names for routines, or translations of programming language keywords, only a similarly localized compiler can parse it. Then, the resulting object code only runs on systems that have the same set of localized names.

Consider these two source code lines:

```
printf("%s %d\n", text, number);
imprimef("%s %d\n", texte, numéro);
```

The first example uses the ISO C-compliant call **printf( )**, while the second uses a localized French name for that call—**imprimef( )** (*imprime fichier*). Both examples use language-specific variable names, with the French version including an accented letter (*é*) in one name. It is possible to compile and run the **printf( )** call on many systems around the world. The **imprimef( )** only works at sites with a compiler that understands French names and allows a larger-than-usual set of characters in variable names, and on a system that contains a routine called **imprimef( )**.

Internationalized software that uses constant, standard routine names and keywords is capable of running in whatever locales a given system supports, but such software does not depend on any locale being present in order to run. If the local system includes Danish, Austrian, French, and Korean locales, the internationalized code can run in any of these. If you remove the French and Korean locales, how-

ever, the software still can run in the remaining locales. In contrast, localized code
only works if the particular version of localized names and keywords it needs exists
on the target system, or if the localized functions have been statically bound into the
object code. Without a localized French system or statically bound code, the
imprimef( ) call fails. Such software therefore is not portable.

10.2.2   Usability

The fact that some names are constant means users can interact with the system
one way instead of having to learn and remember multiple translations of such
names. You can run a command like

```
find *.o -print | sort
```

in any locale, and get results that are specific to that locale. You don't, for example,
have to enter a translation like

```
trouve *.o -imprime | tri
```

when running in a French locale. This consistency helps users who run in multiple
locales. It also helps customer services personnel who may communicate with or
support users from multiple locales.

10.2.3   Maintainability

Chapter 3 describes some of the disadvantages of customized or localized software. That chapter concentrates on program text or logic that only works for a single language or culture—for example, hard-coded messages that mean the program
can only interact with users in a single language, or input formats that expect data in
one culture-specific order. This chapter concentrates on the names of routines or
other keywords that might appear in such programs, but both types of customization
face similar maintenance problems.

If you use localized names in source code, you must create a separate version of
the code for each language or culture you wish to support. Then you must apply all
bug fixes and functional changes to all versions. The high level of maintenance
work is likely to slow down your software's evolution. Instead of keeping up with
changing times, it is likely to fall further and further behind.

10.3   An Advantage for English Speakers

Although there are good reasons for consistency in keywords, commands, and routine names, the plain truth is that most such names are English or English-based, and this gives English speakers a perhaps-unfair advantage. After all, a criterion for naming routines or options is that the name be descriptive and easy to remember. An English word like **date**, an abbreviation like **strcoll( )**, (*str*ing *coll*ate), or acronym like **ftp** (*f*ile *t*ransfer *p*rotocol) usually is easier for English speakers to remember because the name has some meaning for them; it is not just a random collection of letters. It may be more challenging for non-English speakers to learn the same names.

It is possible to maintain consistency while removing the English bias from names, but that requires changing all current names to strings that are language-neutral. (Actually, some might argue that with new functions like **wcsxfrm( )** and **mbstowcs( )**, standards committees have achieved the goal of creating names that are incomprehensible to everyone.) Consider one possible implementation. You might choose that all command names consist of three letters, although for portability reasons, you probably would restrict the set of acceptable letters to those in common portable character sets. Such names might look something like this:

```
aaa
aab
aac
aad
.  .  .
baa
bab
.  .  .
```

Such names remove the advantage English speakers enjoy, but they also provide no clue as to their purpose. Given a choice between names like these and more descriptive but English-biased names, most people choose the English-biased names.

10.4   Breaking Rules

Despite the reasons for maintaining consistency in some names and keywords, there may be circumstances under which you decide against using standard names. If you know that all users of your software speak a single language other than

English, you might choose to use localized names. A compiler that includes Chinese keywords may be easier for Chinese programmers to use than one that uses standard keywords. A set of Portuguese command names may help Portuguese-speaking users learn a new system more quickly.

In cases like these, you may decide that the increased ease of use that localized names provide outweighs the loss of portability and increased maintenance problems you are likely to face. Think very carefully, however, before tying software to a single locale. While you may assume now that your software only needs to run in one locale, today's global economy and the increase in worldwide networks makes it increasingly likely that your assumption will prove false. In most cases, you should *not* create custom versions of standard, constant names.

Documenting the World

11

With all the programmatic changes needed to provide an internationalized system, it should come as no surprise that documentation also needs work before it is ready for an international audience. What may be surprising, though, is the type and extent of changes that are needed.

Just as programmers tend to produce software that includes hard-coded cultural assumptions, writers often produce documentation that is just as biased. In some cases, the documentation merely reflects the software's functionality, so there is nothing really "wrong" with it. But in others, the text adds cultural roadblocks that don't exist in the software. It is a fairly safe assumption that in both situations, the writers are not aware of the biases in the text. It also is true that as software gains I18N support, documentation must change to describe the software's new capabilities.

Chapter 2 described some of the variety in linguistic and cultural conventions that exists around the world. This chapter discusses ways documentation must change to embrace that variety. It covers:

- Design strategies for internationalized documentation
- Methods for making information more accessible to international readers
- Methods for making documentation easier to understand for nonnative readers, and easier to translate
- Methods for removing cultural biases from existing text

11.1 Designing Books for International Audiences

Internationalization produces a major change that affects documentation—it changes the way the system works. This means you must add to or revise existing documentation. However, there are several ways to approach the task.

11.1.1 Customized Manuals

Chapter 3 discusses the differences between customizing (or localizing) software and internationalizing it. Customization usually is the first idea that programmers consider, but internationalization is by far the best long-term solution. The same is true with documentation. Suppose your existing documentation is in German and the text and examples reflect German conventions for sorting, dates and time, numeric formatting, and so on. Now the software that the text describes is internationalized. Your first thought may be to produce custom versions of the books. In this scenario, the German book continues to use German examples, while, say, an American English book uses American conventions, a French book uses French rules, and a Japanese book uses Japanese conventions.

This option seems simple. After all, the system may be internationalized, but most individual users want only one locale—their own. Rather than confusing readers with all the possibilities, each version of a manual is localized to their particular needs.

The logic seems compelling, but it doesn't hold up. Manuals typically do not get translated into every language that the software supports because it costs too much to do so. Suppose the software supports 10 European languages as well as Japanese, Chinese, and Korean. Further suppose you can only afford to do translations into French, American English, and Japanese. What about, say, the Italian users? Or the Korean? Or the Dutch? The original German documentation shows the software handling German only. The customized versions are similarly culture-centric. There is no indication that the software supports additional languages.

Even the translations that are available may not meet users' needs. People typically do most work in their own languages, but they need other languages or cultural conventions from time to time. A customized manual, though, gives no hint that such functionality is available.

Internationalized software is capable of producing variety, and the documentation must reflect that capability. Manuals that show only one possibility are holding back on the users. Instead of customizing documentation, you should internationalize it.

11.1.2 Internationalized Books

Whereas customized manuals focus on one way the system works, internationalized books describe the many ways it can work. Customization and internationalization thus result in very different documentation. Consider these two descriptions of ranges in regular expressions:

American English Customized Text:

You can use a dash (-) to indicate a range of consecutive ASCII characters. For example, **[a-d]** is equivalent to **[abcd]**.

Internationalized Text:

You can use a dash (-) to indicate a range of consecutive characters. The current collating sequence, as defined by LC_COLLATE, determines which characters fall within a range. For example, **[a-d]** is equivalent to **[abcd]** if you are using English collation, but with French rules, it matches **[aàâbcçd]**.

The customized version is briefer, but doesn't let users know the full story on range expressions. The internationalized text is much more complete.

As this book shows, many areas of the system change because of I18N, and so existing descriptions of those areas must change, too. In some cases, the changes are no different from those you make every time software gets updated. Any time there is new functionality, documentation must describe it. Describing three new field descriptors that have been added to a utility for I18N reasons is no different from describing three descriptors that were added for any other reason.

However, internationalization adds much more than just a few new field descriptors. There are several discrete pieces of functionality for which you must supply documentation. The pieces may include:

- **Locales.** Documentation may include a conceptual description of locales and the tools available for defining, building, setting, and managing them.
- **Messaging system.** This includes new interfaces and methods for changing existing programs as well as instructions for obtaining translated messages.
- **Wide characters.** In addition to the **wchar_t** typedef, there are many **wchar_t**-based interfaces.
- **Code sets/encoding methods.** An internationalized system usually supports many sets and methods. Documentation must explain which ones it handles.
- **Input methods.** The system may include input methods for entering additional characters.

What you must document depends on the software you are describing. System documentation of commands and libraries must include information about all of these (except possibly input methods). End-user documentation only needs to describe the effects of I18N. For instance, end-user documentation might define locales, explain how to set them, and demonstrate how locales affect the way the system or a given application works. However, it does not need to include information about defining, building, and managing locales.

In addition to major new parts of the system, I18N typically causes a ripple of other changes throughout the system—and therefore the documentation. Regular expressions, sorting, character classification, date and time formatting, and numeric formatting are among the existing types of functionality that I18N changes dramatically. In addition to these large changes, there are a host of smaller ones. The section Fixing Existing Text later in this chapter covers smaller but essential changes you probably need to make to existing documentation.

As you plan your documentation effort, you must include time for all three types of I18N changes: major new pieces of functionality, significant revisions to existing capabilities, and all the details. You also must decide how detailed you want your internationalized descriptions to be. There are several possibilities.

11.1.3 Endless Possibilities, Endless Manuals?

A customized manual shows only one way to complete a task. Does that mean an internationalized book has to show all possibilities? Not unless you expect users to haul around your manuals in wheelbarrows. They would need to if you described everything because the books would be huge.

Take a simple example. Suppose you are writing documentation for the **date** utility. In pre-I18N days, if a user executed **date** without flags or arguments, the utility printed the date and time using English strings for day and month names. The output looked something like this:

% date
```
Mon Jul 12 15:24:33 EDT 1993
```

An internationalized version of **date** is capable of much more than this single type of string. It uses the current locale to decide how to format information, and to find language-appropriate versions of the day and month names. Still keeping the example simple, assume your company ships locale-specific data for eight Western European locales—British English, Danish, Dutch, French, German, Italian, Spanish, and Swedish—as well as supporting the original American English. If you document all possibilities, the description might look like this:

To display the date and time, enter:

% date

Depending on the current locale, the output looks like one of the following:

Am-English	`Mon Jul 12 15:24:33 EDT 1993`
Br-English	`Mon 12 Jul 15:24:33 BST 1993`
Danish	`man 12 jul 15:24:33 MET 1993`
Dutch	`Ma 12 Jul 15:24:33 MET 1993`
French	`lun 12 jul 15:24:33 MET 1993`
German	`Mo 12 Jul 15:24:33 MET 1993`
Italian	`lun 12 lug 15:24:33 MET 1993`
Spanish	`Lu 12 Jul 15:24:33 MET 1993`
Swedish	`mån 12 jul 15:24:33 MET 1993`

Talk about overkill. While a customized manual provides too little information, this is too much. And remember that this shows a relatively simple example of a system that supports less than 10 locales. Over time, the number of locales on a system grows. Documentation becomes unusable if your strategy is to list every possibility.

The correct approach is to list a representative sample of the internationalized capabilities. For the **date** description, you might include three of the possible outcomes. That lets users know what **date** can do without overwhelming them. And, in fact, this is the same approach you probably already take elsewhere in the documentation. You probably don't provide examples for every utility option. Rather, you pick a few and leave the others as an exercise to the reader.

Choosing some possibilities is a good compromise between the *All* and *One* ends of the spectrum, but even that can become tedious. Suppose you are describing an internationalized **sort** utility. The utility probably includes five to 10 options that users can mix and match. Since sorting is locale-dependent, these options all produce varieties of results. A flag that ignores case can do so in a French locale, a German locale, and others. A flag that removes duplicates can strip them from Spanish output, Japanese output, or any other supported locale. Other flags work in all locales.

It doesn't make sense to include the fact that sorting is locale-dependent in each flag description. Nor is it a good idea to show three or four locales' output for each **sort** example. Instead, the general command description should cover what kinds of sorts the utility performs and explain that the current locale affects sort output. This information is absolutely essential if users are to understand what I18N capabilities exist. Once you have provided the general information, some—but not all—examples should show the different types of sorts and should demonstrate the way output varies depending on the current locale.

11.2   Making Information Accessible

Just as internationalization adds new functionality to the system that must be documented, it also brings new users to the system. Those users have new requirements for the way you document software. This includes enhancing sections like glossaries and indexes to help nonnative readers find information, making sure the text includes international examples, and choosing graphic images that enlighten instead of confuse.

11.2.1   Tools for Finding Information

In some cases, the guidelines for providing well-internationalized documentation seem very much like those for any documentation. This certainly is the case for tools like glossaries, indexes, and tables of contents. It always has been important to stock glossaries with clearly defined terms. Such glossaries help readers learn new and unfamiliar terms. Similarly, writing gurus consistently stress the importance of detailed indexes and tables of contents. Technical documentation isn't supposed to be like a mystery novel that keeps readers guessing. Rather, tools like indexes and tables of contents should help them find information quickly and easily.

If it is possible, internationalization makes it even more important that you do a good job on these parts of the books. As the level of I18N support in software increases, it becomes increasingly likely that people around the world will use the software. The worldwide users probably are not fluent in your language, so they need extra consideration.

You may need to add more terms to your glossary. Technical language changes very quickly, but it doesn't change uniformly. A term that is common to people in your country may not exist yet in other countries. Or separate users may use different terms for a concept. This happens even before software moves outside national boundaries—when starting a new job, one of the first tasks is to learn the local versions of technical terms. What might have been called a *directory* at your last job is now a *queue*, and a *flag* becomes a *switch*.

Same-language vocabularies tend to become more disparate when they move to other countries. An American English term may have a different name in British English and still another name in Australian English. To avoid confusion for readers who use a different technical vocabulary, your glossary should include clear definitions of the way *you* are using a word or phrase. It is particularly important to add entries for terms that either don't appear in an average dictionary for your language or that take on a new meaning in a technical setting.

Consider the English word *construct*. Some dictionaries define this only as a verb that means to build or make. But in technical documentation, *construct* can be a noun that means a structure built from simpler elements (*These data constructs allow you to build arbitrary length records* . . .). Users' English dictionaries may not include *construct*'s meaning as a noun. If you use such a term in your documentation, you need to include the definition in your glossary.

If glossaries need to grow, so too do indexes. An international user may not think of the same name for a concept as does a native-language reader. Therefore, it is important to add more cross-references. Instead of a single listing like this index entry:

> *removing*
>   *characters 35*
>   *directories 24, 115*
>   *files 23-24, 44, 225*
>   *words 35-36*

you should include synonyms like:

> *deleting (see* removing*)*
> . . .
> *erasing (see* removing*)*

Additional entries make it easier for international readers to find the information they need.

11.2.2   International Examples

The fact that your text will have worldwide readership may impact your examples. Documentation often includes references to entities or sample users that are specific to one culture. You should shake loose of such artificial boundaries.

Take names. Early American technical documentation often used male names like *Dan, David,* and *Larry* in examples. Over time, examples changed to include female names like *Marjorie* and *Alice.* Both men and women were using the software, so it was important for the examples to reflect this reality.

Now reality is changing again. Men and women around the world are likely to use manuals that describe an internationalized system. If your documentation includes names from a single culture, you should consider broadening your outlook. Table 11.1 shows examples of male and female given names and of family names (surnames) along with each name's nationality. Note that many names are common in multiple countries; the table just notes the nationality with which the name may be most closely associated.

Table 11.1   Sample International Names

Type	Name	Nationality
Female	Alka	Indian
	Mariko	Japanese
	Mitra	Iranian
	Natalia	Russian
	Simone	French
Male	Antonio	Italian
	Dieter	German
	Stavros	Greek
	Takashi	Japanese
Family	Itoh	Japanese
	Kim	Korean
	Paulsen	Danish
	Richter	German

In addition to names, other examples often are culture-specific. While such examples are not exactly wrong, they may be more useful if they lose some of their home-grown look. Suppose you have an example that produces a sorted list of American states. You should consider changing the example to use a list of countries. Not all international readers know the 50 American states, but nearly all should be familiar with country names.

Another example might be of a utility that compares two sorted lists of data. If you are producing documentation in France, you might use names of French cities for the entries in the two lists (for example, Bordeaux, Calais, Lille, Lyon, Marseille, Orléans, Paris). The example is less limited, however, if you include names from around the world—names like Bangkok, Buenos Aires, Nairobi, New York City, Paris, Sydney, Tokyo, and others.

When creating examples, think beyond your own country's borders.

11.2.3   Not-So-Worldly Symbols

In addition to internationalizing text, you also need to think about the graphic images in your books. Many are culture-specific, and won't always convey your intended message.

Think about a question mark (?). This is an ideograph that in most cultures indicates a question. Suppose your books use an icon with a question mark to denote "Related Information" sections like this:

 time(2), setlocale(3C),
strftime(3C), environ(5),
langinfo(5)

These sections explain where users should look for more information (that is, if they have questions). The icon seems so clear and concise that you see no need for the explicit "Related Information" header. It's understood, right?

Not necessarily. In Greek, the semi-colon (;) denotes a question. That means the question mark icon may not convey the right message to a Greek reader.

Mail-related icons also are good examples of cultural specificity. Mailboxes around the world take an astounding variety of shapes, confounding nonnative visitors. Given these differences, an icon of your country's mailbox may be a mystifying symbol to nonnative readers.

Few graphic symbols are truly global (for instance, there is no single way to indicate a question), but there are steps you can take to ensure that readers understand the ones you use. Consult with users in your target markets to determine which symbols are culture-bound and which are more widely understood. If possible, replace very specific symbols with more international ones. Mailboxes may differ around the world, but envelopes look similar. Instead of using your mailbox in an icon, use an envelope. In addition, you should include a table that lists the graphic symbols used in your book and their interpretation. This information makes sure users get the right message.

11.3   Translation and Understanding

The previous sections concentrate on general design strategies for including both internationalization functionality and international readers in documentation. An offshoot of internationalized software is that as your base of international users grows, there may be more demand for translated versions of your books. In addition, since books often are translated into only a few languages, many users reading the original language documentation will not be native speakers of that language.

There are steps you can take to make manuals easier to translate and easier for nonnative readers to understand, and this section describes some of these steps. However, this section does not include a complete set of guidelines; such completeness is beyond the scope of this book.

Before reading the guidelines, keep in mind that it is your responsibility to produce text that translators and nonnative readers can understand. Translators only translate what appears in the original language document; they do not rewrite text to remove or explain culture-bound references. If you use an example that assumes a high level of familiarity with, say, American geography, the translator does not change that example to use sites in the local country. Similarly, the translator does not add text that explains the nuances of American geography. Even if translators did rewrite text to make it easier for target users, such revisions would not help nonnative readers of the original language documentation. That is why it is so important for your original text to be clear and easy to understand.

11.3.1 Clear Text

The best way to help translators and nonnative readers is to give them clearly written text. Once again, this sounds like general good writing rules, but there is a special emphasis on clarity when you know text will be translated or read by nonnative readers. While translators of technical documentation and international users usually are technically savvy, they often are not experts in the documentation's subject. (This is particularly true for translators.) You can't rely on them to understand what you meant to write; they can only go by what appears in the original language file. The better your writing, the easier it is to understand or translate the text.

One way to improve the clarity of your documentation is to use as little jargon (specialized vocabulary) as possible. Before using the newest term for a given concept, consider whether an existing phrase conveys the same meaning. If so, use the existing term.

Despite the advice to reduce jargon, the nature of technical documentation means that it *must* include new terms or use old ones in ways the dictionary never intended. A jargon-free manual might well be a content-free manual. This book contains dozens of terms that are specific to internationalization. Examples include:

code set
encoding method
locale
messaging
multilevel collation
multibyte character
wide character

Without terms like these, the text would lose much of its precision and content.

Since you probably can't eliminate jargon, you must define it clearly. Good definitions ensure that translators understand your writing. As a side bonus, clear definitions help native readers as well.

Text can be crystal clear to native readers and still cause problems for translators or nonnative readers. That is the case if the text includes slang, puns, or other word play. You may include slang to liven up otherwise dull text, and use word play to express a point more succinctly than plain text allows. Well-used slang and word play help hold native readers' interest, and it is important to remember their needs. (Even with internationalization, they probably outnumber foreign readers.) But efforts to keep native readers interested may confuse others.

If you write something that may be difficult to translate, add comments to the source file. The previous paragraph uses the English idiom *crystal clear*. You might add something like this to the source (*TN* indicates a Translator's Note):

.\" TN -- the phrase "crystal clear" means "completely clear."
.P
Text can be crystal clear to native readers and still cause problems . . .

The comment helps ensure an accurate translation. However, translator notes are only a partial solution to the problems that slang and other similar text cause. Nonnative readers who do not have access to a translation do not see translator notes, so the text still may be confusing to them. Therefore, in most cases, you should avoid slang, idioms, and word play.

11.3.2   Limiting Vocabularies

Since the reason for removing jargon and slang is to simplify text, some writing authorities recommend taking the work a step further and limiting vocabularies. There are many variations of this approach, but most involve strict rules about what text can contain.

The least restrictive approach is to create lists of words that writers must avoid. Such lists include words that are deemed difficult to translate or that have unclear, meanings. Generally, acceptable substitutes for the forbidden words are provided. For example, some major American computer manufacturers forbid the use of contractions in text because they consider contractions to be confusing to translators. Therefore, instead of, say, *don't, can't, won't,* and *it's*, documentation must contain *do not, can not, will not,* and *it is*.

A more far-reaching approach to simplifying text involves sets of usage guidelines. For English, there are several such sets with names like *Controlled English*,

Simplified English, and *International English.* These systems include some or all of these characteristics:

- **No synonyms allowed.** Strictly limited vocabularies designate one way to express a concept. Table 11.2 shows groups of similar terms, and the one that might be chosen for a limited vocabulary list.

Table 11.2   Many Possibilities, One Choice

Synonyms	Approved Term
collate, order, sort	sort
command, utility	utility
display, monitor, screen, tube	screen
display, demonstrate, show	show
delete, erase, remove, strip	delete
documentation, text	text
flag, option, switch	flag

Documentation without synonyms reads differently than less restricted text. Here is part of a paragraph from earlier in this chapter that uses synonyms freely:

> Suppose you are describing an internationalized **sort** utility. The utility probably includes five to 10 options that users can mix and match. Since sorting is locale-dependent, these options all can produce varieties of results. . . . A flag that removes duplicates can strip them from Spanish output, Japanese output, or any other supported locale.

The following shows how you might rewrite this paragraph to use a limited vocabulary. Italics mark changes.

> Suppose you are describing an internationalized **sort** utility. The utility probably includes five to 10 *flags.* Since sorting is locale-dependent, these *flags* all can produce varieties of results. . . . A flag that *deletes* duplicates can *delete* them from Spanish output, Japanese output, or any other supported locale.

- **One meaning allowed per word.** Many limited vocabulary systems prohibit reusing words. For example, the word *display* has multiple meanings including as a noun referring to a computer screen (. . . *the information appears on the display*) and a verb meaning "to show" (*If you want to display the information . . .*).

- **No idioms, abbreviations, acronyms, slang, or jargon allowed.** Previous sections in this chapter describe the problems associated with jargon, slang, and otherwise informal text.
- **Text uses active voice and simple verbs as much as possible.** Here are examples of original and rewritten text:

> **Example 1; passive voice:**
> In order to collate non-ASCII text, *use of* internationalized sort routines *is required.*
>
> **Rewrite using active voice:**
> In order to collate non-ASCII text, *use* internationalized sort routines.
>
> **Example 2; compound verb:**
> The requirements for internationalized collation *can be satisfied* with routines like **strcoll( )** and **wcscoll( )**.
>
> **Rewrite using simple verb:**
> Routines like **strcoll( )** and **wcscoll( )** *satisfy* international collation requirements.

As these examples show, active voice and simple verbs often are easier to understand.

Some aspects of simplified language systems improve text significantly. This includes guidelines limiting passive voice, complicated verbs, idioms, and slang. But there are important disadvantages to limited vocabularies. The disadvantages include:

- **Reducing the text's precision.** Limited vocabularies reduce or eliminate synonyms. This may have no impact on your text if multiple words really have equivalent meanings. However, different words often convey slightly different meanings. Table 11.2 shows *documentation* and *text* as being synonyms. In many ways they are, but *documentation* usually refers only to printed manuals or on-line reference pages. *Text* is a more general term that includes documentation, on-line help, program messages, menus, and other textual data. If writers can use only the general term, there is no easy way to refer specifically to the documentation.

- **Forcing awkward phrasing**. Since limited vocabularies may prohibit using the right word, you may have to use several. Instead of referring to *documentation,* you may write about *the text in books or on-line reference pages.* Such phrases are awkward. They also may increase overall text size.
- **Adding distractions for the reader**. The guideline against using acronyms leads to some interesting anomalies. Words like *radar* (*r*adio *d*etecting *a*nd *r*anging) and *laser* (*l*ight *a*mplification by *s*timulated *e*mission of *r*adiation) are acronyms, but they are accepted as true words and appear in English dictionaries. Most people probably are unaware of their linguistic heritage. Guidelines that force these words to be spelled out distract readers rather than illuminating them. Naturally, it is vital to spell out acronyms that are not as commonly accepted.
- **Producing boring results**. Documentation that uses the same few words may help translators and nonnative readers, but if you simplify text so much that it resembles a child's reading book, your native-language readers may find the text unacceptably dull. Since native-language readers almost always are the largest percentage of your audience, you can't ignore their requirements.

The disadvantages of limited vocabularies may outweigh the small advantage they give translators and nonnative readers. Technical documentation needs to be precise, and that means writers need the freedom to use the right words. However, you must weigh the cost of such freedom against the skills of your translation team and the average fluency of target nonnative readers. In general, the more experienced translators are with the technology your documentation describes, the less the advantage of limited vocabularies. Similarly, the more fluent your nonnative readers are, the less need there is for limited text.

If you decide against limiting vocabularies, that doesn't mean your documentation should resemble a thesaurus. Use the words you need—no more, no less. Don't use words or terms that are easily confused. While the total ban on contractions mentioned earlier probably goes too far, some contractions are confusing or just plain wrong (for example, *he'll* and *shouldn't've*). You should ban such words from your text.

11.3.3 Reordered Text

Some parts of documentation commonly are provided as ordered lists. Glossaries typically include lists of words and phrases in alphabetic order, while reference pages (man pages) also list system commands or interfaces in alphabetic order. Compiler manuals may feature alphabetized lists of programming language key-words, together with descriptions of those words.

Alphabetizing helps users find terms quickly, but it is important to remember that the order changes when text gets translated. Whereas *computer* comes before *software* in English, the order changes for the equivalent French words (*logiciel* is before *ordinateur*). This means entries in ordered documentation must be independent of each other. For example, an entry for *code sets* should not include a statement like: "For more information, see *encoding methods* later in this section." After translation, *encoding methods* may move ahead of *code sets*. To fix this problem, remove position references in ordered lists.

Remember that order is language-specific and thus variable.

11.3.4 That's Not Funny

Since technical documentation tends to be fairly dry and straightforward, you may be tempted to use humor to liven it up. It seems logical that some clever phrases or puns make the text easier to understand and more enjoyable for all readers. You may also reason that humor helps keep readers' attention.

While humor seems like a useful teaching tool—or, at worst, harmless—it actually creates several problems:

- Humor often is difficult or impossible to translate
- Nonnative readers may find the humor incomprehensible or offensive

Humor relies on very detailed knowledge of a language, but more importantly on shared ideas about what is funny. A reader or translator may be fluent in the text's original language, but the humor may fail because it relies on a culture-specific point of view. A joke about one ethnic group usually is offensive to another ethnic group (particularly the joke's target). Similarly, a situation that is funny in one culture isn't in another. This may make the "funny" part of your text untranslatable.

If humor is difficult for people who are fluent in the original language, it is even harder for less-than-fluent readers. For them, the text may simply be incomprehensible. Since the goal of technical documentation is to educate users, you should avoid a writing style that leaves some of them mystified.

11.3.5 Terminology Lists

After deciding whether to use a limited vocabulary, and after removing position dependencies from ordered lists, and after (perhaps reluctantly) removing the puns and other humor from your text, you should do one more thing to help translators. Compile a *terminology list* of the significant words and phrases that appear in your text so the translators can use it to create a *translation table.*

A translation table contains approved translations of the terms in the terminology list. When the translators find a term from the list in your text, they translate it as the table specifies. This avoids inconsistencies within manuals or manual sets. That is because in many cases, multiple translators work on your text. Individuals have distinct vocabularies, so without a translation table they tend to choose multiple ways to translate a given phrase. This could create confusion for readers.

A terminology list should not contain every word that appears in your text. There is no need to include common words like *the, and, of, or, you, we* and others. Similarly, you can omit simple verbs and nouns like *go, do, book,* and *word.* Any competent translator knows how to translate these words. Rather, the terminology list should focus on terms that are specific to your topic, or that have multiple meanings. It should include all glossary terms, but that's just the beginning. For example, most glossaries don't include entries for *computer, file, program,* and *software,* but these words should be on your terminology list.

In general, if you are unsure whether to include a term on the list, add it.

11.3.6 Graphical Changes for Translation

Guidelines about translation often focus on the ordinary text—sentences, paragraphs, section headings, glossary entries—that make up the majority of documentation. However, there is other text that needs special attention. That is the text that appears in tables and illustrations.

The amount of space it takes to express a thought differs from language to language. On average, French and German consume 10 to 30 percent more space than does the equivalent English. For short phrases, the difference may be even higher. (Naturally, there are exceptions, but these percentages reflect averages.) If your original documentation is in English, and the illustrations have hard-coded dependencies on the length of the English text, the French and German (or other language) translations may not fit.

There are several ways to accommodate variable text lengths. Some text formatting tools determine the dimensions of a box or table based on the text that goes in the box. When text changes, the tool recalculates the dimensions. If your formatting tool has this ability, use it. Most tables in this book were created using variable dimensions.

Another way to handle variable text lengths is to move text outside boxes and onto separate lines. Since the words no longer have to fit inside a fixed-width box,

there is no problem if they grow or shrink. Figure 11.1 shows an example of this
kind of illustration.

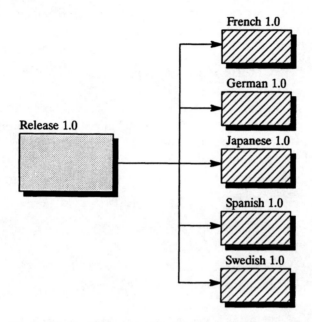

Figure 11.1   Illustration That Allows Text Expansion

With this illustration, it doesn't matter how long the local language equivalents are
for words like *French, German,* and the others. They can expand to the right
beyond the boundaries of the boxes.

11.4   Fixing Existing Text

The internationalization process for documentation often focuses on highly visible issues, including describing major new functionality and preparing books to be
translated. But I18N affects nearly every part of the system, and that includes many
details in existing documentation. Your work is not complete until you find and fix
the small problems.

The details usually are not obvious when you review text. They often include
words, phrases, or examples you have used for years without question. This section
covers some common phrases and examples, explains why they may be incorrect,
and suggests ways to rewrite them. In the revisions, *italic type* marks changes.

You will find that some changes are necessary regardless of whether your software has been internationalized; the current description probably is wrong. Naturally, before making changes, check with your programmer to determine how the software you are documenting works.

11.4.1 ASCII Right and Wrong

When it comes to describing internationalized software, *ASCII* probably is the most misused word in existing documentation. Most of the time that it does appear, it is used incorrectly, and there are many times when it doesn't appear, but should.

Take the first situation. It is extremely common to use *ASCII* as a synonym for *text* or to describe characters. Documentation often contains dozens of such references. Consider these phrases:

1. The utility produces formatted ASCII output . . .
2. Use **lpr** to send ASCII files . . .
3. Words are selected as a range of ASCII characters . . .
4. Comments can include any ASCII character . . .

Before internationalization, these examples probably would have been correct. In general, programs then could only handle ASCII, so it was acceptable to refer to *ASCII files* or *ASCII characters*. However, an internationalized system is capable of handling many code sets and encoding methods. For such a system, *ASCII* is wrong in each of the preceding examples. In the first two, the word is used to mean text or data. In the last two examples, the word is unnecessarily restrictive and must be removed. Here is how you might rewrite each of these phrases:

1. The utility produces formatted *text* output . . .
2. Use **lpr** to send *text* files . . .
3. Words are selected as a range *of characters* . . .
4. Comments can include *any character* . . .

While these examples demonstrate the circumstances under which you should remove *ASCII* from text, there are situations that call for adding it. That is because some software really does handle only ASCII. Consider a compiler. It is common for compilers to allow any character in a comment or string, but to restrict identifiers such as variable and function names to including only a subset of ASCII characters. Suppose your current documentation includes this information:

An identifier must meet the following criteria:

- The first character is a letter
- The remaining characters are any of the following:
    - Letters
    - Digits
    - Underscore (_)
    - Period (.)
- The name must be no more than 32 characters

Assume the identifiers can only include ASCII characters. This description then is far too generous. It allows names like où, nächste, and sí (French, German, and Spanish words, respectively) because it says identifiers can include "letters." Clearly, *ù, ä*, and *í* are letters, but they aren't ASCII letters. For those cases when only specific characters are permitted, the documentation should state this restriction. Here is how to revise the description of valid identifiers:

An identifier must meet the following criteria:

- The first character is *an ASCII letter (A–Z or a–z)*
- The remaining characters are any of the following:
    - *ASCII letters*
    - Digits *(0–9)*
    - . . .

The first reference to ASCII letters clearly specifies the letters that are part of the acceptable set. Since the first reference is so close to the second, it is not necessary to spell out the range the second time.

11.4.2 Characters and Bytes

Just as *ASCII* and *text* have often been used interchangeably, so too have *characters* and *bytes*. The second pair reflects the fact that on many uninternationalized systems, a character consumes one byte. The two words have been intertwined for other reasons. Textual data types in programming languages tend to have names like **char** or **character**, even though these types designate a byte of storage. Consider these array declarations:

C	`char my_array[80];`
FORTRAN	`CHARACTER*80 my_array`
Pascal	`my_array : array[1..80] of CHAR;`

These examples seem to declare arrays of 80 characters, but the arrays really are 80 bytes. That's because each data type assumes all characters are one byte each. However, as you learned in Chapter 4, characters can span multiple bytes. This means a string of, say, five characters consumes at least five and possibly more bytes. The actual amount of space required depends on the number of bytes in each character.

Clearly, in an internationalized system, *characters* and *bytes* no longer are synonyms. This tends to have a significant impact on documentation. The earlier example about identifiers included the phrase

The name must be no more than 32 characters

If the software you are describing handles multiple-byte or wide characters, a phrase like this is incorrect. The length refers to the maximum number of bytes rather than characters. Bytes are fixed units; characters are variable. In most cases, any time documentation includes a specific number before the word *characters*, the word should change to *bytes*. So the phrase above becomes

The name must be no more than *32 bytes*

Statements that refer to specific numbers of characters tend to be sprinkled throughout documentation, so finding and fixing all of them takes some time. Here are a few more examples:

Original: ctime( ) returns a pointer to a 26-character string . . .
Revision: ctime( ) returns a pointer to a *26-byte* string . . .

Original: A path name can contain up to 1024 characters . . .
Revision: A path name can contain up to *1024 bytes* . . .

Original: The editor allocates 128-character buffers . . .
Revision: The editor allocates *128-byte* buffers . . .

The difference between characters and bytes affects other parts of the documentation. Consider the command **wc** (word count). This utility includes a **-c** flag which originally was defined as counting the number of characters in a file. Thus, the flag name was a mnemonic for the task it performed. Unfortunately, **-c** never counted characters; it counted bytes. This difference was insignificant when bytes and characters were the same thing, but that is not the case on an internationalized system. In order to define **wc**'s functionality correctly, the documentation must say that **-c** counts bytes.

Notice that as a result of internationalization, there sometimes is a difference between the obvious and actual meaning of a data type or utility option. There is too much historical baggage to change, for example, **char** to **byte**, even though the latter name is more correct. This means you must be especially careful in documentation to explain actual meanings or behaviors.

You may also need to provide extra background information to readers. While changing specific character counts to byte counts adds accuracy to the text, the counts may confuse some readers. They may not know what bytes are, or how many bytes their characters consume. You either need to describe bytes and characters, or to point readers to another document that contains this information.

11.4.3 "Alphabetic" Order

Internationalization affects few aspects of software as much as it does collation. Naturally, changes to software affect the documentation. Suppose you want to describe the results of a command that produces sorted output. If you write about the **ls** command, your documentation might include this sentence:

By default, the **ls** command lists file names sorted alphabetically.

This seems simple and straightforward enough. What could possibly be wrong? The problem is twofold—one part explicit, one part implicit.

First, the explicit problem. This description is only valid for languages that use an alphabetic writing system. Since Japanese Kanji or Chinese Hanja are ideographs rather than phonetic letters, they can't be sorted "alphabetically." If taken literally, this description says ideographs can't be sorted. However, internationalized versions of **ls** can collate such data, so this description is wrong.

Second, there is an unstated, but implicit assumption that **ls** sorts file names only one way. However, once software includes support for internationalized sorting, data can be collated many ways. The particular way data appears depends on the locale that is active when the sort runs. Suppose you are running a French locale when you use **ls**. The file names appear in French sorted order. Similarly, if your locale is Japanese, the data appears in Japanese sorted order.

In order to fix the explicit and implicit problems in the example text, you can revise it this way:

> By default, the **ls** command lists file names *in sorted order as determined by the current locale.*

This removes the incorrect reference to alphabetic orders, and correctly explains that data may be sorted in many ways. In general, when referring to collation, you must specify that it is a locale-dependent function.

Another sort-related change in documentation has to do with text that ties collation to code set. Some utilities require collated input, and a typical way to describe this is:

> *file1* and *file2* must be in ASCII sorted order . . .

You already have learned that most references to *ASCII* are obsolete, and this one is no exception. Since data can be sorted many ways, it is incorrect to restrict the input to a single order and a single code set. You can reword this as follows:

> *file1* and *file2* must be in *sorted order as determined by the current locale* . . .

11.4.4   Ranges of Characters

The fact that data can be sorted many ways has a direct impact on another common type of phrase in documentation: a range of characters. In English, something is all-inclusive if it includes *everything from A to Z.* Technical documentation tends to reflect the same belief that the range A–Z includes everything, but this isn't true for systems that support more than English.

You learned earlier that some alphabets include letters after Z. For such alphabets, A–Z is a few letters short of the full range. The problem becomes even more acute in languages that don't use Latin letters. A range like A–Z has no meaning when working with Japanese Kanji characters, or with Arabic letters, or with Hindi. And the range has only a misleading relationship to scripts like Greek and Cyrillic. They both begin with letters that look like the Latin A, but are considered separate, different characters. Both end with letters that don't exist in the Latin alphabet. For instance, Greek ends with Ω (omega).

So A–Z isn't the beginning and the end that you might have thought it was. This means you have to revise documentation that includes such a range. Suppose your text includes the following:

A string can contain any valid letter (A–Z, a–z), digit (0–9), or punctuation character.

Assume the software you are describing has been partially internationalized and can accept alphabetic characters from many languages rather than just ASCII letters. The software can't, however, handle ideographs such as Japanese Kanji or Chinese Hanja. In this scenario, the specific range is incorrect, because it doesn't work for languages like Swedish, Danish, Polish, and others that have letters after Z. To describe the software's functionality correctly, simply omit the specific range. The sentence becomes:

A string can contain *any valid letter*, digit (0–9), or punctuation character.

Now take this revision a step further. Suppose the software has additional I18N support and now can accept ideographs. That means the reference to letters is wrong—or at least incomplete—because it doesn't include ideographs. You can rewrite the sentence two ways:

1. A string can contain *any valid graphic character.*
2. A string can contain *any valid graphic character. This includes letters, ideographs, digits, and punctuation.*

The first example is correct, but may not provide enough information. The second spells things out more clearly.

A–Z's change in status probably also affects some existing examples. Consider this example of the **grep** utility:

```
grep '^[A-Z]' my_data
```

This displays all lines in the file my_data that begin with uppercase letters. At least, that's the intention. Since not all uppercase letters fall in the range of *A–Z*, you need to rewrite the example. Assuming your system has internationalized regular expressions, here is how to rewrite it:

```
grep '^[[:upper:]]' my_data
```

Smaller ranges than the formerly all-inclusive *A–Z* also may need to change when you document an internationalized system. Suppose you are describing how to print a subset of file names in a directory. The documentation might include something like this:

To display a subset of files in the current directory, enter:

```
ls [c-f]*
```

This lists all files with names that begin with any of *c, d, e,* or *f.*

The problem is that what falls within a range depends on the collation rules in effect at utility run time. If you run in a case-segregated French locale, [c-f] includes *c, ç, d, e, è, é, ê, ë,* and *f.* In a mixed-case French locale, the range takes in even more letters: *c, C, ç, Ç, d, D, e, E, è, È, é, É, ê, Ê, ë, Ë,* and *f.* In a case-segregated Hungarian locale, the range encompasses *c, d, e, é,* and *f.* For German or English mixed-case locales, the range includes *c, C, d, D, e, E,* and *f.* (Notice that for mixed-case sorts, the range does not include uppercase *F.* These examples assume lowercase letters collate before uppercase.) The documentation should reflect some of this diversity. You can rewrite the text this way:

To display a subset of files in the current directory, enter:

```
ls [c-f]*
```

This lists all files with names that begin with *characters that fall within the listed range as determined by the current locale. For example, in a case-segregated French locale, [c-f] includes c, ç, d, e, è, é, ê, ë, and f. In a similar English locale, the range includes c, d, e, and f.*

This is not the only way to rewrite the text. If you already have provided a description and examples of the effect of locales on range expressions, you might refer readers to that information; it is not necessary to repeat the information in multiple places.

11.4.5 Dates and Time in Text

Nearly all information in a date or time is bound to culture in some way. The Gregorian calendar, according to which this book was written in the 1990s, is the most widespread, but numerous countries and regions use alternate calendars. Differences in dates and times aren't limited to calendars. Each language has its own names for days of the week or months in the year. The 24-hour clock is most popular in some regions; the 12-hour clock in others. Every place has its own ideas about the way to order and format the information in a date or time.

Because these conventions (discussed in more detail in Chapter 2) exist, it is important for documentation to reflect the diversity and to describe any formatting assumptions software makes about dates or times. This applies equally to internationalized and uninternationalized systems. Suppose you are documenting a database program that allows users to make date-based queries. The instructions might include something like this:

> To produce a report of all orders that occurred within a specific time, enter the start and end dates. For example:

```
print orders with entry_date from 10/1 to 10/7
```

> This produces a list of the orders that were placed between October 1 and October 7.

These instructions are incomplete because they don't describe formatting assumptions. The text says the query produces a report of orders between October 1 and October 7, so the dates in the sample query must be in *month/day* order. Depending on the level of I18N support in the program, the text is either incomplete or wrong.

Take the case of the text being incomplete. If the software has not been internationalized and can only accept dates in *month/day* order, you must document this restriction. Without specific instructions, a European user might enter the start and end dates in *day/month* order and get a report covering January 10 (1/10) through July 10 (7/10). Here's how to rewrite the text:

> To produce a report of all orders that occurred within a specific time, enter the start and end *dates in month/day order.* For example: ...

Now consider the case of the text being wrong. Internationalized software can accept dates in different formats, so the text can not say there is one and only one way to input data. In that case, you must revise the text to reflect the functionality. You could rewrite it this way:

> To produce a report of all orders that occurred within a specific time, enter the start and end *dates in the appropriate format for the locale.* For example:

```
print orders with entry_date from 10/1 to 10/7
```

> *If your locale's date format is month/day,* this produces a list of the orders that

were placed between October 1 and October 7. *If the date format is day/month, this produces a report for January 10 through July 10.*

In general, any time software expects dates or times in a specific format, you should provide that information. Alternatively, if your software can accept variety, make that clear.

You should also spell out assumptions about the first value in a date sequence. Consider these date field descriptions:

a   Displays the abbreviated day of the week (locale-specific version of *Sun* to *Sat*)

h   Displays the abbreviated month in the year (locale-specific version of *Jan* to *Dec*)

The references to locales reflect that there are different names for weekdays and months. The descriptions also state that the first day of the week is the *Sunday* equivalent, and the first month of the year is the *January* equivalent. This avoids any confusion for users who are accustomed to different conventions.

Just as you need to spell out assumptions about dates, you also must be careful with times. Nearly all cultures agree there are 24 hours in a day, but some use a 24-hour clock, while others use the 12-hour version. If the software expects times in one or the other, you need to state that in the documentation. Similarly, you must describe the way(s) the software outputs times.

There is one easy aspect to time. While everything else about dates and times is culture-dependent, 60-minute hours and 60-second minutes seem to be nearly universal.

11.4.6   Answering Yes or No

Of all the kinds of input programs expect from users—everything from names and addresses to user names and passwords—there is one kind that turns up most often. It is a question that needs a yes or no answer. Simple commands include yes/no questions (for instance, *Save file foobar? [y or n]* or *rm: remove temp_file?*), as do text editors (*1 modified buffer; do you really want to exit? [yes or no]*), and countless other programs.

The words for *yes* and *no* differ from language to language, and an internationalized system allows users to enter the words that are appropriate for their locale. However, documentation often restricts the software to the English words. For example:

... but if you use the **-i** flag with **rm**, you are prompted, allowing you to answer y(yes) to delete the file, or n(no) to retain it.

In order to reflect the variety an internationalized system includes, you can rewrite this several ways. Here are two possibilities:

1.   ... but if you use the **-i** flag with **rm**, you are prompted, allowing you *to delete* the file, or *to retain* it.
2.   ... but if you use the **-i** flag with **rm**, you are prompted, allowing you *to delete* the file, or *to retain it. Enter the equivalent to yes or no for your locale.*

Both revisions remove the reference to the English words for *yes* and *no*. Both also are correct, but the first may not provide enough information. The second example clearly describes what the user should do.

Although these revisions are enough for many cases, for some software they are too vague. Suppose a Spanish user types *sí* in answer to a yes/no query. Some programs only look at the first character and assume trailing characters are answers to subsequent questions. If that is how your software works, you must document this assumption. Similarly, if your software accepts characters in a specific case, or only takes full strings (*yes, oui, ja, sí*, and so on) rather than abbreviations (*y, o, j, s*), the documentation must include these facts.

11.4.7 Program Messages

While culture-specific software usually can only produce program messages in one language, internationalized products are capable of interacting with users in a variety. Because program messages can appear in several languages, documentation should reflect this diversity. It is not correct for the text to state that a user *will* see a specific message. Remember, too, that documentation often is not translated into all users' languages, so it is very possible that those running in, say, French, German, or Chinese locales may be reading English-language documentation while seeing native-language messages on the screen. Consider this sample text:

To change your password, use the **passwd** command. You will see this message:

```
Please enter current password:
```

Assuming you supply the correct password, you are prompted twice for a new password as follows:

```
Enter new password:
Retype new password:
```

According to this description, **passwd** produces messages in English—and only English. There are two ways to make this text more suitable for an internationalized system. You can change references like *you will see this message* to a less specific *you will see a message like*, or you can remove specific program messages completely and instead paraphrase them. In the latter case, you might revise the documentation this way:

To change your password, use the **passwd** command. *You are prompted for your current password. Assuming you type it correctly, you are prompted twice for a new password.*

The revised text correctly avoids restricting **passwd** to producing English-only messages.

11.4.8 People's Names

If the software you are describing processes people's names, or if you use names in examples, it is likely your documentation contains cultural biases. When describing an internationalized system, it is important to keep cultural differences related to names in mind.

For example, your text may include references to *first names* or *last names*. However, the order of names varies depending on the culture. In most Western cultures, a *first* name is the given name, while the *last* name is the family name (or surname). In some Asian cultures, however, the order is reversed—the family name comes first, followed by a given name. This is the standard order in Japan, the PRC, and South Korea.

If your text refers to names by position, change it to describe the type of name. Suppose your documentation includes something like this:

Enter the last name first, followed by the first name and middle initial.

You can rewrite it this way:

Enter the *family name* first, followed by *any given names*.

This assumes, of course, that the software allows users to enter multiple given names instead of a single name and an initial. As always, make sure your revision correctly describes the software's capabilities.

11.4.9   Other Cultural Assumptions

Writers sometimes assume that everyone who will read their manuals lives in the same country as they do. This assumption creeps into the text in unexpected ways. In some cases, the problem is what the text *doesn't* say, while in others, it is what it *does* say.

Geographic Confusion

References to geography can be maddeningly vague. Suppose your documentation describes how to partition entries in distributed name servers, and uses an example of telephone directories. The documentation might include this:

> A partition or collection of partitions under a single administrative authority is called an administrative *domain*. If the directory servers in San Francisco and Phoenix are part of separate administrative domains, the name entries in San Francisco can be maintained by the California Telephone Company, and the name entries in Phoenix by the Arizona Telephone Company.

This example assumes readers are familiar with American geography. Users in other countries, however, may not know that California and Arizona are U.S. states, much less that San Francisco is in California and Phoenix is in Arizona. You should either change the example to something that is less dependent on American geography, or that explains the relationship between the cities and states.

Geographic references are not limited to cities and states. Suppose your documentation describes the way the system handles time zones. It may include something like:

> The string for the time zone on the east coast is *EST* (Eastern Standard Time). Moving west, the other time zone strings are *CST* (Central Standard Time), *MST* (Mountain Standard Time), and *PST* (Pacific Standard Time).

This text describes continental American time zones, and that would be obvious to nearly every American reader. But the text could be mystifying to someone from another country. *The east coast?* The east coast of *what?* The text doesn't say. Even if a reader can guess correctly that the text refers to American time zones and geography, the information still is annoyingly American-centric. *Eastern* may be the time zone on the east coast of the United States, but not in Canada. The east coast of that country is in the *Atlantic* time zone. The east coast of Japan—for that matter, any coast—is in the *Japan* time zone.

Depending on the level of I18N support in your system, a description like this needs a little or a lot of work. If your software can only handle American time zones, state that clearly. For example:

> Product **foobar** *supports the four continental USA time zones.* The string for the time zone on the east coast *of the USA* is *EST* (Eastern Standard Time) . . .

If your software supports worldwide time zones, replace the U.S.-specific text with a more general description. This might include a table of the supported time zone names.

Tax Examples

The old saying about nothing being certain except death and taxes is almost completely right. Nearly all adults around the world are required to pay taxes of some form. However, there is nearly endless variety in the kinds of taxes they pay and the way they pay them.

Most Americans pay taxes based on income to the federal government and their local state government. A few cities also levy income taxes. In addition to these income taxes, most states have sales taxes (a tax as a percentage of goods sold), but the sales tax rates differ from state to state. Other major taxes include social security (for which all taxpayers have a nine-digit Social Security Number) and property taxes. Americans must calculate the total tax they owe to city, state, and federal governments and file the appropriate tax forms every year. The filing deadline usually is April 15.

If you are an American reading this, you may be yawning about now. *Everyone knows this; why waste space spelling it out?* That is precisely the problem. Documentation that includes examples of tax calculations or tax returns often assumes readers are familiar with the local conventions, so it doesn't bother to explain the basics. But references to tax returns may make little sense in other countries. In Japan, taxpayers usually do not calculate their own taxes; in general, they provide data to their companies and the companies determine how much more they must pay, or how much of a refund they will get back.

Similarly, examples of various tax calculations in text may be confusing. What Americans call a *sales tax*, Europeans call a *value added tax (VAT)*. However, while the sales tax is added on at the time of purchase in the United States, the VAT usually is included in the price of an object in Europe. An example in documentation that calculates the tax due on a purchase may therefore confuse readers. If they live in a country in which taxes are included in an item's price, they may not understand why their documentation is showing them how to calculate taxes due.

You don't have to include your country's entire Tax Code in text when using a tax-related example. Just provide enough information so that people who are not from your country (whatever that is) have a chance of understanding and learning from the documentation. You might also choose to add examples that cover conventions in regions other than your own.

11.5   Reviewing Documentation

This chapter has covered some of the issues and problems you need to keep in mind as you document internationalized and uninternationalized systems. There are significant design and translation issues, but you also must be careful to address the common phrases and culture-specific examples that permeate most manuals. It takes careful, thorough searching to find and fix all of the inappropriate or incorrect text, but the result is documentation that is fit for the world.

Multilingual and Distributed Computing

12

Current internationalization standards add new worlds of functionality to systems. A single well-internationalized program can process English, Japanese, German, Spanish, Korean, and many other languages. This obviously is a huge advance over software that handles only one language or culture, but the existing support implicitly assumes that individuals work in one language and on one computer at a time.

The world isn't that simple.

Many users need access to multiple languages simultaneously, while others want to parcel out processing to multiple computers (or nodes) across networks. This chapter describes some I18N issues resulting from the need to use multiple languages or multiple nodes. It covers:

- Defining distributed computing and multilingual functional requirements
- Limitations in the current standard internationalization model
- Design approaches including a universal code set and tagging models
- New definitions of equality
- Handling locales on local and distributed systems
- Interchanging data

Unlike topics in previous chapters, current standards do not cover most of these issues. That means if you add support for multilingual or distributed computing, you need to decide how to solve these problems. Before deciding how (or if) to solve them, however, you need to understand the problems that exist and some design options for addressing them.

12.1   Words and Meanings

Before examining ways to solve some of the remaining I18N problems, it is important to understand what functionality is missing in current standards-based systems. It also is important to explain what terms like *distributed computing* and *multilingual* mean, because people define them differently. The following describes how this chapter uses these terms.

12.1.1   Distributed Computing

Distributed computing involves the cooperation of two or more nodes communicating over a network. In distributed computing, you start a program on one node, and then distribute parts of the program to other nodes in the network. Using several nodes almost always means the program runs faster, particularly if it takes advantage of individual nodes' strengths. Suppose your program includes some I/O, but spends most of its time doing complex mathematical calculations. You may choose to do the I/O on your local, everyday system, and distribute the number-crunching to the supercomputer or mainframe in your network.

Distributed computing occurs across multiple nodes in a homogeneous or heterogeneous network. A homogeneous network consists of nodes from a single manufacturer or using a single operating system (OS). For example, you can tie together IBM PC and PC-compatible systems to create a homogeneous network. A heterogeneous network includes mixtures—perhaps different types of computers from multiple manufacturers, or nodes from a single manufacturer that run different OSes. An otherwise uniform network with nodes running different locales is an I18N-specific type of heterogeneous network. In general, it is easier to work in a homogeneous network because all nodes represent and process data the same way. In contrast, a heterogeneous network requires software to reconcile differences in data representation and processing methods.

12.1.2   Multilingual Support

Multilingual functionality is the ability to recognize and process correctly an arbitrary mixture of languages. The mixture may be in a network, a local file system, or in a single file. The stipulation that individual files can contain multiple languages is crucial to this definition. According to some definitions, any program that can process multiple languages is multilingual. In that case, software using current internationalization capabilities is multilingual because when you change locales, the software adjusts to process the new locale. However, such programs do not meet this definition of multilingual because they can not process arbitrary mixtures of languages in a file.

To be multilingual (at least, as far as this chapter is concerned), the system must allow combinations of any group of supported languages. If your system supports both German and Japanese, a multilingual system must allow you to combine these two languages in a single file or process. Then, the system must recognize which parts of the data are German and which parts are Japanese, and process each language segment correctly.

Multilingual text already is common in many company publications. The instructions that accompany electronic components such as compact disk players or video cassette recorders (VCRs) often appear in multiple languages. Other companies that do business around the world often need to provide information in multiple languages. Figure 12.1 shows examples from a United Airlines in-flight publication and a Federal Express document envelope.

Although these samples include many of the same languages, there are differences. The first sample includes Thai and Tagalog, which don't appear in the second list. The latter, however, includes Dutch and Italian. (The languages in the second sample are English, French, German, Korean, Japanese, Dutch, Spanish, Italian, Simplified Chinese, and Traditional Chinese, respectively.) According to this chapter's definition of multilingual, these dissimilar mixtures must be supported.

12.1.3   What Software Should Do

Given the descriptions of distributed computing and multilingual support, here's how you might expect the system to work. When you distribute computing, all nodes should use the same rules for locale-sensitive tasks. If application **foo** starts on Node 1 under a French locale, and part of **foo** runs on Nodes 2, 3, and 4, all four nodes should use the same French locale definition to ensure consistent results. Ideally, you should not have to do anything special to ensure this consistency; the system should take care of the job.

Along with letting the system take care of locales, you may also expect it to recognize the difference between the content and encoded representation of data fields. Suppose you search for a file named **bar**. You may expect the system to find any file with that name, regardless of how the characters in the name are encoded. Assuming your network includes both ASCII-based and EBCDIC-based nodes, a single file search could find **bar** on either node types.

Consistent distributed computing and character handling are only two tasks you may expect the system to handle. A third involves recognizing what data is, and then processing it appropriately. If you use a word processor to hyphenate and justify a file that contains Spanish, the system should recognize this fact and process

English

Language Flag-Pins are worn by employees who are able to assist non-English speaking customers.

Korean

언어표시나 핀을 착용한 직원들이 영어를 못하시는 고객들을 도와드립니다.

French

Les insignes-drapeaux sont portés par des employés qui peuvent assister les passagers dans leur langue natale.

Japanese

日本国旗のピンをつけた従業員は、英語をお話しにならないお客様の為に日本語でお手伝いを致しております。

Spanish

Los empleados que pueden asistir a los clientes que no hablan inglés, llevarán una insignia con una bandera indicando qué idioma hablan.

Chinese

Traditional Characters
佩帶外國旗幟徽胸章的機組人員可協助不會說英語的乘客。

Simplified Characters
佩带外国旗帜胸章的机组人员可帮助不会英语的乘客。

German

Angestellte, die Passagieren ohne englische Sprachkenntnisse helfen können, tragen eine Anstecknadel mit der Landesfahne der entsprechenden Sprache.

Thai

ตัวบ่งชี้ภาษาในรูปแบบเข็มกลัดธง จะ ใช้ติดกับเจ้าหน้าที่ช่วยเหลือผู้โดยสาร ที่ไม่พูดภาษาอังกฤษ

Tagalog

Ang mga sagisag ng mga wika ay ginagamit ng mga empleyado upang makatulong sa mga pasaherong hindi bihasa sa wikang Ingles.

DO NOT SEND CASH/CASH EQUIVALENT
NE PAS ENVOYER D'ESPÈCES OU AUTRE NUMÉRAIRE
KEIN BARGELD ODER BARGELDÄHNLICHE ZAHLUNGSMITTEL SENDEN!
현찰 송금 불가／현찰 대체 가능 송금수단 사용
現金および現金に類するものはお取扱いできません。
STUUR GEEN GELD OF IETS DAT DAARAAN GELIJK STAAT
NO ENVIE DINERO EN EFECTIVO O SU EQUIVALENTE
NON INVIARE DENARO IN CONTANTI O SIMILI
不可交运现金／现金相当品
不可交運現金／現金相當品

Figure 12.1 Multilingual Text Samples

326

the data using applicable Spanish rules. If that same file contains an excerpt in Portuguese, the system also should recognize the language shift and make any necessary adjustments in hyphenation and justification rules.

While the system should recognize data's language or encoding, it must still be possible to override default behavior. If (for some reason) you want to use Japanese hyphenation and justification rules on the Spanish file, you must be able to do so.

These tasks may seem logical—even inevitable. Of course distributed applications should use locales consistently. How could they not? And naturally the system should recognize the language in which data is written. Otherwise, it may process the data incorrectly.

Though these tasks seem logical, current I18N standards can't handle them. Individual software packages address some of these issues, but they usually only work on a few computer systems; they are not readily available on heterogeneous networks. That means you may need to write your own software if you want to handle these tasks. First, though, you need to understand what capabilities the current I18N model lacks.

12.2   Locales Aren't Everything

Previous chapters describe the functionality that locales offer and show why they leave single-language systems far behind. But the locale model assumes each process is a separate island rather than one of many fish in the sea.

12.2.1   Locales' Global Reach

Locales are global to the process in which they are invoked. If you set your locale to U.S. English, all locale-sensitive tasks use U.S. English rules. The process shows dates and times using American formats; it displays program messages in U.S. English; it collates data using American rules. The one locale permeates the process (and any child processes as well), with the global rules in effect until you close the process or change locales. Any changes have similarly global effects. If you change from U.S. English to Swiss German, the system discards the U.S. English rules and uses Swiss German conventions instead.

Global locales make it difficult or impossible to process multilingual data. Suppose you have French, Spanish, and Italian text in a single file. The system interprets the text as if it were in the current locale. The locale might be French, in which case the Spanish and Italian sections are processed using French rules. Alternatively, the locale might be Spanish, which means the French and Italian sections are treated as if they were Spanish. It also might be something like Thai or Japanese, in which case *all* sections of the text are processed incorrectly. The global locale provides no way to apply French rules to the French section while simultaneously applying Spanish and Italian rules to the other sections.

Global locales also make it difficult to support multiple locales within a single process. On the X Window System, it is common to have several users (or clients) attached to a single X server. These clients can each be running in different locales. Figure 12.2 shows one such scenario. In this example, Node A has clients running in British English and Hindi, while Nodes B and N are running one application each (in French and Japanese, respectively). One X process serves all four clients. The global locale model wasn't designed for this scenario because while it assumes a process runs in a single locale, this single X server has four different client locales.

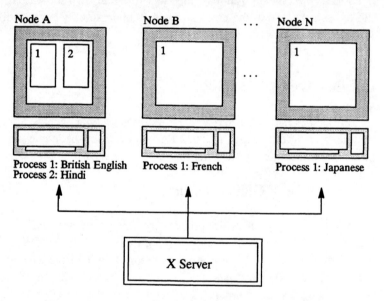

Figure 12.2   One Process, Multiple Locale Clients

12.2.2 Locale and Data Unconnected

With locales, data is what you say it is. If you set your locale to French, the system treats all data as if it were French. If you set your locale to Chinese and reprocess the same data, the system treats it as if it were Chinese. There is no standard way to tie locales to data.

The fact that locales and data are not tied together reflects the UNIX file system philosophy. UNIX text files traditionally have been typeless streams of bytes that contain no identification information. The locale model works within this philosophy, which means that locales have no effect on data. Instead, they only change the way the system interprets data.

The lack of connection between locales and data is both a great strength and great weakness. It means the system can interpret data as many ways as you choose. If you want to sort one set of data repeatedly using French, German, Hungarian, and Dutch rules, you can do so. While this gives great freedom, it also creates tremendous possibilities for errors. You can process Chinese as if it were English, or handle Swedish as if it were Japanese. While some users ask for the ability to process data as if it were in another language, in most cases, such processing is a mistake.

The lack of connection between locales and data isn't much of a problem if you are a single user on a stand-alone system. You probably can remember your files' language and encoding and set your locale appropriately before accessing them. But what about other users or distributed applications? With networks, users often access files on other nodes. Distributed applications reach across the network to share program processing tasks. It is quite possible that the users and nodes are running locales different from yours. When users access files or a distributed application processes data, there is nothing to indicate when locales don't match—except perhaps the results.

Suppose you are a user at a Japanese site. Assume all data is in Japanese, but the local network includes both AJEC- and SJIS-based nodes. If you open a SJIS-encoded file while running an AJEC-based locale, the data appears garbled.

While it is easy to diagnose this problem once you see data displayed in the "wrong" locale, it is common to process data without looking at it. Suppose that while running the AJEC locale, you use **fgrep** to search for a Kanji string in the SJIS-encoded file. The results will be wrong, but you may not realize that. The locale model gives no clue that the locale and data don't match.

The locale model also provides no way to designate a specific locale. Suppose a distributed application begins on a node running in a German locale. When it branches out to other nodes, it would be helpful if the application could send along information about its locale. But since locales and data are not tied together, there is no standard way to do this.

12.2.3 Changing Locales in Mid-Stream

It is theoretically possible to change locales any time and therefore process multilingual data using appropriate linguistic rules. Suppose you have a file that contains French, English, and German versions of the same text as follows:

Beaucoup de choses se sont passées dans notre secteur au cours des dernières années. Les environnements informatiques se sont considérablement diversifiées—machines de bureau, ordinateurs de capacité moyenne et unités centrals à architectures matérielles et systèmes d'exploitation très variés.

Much has happened in our industry during the past few years. Computing environments have become exceedingly diverse—made up of desktop, midrange, and mainframe systems with varied hardware architectures and operating systems.

In unserer Industrie ist in den letzten Jahren viel geschehen. Computerumgebungen sind immer vielfältiger geworden. Sie umfassen Desktop, mittelgroße und Mainframe Systeme mit unterschiedlichen Hardware-Architekturen und Betriebssystemen.

A single program can process the segments in three different locales. All they have to do is call **setlocale( )** when the language changes.

Unfortunately, theoretical possibility collides with practical reality. The vast majority of application programs call **setlocale( )** once—at program start-up. However, to process multilingual data within the locale model, programs must call **setlocale( )** when the data's locale changes. The problem is that data in this model contains no locale information, so there is nothing to indicate when the change takes place. And even if you can determine when to change locales, you might not want to do so. Remember, locales are global. The current setting determines behavior for many tasks including how dates and times appear and the language for messages. Suppose you use a German locale but have some multilingual files. The fact that a file contains a little French or English doesn't mean you want all system messages to change from German to being in French or English, or that you want dates and times to change. If you call **setlocale( )** multiple times in a program, such changes can occur.

In addition to undesired changes that may occur if a program calls **setlocale( )** multiple times, there also is the possibility that locale behavior won't change consistently. If a distributed application runs in multiple processes, there is no standard way to ensure that a mid-program call to **setlocale( )** affects the locale in all the processes.

12.2.4 Locales Aren't Perfect, But . . .

As this section shows, the standard locale model doesn't solve all internationalization problems. The following sections discuss two common options—universal code sets and data tagging—for overcoming the limitations. However, these options are most likely to be used in conjunction with locales rather than replacing them entirely.

Locales let you specify the overall environment in which you want to work. This is all most users need, because average users do most work in a single language or locale. Even the most multilingual users probably want to use a single language or set of cultural rules for some tasks. Some European users may communicate regularly in English, French, and German, but they probably want the date to appear one way on their screen, or they want program messages to be in one language. Locales provide a good mechanism for meeting overall requirements. Keep locales' pluses in mind as you read about ways to address problems they can't solve.

12.3   A Universal Solution?

Computer systems that handle only ASCII data are bad for non-American users, but good for programmers. Since these increasingly obsolete systems handle text that is encoded only one way, programmers often tune their code to this single encoding.

Internationalized systems are different. They must support many code sets and encoding methods, and so must assume that text takes many different forms.

Or must they? Maybe the original model of tuning systems to a single code set is right, and only the code set is wrong. ASCII is far too limited to meet worldwide needs, but how about a set that includes characters for all languages? Wouldn't that solve international needs and avoid forcing software to handle an ever-increasing group of code sets and encoding methods? Some advocates of universal code sets believe so. They feel that a single set is the best solution because it meets international needs while keeping software relatively simple.

12.3.1   Universal Strengths

A universal set solves some multilingual and distributed computing problems easily and neatly. A major obstacle to supporting multilingual text is finding a code set that supports the particular combination of languages you want. Commonly used code sets include characters for one language or a group of related languages. Latin-1, for example, has characters for Western European languages like French, German, Italian, and Swedish. Latin-2 covers Eastern Europe. JIS X0208 contains Japanese Kanji. CNS 11643 contains the Traditional Chinese ideographs that Taiwan uses. If you want to combine French and German in one file, Latin-1 does the job, but if you want to combine French, Japanese, and Chinese, regional code sets aren't good enough.

A universal set like ISO 10646 combines characters from every language you are likely to use, allowing nearly any language mix in a single code set. In addition, if you assume that you will only handle 10646-encoded data, you can tune programs to this single set.

Processing for distributed applications becomes easier as well if all nodes on the network use a single universal set. (Note that such uniformity is hard to achieve. See Other Potential Drawbacks later in this chapter.) With the current group of code sets, a file of Western European text can be encoded in Latin-1, ROMAN8, pc850, an ISO 646 national variant, a form of ISO 10646, or other set. Japanese text may be in AJEC or SJIS. Taiwanese Chinese could be in EUC or Big 5. Because these variations exist, distributed applications need a method for keeping track of data encodings. However, if all data uses a single form of a universal set, there is no need to send along encoding information. Just as in the ASCII-only days, the data has only one possible encoding.

12.3.2 Universal Limitations

While a universal code set solves some multilingual and distributed computing problems, there are others it can't touch. The set gives access to nearly all characters, but it doesn't tell you how to interpret those characters because it has no method for identifying language.

Earlier in this chapter you saw an excerpt from a file containing French, English, and German text. While it is possible to encode this multilingual file using a universal set, a smaller set like Latin-1 also is capable of handling this language mixture. Neither code set tells you where French text ends and English begins, or where English finishes and German starts.

A universal set does let you combine new groups of languages that are not possible in the smaller sets. A single file with Japanese, Simplified Chinese, and Traditional Chinese is beyond the smaller sets, but fine for ISO 10646. However, as with the combination of European languages, there is no way to tell where one language ends and another begins.

The fact that a universal set doesn't identify language does not imply that the set is deficient in some way. Many experts argue that code sets are not the right place to encapsulate linguistic information; that sets simply should encode characters or pieces of characters. However, the absence of linguistic data does mean that a universal set is not a complete solution to multilingual text processing requirements. Instead, you must use it in conjunction with other software that does specify or determine the language of a given text segment. Suppose you want to hyphenate and justify the text in the sample French-English-German file. You need some method for identifying each language segment so that the software can apply the appropriate language's rules.

Suppose you want to do something simpler like display mixed Asian text on your computer screen. As discussed in Chapter 4, ISO 10646 unifies many Han ideographs. The languages that use the ideographs all have, for example, an ideograph for *sun*, so instead of repeating it multiple times in the set, it appears only once. However, the appropriate way to draw a given ideograph depends on the language in which it appears. A file that mixes Japanese, Simplified Chinese, and Traditional Chinese needs to render (draw) each language section using the appropriate fonts. While a universal set contains the ideographs that Asian languages use, it doesn't solve such rendering problems.

Universal sets also don't tell you how to handle other cultural and linguistic tasks. If you want to sort a 10646-encoded file that contains only German text, the universal set can't supply the German rules. Universal sets also don't specify how to format numeric values, what names to use for the months in the year, or the language in which program messages should appear.

12.3.3   Other Potential Drawbacks

The Universal Strengths section notes that a universal code set can simplify distributed computing. If all nodes in a network use a single form of the universal set, there is no need to keep track of encoding information. But that is a huge *if*. There are countless existing data files around the world encoded in almost as many code sets. It is a huge job to unify those encodings, involving both technical effort and a lot of human persuasion.

Think about the technical effort first. You probably need to revise existing programs so they can support data encoded in the universal set. The amount of changes necessary depends on the level of internationalization in those programs; if they already are internationalized, you have fewer changes to make. After fixing the programs, existing data needs to be converted. This actually is a fairly easy job because while many encodings exist, conversion functions are not difficult to write.

These tasks are time-consuming, but nearly insignificant compared to the human persuasion necessary to get them done. Users usually vigorously fight attempts to change code sets. The situation usually goes something like this:

1.   Foo Company has users in several countries, and those users want to work in their own language. No standard code set exists for some user-requested

languages, so Foo creates a proprietary set. (Alternatively, several standard code sets exist, so Foo picks one.)

2.   A standards group creates a code set or sets that covers Foo's language needs. The new set(s) differ from what Foo chose.

3.   Some Foo users ask the company to support the new standards. Foo wants to meet its users' needs, and it also likes the idea of using standards because they increase interoperability in heterogeneous networks. Multiple companies usually support standard sets, but proprietary encodings tend to have much more limited use. For these reasons, Foo decides to replace proprietary sets with standard versions.

4.   Now other Foo users complain. They have existing software that depends on the proprietary set(s) and have terabytes of data encoded in them. They argue that it is too expensive to convert data when they see no direct benefit of doing so, and besides, the standard sets don't contain exactly the same characters as exist in the proprietary version. These users rely on the unique characters, so new software must continue to work with the existing data. In addition, if it takes more space to store data in the new encoding, users are likely to complain even more. (*I have to buy how many more disks to store the same data? Why should I do that?*)

5.   Foo adds support for new sets while retaining support for the old. Those who want to use standard encodings can do so, while those who like the status quo don't have to change. The result is that Foo supports multiple encodings.

A sequence like this has occurred in many companies throughout the world, and it often is true that users have solid reasons for insisting on using older code sets. This is particularly true in the case of Asian ideographic sets. Standard sets include commonly used characters, but often do not include ideographs for company names or other specialized vocabulary. As noted in Chapter 4, Asian encoding methods include provisions for Vendor and User Definable Characters to accommodate Asian customers' requirements for unique characters.

It is not always users who force a company to retain support for multiple code sets. Sometimes the company forces that support on itself because it doesn't fully internationalize its systems. Suppose Foo introduces a new laser printer at the same time it creates a proprietary code set named *Foo-special*, and further suppose it hardcodes knowledge of the new set into the printer. Given that internationalization still is a fairly new programming discipline, it is easy to imagine the company building in such a dependency. However, that dependency means the company can not throw out the proprietary *Foo-special* set when a standard one comes along. Foo can change software to produce text encoded in, say, Latin-1 rather than *Foo-special*, but if installed printers at user sites assume all text is in *Foo-special*, the Latin-1 input becomes garbled *Foo-special* output.

Given that both users and companies often have compelling reasons for supporting multiple sets, is it likely that all companies can force all users to use one single universal set? Don't count on it. And a universal set only simplifies distributed computing software if all nodes on the network use that set. If you can't rely on total consistency, software must be written to handle the inconsistencies. In that case, a universal set becomes just one more set that the distributed computing software must support, instead of a single, unifying set.

Despite the difficulties in changing code sets, companies and users do change. During the 1950s and 1960s, American computer manufacturers used many different sets, but over time, most dropped their proprietary sets and adopted ASCII. However, it usually takes several years—or even a decade—to complete a transition, and you must factor that transition time into your plans.

Table 12.1 summarizes the strengths and limitations of a universal code set.

Table 12.1   Strengths and Limitations of Universal Code Set

Strengths	Limitations
Supports all languages in one set	No method for identifying languages in data stream
Distributed computing easier if all nodes use one set	Difficult to get users to accept a single set
Can tune software to one code set instead of generalizing it	Doesn't handle culture-specific processing

12.4   Tagged Data

A universal set combines all characters into one set, but there is another programming model that takes the opposite approach. It adds *tags* to data that specify the data's characteristics. One tag might designate that the accompanying data is Spanish text encoded in Latin-1. Another might identify the data as being Japanese encoded in AJEC. The tags let you handle many sets because they designate how to interpret text bytes.

Tags—also sometimes called *data handles*—are not an internationalization invention. Many proprietary operating systems use some form of tagging. However, the most common use probably is in word processing packages. These packages use tags to keep track of rendering information. This example shows some pseudo word processing tags using a paragraph from earlier in this book:

> *<paragraph>* `If you are doing any arithmetic-based opera-` `tions on characters, such as indexing into an array,` `you probably should change your data type to` *<bold>*`unsigned char`*<roman>*`.` `Suppose you use a character` `as an index into an array (e.g.,` *<mono-* `space>`*my_array[c]*`<roman>`. `If you declare` *<mono-* *space>*`c`*<roman>* `as a` *<bold>*`signed char`*<roman>*`, . . .` `your` `code does not work properly for characters in the upper` `half of a single-byte set.` *<end_paragraph>*

A word processor uses these tags to decide how to render the text. Here is the processed text:

> If you are doing any arithmetic-based operations on characters, such as indexing into an array, you probably should change your data type to **unsigned char**. Suppose you use a character as an index into an array (e.g., `my_array[c]`). If you declare c as a **signed char**, . . . your code does not work properly for characters in the upper half of a single-byte set.

Tags can and do take many forms. They may look like the pseudotags above, or they may be sequences of code bytes. The ISO 2022 encoding method described in Chapter 4 tags data with escape sequences that identify code sets. For example, the tag sequence `ESC 0x2d 0x41` assigns the right half of Latin-1 to the G1 graphic character slot, and designates SO as the control character that invokes the set. (See Chapter 4 for details on ISO 2022.)

Just as tags take different forms, they also save different information. Tags in word processing packages keep information about font styles and sizes, and other formatting data. ISO 2022 escape sequences keep information about code sets. Internationalized tags need to keep track of code sets and languages, and may also need to identify text direction and territories.

12.4.1 Tagging Models

As the ISO 2022 and pseudo word processing tag examples show, there often are multiple tags within a data stream, and these tags can appear anywhere in that stream. However, more limited tagging models allow only one tag per file. In these models, the system keeps information—perhaps in the file header—that identifies the contents of the file. A non-internationalized example of this model is one that supports flags to identify whether a given file is program source, binary code, formatted text (for example, PostScript output), or unformatted text.

An internationalized system takes identification a bit further. It might specify the language or encoding of unformatted text. The identification makes it possible to determine that one file contains Latin-1-encoded French text while another contains Latin-1-encoded Spanish, and still another has AJEC-encoded Japanese. However, if a tagging system allows only one tag per file, it can't support multilingual text. A single tag allows you to specify if a file contains French *or* Japanese *or* English, but not that a file contains French *and* Japanese *and* English.

A tagged data system is not restricted to specifying file contents. While this is their most common use, it is possible for tags to be attached to other system objects including file or directory names, print resources, or node names. There are several ways to assign tags to such objects. Suppose you want to tag file names. One alternative is to embed the tag in the name. In such a scenario, there is a byte value that signals locale information, followed by pre-assigned sequences that identify specific locales. Suppose that, like ISO 2022, ESC is the signal byte, and sequences like these indicate locales:

Sequence	Locale Name	Designates
0x51 0x51	C	C
0x51 0x52	en_US.ISO8859-1	U.S. English
0x51 0x53	de_DE.ISO8859-1	German
0x51 0x54	fr_FR.ISO8859-1	French
0x51 0x55	pt_BR.ISO8859-1	Brazilian Portuguese

Given this limited list, here are some tagged file names:

```
ESC 0x51 0x53 M a ß
ESC 0x51 0x54 l e ç o n
ESC 0x51 0x55 f r a ç ã o
```

The first name is tagged as German, the second is French, and the third is Brazilian Portuguese.

An alternative to embedding tags within file names is to assign locale information as part of the file header. This is an extension to the tagging model described earlier for file contents. In that design, you save the locale in which the file is written and assume all data in the file matches that one locale. In this model, the file *contents* tag also applies to the file *name*. An implementation might then display this information via an ordinary **ls -l** command. For example:

```
% ls -l
-rw-------  ...  pt_BR.ISO8859-1   3950   31 oct 15:09 fração
-rw-r--r--  ...  fr_FR.ISO8859-1  15928    6 aoû 08:30 leçon
-rw-r--r--  ...  de_DE.ISO8859-1   7944   22 nov 12:22 Maß
```

This example of tagged file names is far-fetched since it is beyond the control of most application developers. Typically, system vendors are the only ones who can choose to add tags to file names, and few have chosen to do so. However, the example does illustrate the way tags might be used and the information they can provide.

Although this section describes possible tagging models, none of these models has been implemented completely in widely available internationalized software. Some electronic mail systems use limited ISO 2022-based tagging to enable exchange of multiple code sets through seven-bit-only electronic mail systems, and other proprietary packages have implemented some tagging features. However, if you want to use tags, you probably have to write the software yourself—or hope that things have changed since this book was written.

12.4.2 Tagging Pluses

Data tags are powerful tools for extending internationalization functionality. Depending on how they might be implemented, they provide the mechanism for solving many of the shortcomings in the global locale model.

Tags allow you to establish a connection between locales and data, making it possible to identify and process multilingual data correctly. With tags, it is possible to determine where each language or encoding segment begins and ends in any file. Using the pseudo tags from the previous section, you might tag text like this:

ESC 0x51 0x54 Beaucoup de choses se sont passées dans notre secteur au cours des dernières années. Les environnements informatiques se sont considérablement diversifiées . . .

ESC 0x51 0x52 Much has happened in our industry during the past few years. Computing environments have become exceedingly diverse . . .

ESC 0x51 0x53 In unserer Industrie ist in den letzten Jahren viel geschehen. Computerumgebungen sind immer vielfältiger geworden . . .

These tags identify that the first paragraph is French, the second is English, and the third, German. Since tags identify language boundaries, they provide a way to solve some problems that code sets alone cannot. For example, remember that ISO 10646 unifies many Han ideographs. The proper way to render a unified character depends on the language in which it appears. A tag gives that information.

Not only do the tags clearly designate language or encoding boundaries, they also make it possible to pass multilingual text independent of the global locale. Remember that with the global locale model, data is whatever your locale says it is. If the locale doesn't match your data, the data may be processed inappropriately. However, if tags are available, software can use them to determine the "right" thing to do. While the global locale model lets you make incorrect assumptions about data, tags let you avoid assumptions.

While tags have the potential to solve requirements for multilingual processing, whether they really do depends on how they are implemented. A tagging system that allows only one tag per object cannot provide true multilingual support. A single tag—for example, a locale field in a file header—does not support locale mixtures within a single file. However, a system that allows multiple tags to appear in arbitrary places within a file is equal to the multilingual requirement.

In addition to handling some multilingual issues, tags are a natural solution to distributed computing problems. Consider a distributed application that performs some locale-specific tasks. To ensure that all nodes active in a given run use the same locale, the application can send along the data's tag to remote nodes. This lets them know the locale in which they should process the data.

12.4.3 Tagging Minuses

Data tags have significant advantages, but they also have serious drawbacks.

The previous section notes that tags provide the capability of solving many remaining I18N-related problems, but the capability comes with a high cost. You either must modify every piece of software that currently assumes untagged data to understand the tags, or else provide new software for handling the tags. That may be a huge task. This is particularly true for UNIX-like systems since they assume data is a stateless stream of bytes. Most utilities implemented on POSIX.2- or XPG-compliant systems have no idea how to handle tag bytes. Suppose you want to search for the string *école* in all files in the current directory. Normally, a simple command like this is all you need:

```
fgrep 'école' *
```

However, assume your directory contains some ISO 2022-encoded files. The tagged word might look like this:

SO	é	SI	c	o	l	e

Given this data, **fgrep** fails to recognize it as matching *école*. The command easily scans past the SO control character and finds the *é*, but it doesn't know how to ignore the SI. To handle tagged data, **fgrep** and every other utility that parses or processes data needs to be revised.

Besides the fact that this is a lot of work, you may be unwilling to do it. Many UNIX supporters believe one of the strengths of its model is that data is a simple, stateless stream of bytes. Because it makes a simplifying assumption about data, UNIX eliminates some of the overhead associated with systems that do handle tags. Of course, a counterargument is that UNIX's simplifying assumption was valid for ASCII-only data, but is not for today's internationalized systems. The question then becomes whether you want a simple system that handles only certain tasks, or a complex system with more capabilities.

Before deciding whether you want the richer capabilities that data tagging makes possible, you should be aware of its other drawbacks. With untagged data, data parsing is relatively simple. Depending on the way the data is encoded, it might be possible to begin parsing data at any random point in the stream. Single-byte encodings and wide character forms are particularly easy because each byte or **wchar_t** is a character. With encoding methods like EUC, finding character boundaries requires more logic, but you may be able to find a boundary after searching backward only a few bytes. Tagged data, however, throws a monkey wrench into search algorithms. Assume your data is this list of English and French words:

```
<english>
apple
<french>
banane
cerise
fraise
framboise
<english>
grapefruit
kiwi
orange
<french>
pamplemousse
```

In this example, the italicized pseudotags indicate where the language changes. Suppose you want to determine how many words from each language appear on the list. The only effective way to complete this task is to do a linear search from the beginning of the list. If you start anywhere else, you must search backward an arbitrary number of entries to determine the current language. This may not seem costly—in this example, *framboise* is the worst case, because it is four entries away from its language tag—but suppose you need to search a database with thousands of entries. It might take a long time to determine the state of the data.

12.4.4 Adding Support for Tags

If you add tags to data, you also must have functions to handle them. You might choose to revise existing functions to add appropriate tag parameters, or add new functions. Suppose your software includes this function:

int foo(const char *string1*, **const char** *string2*);

These are some ways to add tagging support:

1. **int bar(LocaleHandle** *locale*, **const char** *string1*, **const char** *string2*);
2. **int foo(const char** *string1*, **const char** *string2*,
    tag_type *tag1*, **tag_type** *tag2*);
3. **int t_foo(const char** *string1*, **const char** *string2*,
    tag_type *tag1*, **tag_type** *tag2*);
4. **int foobar(TagObject** *string1*, **TagObject** *string2*);

In this example, the **bar( )** function performs exactly the same function as the original **foo( )**, but it includes the *locale* parameter which functions as a tag. While the original **foo( )** simply looks at the current locale, **bar( )**'s extra parameter designates the locale in which the function should run. This is particularly useful for distributed programs that begin on one node but may continue on other nodes running other locales. The *locale* parameter provides a way to designate that locale-specific operations should be performed in the locale in which the program began running.

The next two examples add *tags* of type **tag_type** to the parameter lists, but the first adds them to the existing **foo( )** function, while the second creates a new **t_foo( )** (tagged foo) version. The *tag1* parameter applies to *string1*, and *tag2* applies to *string2*. These examples result in functions that do almost exactly what the original **foo( )** function did, except that each string has an explicit tag.

The last example defines the new function **foobar( )**. This function differs from the other examples because the strings now are of an opaque data type **TagObject**. The opaque type contains both the data and information about the data—that is, the tag. An opaque type lets you add more attributes over time because it separates implementation details from the interface definition.

The way you choose to support tags depends on your software. If you support standards-defined functions, you can't choose the second option listed above (adding parameters to an existing function) because you don't have the freedom to change the interface definitions. However, if you control your interfaces, you can change them as you see fit—assuming you take care of backward compatibility issues.

12.4.5 Applying the Options

As systems gain internationalized functionality, they have to solve problems that don't exist in earlier, less complex versions of the software. A universal code set and data tagging are two common design options that may be used separately or together to handle some of these problems. Now that you understand what the options are, it is time to look at how you might apply them to specific multilingual or distributed computing issues including:

- defining equality in new ways
- handling multiple local locales
- handling distributed locales
- interchanging data

The rest of this chapter covers these issues.

12.5 Defining Equality

Equality on noninternationalized systems is easy to define and easy to implement. The same is not true, however, for systems that take a broader outlook on what data is.

First, consider noninternationalized systems. Objects such as data strings, file names, node names, and others are equal if their encoded values match. When you use a command like **fgrep** to search a file for a specific string, the command looks for bit patterns in the file that are the same as the input string's bit pattern. The command reports success when it finds an exact match.

When all data is encoded one way (usually, in ASCII), simple bit-matching operations make sense, but it is more complicated on an internationalized system. Suppose you have an ASCII-encoded file name **foo** and a U.S. EBCDIC-encoded file name **foo**. Are they the same? On many systems they are not because their encodings don't match. They have these encodings:

ASCII   `0x66 0x6f 0x6f`
U.S. EBCDIC   `0x86 0x96 0x96`

Some software packages, however, do consider the two **foo**s to be the same because they do automatic conversions between encodings. If a user on an ASCII-based client asks to open **foo** and there happens to be a **foo** file on a U.S. EBCDIC-based server, the software automatically converts the name from its U.S. EBCDIC encoding to ASCII and opens the file.

From a user's perspective, the latter behavior makes a lot of sense. Many are not aware of how data is encoded. If they use ASCII-based terminals and access files on an IBM mainframe, they simply expect to be able to open file **foo**. In fact, if the system already takes care of this for them, they probably aren't aware that conversions are taking place. But consider a more complicated example involving a string **bár**. Table 12.2 shows some ways the string can be encoded on an internationalized system. In the table, the UCS entries are forms of ISO 10646. In addition, the third column lists the characters encoded in the data stream. Some sets include the complete letter-with-diacritic *á*, while others require or allow you to combine two code values to make the accented letter.

Table 12.2   Sample Encodings of 'bár'

Code Set	Encoding	Contents
ISO 8859-1	0x62 0xe1 0x72	bár
ISO 6937	0x62 0xc2 0x61 0x72	b'ar
HP ROMAN8	0x62 0xc4 0x72	bár
IBM pc850	0x62 0xa0 0x72	bár
UCS-2, Level 1	0x00 0x62 0x00 0xe1 0x00 0x72	bár
UCS-2, Level 3*	0x00 0x62 0x00 0x61 0x03 0x01 0x00 0x72	ba'r

* encoded using combining characters

While Table 12.2 shows numerous encodings, many other code sets exist, giving **bár** even more possible encodings. Now, are all these **bár** strings the same? That is, should a string comparison function return true when given any two of these encodings? Taking a user's perspective again, they probably should be, but this functionality is difficult to deliver. It requires a fundamental change in the definition of equality. Instead of matching based on encoded values, this requires matching based on semantic values.

Semantic equality refers to equality based on meaning rather than implementation details. If two entities contain the same semantic characters, a semantic match returns true. Semantic matching as defined here does not refer to matching based on equivalent meaning. While the ASCII- and U.S. EBCDIC-encoded strings **book** are semantically equivalent because they contain the same characters, a French-tagged string **livre** and an English-tagged string **book** are not semantically equivalent. Rather, the French and English strings are translations of each other.

Semantic matching already is common for some tasks. Users recognize the font glyphs **a,** *a,* and a as being the same character, even though they look different. Similarly, Europeans and Americans accept that *7* and a *7* with a cross-bar both represent the digit seven.

While users typically have little trouble with semantic equality, computers do. Software that relies on encoded values doesn't consider separate encodings of the string **bár** to be the same, but it does make other matches that seem odd at first glance. Most users wouldn't think **bár** and **bαr** are the same, but they are if the first is encoded in ISO 8859-1 and the second in ISO 8859-7 because both strings have the same encoded value (`0x62 0xe1 0x72`). Table 12.3 shows several interpretations of `0x62 0xe1 0x72`.

Table 12.3   Sample Interpretations of One Encoded Value

Code Set	Contents
ISO 8859-1	bár
ISO 8859-5	bcr*
ISO 8859-7	bαr
HP ROMAN8	bÃr
IBM pc850	bßr

* second letter is Cyrillic lowercase es

While users might agree that semantic equality is more important than encoded equality, possible implementations of such support all have pros and cons. The following describes some possibilities.

- **Convert all data to one format.** This is the simplest implementation, and it removes the need for semantic matching. You drop support for all existing code sets and move to a single universal set. With a single set, matching can continue to be based on encoded values because data has only one representation. While this is simple, it may not be realistic. As noted earlier, getting agreement on a single code set and converting all data to that set is a time-consuming process.

- **Convert to one format for matching only.** Instead of forcing all data to one code set, permit multiple encodings but convert to a single representation (like a form of ISO 10646) before doing any matches. With all data in the same format, you use encoded values for comparisons. This model works well, but is inefficient. Most users handle data that is encoded in one way. For American users, that one way may be ASCII. For European users, it may be Latin-1. For Japanese users, it may be AJEC or SJIS. These users may occasionally work with data encoded in different ways, but diversity is the exception rather than the rule. However, if you use a single format for matching, the software must convert all data to that format—even when you only want an ASCII-to-ASCII comparison. Conversions take time, so all comparisons are slower.

  One significant problem with this design is determining data's encoding so you know how to convert it. You can use the current locale, but that may not be correct. This is especially true in a network. Just because the user on a node is running an AJEC-based Japanese locale doesn't mean that all files on other nodes are in AJEC. In addition, there currently is no way to reach across a network and find out what locale other nodes are running, so you can't even get the perhaps-incorrect information.

- **Use data tags.** Data tags let you reliably determine how a given piece of data is encoded. They also let you refine the conversion design to eliminate unnecessary conversions. In this case, you examine tags before examining data. If the tags don't match, you convert one string to the other's encoding, or convert both to an agreed-upon, single encoding. After conversion (or if no conversion is necessary), you compare the bits.

  A disadvantage to this approach is the overhead of finding and processing tags. If the implementation allows tags to appear anywhere in a file, you may have to search the entire file to find your data's tag. A worst-case scenario is having one tag at the beginning of the file, and the potential matching string at the end. There is no way to know that no other tags exist, so you have to scan the whole file. A tagging design that allows only one tag per file is much simpler and faster, but it doesn't completely handle multilingual text.

Current standards-based functions perform matching based on encoded equality only, but a matching design like one of these may have to be added in the future. If you need such functionality now, you must write your own functions.

12.6   Multiple Local Locales

Just as multilingual and distributed computing requirements add new questions about defining equality, they also create locale handling problems that the global model doesn't have to address. If software is capable of recognizing multiple locales, it must also include routines for managing the interactions between them. This assumes such support includes data tagging and appropriate routines to handle the tags. As noted earlier, a universal set by itself is not enough to provide true multilingual support.

Given this assumption, individual files may contain multiple languages and have tags to identify each language segment boundary. An implementation may add locale tags to file names so that it is possible to determine which fonts to use in displaying a possibly mixed group of names in a directory. In both cases, tags allow variety to exist on a local system, so software needs policies for handling the diversity. Diversity is not confined to far-flung heterogeneous networks; it can exist on a single desktop.

12.6.1   "Simple" Multiple-Locale Tasks

Tagged diversity does not automatically add significant complexity. For many locale-sensitive tasks, you can simply examine a tag to decide how to complete the task. Suppose you are doing numeric formatting. If the numeric data's tag says it is a British quantity, you format using British rules. If the next tag shows the data is a Danish quantity, use Danish rules.

Character classification and conversion functions are also easy in a tagged environment. Functions similar to **isalpha( )**, **iswalpha( )**, or **toupper( )**, only need to examine a tag to decide which locale's rules to use. This assumes, of course, that your implementation includes such tag-sensitive functions.

In general, stand-alone operations—those that do not involve comparisons between objects—are fairly easy in a local tagged environment. Such operations include:

- Character classification
- Date and time formatting
- Numeric and monetary formatting
- Message handling
- String functions that operate on a single character or string. This includes:
  - I/O functions (examples: **fputs( )**, **getc( )**, **getwc( )**, **printf( )**, **scanf( )**)
  - Character and number conversion functions (examples: **mbtowc( )**, **strtod( )**, **wcstod( )**, **wcstombs( )**)
  - Length functions (examples: **mblen( )**, **wcslen( )**)

12.6.2   Collation in a Multiple-Locale Environment

While tagging adds relatively simple requirements to many locale-sensitive tasks, it adds great complexity to those that involve multiple objects. If tags exist, and an operation includes two or more objects, those objects may have different tag values. That means you must decide how to handle situations when tags don't match and then add the appropriate logic for those cases. One of the most challenging examples of a multiple object task is collation.

Taking a simple example, suppose you have a group of tagged file names in a directory. The tags show that the names all share the same encoding—Latin-1—but are in two languages. These are the names and language tags:

Name	Tag
adjö	*Swedish*
andere	*German*
ändern	*German*
äppelblom	*Swedish*
trafik	*Swedish*
züruck	*German*

Assume you want to list the directory contents. What order should a command like **ls** produce? The two languages use almost the same alphabet, but have differing rules for sorting some letters. German groups *ä* and *ö* with the plain *a*'s and *o*'s while Swedish puts them after *z* (. . . *x,y,z,å,ä,ö*).

There are several possible designs for handling these unmatched tags, and as always, each has pros and cons. The approaches include:

* **Sort the two languages separately**. Group all German-tagged names and all Swedish-tagged names and perform two separate sorts. Add logic for deciding which language appears first. This method produces results like one of these:

German First	Swedish First
andere	adjö
ändern	trafik
züruck	äppelblom
adjö	andere
trafik	ändern
äppelblom	züruck

In addition to slowing down **ls** as it does two sorts, these results probably aren't what most people would expect. The orders look illogical.

- **Sort using one language's rules.** Instead of doing two sorts, use one language's rules and produce results like one of these:

German	Swedish
adjö	adjö
andere	andere
ändern	trafik
äppelblom	züruck
trafik	ändern
züruck	äppelblom

This is easy to implement since it involves using only one set of rules. You don't even have to worry much about whether the rules being used include specific provisions for all the characters in the second language. POSIX.2's **localedef** includes default ordering rules for characters that don't specifically appear in the collation section. If the Swedish words included *å*, which doesn't exist in German, a German sort might fall back to those default rules.

While this alternative is simple, it seems to defeat the purpose of adding multilingual support. If you are going to pretend that everything is the same, you might as well use the global locale and forget about tags.

- **Sort the two languages together.** Since the two languages use similar collation rules, merge those rules to put words in the correct order for each language. The result might look like this:

```
adjö
andere
ändern
trafik
züruck
äppelblom
```

This might be what users expect, but it is a lot harder to achieve. You must determine how to merge multiple languages' collation rules while maintaining acceptable system performance. Remember, too, that merging rules gets more complicated as the number of locales increases and as the locales become more divergent. This example shows a directory with files in one encoding of two European languages, but imagine if the directory also contained Japanese, Russian, and Greek names. Besides solving collation problems, your software also would have to be capable of displaying such a mixture of languages and writing systems.

The German and Swedish example poses interesting locale-interaction questions, but at least the languages both use the same encoding. Now suppose the directory contains German and Greek names. The former uses Latin letters (encoded in a set like Latin-1), while the latter uses Greek characters (present in ISO 8859-7). When listing the directory contents, you must decide whether Latin letters come before, after, or interspersed with Greek letters. You may also want a policy for Latin and Greek letters that look exactly alike. Both Latin-1 and ISO 8859-7 contain the Latin-based letters A–Z and a–z, and in addition, the latter set contains Greek characters. Some uppercase letters are common to Latin and Greek scripts, and so appear to be repeated in ISO 8859-7. These are the code values for a few related letters:

Letter	Latin Encoding	Greek Encoding
A	0x41	0xb1
B	0x42	0xb2
H	0x48	0xb7
Z	0x5a	0xb6

The options for handling mixed Latin and Greek text (or any other writing system mixtures) are similar to those for the German and Swedish example. You can sort the scripts separately, sort according to one language's rules, or try to intersperse the two. In general, the more dissimilar two scripts are, the less sense it makes to intersperse them. For example, it is hard to imagine a logical way to mix English and Japanese Kanji in a sort. One should simply follow the other. Similarly, French and Arabic are so different that it probably is best to sort them separately.

12.6.3   Strings in a Multiple-Locale Environment

Sorting isn't the only operation that needs new functionality to handle multilingual text. Suppose you do a string compare on a French *ch* and a Spanish *ch*. Are they equal? Probably, although one could argue that because Spanish *ch* is a single collating element, it is not the same as the individual French letters.

Concatenation also needs additional logic to handle new functional requirements, although the logic depends on how data is tagged. If the implementation embeds tags within data, a concatenation operation needs to handle redundant tags.

However, if tags appear only in the file header, the operation needs rules for mis-matched tags.

Take the first possibility—tags within data. Suppose a database includes cus-tomers' names and addresses. Addresses consist of two parts: street address and city (including postal codes). Since the database entries may come from a variety of locales, you decide to tag each field. A complete entry might be stored like this:

\<french\>	François Depardieu
\<french\>	15 Avenue de la Paix
\<french\>	12345 Paris

Now suppose you want to concatenate the three fields together to produce a printed report. The *\<french\>* pseudotags all match. You could simply tack the fields together, retaining all three tags like this:

\<french\>	François ...	*\<french\>*	15 Ave ...	*\<french\>*	12345 Paris

However, it clearly is wasteful to repeat the tags inside the concatenated string. A more efficient way to store the string is for the concatenation operation to include logic for recognizing and then deleting redundant tags. In that case, the concate-nated string looks like this:

\<french\>	François Depardieu	15 Avenue de la Paix	12345 Paris

While tags within data create the possibility of redundant tags in concatenated strings, an implementation that only allows a single tag in the file header poses a dif-ferent set of possibilities. In that case, you may decide to concatenate strings only if their tags match. Suppose you have these files:

File Name	Tagged As
file1	French
file2	German
file3	French
file4	Japanese

Since `file1` and `file3` have the same tag, you can easily concatenate strings from these files and (if necessary) direct the output to a separate file that you also tag as being French. However, you need another way to handle other combinations.

Given the one-locale-per-object limitation, you can either return an error on requests to concatenate mixed-locale strings, or ignore all but one of the source locales and designate the result as being in the remaining locale. In the latter case, suppose there is a request to concatenate strings from `file1`, `file2`, and `file4`. You would save the locale from the first string (French), and ignore the German and Japanese locale designations. The concatenated string would be considered all French—as illogical as that might seem.

12.6.4   Designing a Usable System

Collation, string comparison, and concatenation are among the significant issues to address when handling multilingual or multilocale text, but the common thread that runs through all of them is that if you support tags, you must decide what to do when tags don't match. Tags allow any mixture of locales, creating endless interactions to codify and manage. However, performance would probably slow to a crawl if you tried to manage all interactions. A more realistic approach might be to merge characteristics of the existing global locale model with data tags.

Here is a possible design. Since a typical user does most work in a single language or locale, he or she can set the global locale to match that choice. This locale could be considered the *primary locale*. Tags that do not match the current primary locale are *secondary locales*. For locale-sensitive operations, here are the possible combinations and how software might handle them:

- **All locales in the operation match**. Do the operation according to the locale's rules. If the primary locale is German, and you want to collate two Swedish strings, the operation ignores the primary locale and uses Swedish rules.

- **Locales differ, but one is the primary locale**. The operation ignores any secondary locales and uses the primary locale's rules. If the primary locale is German and you collate German and Swedish strings, the operation uses German rules.

- **Locales differ, and none is the primary locale**. If the primary locale is German and you collate Swedish and French strings, the operation uses the rules of the first locale it encounters.

These rules are arbitrary—an obvious addition is to support merging locales' rules when appropriate. However, this model uses tags to provide some real multilingual capabilities while not taking on the almost-impossible task of codifying all interactions among locales.

12.7 Distributed Locales

While multiple locales on a single system add complexity to local processing, there are a different set of issues when those locales are distributed across a network. When distributing an application, one goal is to ensure consistent handling of similar operations. Users should not be aware that multiple nodes are involved in the results, and should get the same answers regardless of the nodes involved in a given program run. For locale-dependent tasks, this means distributed applications must have a way to track locales.

Suppose an application starts on Node 1 under the **foo** locale and it sends part of its work over to Node 2. The application needs some way to ensure that Node 2 also uses **foo**. Among the available options are:

- **Ask what locale Node 2 is running**. Node 1 sends a query to Node 2 about its current locale. If the two locale names match, Node 1 sends over processing tasks. If the names differ, Node 1 chooses among the remaining options.
- **Ask Node 2 to process using 'foo.'** Node 1 sends an announcer that defines which locale its application needs. Node 2 changes its locale to **foo**—that is, it does the equivalent of:

```
(void) setlocale(LC_ALL, "foo");
```

The operation fails if Node 2 doesn't have the proper locale, and Node 1 chooses among the remaining options.

- **Build a new foo locale on Node 2**. One way to ensure that all nodes run the same locale is to send that locale over with the processing request. However, this is extremely inefficient. Standards exist for locale source formats, but not for their object formats, so locale objects are not exchangeable across a heterogeneous network. This means your application must send source to Node 2 and wait for a new object to build. In nearly all cases, this slows performance to unacceptable levels.
- **Ask other nodes**. If Node 2 isn't running **foo** and you decide against strategies for getting it to run that locale, you can take your request to other nodes. In this case, Node 1 continues looking until it finds a node running **foo**.

In order for any of these options to work correctly, locale names and contents must be consistent across nodes. If you are running a French Canadian locale and want other nodes to run it, you need to find out whether they have that same locale. Unfortunately, locale names show a maddening amount of variety. Here are some names for a French Canadian locale:

```
c-french
c-french.iso8859-1
fr_CA
fr_CA.ISO8859-1
Fr_CF
```

In addition to names being different, locale contents often show individuality. For these French Canadian locales, some define case-segregated sorting, while others define mixed-case collation. Several are based on the standard Latin-1 code set, while others use company-specific sets. Even those that agree on Latin-1 may differ—one including information for all Latin-1 characters, another cataloging only a subset.

The differences in locale names and contents greatly complicate distributed computing. Assume your network includes the three nodes running the locales shown in Figure 12.3. Further assume all three nodes are from different manufacturers; that this is a heterogeneous cluster.

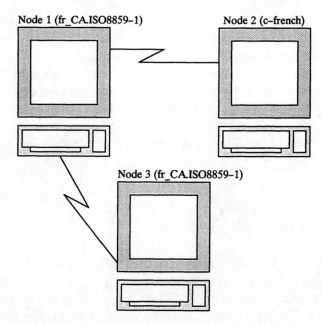

Figure 12.3   Multiple Nodes, Multiple Locales

An application starts on Node 1 and it wants to distribute some tasks to other nodes. Depending on the specific tasks, the variety in locales may make the distributed computing software reject some suitable nodes or accept unsuitable ones. Consider two scenarios:

1. **Distributed tasks include collation.** The distributed computing software checks the locale on Node 2 and concludes that it is completely different from what Node 1 is running, so it moves on to Node 3. This time the names match, so processing starts on Node 3. Although the names match, different companies created the two locales and they defined collation differently, resulting in inconsistent answers.

2. **Distributed tasks include numeric formatting.** As before, the distributed computing software checks and rejects Node 2 because its locale seems so obviously different from that on Node 1. However, both locales happen to include the same definition for simple numeric formatting, so Node 2's locale would have been acceptable. Since there is no way to peek inside locales—and it would be time-consuming to do so—the software moves on to Node 3. This time, the names match and the formatting gets done correctly.

One solution to these problems is to define standard locale contents with predictable, consistent names, and then to add interfaces for sending this information across the network. That way distributed applications (and even local ones) know what each locale name signifies and have a way of ensuring consistent results. Some national groups already have created standard locales (including Japan and Denmark), while others are in the process of doing so. In addition, standards groups are developing announcement mechanisms for sending locale or language information around a network.

12.8   Interchanging Data

Data is the fuel for most programs, but the various blends available on internationalized systems can be confusing. You might store a Japanese database on a server node in AJEC form, but access it from nodes that expect data in SJIS. A network in Europe may include nodes using code sets like Latin-1, Latin-2, pc850, ROMAN8, and others. A company with multinational employees may have files in languages from English to Japanese to Arabic.

When programs process data, they need some way to ensure they process it consistently. The global locale model provides a way to do this for individual systems, even if it doesn't always do the job correctly. If your locale is U.S. English and you access two files—one in U.S. English, the other in Japanese—the program processes both as if they were English. That's not right, but it is predictable.

It is desirable for there to be a method for processing data both predictably *and* correctly. That requires the ability to convert data automatically to and from multiple encodings when appropriate. In other words, it requires some sort of *data interchange* procedure.

Data interchange is different from exchanging locale information. When exchanging locale names, the goal is to ensure that all nodes involved in a single run of a distributed application use the same locale. However, separate programs (or program runs) can access the same data, but need it in different formats. With data interchange support, data becomes available in the format in which users need it.

Consider a Japanese database application. Assume the data is encoded in AJEC, and that users with both AJEC- and SJIS-based locales run the application. There are two ways the SJIS users can access the data: they can change to an AJEC-based locale, or the data can be converted to SJIS.

The first option isn't always feasible. It takes a considerable amount of software to support a locale, including the appropriate screen fonts, input methods, and locale definitions. If the SJIS nodes don't have all the required pieces, the users can't switch their locales and therefore can't run the application. However, if they can get the data in SJIS form, they can run the application without problems.

There are ways to convert data manually from one encoding to another, but networks and distributed computing make it desirable for the system to take care of such tasks automatically. Most interchange designs represent variations on two basic algorithms. The first reduces the number of converter modules required at the cost of increasing the number of conversions the software performs. The second reduces the number of conversions while increasing the converter modules required. Each algorithm has merit, but the best solution may be a combination of the two. This section describes all three possibilities. In the descriptions, when data is traveling across the network it is defined as being in a Network Interchange Encoding (NIE).

12.8.1   Universal Data Interchange

The simplest way to implement data interchange is to convert all data to a single, universal NIE before sending it across the network. When it reaches its destination, you convert it from the universal to the local encoding (whatever that is). Figure 12.4 illustrates the model.

The advantage of using a single NIE is that it only requires a few conversion routines. It is a $2n$ algorithm because it requires two converters per file code—into and out of the interchange code. However, as Figure 12.4 shows, a universal NIE

Figure 12.4   Universal NIE in Data Interchange

reduces the converter modules at the expense of increasing the number of conversions the software must do. It also sometimes wastes conversions, because it allows you to start an "inappropriate" conversion. Assume you have source data encoded in Latin-1. These are some possible results for target nodes that expect data encoded as listed:

- **pc850**. The universal interchange set works well for this conversion. It converts from Latin-1 into the single NIE and then from the NIE to pc850. A user might not even be aware the conversion has taken place.
- **Latin-1**. There is no technical problem with this scenario, but it obviously is inefficient because the system does two conversions (Latin-1 to NIE and NIE to Latin-1) when none is necessary.
- **Latin-2**. The conversion from Latin-1 to NIE works fine, but problems may arise when the data reaches the target node. Latin-2 contains some, but not all, of the characters in Latin-1. Among the Latin-1 entries missing in Latin-2 are uppercase and lowercase *à, å, è, ê, ì*, and *û*. If the original data contains these or any other characters that are unique to Latin-1, the conversion has problems because there is no way to convert them from the NIE to Latin-2. In that case, you can either reject the data or use a substitute character (usually a space or question mark) in place of unconvertable characters. If you reject the data, that means you waste two conversions. If you use a substitute character, there is partial data loss.

These three examples require a total of four converter modules (from Latin-1 to NIE, and from NIE to pc850, Latin-1, and Latin-2), and six actual conversions (two for each scenario).

12.8.2 Negotiated Conversions

Instead of converting data into another format before sending it across the network, you can use tags to determine when to convert and which conversions are appropriate. A tag may be a physical tag within the data, or it may be as simple as the value of the current global locale on a source or target node. This algorithm allows many NIEs because data may be encoded in a variety of ways for the trip across the network.

Using data tags to negotiate conversions greatly reduces the number of conversions software must perform, but creates the possibility of *n to n* converter modules. Theoretically, you need converters from *n* file codes to all other *n* file codes. Suppose you want to support data encoded in Latin-1, Latin-2, pc850, and Japanese AJEC. To cover these possibilities, it may appear you need these 12 converters:

```
Latin-1 to Latin-2        pc850 to Latin-1
Latin-1 to pc850          pc850 to Latin-2
Latin-1 to AJEC           pc850 to AJEC
Latin-2 to Latin-1        AJEC to Latin-1
Latin-2 to pc850          AJEC to ROMAN8
Latin-2 to AJEC           AJEC to pc850
```

However, theory and reality are two different things because most of these conversions don't make sense. Conversion is useful only if two code sets encode the same (or nearly the same) character set. Latin-1 and Latin-2 encode different character sets so you may decide it is inappropriate to convert data between the two. Similarly, an AJEC to Latin-1 conversion is likely to lose a significant amount of data. However, it is appropriate to convert between Latin-1 and pc850 because they encode nearly the same characters. If you only write converters for code sets that include the same characters, you reduce the theoretical 12 converters down to these practical two:

```
Latin-1 to pc850
pc850 to Latin-1
```

Data interchange works differently if you negotiate conversions rather than always converting into and out of a universal NIE. As in the previous section, assuming the source data is encoded in Latin-1, these are some results when using tags to negotiate data conversions:

- **pc850**. The source and target tags differ. You send the data over the network in Latin-1, and convert it to pc850 when it reaches the target.
- **Latin-1**. The source and target tags are the same, so you send the data over the network. No conversion is necessary.

- **Latin-2**. The source and target differ, and the characters in the two sets differ. There are two possible design choices. In the first, the conversion request returns an error and does no conversion. The alternate design is for the converter to transform as much data as possible and use a substitute for characters that don't exist in the target code set. In this scenario, the converter might also return a count of the number of characters it was not able to convert, thus giving users information about the amount of data loss.

If you choose to do a Latin-1 to Latin-2 conversion using a substitute character, these three examples require a total of two converter modules (Latin-1 to pc850 and to Latin-2), and two actual conversions (again, Latin-1 to pc850 and to Latin-2). If you decide a Latin-1-to-Latin-2 conversion is inappropriate, these examples require only one converter module and one conversion.

12.8.3 A Compromise Model

Given the examples listed above, negotiated data interchange may seem a clear winner. After all, it requires fewer converter modules and performs fewer actual conversions. However, unrestricted negotiation does have a significant drawback: conversion is only possible when there is a module between the source and target encodings. If there is no Latin-1-to-pc850 converter, you can't convert source data from Latin-1 to the pc850 form that a target might want.

This situation also holds true when using a universal NIE for interchange, but it is much more likely to be a problem for the negotiation model. That is because in addition to the large group of standard code sets and encoding methods available, many company-specific sets exist. It is impractical to assume all systems will have converters to and from every standard and proprietary encoding. For example, assume two companies support the mostly-pseudo code sets for Western European languages listed in Table 12.4.

Assume, as is common, that each company has converters to and from Latin-1 and all its proprietary sets. **Foo** and **Bar** even have converters for each others' general, proprietary sets (to and from `foo_weuropean` and `bar_weuropean`). However, assume there are no converters between the individual language sets because these sets have only limited use. That is, assume there is no `foo_french` to `bar_french` or `bar_spanish` to `foo_spanish`. That means a request to convert between these sets fails.

Negotiated conversions assume every source and every target know each others' encodings and so require too many converter modules. An unnegotiated universal

Table 12.4   Pseudo Sample Code Sets

Company	Code Sets
Foo	ISO 8859-1 (Latin-1)
	foo_weuropean
	foo_french
	foo_german
	foo_italian
	foo_spanish
Bar	ISO 8859-1
	bar_weuropean
	bar_french
	bar_german
	bar_italian
	bar_spanish

NIE results in excessive conversions. Therefore, it may make sense to compromise between the two models.

Suppose your network includes nodes using Latin-1, ROMAN8, pc850, and ISO 6937. These sets all encode Western European characters, and in the negotiation model, you need converters to and from each set. That's these 12 converters:

```
Latin-1 to ROMAN8     pc850 to Latin-1
Latin-1 to pc850      pc850 to ROMAN8
Latin-1 to ISO 6937   pc850 to ISO 6937
ROMAN8 to Latin-1     ISO 6937 to Latin-1
ROMAN8 to pc850       ISO 6937 to ROMAN8
ROMAN8 to ISO 6937    ISO 6937 to pc850
```

In contrast, a universal NIE requires these eight converters:

```
Latin-1 to NIE     NIE to Latin-1
ROMAN8 to NIE      NIE to ROMAN8
pc850 to NIE       NIE to pc850
ISO 6937 to NIE    NIE to ISO 6937
```

A compromise alternative, however, is to choose an NIE per character set. You might refer to this as a regional NIE. For sets that encode Western European characters (as in these examples), you might choose Latin-1. Among the common

Japanese encodings—AJEC, and UJIS or SJIS varieties—you might choose AJEC. For Taiwanese Chinese, you might choose the EUC encoding over a Big 5 implementation.

Assuming you pick Latin-1 as the Western European NIE, you reduce the converter modules needed from 12 (with negotiation) or eight (with a universal NIE) down to these six:

```
Latin-1 to ROMAN8
ROMAN8 to Latin-1
Latin-1 to pc850
pc850 to Latin-1
Latin-1 to ISO 6937
ISO 6937 to Latin-1
```

While the universal NIE always requires two conversions per operation (into and out of the NIE), this compromise requires significantly fewer. If the source and target match, there is no conversion. If they differ, but either the source or target uses the regional NIE, one conversion takes place—into or out of that NIE. The results of both these scenarios is the same as that for the negotiation model. The difference comes when the source and target differ and neither uses the regional NIE. For example, assume the source is ISO 6937 and the target is ROMAN8. As with the universal NIE model, in that case you do two conversions—from ISO 6937 to Latin-1 (the regional NIE) and from Latin-1 to ROMAN8.

With this compromise model or with a universal NIE, there is no need for converters between probably limited-use proprietary sets. Instead, each company can write modules to and from its sets to the appropriate regional or universal NIE. Reducing the number of possibilities streamlines the conversion process.

12.9   Looking to the Future

As requirements from worldwide users and distributed applications grow and change, it becomes increasingly necessary to provide functionality that is beyond the ability of current standards to handle. This chapter has provided a look at some of the issues, and an analysis of some potential solutions. When new functionality becomes available, it will give programmers and users access to even greater levels of I18N support. However, even without enhanced functionality, present internationalized interfaces, code sets, and programming techniques make software capable of meeting many more users' needs than does ASCII-only, or single-language software. When writing programs, keep the world in mind.

Defining a Locale

Most locales consist of a charmap and a locale definition (**localedef**). This appendix contains a charmap for the ISO 8859-1 (Latin-1) code set, and French **localedef** source file. Both follow POSIX.2-defined syntax.

A.1   ISO 8859-1 Charmap

This is the source for a ISO 8859-1 charmap. This uses the symbolic names defined in the POSIX.2 Portable Character Set for all portable characters. Other symbolic names are implementation-defined.

```
#
#    Charmap for ISO 8859-1 code set
#
<code_set_name>        "ISO8859-1"
<mb_cur_max>           1
<mb_cur_min>           1

CHARMAP
#    Portable characters and other
#    standard controls
<NUL>                  \x00
<SOH>                  \x01
<STX>                  \x02
<ETX>                  \x03
<EOT>                  \x04
<ENQ>                  \x05
```

<ACK>	\x06
<BEL>	\x07
<alert>	\x07
<backspace>	\x08
<tab>	\x09
<newline>	\x0a
<vertical-tab>	\x0b
<form-feed>	\x0c
<carriage-return>	\x0d
<SO>	\x0e
<SI>	\x0f
<DLE>	\x10
<DC1>	\x11
<DC2>	\x12
<DC3>	\x13
<DC4>	\x14
<NAK>	\x15
<SYN>	\x16
<ETB>	\x17
<CAN>	\x18
<EM>	\x19
<SUB>	\x1a
<ESC>	\x1b
<IS4>	\x1c
<IS3>	\x1d
<IS2>	\x1e
<IS1>	\x1f
<SP>	\x20
<space>	\x20
<exclamation-mark>	\x21
<quotation-mark>	\x22
<number-sign>	\x23
<dollar-sign>	\x24
<percent-sign>	\x25
<ampersand>	\x26
<apostrophe>	\x27
<left-parenthesis>	\x28
<right-parenthesis>	\x29
<asterisk>	\x2a

```
<plus-sign>              \x2b
<comma>                  \x2c
<hyphen>                 \x2d
<hyphen-minus>           \x2d
<period>                 \x2e
<full-stop>              \x2e
<slash>                  \x2f
<solidus>                \x2f
<zero>                   \x30
<one>                    \x31
<two>                    \x32
<three>                  \x33
<four>                   \x34
<five>                   \x35
<six>                    \x36
<seven>                  \x37
<eight>                  \x38
<nine>                   \x39
<colon>                  \x3a
<semicolon>              \x3b
<less-than-sign>         \x3c
<equals-sign>            \x3d
<greater-than-sign>      \x3e
<question-mark>          \x3f
<commercial-at>          \x40
<A>                      \x41
<B>                      \x42
<C>                      \x43
<D>                      \x44
<E>                      \x45
<F>                      \x46
<G>                      \x47
<H>                      \x48
<I>                      \x49
<J>                      \x4a
<K>                      \x4b
<L>                      \x4c
<M>                      \x4d
<N>                      \x4e
```

<O>	\x4f
<P>	\x50
<Q>	\x51
<R>	\x52
<S>	\x53
<T>	\x54
<U>	\x55
<V>	\x56
<W>	\x57
<X>	\x58
<Y>	\x59
<Z>	\x5a
<left-square-bracket>	\x5b
<backslash>	\x5c
<reverse-solidus>	\x5c
<right-square-bracket>	\x5d
<circumflex>	\x5e
<circumflex-accent>	\x5e
<underscore>	\x5f
<low-line>	\x5f
<grave-accent>	\x60
<a>	\x61
<b>	\x62
<c>	\x63
<d>	\x64
<e>	\x65
<f>	\x66
<g>	\x67
<h>	\x68
<i>	\x69
<j>	\x6a
<k>	\x6b
<l>	\x6c
<m>	\x6d
<n>	\x6e
<o>	\x6f
<p>	\x70
<q>	\x71
<r>	\x72

```
<s>                          \x73
<t>                          \x74
<u>                          \x75
<v>                          \x76
<w>                          \x77
<x>                          \x78
<y>                          \x79
<z>                          \x7a
<left-brace>                 \x7b
<left-curly-bracket>         \x7b
<vertical-line>              \x7c
<right-brace>                \x7d
<right-curly-bracket>        \x7d
<tilde>                      \x7e
<DEL>                        \x7f
#
# Extended control characters
# (names taken from ISO 6429)
#
<PAD>                        \x80
<HOP>                        \x81
<BPH>                        \x82
<NBH>                        \x83
<IND>                        \x84
<NEL>                        \x85
<SSA>                        \x86
<ESA>                        \x87
<HTS>                        \x88
<HTJ>                        \x89
<VTS>                        \x8a
<PLD>                        \x8b
<PLU>                        \x8c
<RI>                         \x8d
<SS2>                        \x8e
<SS3>                        \x8f
<DCS>                        \x90
<PU1>                        \x91
<PU2>                        \x92
<STS>                        \x93
```

```
<CCH>                      \x94
<MW>                       \x95
<SPS>                      \x96
<EPA>                      \x97
<SOS>                      \x98
<SGCI>                     \x99
<SCI>                      \x9a
<CSI>                      \x9b
<ST>                       \x9c
<OSC>                      \x9d
<PM>                       \x9e
<APC>                      \x9f
#
# Other graphic characters
#
<nobreakspace>             \xa0
<exclamation-down>         \xa1
<cent>                     \xa2
<sterling>                 \xa3
<currency>                 \xa4
<yen>                      \xa5
<broken-bar>               \xa6
<section>                  \xa7
<diaresis>                 \xa8
<copyright>                \xa9
<feminine>                 \xaa
<guillemot-left>           \xab
<not>                      \xac
<dash>                     \xad
<registered>               \xae
<macron>                   \xaf
<degree>                   \xb0
<plus-minus>               \xb1
<two-superior>             \xb2
<three-superior>           \xb3
<acute>                    \xb4
<mu>                       \xb5
<paragraph>                \xb6
<dot>                      \xb7
```

```
<cedilla>                    \xb8
<one-superior>               \xb9
<masculine>                  \xba
<guillemot-right>            \xbb
<one-quarter>                \xbc
<one-half>                   \xbd
<three-quarters>             \xbe
<question-down>              \xbf
<A-grave>                    \xc0
<A-acute>                    \xc1
<A-circumflex>               \xc2
<A-tilde>                    \xc3
<A-diaresis>                 \xc4
<A-ring>                     \xc5
<AE>                         \xc6
<C-cedilla>                  \xc7
<E-grave>                    \xc8
<E-acute>                    \xc9
<E-circumflex>               \xca
<E-diaresis>                 \xcb
<I-grave>                    \xcc
<I-acute>                    \xcd
<I-circumflex>               \xce
<I-diaresis>                 \xcf
<Eth>                        \xd0
<N-tilde>                    \xd1
<O-grave>                    \xd2
<O-acute>                    \xd3
<O-circumflex>               \xd4
<O-tilde>                    \xd5
<O-diaresis>                 \xd6
<multiply>                   \xd7
<O-slash>                    \xd8
<U-grave>                    \xd9
<U-acute>                    \xda
<U-circumflex>               \xdb
<U-diaresis>                 \xdc
<Y-acute>                    \xdd
<Thorn>                      \xde
```

```
<s-sharp>               \xdf
<a-grave>               \xe0
<a-acute>               \xe1
<a-circumflex>          \xe2
<a-tilde>               \xe3
<a-diaresis>            \xe4
<a-ring>                \xe5
<ae>                    \xe6
<c-cedilla>             \xe7
<e-grave>               \xe8
<e-acute>               \xe9
<e-circumflex>          \xea
<e-diaresis>            \xeb
<i-grave>               \xec
<i-acute>               \xed
<i-circumflex>          \xee
<i-diaresis>            \xef
<eth>                   \xf0
<n-tilde>               \xf1
<o-grave>               \xf2
<o-acute>               \xf3
<o-circumflex>          \xf4
<o-tilde>               \xf5
<o-diaresis>            \xf6
<divide>                \xf7
<division>              \xf7
<o-slash>               \xf8
<u-grave>               \xf9
<u-acute>               \xfa
<u-circumflex>          \xfb
<u-diaresis>            \xfc
<y-acute>               \xfd
<thorn>                 \xfe
<y-diaresis>            \xff

END CHARMAP
```

A.2 Sample French localedef

This is an example locale definition source file for a French locale. Because user preferences vary, there are many equally correct ways to define a locale. The information in this **localedef** is an example of one way to do so, but the version your vendor supplies or that you write yourself may differ.

```
############################################################
# Localedef source for fr_FR (French in France) locale  #
############################################################

#############
LC_CTYPE
#############

upper       <A>;<B>;<C>;<D>;<E>;<F>;<G>;<H>;<I>;<J>;<K>;\
            <L>;<M>;<N>;<O>;<P>;<Q>;<R>;<S>;<T>;<U>;<V>;<W>;\
            <X>;<Y>;<Z>;\
            <A-grave>;<A-circumflex>;<AE>;<C-cedilla>;\
            <E-grave>;<E-acute>;<E-circumflex>;<E-diaresis>;\
            <I-circumflex>;<I-diaresis>;<O-circumflex>;\
            <U-grave>;<U-circumflex>;<U-diaresis>

lower       <a>;<b>;<c>;<d>;<e>;<f>;<g>;<h>;<i>;<j>;<k>;\
            <l>;<m>;<n>;<o>;<p>;<q>;<r>;<s>;<t>;<u>;<v>;<w>;\
            <x>;<y>;<z>;\
            <a-grave>;<a-circumflex>;<ae>;<c-cedilla>;\
            <e-grave>;<e-acute>;<e-circumflex>;<e-diaresis>;\
            <i-circumflex>;<i-diaresis>;<o-circumflex>;\
            <u-grave>;<u-circumflex>;<u-diaresis>

space       <tab>;<newline>;<vertical-tab>;<form-feed>;\
            <carriage-return>;<space>

cntrl       <NUL>;<SOH>;<STX>;<ETX>;<EOT>;<ENQ>;<ACK>;\
            <alert>;<backspace>;<tab>;<newline>;\
            <vertical-tab>;<form-feed>;<carriage-return>;\
            <SO>;<SI>;<DLE>;<DC1>;<DC2>;<DC3>;<DC4>;<NAK>;\
            <SYN>;<ETB>;<CAN>;<EM>;<SUB>;<ESC>;<IS4>;\
            <IS3>;<IS2>;<IS1>;<DEL>;\
```

```
              <PAD>;<HOP>;<BPH>;<NBH>;<IND>;<NEL>;<SSA>;<ESA>;\
              <HTS>;<HTJ>;<VTS>;<PLD>;<PLU>;<RI>;<SS2>;<SS3>;\
              <DCS>;<PU1>;<PU2>;<STS>;<CCH>;<MW>;<SPS>;<EPA>;\
              <SOS>;<SGCI>;<SCI>;<CSI>;<ST>;<OSC>;<PM>;<APC>


graph         <exclamation-mark>;<quotation-mark>;<number-sign>;\
              <dollar-sign>;<percent-sign>;<ampersand>;<apostrophe>;\
              <left-parenthesis>;<right-parenthesis>;<asterisk>;\
              <plus-sign>;<comma>;<hyphen>;<period>;<slash>;\
              <zero>;<one>;<two>;<three>;<four>;<five>;\
              <six>;<seven>;<eight>;<nine>;\
              <colon>;<semicolon>;<less-than-sign>;<equals-sign>;\
              <greater-than-sign>;<question-mark>;<commercial-at>;\
              <A>;<B>;<C>;<D>;<E>;<F>;<G>;<H>;<I>;<J>;<K>;<L>;<M>;\
              <N>;<O>;<P>;<Q>;<R>;<S>;<T>;<U>;<V>;<W>;<X>;<Y>;<Z>;\
              <left-square-bracket>;<backslash>;\
              <right-square-bracket>;<circumflex>;\
              <underscore>;<grave-accent>;\
              <a>;<b>;<c>;<d>;<e>;<f>;<g>;<h>;<i>;<j>;<k>;<l>;<m>;\
              <n>;<o>;<p>;<q>;<r>;<s>;<t>;<u>;<v>;<w>;<x>;<y>;<z>;\
              <left-brace>;<vertical-line>;<right-brace>;<tilde>;\
              <exclamation-down>;<cent>;<sterling>;<currency>;\
              <yen>;<broken-bar>;<section>;<diaresis>;<copyright>;\
              <feminine>;<guillemot-left>;<not>;<dash>;\
              <registered>;<macron>;<degree>;<plus-minus>;\
              <two-superior>;<three-superior>;<acute>;<mu>;\
              <paragraph>;<dot>;<cedilla>;<one-superior>;\
              <masculine>;<guillemot-right>;<one-quarter>;\
              <one-half>;<three-quarters>;<question-down>;\
              <A-grave>;<A-acute>;<A-circumflex>;<A-tilde>;\
              <A-diaresis>;<A-ring>;<AE>;<C-cedilla>;<E-grave>;\
              <E-acute>;<E-circumflex>;<E-diaresis>;<I-grave>;\
              <I-acute>;<I-circumflex>;<I-diaresis>;<Eth>;\
              <N-tilde>;<O-grave>;<O-acute>;<O-circumflex>;\
              <O-tilde>;<O-diaresis>;<multiply>;<O-slash>;\
              <U-grave>;<U-acute>;<U-circumflex>;<U-diaresis>;\
              <Y-acute>;<Thorn>;<s-sharp>;<a-grave>;<a-acute>;\
              <a-circumflex>;<a-tilde>;<a-diaresis>;<a-ring>;<ae>;\
              <c-cedilla>;<e-grave>;<e-acute>;<e-circumflex>;\
```

```
                <e-diaresis>;<i-grave>;<i-acute>;<i-circumflex>;\
                <i-diaresis>;<eth>;<n-tilde>;<o-grave>;<o-acute>;\
                <o-circumflex>;<o-tilde>;<o-diaresis>;<divide>;\
                <o-slash>;<u-grave>;<u-acute>;<u-circumflex>;\
                <u-diaresis>;<y-acute>;<thorn>;<y-diaresis>
#
# print category omitted to save space. It includes
# everything in graph plus <space>.

punct           <exclamation-mark>;<quotation-mark>;\
                <number-sign>;<dollar-sign>;<percent-sign>;\
                <ampersand>;<apostrophe>;<left-parenthesis>;\
                <right-parenthesis>;<asterisk>;<plus-sign>;<comma>;\
                <hyphen>;<period>;<slash>;<colon>;<semicolon>;\
                <less-than-sign>;<equals-sign>;<greater-than-sign>;\
                <question-mark>;<commercial-at>;\
                <left-square-bracket>;<backslash>;\
                <right-square-bracket>;<circumflex>;\
                <underscore>;<grave-accent>;<left-brace>;\
                <vertical-line>;<right-brace>;<tilde>

digit           <zero>;<one>;<two>;<three>;<four>;\
                <five>;<six>;<seven>;<eight>;<nine>

xdigit          <zero>;<one>;<two>;<three>;<four>;\
                <five>;<six>;<seven>;<eight>;<nine>;\
                <A>;<B>;<C>;<D>;<E>;<F>;\
                <a>;<b>;<c>;<d>;<e>;<f>

blank           <space>;<tab>

toupper         (<a>,<A>);(<b>,<B>);(<c>,<C>);(<d>,<D>);(<e>,<E>);\
                (<f>,<F>);(<g>,<G>);(<h>,<H>);(<i>,<I>);(<j>,<J>);\
                (<k>,<K>);(<l>,<L>);(<m>,<M>);(<n>,<N>);(<o>,<O>);\
                (<p>,<P>);(<q>,<Q>);(<r>,<R>);(<s>,<S>);(<t>,<T>);\
                (<u>,<U>);(<v>,<V>);(<w>,<W>);(<x>,<X>);(<y>,<Y>);\
                (<z>,<Z>);(<a-grave>,<A-grave>);\
                (<a-circumflex>,<A-circumflex>);\
                (<ae>,<AE>);(<c-cedilla>,<C-cedilla>);\
```

```
                    (<e-grave>,<E-grave>);\
                    (<e-acute>,<E-acute>);\
                    (<e-circumflex>,<E-circumflex>);\
                    (<e-diaresis>,<E-diaresis>);\
                    (<i-circumflex>,<I-circumflex>);\
                    (<i-diaresis>,<I-diaresis>);\
                    (<o-circumflex>,<O-circumflex>);\
                    (<u-grave>,<U-grave>);\
                    (<u-circumflex>,<U-circumflex>);\
                    (<u-diaresis>,<U-diaresis>)

END LC_CTYPE

############
LC_COLLATE
############
#
#  Order is control characters followed by punctuation
#  (including digits) and then letters. The letters
#  have a multi-level sort with diacritics and case
#  being ignored on the first pass, then a
#  sort-by-diacritics on the second pass, and
#  sort-by-case on the third (last).
#
order_start                    forward;backward;forward

<NUL>
<SOH>
<STX>
<ETX>
<EOT>
<ENQ>
<ACK>
<alert>
<backspace>
<tab>
<newline>
<vertical-tab>
<form-feed>
<carriage-return>
```

```
<SO>
<SI>
<DLE>
<DC1>
<DC2>
<DC3>
<DC4>
<NAK>
<SYN>
<ETB>
<CAN>
<EM>
<SUB>
<ESC>
<IS4>
<IS3>
<IS2>
<IS1>
<PAD>
<HOP>
<BPH>
<NBH>
<IND>
<NEL>
<SSA>
<ESA>
<HTS>
<HTJ>
<VTS>
<PLD>
<PLU>
<RI>
<SS2>
<SS3>
<DCS>
<PU1>
<PU2>
<STS>
<CCH>
```

```
<MW>
<SPS>
<EPA>
<SOS>
<SGCI>
<SCI>
<CSI>
<ST>
<OSC>
<PM>
<APC>
<space>                    <space>;<space>;<space>
<exclamation-mark>         <exclamation-mark>;<exclamation-mark>;\
                           <exclamation-mark>
<quotation-mark>           <quotation-mark>;<quotation-mark>;\
                           <quotation-mark>
<number-sign>              <number-sign>;<number-sign>;<number-sign>
<dollar-sign>              <dollar-sign>;<dollar-sign>;<dollar-sign>
<percent-sign>             <percent-sign>;<percent-sign>;\
                           <percent-sign>
<ampersand>                <ampersand>;<ampersand>;<ampersand>
<apostrophe>               <apostrophe>;<apostrophe>;<apostrophe>
<left-parenthesis>         <left-parenthesis>;<left-parenthesis>;\
                           <left-parenthesis>
<right-parenthesis>        <right-parenthesis>;<right-parenthesis>;\
                           <right-parenthesis>
<asterisk>                 <asterisk>;<asterisk>;<asterisk>
<plus-sign>                <plus-sign>;<plus-sign>;<plus-sign>
<comma>                    <comma>;<comma>;<comma>
<hyphen-minus>             <hyphen-minus>;<hyphen-minus>;\
                           <hyphen-minus>
<period>                   <period>;<period>;<period>
<slash>                    <slash>;<slash>;<slash>
<zero>                     <zero>;<zero>;<zero>
<one>                      <one>;<one>;<one>
<two>                      <two>;<two>;<two>
<three>                    <three>;<three>;<three>
<four>                     <four>;<four>;<four>
<five>                     <five>;<five>;<five>
```

```
<six>                 <six>;<six>;<six>
<seven>               <seven>;<seven>;<seven>
<eight>               <eight>;<eight>;<eight>
<nine>                <nine>;<nine>;<nine>
<colon>               <colon>;<colon>;<colon>
<semicolon>           <semicolon>;<semicolon>;<semicolon>
<less-than-sign>      <less-than-sign>;<less-than-sign>;\
                      <less-than-sign>
<equals-sign>         <equals-sign>;<equals-sign>;<equals-sign>
<greater-than-sign>   <greater-than-sign>;<greater-than-sign>;\
                      <greater-than-sign>
<question-mark>       <question-mark>;<question-mark>;\
                      <question-mark>
<commercial-at>       <commercial-at>;<commercial-at>;\
                      <commercial-at>
<left-square-bracket> <left-square-bracket>;\
                      <left-square-bracket>;\
                      <left-square-bracket>
<backslash>           <backslash>;<backslash>;<backslash>
<right-square-bracket><right-square-bracket>;\
                      <right-square-bracket>;\
                      <right-square-bracket>
<circumflex>          <circumflex>;<circumflex>;<circumflex>
<underscore>          <underscore>;<underscore>;<underscore>
<grave-accent>        <grave-accent>;<grave-accent>;\
                      <grave-accent>
<left-brace>          <left-brace>;<left-brace>;<left-brace>
<vertical-line>       <vertical-line>;<vertical-line>;\
                      <vertical-line>
<right-brace>         <right-brace>;<right-brace>;<right-brace>
<tilde>               <tilde>;<tilde>;<tilde>
<DEL>                 <DEL>;<DEL>;<DEL>
<nobreakspace>        <nobreakspace>;<nobreakspace>;\
                      <nobreakspace>
<exclamation-down>    <exclamation-down>;<exclamation-down>;\
                      <exclamation-down>
<cent>                <cent>;<cent>;<cent>
<sterling>            <sterling>;<sterling>;<sterling>
<currency>            <currency>;<currency>;<currency>
```

```
<yen>                     <yen>;<yen>;<yen>
<broken-bar>              <broken-bar>;<broken-bar>;<broken-bar>
<section>                 <section>;<section>;<section>
<diaresis>                <diaresis>;<diaresis>;<diaresis>
<feminine>                <feminine>;<feminine>;<feminine>
<copyright>               <copyright>;<copyright>;<copyright>
<guillemot-left>          <guillemot-left>;<guillemot-left>;\
                          <guillemot-left>
<not>                     <not>;<not>;<not>
<dash>                    <dash>;<dash>;<dash>
<registered>              <registered>;<registered>;<registered>
<macron>                  <macron>;<macron>;<macron>
<degree>                  <degree>;<degree>;<degree>
<plus-minus>              <plus-minus>;<plus-minus>;<plus-minus>
<two-superior>            <two-superior>;<two-superior>;\
                          <two-superior>
<three-superior>          <three-superior>;<three-superior>;\
                          <three-superior>
<acute>                   <acute>;<acute>;<acute>
<mu>                      <mu>;<mu>;<mu>
<paragraph>               <paragraph>;<paragraph>;<paragraph>
<dot>                     <dot>;<dot>;<dot>
<cedilla>                 <cedilla>;<cedilla>;<cedilla>
<one-superior>            <one-superior>;<one-superior>;\
                          <one-superior>
<masculine>               <masculine>;<masculine>;<masculine>
<guillemot-right>         <guillemot-right>;<guillemot-right>;\
                          <guillemot-right>
<one-quarter>             <one-quarter>;<one-quarter>;\
                          <one-quarter>
<one-half>                <one-half;<one-half>;<one-half>
<three-quarters>          <three-quarters>;<three-quarters>;\
                          <three-quarters>
<question-down>           <question-down>;<question-down>;\
                          <question-down>
<multiply>                <multiply>;<multiply>;<multiply>
<division>                <division>;<division>;<division>
<a>                       <a>;<a>;<a>
<A>                       <a>;<a>;<A>
```

```
<a-acute>             <a>;<a-acute>;<a-acute>
<A-acute>             <a>;<a-acute>;<A-acute>
<a-grave>             <a>;<a-grave>;<a-grave>
<A-grave>             <a>;<a-grave>;<A-grave>
<a-circumflex>        <a>;<a-circumflex>;<a-circumflex>
<A-circumflex>        <a>;<a-circumflex>;<A-circumflex>
<a-ring>              <a>;<a-ring>;<a-ring>
<A-ring>              <a>;<a-ring>;<A-ring>
<a-diaresis>          <a>;<a-diaresis>;<a-diaresis>
<A-diaresis>          <a>;<a-diaresis>;<A-diaresis>
<a-tilde>             <a>;<a-tilde>;<a-tilde>
<A-tilde>             <a>;<a-tilde>;<A-tilde>
<ae>                  <a>;<a><e>;<a><e>
<AE>                  <a>;<a><e>;<A><E>
<b>                   <b>;<b>;<b>
<B>                   <b>;<b>;<B>
<c>                   <c>;<c>;<c>
<C>                   <c>;<c>;<C>
<c-cedilla>           <c>;<c-cedilla>;<c-cedilla>
<C-cedilla>           <c>;<c-cedilla>;<C-cedilla>
<d>                   <d>;<d>;<d>
<D>                   <d>;<d>;<D>
<eth>                 <d>;<eth>;<eth>
<Eth>                 <d>;<eth>;<Eth>
<e>                   <e>;<e>;<e>
<E>                   <e>;<e>;<E>
<e-acute>             <e>;<e-acute>;<e-acute>
<E-acute>             <e>;<e-acute>;<E-acute>
<e-grave>             <e>;<e-grave>;<e-grave>
<E-grave>             <e>;<e-grave>;<E-grave>
<e-circumflex>        <e>;<e-circumflex>;<e-circumflex>
<E-circumflex>        <e>;<e-circumflex>;<E-circumflex>
<e-diaresis>          <e>;<e-diaresis>;<e-diaresis>
<E-diaresis>          <e>;<e-diaresis>;<E-diaresis>
<f>                   <f>;<f>;<f>
<F>                   <f>;<f>;<F>
<g>                   <g>;<g>;<g>
<G>                   <g>;<g>;<G>
<h>                   <h>;<h>;<h>
```

```
<H>                   <h>;<h>;<H>
<i>                   <i>;<i>;<i>
<I>                   <i>;<i>;<I>
<i-acute>             <i>;<i-acute>;<i-acute>
<I-acute>             <i>;<i-acute>;<I-acute>
<i-grave>             <i>;<i-grave>;<i-grave>
<I-grave>             <i>;<i-grave>;<I-grave>
<i-circumflex>        <i>;<i-circumflex>;<i-circumflex>
<I-circumflex>        <i>;<i-circumflex>;<I-circumflex>
<i-diaresis>          <i>;<i-diaresis>;<i-diaresis>
<I-diaresis>          <i>;<i-diaresis>;<I-diaresis>
<j>                   <j>;<j>;<j>
<J>                   <j>;<j>;<J>
<k>                   <k>;<k>;<k>
<K>                   <k>;<k>;<K>
<l>                   <l>;<l>;<l>
<L>                   <l>;<l>;<L>
<m>                   <m>;<m>;<m>
<M>                   <m>;<m>;<M>
<n>                   <n>;<n>;<n>
<N>                   <n>;<n>;<N>
<n-tilde>             <n>;<n-tilde>;<n-tilde>
<N-tilde>             <n>;<n-tilde>;<N-tilde>
<o>                   <o>;<o>;<o>
<O>                   <o>;<o>;<O>
<o-acute>             <o>;<o-acute>;<o-acute>
<O-acute>             <o>;<o-acute>;<O-acute>
<o-grave>             <o>;<o-grave>;<o-grave>
<O-grave>             <o>;<o-grave>;<O-grave>
<o-circumflex>        <o>;<o-circumflex>;<o-circumflex>
<O-circumflex>        <o>;<o-circumflex>;<O-circumflex>
<o-diaresis>          <o>;<o-diaresis>;<o-diaresis>
<O-diaresis>          <o>;<o-diaresis>;<O-diaresis>
<o-tilde>             <o>;<o-tilde>;<o-tilde>
<O-tilde>             <o>;<o-tilde>;<O-tilde>
<o-slash>             <o>;<o-slash>;<o-slash>
<O-slash>             <o>;<o-slash>;<O-slash>
<p>                   <p>;<p>;<p>
<P>                   <p>;<p>;<P>
```

```
<q>                   <q>;<q>;<q>
<Q>                   <q>;<q>;<Q>
<r>                   <r>;<r>;<r>
<R>                   <r>;<r>;<R>
<s>                   <s>;<s>;<s>
<S>                   <s>;<s>;<S>
<s-sharp>             <s>;<s><s>;<s><s>
<t>                   <t>;<t>;<t>
<T>                   <t>;<t>;<T>
<thorn>               <t>;<t><h>;<t><h>
<Thorn>               <t>;<t><h>;<T><h>
<u>                   <u>;<u>;<u>
<U>                   <u>;<u>;<U>
<u-acute>             <u>;<u-acute>;<u-acute>
<U-acute>             <u>;<u-acute>;<U-acute>
<u-grave>             <u>;<u-grave>;<u-grave>
<U-grave>             <u>;<u-grave>;<U-grave>
<u-circumflex>        <u>;<u-circumflex>;<u-circumflex>
<U-circumflex>        <u>;<u-circumflex>;<U-circumflex>
<u-diaresis>          <u>;<u-diaresis>;<u-diaresis>
<U-diaresis>          <u>;<u-diaresis>;<U-diaresis>
<v>                   <v>;<v>;<v>
<V>                   <v>;<v>;<V>
<w>                   <w>;<w>;<w>
<W>                   <w>;<w>;<W>
<x>                   <x>;<x>;<x>
<X>                   <x>;<x>;<X>
<y>                   <y>;<y>;<y>
<Y>                   <y>;<y>;<Y>
<y-acute>             <y>;<y-acute>;<y-acute>
<Y-acute>             <y>;<y-acute>;<Y-acute>
<y-diaresis>          <y>;<y-diaresis>;<y-diaresis>
<z>                   <z>;<z>;<z>
<Z>                   <z>;<z>;<Z>
order_end
END LC_COLLATE
############
LC_MONETARY
############
```

```
int_curr_symbol        "<F><R><F><space>"
currency_symbol        "<F>"
mon_decimal_point      "<comma>"
mon_thousands_sep      ""
mon_grouping           3
positive_sign          ""
negative_sign          "<hyphen>"
int_frac_digits        2
frac_digits            2
p_cs_precedes          0
p_sep_by_space         1
n_cs_precedes          0
n_sep_by_space         1
p_sign_posn            1
n_sign_posn            1

END LC_MONETARY


############
LC_NUMERIC
############

decimal_point          "<comma>"
thousands_sep          ""
grouping               3

END LC_NUMERIC


############
LC_TIME
############
#  abbreviated day names
abday      "<d><i><m>";"<l><u><n>";\
           "<m><a><r>";"<m><e><r>";\
           "<j><e><u>";"<v><e><n>";\
           "<s><a><m>"
```

```
#  full day names
day          "<d><i><m><a><n><c><h><e>";\
             "<l><u><n><d><i>";\
             "<m><a><r><d><i>";\
             "<m><e><r><c><r><e><d><i>";\
             "<j><e><u><d><i>";\
             "<v><e><n><d><r><e><d><i>";\
             "<s><a><m><e><d><i>"


             #  abbreviated month names
abmon        "<j><a><n>";"<f><e-acute><v>";\
             "<m><a><r>";"<a><v><r>";\
             "<m><a><i>";"<j><u><n>";\
             "<j><u><l>";"<a><o><u-circumflex>";\
             "<s><e><p>";"<o><c><t>";\
             "<n><o><v>";"<d><e-acute><c>"


             #  full month names
mon          "<j><a><n><v><i><e><r>";\
             "<f><e-acute><v><r><i><e><r>";\
             "<m><a><r><s>";\ '
             "<a><v><r><i><l>";\
             "<m><a><i>";\
             "<j><u><i><n>";\
             "<j><u><i><l><l><e><t>";\
             "<a><o><u-circumflex><t>";\
             "<s><e><p><t><e><m><b><r><e>";\
             "<o><c><t><o><b><r><e>";\
             "<n><o><v><e><m><b><r><e>";\
             "<d><e-acute><c><e><m><b><r><e>"


#  date/time format. The following designates this
#  format: "%a %e %b %H:%M:%S %Z %Y"

d_t_fmt      "<percent-sign><a><space><percent-sign><e>\
             <space><percent-sign><b><space><percent-sign><H>\
             <colon><percent-sign><M><colon><percent-sign><S>\
             <space><percent-sign><Z><space><percent-sign><Y>"
```

```
#   date format. The following designates this
#   format: "%d.%m.%y"
d_fmt       "<percent-sign><d><period><percent-sign><m>\
            <period><percent-sign><y>"


#   time format. The following designates this format:
#   "%H:%M:%S"
t_fmt       "<percent-sign><H><colon><percent-sign><M>\
            <colon><percent-sign><S>"


am_pm       "<semicolon>"
#   12-hour time representation. This is empty, meaning
#   this locale always uses the 24-hour format.
t_fmt_ampm  ""


END LC_TIME


#############
LC_MESSAGES
#############


# yes expression. The following designates:
# "^([oO]|[oO][uU][iI])"
#
yesexpr    "<circumflex><left-parenthesis>\
           <left-square-bracket><o><O><right-square-bracket>\
           <vertical-line><left-square-bracket><o><O>\
           <right-square-bracket><left-square-bracket><u><U>\
           <right-square-bracket><left-square-bracket><i><I>\
           <right-square-bracket><right-parenthesis>"


# no expression. The following designates:
# "^([nN]|[nN][oO][nN])"
#
noexpr     "<circumflex><left-parenthesis>\
           <left-square-bracket><n><N><right-square-bracket>\
           <vertical-line><left-square-bracket><n><N>\
           <right-square-bracket><left-square-bracket><o><O>\
           <right-square-bracket><left-square-bracket><n><N>\
           <right-square-bracket><right-parenthesis>"
```

```
# yes string. The following designates: "oui:o:O"
#
yesstr     "<o><u><i><colon><o><colon><O>"

# no string. The following designates: "non:n:N"
#
nostr      "<n><o><n><colon><n><colon><N>"

END LC_MESSAGES
```

Input Methods

B

Internationalized software lets users manipulate and process characters from many languages. In order to work with these characters, however, users almost certainly need the ability to input them from a keyboard or other device. Software-based input methods and (sometimes) revised hardware give users and application programmers this ability. In most cases, application developers can not provide the appropriate software and certainly not the hardware; it is up to system vendors to supply these pieces. However, it is helpful to understand how input works for languages around the world, and to learn why common assumptions about input such as *you can't input a character unless it is stamped on your keyboard* are wrong.

This appendix describes some hardware available for enabling input of various languages, as well as common software-based input methods (IMs). Given the variety of letters and languages that exist, it probably comes as no surprise to learn that there are many, many ways to type, construct, or choose the characters you want.

B.1 English Input

Input on American English systems is simple and straightforward. The keyboard has keys for all the English letters, as well as numbers and commonly used symbols. To enter characters, users simply press the keys that match the characters they want. If you want to enter an *a*, you press the key labeled *A*. If you want an *A*, you press <SHIFT> and the *A* key.

American keyboards almost always are laid out in the QWERTY format (named after the first six letters on the top alphabetic row). That layout, shown in Figure B.1, is a holdover from typewriters. Although other keyboard layouts exist—for example, the Dvorak layout—the overwhelming majority of computer keyboards use QWERTY.

385

While letters and numbers on QWERTY keyboards generally show up in consistent, familiar places, the same is not true for symbols. They may appear in different places on different keyboard models, to the eternal consternation of touch-typists. In addition, computer manufacturers almost always add a variety of special keys to their keyboards. These keys handle anything from cursor movement to editing to user-defined functions.

While American English keyboards are fairly uniform, there are a variety of ways to enter characters in other languages. In some cases, there are hardware changes, and often, software changes as well.

B.2   Country-Specific Keyboards

Most countries have standard keyboard layouts that differ to some extent from QWERTY. Like QWERTY, they often are descendants of local typewriter layouts and typically include some or all of the characters that the local language uses. For a Western European country, keyboards include some or all of the letters-with-diacritics familiar in that country. Plain letters and numbers also are sometimes (for those accustomed to English keyboards) in unexpected places.

Of the Western European keyboard layouts, the French standard probably causes the most frustration for an English touch-typist. The layout is called AZERTY (like QWERTY, it is named after the first six letters on the top alphabetic row, but notice that the letters are a bit different). Numbers are in the same order as on QWERTY, but you must press <SHIFT> to get them. The unshifted section of the numeric row includes letters with diacritics and assorted symbols. Other letters and symbols are at different locations on the keyboard. Figure B.2 shows the French AZERTY layout.

For those countries that have writing systems other than one based on the Latin script, keyboards change in different ways. Since computer users still need access to portable characters, such keyboards often include both portable characters and characters from the local phonetic script. (See Chapter 4 for information on portable characters.) For example, on Japanese keyboards, most keys have dual purposes—in one mode they produce Latin letters, and in another they produce kana characters. Korean keyboards usually include Hangul characters along with Latin letters.

To support local users' needs, computer manufacturers often supply a variety of country-specific keyboards. This hardware solution is fine for some countries, but it doesn't solve the whole input problem. Languages like French and Italian include many letters with diacritics, and there isn't enough room on a standard keyboard for all of them. In addition, even when country-specific keyboards do include all of a

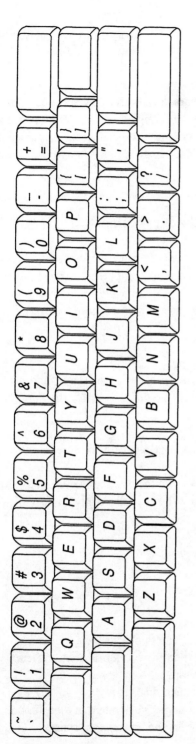

Figure B.1 QWERTY Keyboard Layout

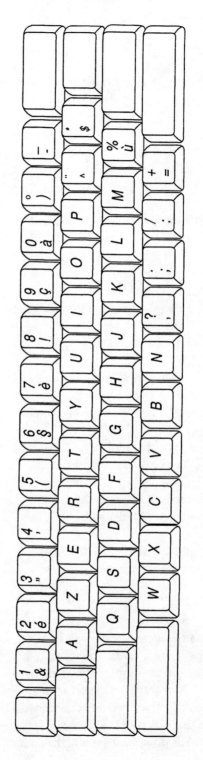

Figure B.2 French AZERTY Keyboard Layout

given language's characters, they don't have the letters for other languages. A German keyboard typically does not have French characters, while a Japanese keyboard doesn't include Hangul. English keyboards just have English characters. Given the multilingual nature of much business, it is very common to need to enter characters other than those stamped on your keyboard. Since hardware can't solve the whole problem, software rides to the rescue.

B.3   Entering Characters That Aren't on the Keyboard

Just as there is a group of country-specific keyboards, there also are several software-related input methods. As with everything else in computers, all have advantages and disadvantages. Depending on the languages for which a system vendor wants to allow input, the vendor needs to provide one or more of these methods.

B.3.1   Dead Keys

Dead-key IMs are common for languages that use the Latin script, and are a holdover from typewriter days. A group of keys is defined as "dead," or nonspacing. To enter a full character, you:

- Type the dead key. The dead-key character may appear on the screen, but the cursor does not advance.
- Type the second character. Assuming the two-character combination you have entered is legal, the display changes to show the completed glyph—usually a letter-with-diacritic.

In a dead key IM, to enter an é, you type:

'

e

and the appropriate glyph appears on the screen. The two-keystroke sequences for producing a given character are not standardized, so there often is some difference between the sequences that different vendors support.

Most often, the dead keys are those that produce diacritics (´ , ` , ˆ , ˜, and others). However, these characters also have meanings independent of their function as diacritics—particularly in computer programs and command syntax. On a POSIX-compliant system, the command

```
% cd ~/foo
```

moves you to the `foo` directory under your home directory. The tilde (~) character is part of the syntax that designates the home directory. Just as the tilde may be a diacritic or part of command syntax, the apostrophe (') has uses ranging from as an apostrophe to a single quote to an acute accent. It may appear in user text (*This report can't show* . . .) or in a command like this:

```
% fgrep 'string' *
```

Since characters have multiple uses, that means there has to be a way enter each dead key character without connecting it to a letter. For most dead key IM implementations, you press the dead key and then press <SPACE> when the character is not being used as a diacritic.

The advantage to a dead-key IM is that it lets you enter characters that aren't on your keyboard with a minimum of keystrokes. In addition, the two-key combinations are fairly easy to learn. Once you know how to enter one letter-with-an-acute-accent, it is easy to predict how to enter any valid letter-with-an-acute-accent. In addition, since dead keys were and are used on typewriters, they are familiar to European touch-typists.

But the IM does have disadvantages. It forces a somewhat-awkward ordering of keystrokes—most people who haven't learned to type instinctively add diacritics *to* letters rather than adding letters to diacritics. A dead-key IM reverses that order. In addition, when a key is dead, that means all users must enter two keystrokes when they want to use the dead character as itself. For example, it is no longer possible for users to press the <circumflex> key (^) once when they need that character. Instead, they must press <circumflex> and <SPACE>. Finally, not all characters lend themselves to a dead-key approach. Dead keys obviously are unsuitable for scripts such as Japanese Kanji or kana, and do not work for other phonetic scripts such as Arabic. They work best for languages that use Latin scripts, but even then are not always suitable. What key would you deaden to produce the German *ß*?

B.3.2 Composing Characters

If dead keys sometimes seem awkward, another common input method is to compose characters. As with dead keys, this IM is most common for languages that use the Latin script, and it features a predefined <compose> key, along with a set of two-keystroke sequences for producing all supported characters. To enter one of these characters, you:

- Press the predefined <compose> key. This signals the system that it should use the next two keystrokes to form a single character.
- Type the first character in the two-keystroke sequence. This usually is the base letter, but it can be something else. Nothing appears on the screen.
- Type the second character (usually the diacritic). The completed character appears on the screen.

Under this approach, to enter *é*, you type:

```
<compose>
e
'
```

Although there are no standards for compose sequences, there are some commonly used sequences for the ISO 8859-1 (Latin-1) characters. Table B.1 shows a few of those sequences.

Table B.1   Compose Sequence Examples

Compose Sequence	Character
ae	æ
a `	à
a'	á
c,	ç
E `	È
E'	É
ss	ß

As with dead keys, the compose method is fairly logical. Once you know how to type one letter with, say, an acute accent, you can easily predict how to type any letter that takes an acute accent. Unlike a dead keys IM, which forces all users to press <SPACE> if they want to use a diacritic as itself, a compose-based IM only impacts users when they enter characters that aren't on the keyboard. The disadvantage, however, is that instead of two keystrokes per character, this IM requires three.

B.3.3   Extra Characters on Every Key

Dead-keys and compose IMs require you to build characters with multiple keystrokes, but there is another alternative. You can map additional characters directly onto the keyboard and define a key (for example, <ALT> or <OPTION>) to signal the change to the new set. With this IM, each key produces up to four characters. Consider the *c* key. Using this IM, it could produce:

- Lowercase *c*. Simply press the key.
- Uppercase *C*. Press <SHIFT> and the key.
- Lowercase *ç*. Press <ALT> and the key.
- Uppercase *Ç*. Press <ALT>, <SHIFT>, and the key.

With this IM, extra characters are mapped as logically as possible on the keyboard. For instance, an *ñ* usually gets assigned to the same key as the plain *n*. Likewise, the *a* key gets some version of an a-with-diacritic. However, some letters take many different diacritics, while others take none. The letter *a* takes one or more of these diacritics in European languages: grave, acute, or circumflex accent, diaeresis, tilde, breve, ring, macron, or ogonek. In contrast, no European language adds a diacritic to *f*. This means the IM must make some fairly arbitrary assignments—an *à* might get assigned, say, to the *f* key.

This IM requires fewer keystrokes than either dead keys or compose. (Both dead keys and this approach take two keystrokes to enter a typical non-English character, but dead keys requires two keystrokes to enter diacritics as themselves, while this only requires one.) A disadvantage is that it is not as logical as either of the first two methods. While it is fairly easy to learn and remember the dead key and compose sequences, there is no mnemonic way to remap the whole keyboard. Key label overlays can solve the problem, but they are not always used because users often find them annoying.

B.4   Phonetic Conversion Input Methods

The input methods described so far work well for languages that use Latin scripts, as well as some other alphabetic scripts like Greek and Cyrillic. But languages written with ideographs, such as Japanese and Chinese, require a good bit more sophistication from input methods. Contrary to popular belief, computer keyboards for these languages do not have individual keys for each of the thousands of ideographs. Instead, IMs for these languages include a variety of alternate methods. In some cases, as you shall see, there is almost too much variety.

B.4.1 Japanese

Probably in part because there are commonly used phonetic scripts for Japanese (hiragana and katakana), the computer input method is fairly uniform. Keyboard keys typically have both Latin characters and kana characters engraved on them. You can toggle the keyboard between Latin and kana mode.

Then, in addition to the Japanese keyboard hardware, there is Japanese IM software. With it, you enter text using either Latin letters (sometimes called *Romaji*) or katakana characters. Here is how it works. As you enter phonetic characters, the IM may convert them to hiragana. After entering the phonetic version of a word or phrase, you press a key that signals the IM to convert the characters to Kanji. The input software looks up the phonetic string in a dictionary and finds the Kanji that match it.

If only one Kanji matches your string, the software replaces the string with that Kanji. However, it is common for a phonetic string to match multiple Kanji. This is analogous to English homonyms such as *meet, meat,* and *mete*, which are three different words that all have the same pronunciation. When the kana or Romaji string matches multiple Kanji, you get a menu of candidates, from which you choose the appropriate one. Figure B.3 shows an example of this IM. In this example, the first line shows phonetic kana input. On the second line, the IM shows the three Kanji strings (numbered 0, 1, and 2) that match the phonetic kana, and the user has selected the initial entry on the list. On the third line, the selected Kanji is now in place.

$ こくさいか

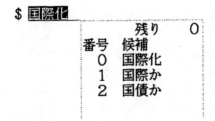

$ 国際化

Figure B.3   Inputting Japanese Text

It is not always the case that Romaji or kana characters in Japanese text should be converted to Kanji. There may be a computer-related string in the text that can not be converted to Kanji. Similarly, the text may include Japanese words that are more commonly written in kana than Kanji. Because of this, Japanese and other phonetic conversion IMs require that you define the region you want to convert.

This basic phonetic-to-ideographic input method is the most commonly used one in Japan. Different manufacturers add their own special touches to it—arranging dictionaries to increase the chances of finding the correct character quickly, teaching the lookup routine to learn from your pattern of usage, and so on—but the basic mechanics are the same on most systems.

B.4.2 Chinese Variety

Unlike Japanese, with its kana, there is no single phonetic system for the varieties of Chinese. In part because of this, there is no single common way of entering Chinese text. Vendors often supply five or six of the most common methods with their products because they know users may be familiar with any one of those methods. Among the methods may be:

- **Phonetic conversion**. As with a Japanese kana-to-Kanji conversion IM, you input phonetic strings and signal that you want to convert them to ideographs. However, instead of there being a single phonetic system, there may be several. There may be a *Pinyin*-based system, which uses the letters in the Latin script, or an alternate system called *BoPoMoFo*. (Like Japanese kana, BoPoMoFo uses its own set of phonetic symbols to build words.) Or there may be both. Pinyin is most common in the PRC, with BoPoMoFo being more prevalent in the ROC (Taiwan), but even inside a single country the details of these systems may vary significantly from vendor to vendor. For example, some Pinyin-based IMs let you collapse common substrings such as *ing* down to the single letter *g*. Others do not.

- **Radical selection**. Along with a phonetic conversion system, there may be an IM that lets you choose ideographs directly. An on-screen menu shows some or all of the radicals from which ideographs are built. You select one or more radicals, and the IM produces a second menu of ideographs that contain the radical(s). You then choose the ideograph you want.

- **Character code**. Instead of converting phonetic strings to ideographs, or selecting characters based on radicals, a character code IM lets you enter the decimal or hexadecimal encoded value of a character. For example, if the encoded value of the "sun" ideograph is 0xc6fc, you enter that value, and the ideograph appears on the display. This IM is also known as *telegraph code*, because telegraph operators used to transmit characters using numeric codes, and it still is used occasionally for Traditional and Simplified Chinese (or Japanese). It minimizes keystrokes and so is handy if you happen to remember the encoded value of a given ideograph. However, it isn't practical as a single IM on a system because most people don't know the encoded values of the thousands of ideographs.

Along with these Chinese IMs, there are others that do not involve a keyboard. See Breaking Free of the Keyboard later in this appendix for more information.

B.5   Other Input Styles

Input methods for Latin scripts or those that convert phonetic strings to ideographs are one thing, but they don't meet the needs of other scripts. Here are examples of other input styles:

- **Korean Hangul.** In a typical Korean IM, you type the Hangul characters that make up the syllables of a given word. The display may change as you enter each Hangul character. Suppose you are entering a syllable. When you type the second character, the first may change its shape and size. Likewise, when you enter the third, the first two may again change their shape and size. This continues until you complete the syllable.

  It is very common to keep all Korean text in Hangul form, but there are times when a user may choose to convert some words from Hangul to the equivalent Hanja ideographs. To change Hangul to Hanja, you define the region to be converted, and follow the same basic phonetic conversion IM as described for Japanese.

- **Hebrew.** Since the majority of Hebrew text omits vowels and instead consists of consonants only, most IMs are fairly straightforward. The Hebrew script includes 22 consonants, five of which have alternate forms when they appear at the end of a word. The keyboard contains keys for each consonant, and the equivalent of a <SHIFT> key lets you enter the final-form version of one of the five consonants when appropriate. This is analogous to English users pressing <SHIFT> when they want to enter an uppercase letter.

  Although Hebrew letters go right-to-left, numbers and any Latin characters go left-to-right, so the IM also usually includes a key for changing direction. By default, the initial direction is right-to-left, and the direction key toggles from the current direction to the other.

- **Arabic**. Context-dependent scripts such as Arabic require input systems that can determine which form (or shape) of a character to use. Most Arabic characters have four forms, with the position the character has in a word dictating which form—initial, medial, final, or isolated—to use. In addition, it is common to convert some sequences of characters into joined ligatures.

  Some IMs for Arabic scripts include context analyzers that attempt to determine which form of characters they should display on the screen. The display changes interactively as a character's context changes. Assume you have entered the fourth character of a five-letter word. The fourth letter appears on the display in its final form. Then, when you type the fifth letter, the fourth changes to medial form—because it no longer is the final letter in the word—and the fifth appears in final form. Such context analysis for some Arabic IMs differs from the norm for Latin and Hebrew scripts. In the latter scripts, users must manually choose which form of character they want to input. For example, English computer users must press `<SHIFT>` when they want to enter uppercase letters. A sophisticated Arabic IM chooses the correct form for its users.

  Note that changes in an Arabic letter's form do not usually affect its internal encoded value because such changes are at a glyph level. This is similar to a German user changing a Latin-1-encoded bold *ä* to an italic *ä*. Only the character's appearance changes; its Latin-1 0xe4 code value remains constant. The various graphic forms that scripts like Arabic use are called *presentation forms*.

  Since the Arabic script, like Hebrew, is right-to-left, an Arabic IM also typically includes a toggle key for changing direction.

- **Thai**. Latin scripts include a fair amount of diacritics, but their use of modifying marks is clearly in the amateur ranks compared to Thai. While most languages that use the Latin script only put one diacritic at a time on a letter, Thai base characters can take multiple modifiers, including vowel and tone marks. Among the existing Thai IMs is a system that works like this:

- You type a base character. The cursor advances.
- To add vowels or tone marks to a base character, you type each of them, and they appear above or below the base as appropriate. The cursor remains where it was—beside the character being modified—until you type another base character.

B.6   Breaking Free of the Keyboard

The input methods discussed so far are alike in one way: they all use keyboards. Although keyboard-based IMs are by far the most commonly used, other systems exist or are under development.

Mouse-based systems are the most developed of the nonkeyboard solutions, although they sometimes are used in conjunction with traditional keyboard systems. One Chinese input method lets you press a mouse button to choose a radical (or group of radicals) from a menu. The system then finds all the Hanzi ideographs that include the radical(s), and presents a menu of choices. You use the mouse to select the one you want. This system is faster than phonetic-conversion systems in certain situations, but it is too cumbersome for all input chores.

Other mouse-based systems include building a "better" mouse. The new and improved mouse usually includes five or six buttons which typically are used to construct ideographs by breaking each character down into pre-defined regions and then entering the strokes for a given region.

Other nonkeyboard IMs include voice recognition systems and light pens. The latter allows you to write characters on a light-sensitive tablet that then appear on the screen. Obviously, the obstacles to both systems involve handling differences: in individuals' ways of speaking for the first, and in handwriting for the second.

B.7   Inside Input

As with other internationalized software, many IMs use the current locale to determine how to perform a given task. Suppose an IM is capable of supporting multiple encodings of Japanese. The code values that go into a data stream match that of the user's current locale. That means if a user inputs the ideograph for sun while running in an AJEC-based locale, the code value 0xc6fc goes into the stream, while if the user is running in a SJIS-based locale, sun's SJIS value of 0x93fa goes into the stream. These internal differences are invisible to the user, however.

Many existing IMs have not been internationalized, and so are capable of handling only one code set or encoding method. These IMs ignore the current locale.

B.8   IM Summary

When enabling input, the best solution for system vendors to provide actually is a combination of solutions. It usually is most convenient to provide country-specific keyboards so that local users can have easy access to the characters they need for their language. In addition to the hardware-based solution, however, an internationalized system also must provide one or more software-based IMs. With the appropriate software, it is possible to input nearly any language from nearly any keyboard.

For More Information

C

Since internationalization has an impact on so many types of software (and, occasionally, hardware), you may need additional information about particular standards or culture-specific conventions. Further, when designing an application, you may need very specific information about an individual country's conventions or a language's characteristics. This appendix lists relevant standards, specifications, and books, and also provides addresses of organizations that may be able to provide more specific information.

C.1 Standards and Specifications

These are some international and national standards and industry specifications that are related to internationalization. For ISO standards, the number that follows the colon (:) indicates either the year the standard was adopted, or the most recent update. An asterisk (*) after a name indicates that the standard or specification was a draft when this book was written.

- **ASMO 449-1982.** Arab Organization for Standardization and Metrology. Data processing—7-bit coded character set for information interchange.
- **CNS 11643-1992.** Chinese National Standard—Han Character Standard Interchange Code for General Use.
- **GB 2312-1980.** Code of Chinese Graphic Character Set for Information Interchange: Jishu Biao-zhun Chubanshe (Technical Standards Publishing).
- **ISO 639:1988.** Code for the representation of names of languages.
- **ISO 646:1990.** Information processing—7-bit coded character set for information processing interchange.
- **ISO 2022:1986.** Information processing—ISO 7-bit and 8-bit coded character sets—Code extension techniques.

397

- **ISO 3166:1988.** Codes for the representation of names of countries.
- **ISO 4217:1990.** Codes for the representation of currencies and funds.
- **ISO 6429:1988.** Control functions for 7-bit and 8-bit coded character sets.
- **ISO 6937-1:1983.** Information processing—Coded character sets for text communication. Part 1: General introduction.
- **ISO 6937-2:1983.** Information processing—Coded character sets for text communication. Part 2: Latin alphabetic and nonalphabetic graphic characters.
- **ISO 8601:1988.** Data elements and interchange formats—Information interchange—Representation of dates and times.
- **ISO 8824:1990.** Information processing systems—Open Systems Interconnection—Specification of Abstract Syntax Notation One (ASN.1).
- **ISO 8825:1990.** Information processing systems—Open Systems Interconnection—Specification of Basic Encoding Rules for Abstract Syntax Notation One (ASN.1).
- **ISO 8859-1:1987.** Information processing—8-bit single-byte coded graphic character sets. Part 1: Latin alphabet No. 1.
- **ISO 8859-2:1987.** Information processing—8-bit single-byte coded graphic character sets. Part 2: Latin alphabet No. 2.
- **ISO 8859-3:1988.** Information processing—8-bit single-byte coded graphic character sets. Part 3: Latin alphabet No. 3.
- **ISO 8859-4:1988.** Information processing—8-bit single-byte coded graphic character sets. Part 4: Latin alphabet No. 4.
- **ISO/IEC 8859-5:1988.** Information processing—8-bit single-byte coded graphic character sets. Part 5: Latin/Cyrillic alphabet.
- **ISO 8859-6:1987.** Information processing—8-bit single-byte coded graphic character sets. Part 6: Latin/Arabic alphabet.
- **ISO 8859-7:1987.** Information processing—8-bit single-byte coded graphic character sets. Part 7: Latin/Greek alphabet.
- **ISO 8859-8:1988.** Information processing—8-bit single-byte coded graphic character sets. Part 8: Latin/Hebrew alphabet.
- **ISO/IEC 8859-9:1989.** Information processing—8-bit single-byte coded graphic character sets. Part 9: Latin alphabet No. 5.
- **ISO/IEC 8859-10:1992.** Information processing—8-bit single-byte coded graphic character sets. Part 10: Latin alphabet No. 6.
- **ISO/IEC 9899:1990.** Programming languages—C. Also known as ANSI X3.159-1989.
- **ISO/IEC 9945-1:1990.** Information technology—Portable Operating System Interface (POSIX) Part 1: System Application Program Interface (API) [C Language]. Also known as IEEE 1003.1-1990 or POSIX.1.

- **ISO/IEC 9945-2:1992.** Information technology—Portable Operating System Interface (POSIX) Part 2: Shells and Utilities. Also known as IEEE 1003.2-1992 or POSIX.2.
- **ISO/IEC 10646-1:1993.** Information technology—Universal multiple-octet coded character set (UCS). Part 1: Architecture and Basic Multilingual Plane.
- **JIS X0201-1976.** Japanese Standards Association Jouhou koukan you fugou (Code for Information Interchange).
- **JIS X0208-1990.** Japanese Standards Association Jouhou koukan you kanji fugoukei (Code of the Japanese Graphic Character Set for Information Interchange).
- **JIS X0212-1990.** Japanese Standards Association Jouhou koukan you kanji fugou-hojo kanji (Code of the supplementary Japanese Graphic Character Set for Information Interchange).
- **KS C 5601-1987.** Korea Industrial Standards Association. Jeongho gyohwanyong buho (Hangul mit Hanja). [Code for Information Interchange (Hangul and Hanja)].
- **KS C 5657-1991.** Korea Industrial Standards Association. Jeongho gyohwanyong buho hwakjang saten (Code of the supplementary Korean graphic character set for information interchange).
- **LTD 37(1610)-1988.** Indian Standard Code for Information Interchange.
- **Multibyte Support Extensions (MSE) to ISO C (ISO/IEC 9899).*** Contains **wchar_t**-based interfaces.
- **TIS 620-2529:1986.** Thai Industrial Standard for Thai Character Code for Computers.
- **X/Open Portability Guide.** The XSH4 volume (X/Open System Interfaces and Headers, Issue 4) contains **wchar_t**-based interfaces. XPG3 (X/Open Portability Guide, Issue 3) contains **char**-based interfaces.

C.2   Further Reading

These books provide more information about internationalization, localization, linguistics, or other culture-specific topics.

- Apple Computer; **Guide to Macintosh Software Localization**, Addison-Wesley, Inc., Reading, MA, 1992.
- Crystal, David; **An Encyclopedic Dictionary of Language and Languages**, Blackwell Publishers, Oxford, UK, 1992.

- Digital Equipment Corporation; **Digital Guide to Developing International Software**, Digital Press, Bedford, MA, 1991.
- Gaur, Albertine; **A History of Writing**, Cross River Press, New York, 1984, revised 1992.
- Katzner, Kenneth; **The Languages of the World**, Routledge and Kegan Paul Ltd., New York, 1977, revised 1986.
- Nakanishi, Akira; **Writing Systems of the World**, Charles E. Tuttle Company, Rutland, VT, 1980.
- Taylor, Dave; **Global Software: Developing Applications for the International Market**, Springer-Verlag, New York, 1992.
- The Unicode Consortium; **The Unicode Standard: Worldwide Character Encoding**, Version 1.0, Addison-Wesley, Reading, MA, 1991.
- X/Open Company; **Internationalisation Guide**, Version 2, X/Open Company Ltd., Reading, UK, 1993.
- X/Open Company; **X/Open Portability Guide, Issue 4**, X/Open Company Ltd., Reading, UK, 1992.

C.3 Organizations

There are numerous organizations that produce standards, specifications, or software with internationalized capabilities. In addition, many national standards groups produce national standards and may be able to provide specific information about cultural conventions or linguistic requirements. Following are the addresses of several such organizations. Contact ISO for a more complete list of national standards groups.

C.3.1 International and Regional Standards Groups

International Organization for Standardization (ISO)
1, Rue de Varembé
Case postale 56
CH-1211 Genève 20
Switzerland

European Computer Manufacturers Association (ECMA)
114, Rue du Rhône
CH-1204 Genève
Switzerland

Arab Standards and Metrology Organization (ASMO)
P.O. Box 926161
Amman
Jordan

C.3.2   National Standards Groups

Australia
Standards Association of Australia (SAA)
Standards House
80-86 Arthur Street
North Sydney -- N.S.W. 2060
Australia

Austria
Österreichisches Normungsinstitut (ON)
Heinestraße 38
Postfach 130
A-1021 Wien
Austria

Belgium
Institut Belge de Normalisation (IBN)
Avenue de la Brabançonne
B-1040 Bruxelles
Belgium

China, People's Republic of
China State Bureau of Standards (CSBS)
P.O. Box 820
Beijing
People's Republic of China

Denmark
Dansk Standardiseringsraad (DS)
Aurehøjvej 12
Postbox 77
DK-2900 Hellerup
Denmark

Egypt
Egyptian Organization for Standardization and Quality Control (EOS)
2 Latin America Street
Garden City
Cairo
Egypt

Finland
Suomen Standardisoimisliitto (SFS)
P.O. Box 205
SF-00121 Helsinki
Finland

France
Association Française de Normalisation (AFNOR)
Tour Europe
Cedex 7
F-92049 Paris La Défense
France

Germany
Deutsches Institut für Normung (DIN)
Burggrafenstraße 6
Postfach 1107
D-1000 Berlin 30
Germany

India
Bureau of Indian Standards (BIS)
Manak Bhavan
9 Bahadur Shah Safar Marg
New Delhi 110002
India

Israel
Standards Institution of Israel (SII)
42 Chaim Levanon Street
Tel Aviv 69977
Israel

Italy
Ente Nazionale Italiano di Unificazione (UNI)
Piazza Armando Diaz, 2
I-20123 Milano
Italy

Japan
Japanese Industrial Standards Committee (JISC)
c/o Standards Department
Agency of Industrial Science and Technology
Ministry of International Trade and Industry
1-3-1, Kasumigaseki
Chiyoda-ku
Tokyo 100
Japan

Korea, Republic of
Korean Bureau of Standard (KBS)
Indusrial Advancement Administration
Chungang-Dong
Kwachon City, Kyonggi-Do
427-010
Republic of Korea

The Netherlands
Nederlands Normalisatie-Instituut (NNI)
Kalfjeslaan 2
P.O. Box 5059
2600 GB Delft
The Netherlands

Norway
Norges Standardiseringsforbund (NSF)
Postboks 7020 Homansbyen
N-0306 Oslo 3
Norway

Portugal
Instituto Português da Qualidade (IPQ)
Rua José Estêvão, 83-A
P-1199 Lisboa
Portugal

Singapore
Singapore Institute of Standards and Industrial Research (SISIR)
1 Science Park Drive
Singapore 0511

Spain
Instituto Español de Normalización (IRANOR)
Calle Fernández de la Hoz, 52
28010 Madrid
Spain

Sweden
Standardiseringskommissionen i Sverige (SIS)
Box 3295
S-103 66 Stockholm
Sweden

Switzerland
Swiss Association for Standardisation (SNV)
Kirchenweg 4
Postfach
CH-8032 Zurich
Switzerland

Taiwan (Republic of China)
National Bureau of Standards
12th Floor, 333 Tung-Hua South Road,
Section 2, Taipei, 105
Taiwan, R.O.C.

Thailand
Thai Industrial Standards Institute (TISI)
Ministry of Industry
Rama VI Street
Bangkok 10400
Thailand

Turkey
Türk Standardlari Enstitüsü (TSE)
Necatibey Cad. 112
Bakanliklar
Ankara
Turkey

United Kingdom
British Standards Institution (BSI)
2 Park Street
London
W1A 2BS
United Kingdom

United States
American National Standards Institute (ANSI)
11 West 42nd Street
New York, NY 10036
USA

C.3.3   Other Relevant Organizations

Institute of Electrical and Electronics Engineers (IEEE)
IEEE Standards Office
P.O. Box 1331
445 Hoes Lane
Piscataway, NJ 08855
USA

X Consortium
One Memorial Drive
P.O. Box 546
Cambridge, MA 02142
USA

Open Software Foundation (OSF)
11 Cambridge Center
Cambridge, MA 02142
USA

Unicode, Inc.
1965 Charleston Road
Mountain View, CA 94043
USA

UniForum
2901 Tasman Drive
Suite 201
Santa Clara, CA 95054
USA

UNIX International (UI)
20 Waterview Boulevard
Parsippany, NJ 07054
USA

X/Open Company Limited
Apex Plaza
Forbury Road
Reading
Berkshire RG1 1AX
England

Acronyms

These acronyms appear in this book.

Acronym	Meaning
AJEC	Advanced Japanese EUC Code
ANSI	American National Standards Institute
ASCII	American Standard Code for Information Interchange
ASMO	Arab Organization for Standardization and Metrology
ASN.1	Abstract Syntax Notation 1
BMP	Basic Multilingual Plane
C0	Control set 0
C1	Control set 1
CNS	Chinese National Standard
CS	Compound Strings
CSI	Code Set Independence
CT	Compound Text
DEC	Digital Equipment Corporation
DIS	Draft International Standard
DST	Daylight Savings Time
EBCDIC	Extended Binary Coded Decimal Interchange Code
ECMA	European Computer Manufacturers Association
EOF	End of file
ESC	Escape
EUC	Extended UNIX Code
FSS-UTF	File System Safe UCS Transformation Format
G0	Graphic set 0
G1	Graphic set 1
G2	Graphic set 2

G3	Graphic set 3
GUI	Graphical User Interface
GMT	Greenwich Mean Time
HP	Hewlett-Packard, Inc.
I18N	Internationalization
IBM	International Business Machines, Inc.
IEC	International Electrotechnical Commission
IEEE	Institute of Electrical and Electronics Engineers
IM	Input method
I/O	Input/output
IRV	International Reference Version
ISO	International Organization for Standardization
JIS	Japanese Industrial Standard
KS	Korean Standard
LS2	Locking shift 2
LS3	Locking shift 3
LSB	Least Significant Bit
MSB	Most Significant Bit
MSE	Multibyte Support Extensions
NIE	Network Interchange Encoding
NLS	National Language Support, Native Language System
PC	Personal Computer
PCS	Portable Character Set
POSIX	Portable Operating System Interface
PRC	People's Republic of China
RE	Regular expression
ROC	Republic of China (Taiwan)
SJIS	Shift Japanese Industrial Standard
SO	Shift Out
SI	Shift In
SS2	Single shift 2
SS3	Single shift 3
TIS	Thai Industrial Standard
UCS	Universal Coded Character Set
UCS-2	Universal Coded Character Set (2-Octet Form)
UCS-4	Universal Coded Character Set (4-Octet Form)
UDC	User-definable character
UTC	Coordinated Universal Time
UTF-1	UCS Transformation Format-1
UTF-2	UCS Transformation Format-2
VDC	Vendor-definable character
WEOF	Wide character end of file
XPG	X/Open Portability Guide

Standard Control Characters

Control assigments for most ISO and even proprietary code sets used throughout the world come from ISO 6429:1988. The standard defines control functions for seven- and eight-bit code sets. Table E.1 shows the assignments that ISO 6429 makes in the C0 space.

Table E.2 shows the assignments ISO 6429 makes for the C1 control space. C1 control characters may have the same encoding as C0, but it is more common for them to have encodings in the range 0x80-0x9f as this table shows.

ISO 6429 defines many other control characters, several of which are significant when encoding data using ISO 2022 rules. Table E.3 shows these additional control characters.

See ISO 6429 for details on these control characters.

Table E.1   ISO 6429 Control Assignments for C0

Code Value	Abbreviation(s)	Name(s)
0x00	NUL	Null
0x01	SOH	Start of heading
0x02	STX	Start of text
0x03	ETX	End of text
0x04	EOT	End of transmission
0x05	ENQ	Enquiry
0x06	ACK	Acknowledge
0x07	BEL	Bell
0x08	BS	Backspace
0x09	HT	Character tabulation
0x0a	LF	Line feed.
0x0b	VT	Line tabulation
0x0c	FF	Form feed
0x0d	CR	Carriage return
0x0e	SO or LS1	Shift out, Locking shift 1
0x0f	SI or LS0	Shift in, Locking shift 0
0x10	DLE	Data link escape
0x11	DC1	Device control 1
0x12	DC2	Device control 2
0x13	DC3	Device control 3
0x14	DC4	Device control 4
0x15	NAK	Negative acknowledge
0x16	SYN	Synchronous idle
0x17	ETB	End of transmission block
0x18	CAN	Cancel
0x19	EM	End of medium
0x1a	SUB	Substitute
0x1b	ESC	Escape
0x1c	IS4	Information separator 4
0x1d	IS3	Information separator 3
0x1e	IS2	Information separator 2
0x1f	IS1	Information separator 1
0x7f	DEL	Delete

Table E.2   ISO 6429 Control Assignments for C1

Code Value	Abbreviation	Name
0x80	—	—
0x81	—	—
0x82	BPH	Break permitted here
0x83	NBH	No break here
0x84	IND	Index
0x85	NEL	Next line
0x86	SSA	Start of selected area
0x87	ESA	End of selected area
0x88	HTS	Character tabulation set
0x89	HTJ	Character tabulation w/justification
0x8a	VTS	Line tabulation set
0x8b	PLD	Partial line forward
0x8c	PLU	Partial line backward
0x8d	RI	Reverse line feed
0x8e	SS2	Single shift 2
0x8f	SS3	Single shift 3
0x90	DCS	Device control string
0x91	PU1	Private use 1
0x92	PU2	Private use 2
0x93	STS	Set transmit state
0x94	CCH	Cancel character
0x95	MW	Message waiting
0x96	SPA	Start of guarded area
0x97	EPA	End of guarded area
0x98	SOS	Start of string
0x99	—	—
0x9a	SCI	Single character introducer
0x9b	CSI	Control sequence introducer
0x9c	ST	String terminator
0x9d	OSC	Operating system command
0x9e	PM	Privacy message
0x9f	APC	Application program command

Table E.3   Additional Control Assignments

Code Value	Abbreviation	Name
ESC 0x6e	LS2	Locking shift 2
ESC 0x7d	LS2R	Locking shift 2 right
ESC 0x6f	LS3	Locking shift 3
ESC 0x7c	LS3R	Locking shift 3 right

Glossary

ASCII The American Standard Code for Information Interchange. ASCII is a code set that is common on computer systems around the world. It includes the English letters **A–Z** and **a–z**, as well as digits, symbols, punctuation, and control characters.

ASCII-transparent A code set or encoding method implementation that restricts byte values in the range 0x00-0x7f to containing ASCII characters only. Although fully internationalized code should not have dependencies on ASCII and thus should not care whether the code sets it supports are ASCII-transparent, much existing software does.

Byte An individually addressable unit of data storage. A byte is composed of a contiguous sequence of bits, the number of which may differ by implementation. However, the most common size for a byte is eight bits. See also *octet*.

Character An independent member of a set of elements used to represent data within a script or natural language. Examples include a letter, a letter with diacritic, an ideograph, a digit, or a punctuation symbol.

Character class A named set of characters, such as **alpha** or **digit**, sharing an attribute and into which individual characters can be classified. Standard functions (e.g., **iswalpha()**, **isdigit()**) and regular expression syntax determine whether input characters belong to a named character class.

Character printer A printer on which a physical object strikes an inked ribbon to produce a character on paper. Also known as an *impact*

413

printer. Some such printers can produce several characters— or even a whole line—simultaneously, but the repertoire of what they can print is tied tightly to the characters molded in metal or plastic. It therefore tends to be difficult for a character printer to support the wide repertoire of characters that an internationalized system needs. See also *intelligent printer.*

Character set   A set that may consist of letters, ideographs, digits, symbols, and/or control functions used to construct words and concepts of natural or computer languages.

Charmap   A source file that lists symbolic character names and associates an encoded value with each of the symbolic names. Abbreviation for *character map.*

Closed repertoire   A code set or encoding method implementation that defines a finite set of valid characters. The ISO 8859 sets and ISO 6937 are examples of closed repertoire sets. For example, since no European language contains an f with an acute accent, <f-acute> does not appear in the ISO 8859 sets, and is not a valid combination in ISO 6937. See also *open repertoire.*

Code set   Abbreviated version of the term *coded character set.*

Code Set Independence   A programming design that involves removing dependencies on specific code sets or encoding methods and replaces them with routines that theoretically can handle any encoding. While no standard interfaces are completely code set independent, the **wchar_t** interfaces are the closest.

Code value   The numeric value assigned to a character in a code set. For example, *A* has a code value of 0x41 (65 decimal) in ASCII. Also called *code position* or *code point.*

Coded character set   An unambiguous mapping of the members of a character set to specific numeric code values.

Collation   Sorting; using linguistic or cultural rules to order data in a list.

Collating symbol   A character or group of characters that must be treated as a unit for collation (sorting) purposes. Also called a *collating element.*

Combining character	A member of a code set that is intended to be combined with one base character and zero or more other combining characters. The universal code sets ISO 10646 and Unicode include combining characters.
Compose sequence	A series of keystrokes that creates a character.
Composite sequence	A character whose encoding consists of a base character followed by one or more combining characters. The universal code sets ISO 10646 and Unicode allow such sequences.
Context dependence	An attribute of some scripts in which individual characters take different forms depending on their location within a word. Examples include Arabic and Hebrew. Most Arabic consonants take four forms—initial, medial, final, and isolated.
Data interchange	The exchange of data across a network. In an internationalized environment, this may involve manual or automatic conversion of the data from one encoding to another.
Data transparent	A program or routine that allows all bits of all data bytes to pass through without alteration, and that, when examining data bytes, looks at all bits instead of ignoring one or more bits. Providing data transparency is one of the first steps in internationalizing source code. Also called *eight-bit clean*.
Dead keys	An input method in which some keys are only capable of producing a character when combined with another key or keys. By themselves, these keys are "dead"; when combined with another key, they can produce characters that do not appear on a keyboard. Typical dead keys are the diacritics. In most dead-key implementations, after pressing a dead key, the system waits for a second keystroke to complete a character. To enter *á* using a dead-key IM, you might type ′ followed by *a*.
Diacritic	A mark added to a letter that usually provides information about pronunciation or the stress that should be given to a syllable. Examples include acute (′) and grave (‵) accents, and diaereses (¨).
DIS	An ISO *Draft International Standard*. Before becoming a full ISO standard, proposals must be circulated as a DIS and comments or suggested revisions requested. Member nations vote on whether a DIS becomes a full standard. See also *ISO*.

Display order   A data storage strategy in which data is stored such that the order of each line matches the way it is displayed (or presented) on a left-to-right output device. For left-to-right scripts, display order matches the order in which data is entered (keyboard order), but for right-to-left or mixed-direction scripts, display order differs considerably from keyboard order. Also known as *presentation order*. See also *keyboard order*.

Display width   The number of columns a character consumes in a monospaced font. Most characters in Latin scripts consume one column, while most Asian ideographs consume two columns. The number of columns a character consumes is unrelated to the number of bytes it takes to encode that character.

Distributed computing The cooperation of two or more nodes communicating over a network. A distributed computing program starts on one node and then may continue on other nodes in the network. The network can be homogeneous or heterogeneous.

Downloaded fonts   Printer fonts that are maintained somewhere on the system, and sent to the printer at different times. The printer may specifically request a given font, or a document may carry along its own fonts when it goes to the printer. The downloaded fonts can supplement or replace resident fonts. See also *resident fonts*.

EBCDIC   Extended Binary Coded Decimal Interchange Code. EBCDIC is a family of code sets used primarily on IBM systems.

Eight-bit clean   See *data transparent*.

Encoding method   A collection of rules for combining and identifying multiple code sets in a single data stream.

Equivalence class   A group of characters or collating symbols that sort to the same primary location. For example, a French locale might define *a, A, à, À, â* and *Â* as sorting to the same primary location and therefore being members of an equivalence class.

Explicit directionality A method for determining the direction in which text should be displayed that uses tags or specific signal sequences embedded in the data stream. See also *implicit directionality*.

Extended UNIX Codes (EUC)	A common encoding method used on Asian UNIX-based systems. Up to four code sets can be combined in a single data stream using EUC.
External code	See *file code*.
File code	The representation of data when it is stored to disk. Also known as the *external code*.
Font	An ordered collection of character glyphs with a common graphic representation. Systems may provide fonts in a variety of sizes, typefaces, and styles. Examples of font styles are **bold**, roman, and *italic*.
Glyph	The graphic representation of a character on a display device or on paper. For example, **g,** g, g, and *g* all are different glyphs of the same character.
Han	Collective name for the ideographs used in Asian writing systems such as Japanese and Chinese.
Hangul	The Korean phonetic script.
Hanja	Korean ideographs. See also *Han*.
Hanzi	Chinese ideographs. See also *Han*.
Hiragana	One of two Japanese phonetic scripts. Somewhat cursive in appearance, hiragana is used for words of Japanese origin. Hiragana may also be combined with Kanji ideographs to form varieties of a single word. When used this way, the hiragana characters provide much the same function as common English word endings (*-ing, -ment, -ed* and so on). See also *katakana*.
I18N	A common abbreviation for the term *internationalization*. The word has 18 letters between the initial 'I' and final 'N.'
Ideograph	A character or symbol representing an idea. Some writing systems, including those for Japanese and Chinese, use thousands of such symbols. Also known as an *ideogram*.
Implicit directionality	A method of determining the direction in which text should be displayed that relies on the characters in the data stream. Since the context in which characters are used affects their direction, this method may result in errors. See also *explicit directionality*.

Input method   A procedure for allowing users to enter characters into a data stream. Methods differ significantly depending on the characteristics of a given writing system.

Intelligent printer   A printer that uses a page description language. The description language includes methods for interpreting characters and code sets and may also include functionality for handling mixed-direction text. Most laser printers are intelligent printers. See also *character printer*.

Internal code   See *process code*.

Internationalization The process of generalizing computer systems so that they can handle a variety of linguistic and cultural conventions.

ISO   International Organization for Standardization. This organization creates international standards for a wide variety of industries and topics, including information processing.

ISO 8859   A family of eight-bit code sets for graphic characters covering many alphabetic scripts. The most commonly used set is ISO 8859-1 (Latin-1), which includes characters for Western European languages.

ISO 10646   A universal code set covering most modern phonetic and ideographic scripts and containing over 33,000 encoded entities. Entities may be encoded in two octets (16 bits) each, or in four octets (32 bits). The set is related to the Unicode code set. See also *Unicode*.

Jargon   Specialized vocabulary, the definitions of which may not be in a standard dictionary. Examples in this book include terms like *code set*, *locale*, *wide character*, and *encoding method*. Text that includes jargon typically is more difficult to translate than text that avoids it, but some amount of jargon is necessary in technical documentation.

Kana   Collective name for the two Japanese phonetic scripts: *katakana* and *hiragana*.

Kanji   Japanese ideographs. See also *Han*.

Katakana   One of two Japanese phonetic scripts. Somewhat angular in appearance, katakana is used for words of foreign origin.

Keyboard order   A data storage strategy in which data is stored in the same order as it was entered from the keyboard or other input device. Also known as *logical order*. See also *display order*.

Latin-1   Common nickname for the ISO 8859-1 code set. This set contains characters for many Western European languages including English, French, German, Spanish, and others.

Latin script   The system of writing that uses the Latin letters. Many languages that use the Latin script add diacritics to some letters. The fact that a language uses the Latin script does not imply that it is linguistically related to Latin.

Ligature   Sequences of characters that must be treated as a unit rather than as the individual characters in the ligature. Latin scripts contain a few ligatures (for example, *ff* and Dutch *ij*), but they are very common in the Arabic script.

Limited vocabulary   A technique for simplifying text that places limits on the words that are permissible. The goal is to make text more comprehensible to nonnative readers and to translators. Limits range from small lists of words that can't appear in text to longer lists comprising the only words from which writers can choose. Examples of English limited vocabularies are Controlled English, Simplified English, and International English.

Locale   The collection of rules and text that represent linguistic and cultural conventions for a specific language and/or region.

Localization   The process of providing language- or culture-specific information for computer systems. Either software or data can be localized, but it is almost always more efficient to localize data rather than software. Localized software is also known as *customized* software.

Locking shift   A control character sequence in a data stream that initiates a state that applies to all following data. The state persists until another locking shift or an end shift control is encountered. A locking shift is one part of a *stateful encoding* method. See also *single shift*.

Logical order   See *keyboard order*.

Lower half   The region in an eight-bit code set containing the code values 0x00-0x7f (0-127 decimal). Also known as the *left half*.

Message catalog A file or other storage area containing program messages for a particular locale.

Messaging system A collection of interfaces for creating, storing, accessing, and updating program text in a variety of languages.

Multibyte character A coded character that consumes one or more bytes and that can be represented with ISO C's **char** data type. Multibyte data streams can include characters with varying widths.

Multilingual The ability to recognize and correctly process text containing arbitrary mixtures of languages. The mixture may be in a network, a local file system, or in a single file.

Network Inter-change Encoding The format data takes in a distributed application when traveling between nodes.

NLS An old, increasingly obsolete term for internationalization. Stands for either *Native Language System*, or *National Language Support*.

NLSPATH An environment variable defined in the X/Open messaging system that designates the search path for message catalogs.

Octet An ordered sequence of eight bits considered to be a unit. An octet is synonymous with the de facto standard definition of a *byte*. See also *byte*.

Open repertoire A code set or encoding method that places no restrictions on its set of valid characters. In such a code set/method, it is permissible to join a base character with any diacritic(s) or combining character(s), even if the resulting character does not exist in any language. For example, although no European language contains an f with an acute accent, a code set or encoding method with an open repertoire would consider such a character valid. See also *closed repertoire*.

Portable Character Set A minimum set of characters guaranteed to exist on the system supporting the set. Portable character sets exist because it is not feasible to expect every system to understand every existing character or code set, but software does need to count on some characters being understood. A portable set only defines characters, not the encoded value of those characters.

POSIX	Portable Operating System Interface. Sponsored by the Institute of Electrical and Electronics Engineers (IEEE), it is a UNIX-like operating system specification that includes significant internationalization support.
Presentation form	A form of a graphic symbol representing a character whose appearance depends on its position within a word. Most consonants in the Arabic script have four presentation forms— initial, medial, final, and isolated.
Presentation order	See *display order*.
Process code	The representation of data when programs are manipulating it. Also known as the *internal code*.
Radical	One of the basic building blocks of ideographs. Radicals provide information about the meaning of an ideograph. For example, the radical that means *wood* appears in all ideographs related to that subject (*tree, table, forest* and so on).
Radix character	The character that separates whole and fractional quantities in a floating point number. Common radix characters are a period (for example, 12.34) and a comma (12,34).
Resident fonts	Fonts that are physically tied to a specific printer. They may be part of the printer's read-only memory, or may be in a cartridge or other device that gets plugged into the printer. See also *downloaded fonts*.
Romaji	Japanese name for the Latin (or Roman) letters. Japanese technical text often includes some Romaji characters, and it also is relatively common to use Romaji when inputting Japanese text. Users can enter the phonetic representation of Japanese words in Romaji and the input method software converts Romaji to the appropriate Kanji and kana.
Script	A collection of related graphic symbols used for writing. Examples include Latin, Arabic, Devanagari, and ideographic Han. Some scripts are used for multiple languages, and some languages use multiple scripts. An example of the former is Latin, which is the script for many languages including English, French, German, Swahili, and Vietnamese. Languages that use multiple scripts include Japanese, which uses Kanji, hiragana, katakana, and Latin (Romaji).

Semantic equality   Equality based on meaning rather than implementation details. If two entities are semantically equal, a semantic match returns true. For example, the font glyphs **a**, *a,* and a represent the same character and thus are semantically equal, even though they look different. Most current implementations of equality are based on encoded values rather than semantic meaning.

Simplified Chinese   The ideographic script in the People's Republic of China, which consists of a streamlined set of Han ideographs.

Single shift   A control character sequence in a data stream that applies to the next character in the stream. The single shift usually provides information about the way in which the following character should be interpreted or the code set to which it belongs. The EUC encoding method uses single shifts. See also *locking shift.*

Stateful encoding   An encoding method that contains sequences embedded in the data that describe how to interpret the data. Such sequences may designate the code set to which the following data belongs, or may include information about the direction in which the text should be displayed. Fully specified ISO 2022-encoded data is a stateful encoding. A stateful encoding is an example of *tagged data.*

Symbolic name   A name that represents an actual character in a charmap and a locale definition source file. Examples include <space>, <A>, and <left-curly-bracket>.

Tagged data   A data stream that includes sequences that provide information about the data in it. Tags, which also are known as *handles*, can specify a wide range of information including the data's code set, text direction, font size and style, and the text unit (paragraph, bulleted list, etc.) to which the data belongs. One tag might designate that the accompanying data is Spanish text encoded in Latin-1. Another might identify the data as being Japanese encoded in AJEC. See also *stateful encoding.*

Terminology list   A list of the significant words or phrases that appear in documentation or program messages. Translators use the list to construct a *translation table.*

Text element	A Unicode-specific term for characters or code values that must be treated as a unit. A character encoded as a base character plus zero or more combining characters is a text element, as is a multicharacter collating symbol.
Traditional Chinese	The ideographic script in the Republic of China (Taiwan), which uses older, more complex versions of Han ideographs.
Translation table	Accepted translations of the words or phrases in a terminology list. Translators use such tables to produce consistent translations of documentation or other program text. When a term from the terminology list occurs in the text they are translating, they use the accepted translation from the table. See also *terminology list*.
Unicode	A universal code set that has much in common with ISO 10646. Unicode contains over 30,000 entities encoded as 16-bit values. See also *ISO 10646*.
Upper half	The region in an eight-bit code set containing the code values 0x80-0xff (128-255 decimal). Also known as the *right half*.
WEOF	Wide character end-of-file macro.
Wide character	A fixed-width character that is wide enough to hold any coded character an implementation supports. It is an object of the **wchar_t** type definition.
Writing system	The script or collection of scripts used to write a natural language. Some writing systems consist of a single script while others combine multiple scripts. For example, English uses only the Latin script, but Japanese uses katakana, hiragana, and Kanji, and often also includes Latin (Romaji).
XPG	X/Open Portability Guide. This is an industry specification the X/Open Company produces. Numbers designate versions of the specification. For example, the X/Open Portability Guide, Issue 4 is called **XPG4**.

Index